The Glannon Guide
to Commercial Paper
and Payment Systems

The Glannon Guide to Commercial Paper and Payment Systems

Learning Commercial Paper and Payment Systems Through Multiple-Choice Questions and Analysis

Second Edition

Stephen M. McJohn
Professor of Law
Suffolk University Law School

Wolters Kluwer
Law & Business

To contact Customer Service, e-mail customer.service@wolterskluwer.com,
call 1-800-234-1660, fax 1-800-901-9075, or mail correspondence to:

> Wolters Kluwer Law & Business
> Attn: Order Department
> PO Box 990
> Frederick, MD 21705

Printed in the United States of America.

1 2 3 4 5 6 7 8 9 0

ISBN 978-1-4548-0405-5

Library of Congress Cataloging-in-Publication Data

McJohn, Stephen M., 1959-
 The Glannon guide to commercial paper and payment systems : learning commercial paper and
payment systems through multiple-choice questions and analysis / Stephen M. McJohn. — 2nd ed.
   p. cm.
 Includes bibliographical references and index.
 ISBN 978-1-4548-0405-5 (alk. paper)
 1. Negotiable instruments — United States — Problems, exercises, etc.   2. Checks — United
States — Problems, exercises, etc.   3. Payments — United States — Problems, exercises, etc.   I. Title.
II. Title: Guide to commercial paper and payment systems.
 KF957.M39 2011
 346.73'096—dc23
                                                                                    2011041414

About Wolters Kluwer Law & Business

Wolters Kluwer Law & Business is a leading global provider of intelligent information and digital solutions for legal and business professionals in key specialty areas, and respected educational resources for professors and law students. Wolters Kluwer Law & Business connects legal and business professionals as well as those in the education market with timely, specialized authoritative content and information-enabled solutions to support success through productivity, accuracy and mobility.

Serving customers worldwide, Wolters Kluwer Law & Business products include those under the Aspen Publishers, CCH, Kluwer Law International, Loislaw, Best Case, ftwilliam. com and MediRegs family of products.

CCH products have been a trusted resource since 1913, and are highly regarded resources for legal, securities, antitrust and trade regulation, government contracting, banking, pension, payroll, employment and labor, and healthcare reimbursement and compliance professionals.

Aspen Publishers products provide essential information to attorneys, business professionals and law students. Written by preeminent authorities, the product line offers analytical and practical information in a range of specialty practice areas from securities law and intellectual property to mergers and acquisitions and pension/benefits. Aspen's trusted legal education resources provide professors and students with high-quality, up-to-date and effective resources for successful instruction and study in all areas of the law.

Kluwer Law International products provide the global business community with reliable international legal information in English. Legal practitioners, corporate counsel and business executives around the world rely on Kluwer Law journals, looseleafs, books, and electronic products for comprehensive information in many areas of international legal practice.

Loislaw is a comprehensive online legal research product providing legal content to law firm practitioners of various specializations. Loislaw provides attorneys with the ability to quickly and efficiently find the necessary legal information they need, when and where they need it, by facilitating access to primary law as well as state-specific law, records, forms and treatises.

Best Case Solutions is the leading bankruptcy software product to the bankruptcy industry. It provides software and workflow tools to flawlessly streamline petition preparation and the electronic filing process, while timely incorporating ever-changing court requirements.

ftwilliam.com offers employee benefits professionals the highest quality plan documents (retirement, welfare and non-qualified) and government forms (5500/PBGC, 1099 and IRS) software at highly competitive prices.

MediRegs products provide integrated health care compliance content and software solutions for professionals in healthcare, higher education and life sciences, including professionals in accounting, law and consulting.

Wolters Kluwer Law & Business, a division of Wolters Kluwer, is headquartered in New York. Wolters Kluwer is a market-leading global information services company focused on professionals.

For the Green RV: Keep moving forward

Table of Contents

Acknowledgments

I owe thanks to my terrific students, who find so many possibilities in every case. Thanks are also due to the great team at Aspen Publishers (including Lynn Churchill, Christine Hannan, Carol McGeehan, and Dana Wilson), and to the reviewers for their astute comments (and the Soia Mentschikoff precedent). Thanks, of course, to my family, not to mention electricity.

The Glannon Guide
to Commercial Paper
and Payment Systems

1

A Very Short Introduction

This book is about payments law, including commercial paper. Transactions involve payment, whether buying an iPod, buying stock in Apple Corporation, or buying the whole corporation. An attorney should be aware of the benefits and risks of a transaction, not only to help the clients plan, negotiate, and execute transactions, but also to aid them if something goes awry. Clients want to get paid, and to avoid paying if they do not get what is promised. Clients also have concerns about theft, forgery, embezzlement, and other misdirecting of money. Payments law is the tool that addresses these issues.

The payments systems covered are the following:

Checks — orders to pay from bank accounts
Promissory notes — promise to pay, a key part of many commercial transactions
Credit cards — loans made instantly and electronically
Debit cards, ACH (Automated Clearing House), online bill paying — consumer wire transfers
Commercial wire transfers — used to move large sums between accounts
Letters of credit — a bank's conditional promise to pay, especially used in international business transactions and in financing transactions
Guaranties — backup promises to pay

The legal issues covered include the following:

Unauthorized use (stolen and forged checks, cards, letters of credit, etc.; bank accounts depleted by wire transfers by unknown hackers)
Mistaken payment by bank
Wrongful failure to pay by bank
Defenses from underlying transaction (If the iPod does not work, can consumer get the charge taken off her account?)
Finality versus stop payment, cancellation (Can we please cancel that wire transfer to San Francisco?)

All of these issues carry various risks, from the points of view of customers, merchants, and financial institutions. One key risk in payments law and practice is that a party that has received money may be obliged to return it. A

1

merchant that honors a credit card may be subject to a chargeback, if the buyer has a defense. A bank that receives payment on a check may have breached a presentment warranty. A bank that has improperly paid a check may have to put the money back in its customer's account.

Another key principle of payments law is that sometimes you cannot get your money back. There is no right to cancel that payment order to San Francisco. A lawyer that understands those risks can do a lot for a client, whether in advising, negotiating, or litigating an issue—and also in changing public policy.

This book analyzes payments law and practice with multiple-choice questions. The key analytic ability of a lawyer is to apply the law to new fact patterns, real or hypothetical. Multiple-choice questions provide a nice medium for learning and for testing. Commercial law legend, Professor Soia Mentschikoff, used multiple-choice tests with a special format. The test-taker would choose one answer, and support it with a short comment. The questions in this book likewise use short fact patterns with several possible answers to bring the rules into sharp focus.

Thoughts, comments, suggestions, cases real or hypothetical, and payment system poetry are always welcome at smcjohn@suffolk.edu.

2

Negotiability

Instruments negotiable,
Itinerant and sociable.
An order or a promise
To pay moneys (not pajamas).
Money in a fixed amount,
Something you can really count.
To bearer or to "order,"
For a real marching hors d'ouevre.
Unconditional,
No promises additional,
At a time or on demand,
Two by sea or one by land.

CHAPTER OVERVIEW
A. Negotiability
B. Article 3 of the Uniform Commercial Code applies only to negotiable instruments
C. Requirements to be a negotiable instrument
   1. Promise (e.g., promissory note) or order (e.g., check) to pay, in a signed writing
   2. A fixed amount of money, with or without interest or other charges
   3. Unconditionally (the "unconditional" condition)
   4. Consumer credit sale notes: may be negotiable but must preserve defenses
   5. Payable to bearer or to order (checks don't need the word "order")
   6. Payable on demand or at a definite time

7. No extra promises (does not state any other undertaking or instruction by the issuer)
8. The issuer may opt out of Article 3: "NON-NEGOTIABLE"
9. Longevity of negotiability

D.   The closer

 McJohn's picks

A.   Negotiability

Some written obligations to pay money are freely transferable and collectible, not dependent on the underlying transaction. Article 3 of the Uniform Commercial Code (UCC) sets out a special set of rules for negotiable instruments (i.e., negotiable promissory notes, checks, and similar items). This article contains rules on how such instruments are transferred from party to party, who is entitled to payment, how to enforce liability of parties that sign them, when a party that signs must pay, how to present the instrument for payment, who takes the loss for forgeries and other misdeeds, and so on. The set of rules is tailored to apply to negotiable instruments. This book will deal mainly with the two most common negotiable instruments: negotiable promissory notes and ordinary checks. There are a number of other negotiable instruments—such as cashier's checks, traveler's checks, teller's checks, and non-bank drafts—and the same rules generally apply to them, but with some special provisions.

The following hypothetical transaction shows that it can make a big difference whether Article 3 applies to a case. Suppose Griffin School signs a piece of paper, promising to pay $10,000, as part of a deal to buy 50 antique swords. Sword Seller sells the piece of paper to Finance Company. Sword Seller never delivers the swords. Does Griffin School have to pay Finance Company anyway? It will depend on whether the piece of paper was a negotiable instrument.

Griffin School → Sword Seller → Finance Company
Assignee under contract law, or
Holder in due course under UCC Article 3?

If contract law governs the case, then Griffin School will not have to pay Finance Company. Under contract law, an assignee of a contract gets whatever right to payment the assignor had. Finance Company would have Sword Seller's right to receive zero dollars. If the piece of paper is a negotiable promissory note, however, the result is quite different. One of the rules in UCC Article 3 is the holder in due course rule, under which a party may have to pay even if they did not get what they were promised (even if they were defrauded). If Finance Company qualifies as a holder in due course (a holder that took in good faith, for value, with no notice of the problem), it can collect on the note and is insulated from the underlying transaction between Griffin School and Sword Seller.

Negotiability allows parties to structure commercial transactions so that the means of payment (such as a check or note) may be freely transferred by the payee and the right to payment is not tied to the underlying transaction. If Griffin School pays with a negotiable note, then Sword Seller can sell the note to Finance Company and presumably receive more. A $10,000 negotiable note is worth more than a $10,000 non-negotiable note (because the negotiable note is freely transferable and can be collected without delving into the details of the underlying transaction). If Finance Company buys a sale contract or a non-negotiable note, it will likely discount the price it pays by the cost and risk of enforcing the rights of the seller (proving that the promised swords were delivered in the promised manner at the promised time) and take the risk that the swords were not delivered as promised.

Why would Griffin School sign a negotiable note, surrendering its defenses against a future holder in due course? Presumably it chose those terms over the alternatives. If Griffin School paid cash, or paid with a wire transfer, it would have to pay now, as opposed to when the note was due. If Griffin School offered to sign only a non-negotiable note, Sword Seller would likely charge a higher price (or higher interest rate, which amounts to the same thing). So Griffin School takes on the risks of negotiability (including the holder in due course doctrine) as part of the overall terms, just as parties to commercial transactions allocate all kinds of risks. We will see that with respect to consumers, certain rights are not waivable, on the theory that consumers may not appreciate the risks. If a consumer buys a sword on credit, the consumer will retain the right not to pay if the sword is not delivered as promised.

B.   Article 3 of the Uniform Commercial Code applies only to negotiable instruments

The holder in due course is just one of the rules of UCC Article 3. Article 3 provides a comprehensive set of rules allowing parties to use negotiable instruments in all kinds of transactions and to transfer the instruments freely. Like the rest of the UCC, Article 3 serves to encourage commercial transactions by providing a comprehensive set of clear rules. A market economy relies on transactions.

Section 3-102 is the scope provision of Article 3, which tells us when Article 3 applies:

§ 3-102. **Subject Matter**

(a) This Article applies to negotiable instruments. It does not apply to money, to payment orders governed by Article 4A, or to securities governed by Article 8.

Section 3-104 acts as a sorting hat, distinguishing the pieces of paper that qualify as negotiable instruments from the many other pieces of paper out there. It would not make sense to apply the rules of Article 3 to sales contracts, wills, letters of credit, invoices, trusts, or bills of lading. Even non-negotiable promissory notes, which are quite similar to negotiable promissory notes, should not be covered by some rules of Article 3 (especially the holder in due course rule, which is quite different from the rules in other areas and is designed to apply only to negotiable instruments). Section 3-104 sets out a detailed definition of "negotiable instrument," to make sure that Article 3 applies only to the instruments it is intended to govern.

> **§ 3-104.** "Negotiable instrument" means an unconditional promise or order to pay a fixed amount of money, with or without interest or other charges described in the promise or order, if it:
>   (1) Is payable to bearer or to order at the time it is issued or first comes into possession of a holder;
>   (2) Is payable on demand or at a definite time; and
>   (3) Does not state any other undertaking or instruction by the person promising or ordering payment to do any act in addition to the payment of money. . . .

Section 3-104 tells us the conditions needed for something to be considered a negotiable instrument, and also gives a sense of what negotiable instruments are and what kind of transactions they are used in. If someone promises to pay, § 3-104 tells us whether that promise is in a negotiable instrument (subject to UCC Article 3) or some other promise (subject to another area of law, such as contract law).

QUESTION 1. Into the pit of despair?   Looney Tunes Music signs a promissory note, in exchange for a delivery of sheet music from Sheets in the Wind. The note states that it is "payable to Sheets in the Wind," which makes it not a negotiable instrument, as we will see (as opposed to if it were "payable to order of Sheets in the Wind" or "payable to bearer"). What is the effect of the instrument being non-negotiable?

A. It is invalid and Looney has no liability on the note.
B. UCC Article 3 does not apply to the note.
C. It is probably governed by common law contract law.
D. It is not subject to the holder in due course doctrine.
E. All of B-D above.

ANALYSIS.   Non-negotiable does not mean invalid. The issue of negotiability is an issue of scope: UCC Article 3 applies to negotiable instruments. If a note or check is negotiable, then UCC Article 3 supplies a comprehensive set of rules, governing such things as who must pay the note, how it may be transferred, who is liable in the event of theft or forgery, and how to discharge liability. If the note is non-negotiable, then the rules of UCC Article 3 do not apply. The question then becomes, what law *does* apply? A court is likely to apply contract law, which generally governs promises. Or, a court might apply UCC Article 3 by analogy, to the extent that it makes sense. The court might reason: UCC Article 3 gives a nice set of rules for promissory notes, and I do not have a better alternative, so I will apply UCC Article 3 for lack of anything better. This would make sense for such issues as the obligations when presenting a note for payment, because those would likely be the same for negotiable and non-negotiable notes. Some rules of UCC Article 3 (especially the holder in due course doctrine) are specially designed for negotiable notes, however, so a court would likely not apply them to a non-negotiable instrument.

A, "It is invalid and Looney has no liability on the note," is definitely wrong. Whether a note is negotiable or not does not govern its validity. A non-negotiable note can still be a perfectly enforceable obligation.

B, "UCC Article 3 does not apply to the note," is true. UCC Article 3 governs if and only if the note is negotiable (although a court might apply some UCC Article 3 rules by analogy to a non-negotiable note or check).

C, "It is probably governed by common law contract law," is also true. The document at issue is a promise to pay money, so contract law would probably apply.

D, "It is not subject to the holder in due course doctrine," is also true. Courts will apply some rules of UCC Article 3 to non-negotiable notes, for lack of an alternative, but some rules should only apply to negotiable instruments.

So **B**, **C**, and **D** are all true, which makes answer **E** ("All of B-D above") the best answer.

Note that although the note is not negotiable, it can probably still be assigned. If Sheets in the Wind assigned the note to Orpheum Finance, Orpheum Finance would be entitled, under contract law, to collect from Looney Tunes (assuming Sheets performed and Looney Tunes has no reason to avoid payment on the note). Orpheum Finance would not, however, be able to use the rules of Article 3, which as we will see often make it easier to collect.

C.   Requirements to be a negotiable instrument

1. *Promise (e.g., promissory note) or order (e.g., check) to pay, in a signed writing*

Under § 3-104, a negotiable instrument must be a promise or order to pay money. That tells us the two categories of negotiable instruments. If I sign a promissory note, I expect that somebody, at some point in time, will come back to me and demand payment. If I write a check, I'm ordering my bank to pay that amount of money to the holder of the check. Unlike the promissory note, I don't expect anyone to come back to me with the check and present it for payment. Instead, I expect that my bank will pay it and that I will reimburse my bank.

"Promise," as defined in § 3-103, means a "written undertaking to pay money signed by the person undertaking to pay. An acknowledgment of an obligation by the obligor is not a promise unless the obligor also undertakes to pay the obligation."

QUESTION 2. When is a promise not a promise? Which of the following would qualify as a "promise"?

A. Bruce, a delinquent customer of Banana Bread Bakers, signs the following: "I, Bruce, acknowledge that I am 50 days behind on my BBB Bill of $150. IOU $150, signed, Bruce."

B. Lilac, another customer, writes on a piece of paper: "I hereby promise to pay to the order of BBB $150."

C. Layla, another customer, writes on a piece of paper: "I hereby promise to pay to the order of BBB $150. Signed, Layla."

D. Pumpkin, a wealthy customer, writes the following on a piece of paper: "I hereby bequeath $150, upon my demise, to the order of BBB. Signed, Pumpkin."

ANALYSIS. This question illustrates that defined terms often give quite clear direction to otherwise tricky issues.

The statement in **A**, "I, Bruce, acknowledge that I am 50 days behind on my BBB Bill of $150. Signed, Bruce," is not a promise. In the abstract, we could look at the words in the context and argue whether they would be considered a promise, as that term is generally understood. But where the statute defines a term, that definition governs. The § 3-103 definition of "promise" states clearly: "An acknowledgment of an obligation by the obligor is not a promise unless the obligor also undertakes to pay the obligation." So this note is not a promise (as defined by UCC Article 3) and therefore is not a negotiable note.

The statement in **B**, "I hereby promise to pay to the order of BBB $150," sounds like a promise, but the definition in UCC Article 3 requires the promise to be signed by the person undertaking to pay. Lilac did not sign the note, so it is not a promise. This is no mere formality. A negotiable instrument is a serious obligation, not imposed unless one takes the step of making a formal step of signing the note or check, thereby authenticating it.

C is a promise, as defined by UCC Article 3. A promise is "a written undertaking to pay money signed by the person undertaking to pay." Layla's note reads, "I hereby promise to pay to the order of BBB $150. Signed, Layla." The note is written, she undertakes to pay money, and she signed it. We have a promise; therefore, **C** is the best answer.

D is not a UCC Article 3 promise. Again, it uses the word "promise": "I hereby promise to bequeath $150, upon my demise, to the order of BBB. Signed, Pumpkin." It may well qualify as some other type of promise, such as a promise to make a bequest. It is not, however, a definite undertaking to pay money; rather, it is a definite undertaking to make a bequest in a will, a slightly different sort of promise. Enforcement of such promises is not the sort of thing for which UCC Article 3 is designed.

A, **B**, and **D** are not negotiable notes, so they are not subject to the rules of UCC Article 3. They may well be enforceable, but that is a matter for another body of law such as contract law or trust law. As with other rules discussed in this chapter, the formal definition of "promise" serves a key functional role of sorting out which pieces of paper are appropriately governed by the rules in UCC Article 3.

The other type of negotiable instrument is an order. A check (i.e., an order to a bank to pay the holder of the check on demand) is the most common type of order. Non-check drafts are useful in some commercial transactions, especially sales of goods.

"Order" means "a written instruction to pay money signed by the person giving the instruction. The instruction may be addressed to any person, including the person giving the instruction, or to one or more persons jointly or in the alternative but not in succession. An authorization to pay is not an order unless the person authorized to pay is also instructed to pay." UCC § 3-103(8).

An order, like a promise, must be "written," which is defined as follows in § 1-201: "'Writing' includes printing, typewriting, or any other intentional reduction to tangible form. 'Written' has a corresponding meaning."

The writing must be signed, which means the person or their authorized representative made (by hand or with a machine), any symbol intending to authenticate the writing. UCC § 3-401.

QUESTION 3. Which of the following would qualify as an "order"?

A. Dash writes on a piece of paper: "To Dash: Pay $1,000 to the bearer of this check. Signed, Dash."

B. The same, except Dash's secretary wrote it, with the authorization of Dash.

C. Dash writes: "To Bank of Boston: Pay $1,000 to the bearer of this check. Signed, Dash."

D. Dash writes: "To Bank of Boston: I hereby authorize you to pay $1,000 to the bearer of this check. Signed, Dash."

D. All of A-C above.

ANALYSIS. This question likewise requires reading a statutory definition carefully and applying it.

A looks like a good abstract, even a philosophical question. Can Dash write an order to himself? One might argue no, on the grounds that he cannot bind himself, or that he could easily stop payment on such an order, or that he does not keep a checking account with himself, or that such an "order" is really a promise. The definition answers the question specifically, however: "'Order' means a written instruction to pay money signed by the person giving the instruction. The instruction may be addressed to any person, including the person giving the instruction." So a writing from Dash telling Dash to pay money to the bearer of the paper is an order. This is not so fanciful. Banks write checks on themselves all the time.

In **B**, Dash did not personally sign the check, so that might raise the question of whether it meets the definition of "order." A person need not personally make the signature, however. The definition of "signature" includes an authorized signature.

The example in **C** is another order, in fact the most typical order — a check. A check is simply an order to a bank to pay money to the holder of the check.

D does not meet the definition of order: "An authorization to pay is not an order unless the person authorized to pay is also instructed to pay."

A–C are true, making **E** the best answer.

2. *A fixed amount of money, with or without interest or other charges*

A negotiable instrument must be a promise or order *to pay a fixed amount of money.* A written promise to pay to paint the house is not a negotiable instrument; rather, it is a contract or offer to make a contract or something else. The rules of Article 3 are tailored to specified monetary obligations. Contract law is better designed to deal with other types of promises.

The amount of money must be fixed. A promise to pay one-half of the profit from my business next year to the holder of this note is not negotiable. The policy is that the holder of the instrument should be able to just look at the instrument and figure out what they are entitled to receive. The rules that cover negotiability say, if you can't look at it and figure out how much money you are entitled to, then it is not a negotiable instrument. If it represents the right to one-half of the profits of a business or the proceeds from the sale of painting, that is not a negotiable instrument, it is something else. However, there is some leeway for typical provisions on promissory notes that do not interfere with negotiability. Article 3 permits a promise to pay interest at a variable rate:

> § 3-312(b). Interest may be stated in an instrument as a fixed or variable amount of money or it may be expressed as a fixed or variable rate or rates. The amount or rate of interest may be stated or described in the instrument in any manner and may require reference to information not contained in the instrument.

> **QUESTION 4. Promise to split.** Bob the Builder agrees to help Noah renovate his old summer house at the beach. In return, Noah signs and delivers to Bob the following promissory note: "I hereby promise unconditionally to pay to the order of Bob the Builder one-third of the proceeds of the sale of my old summer house. Signed, Noah." Is the note negotiable?
>
> A. No. It is not payable for a fixed amount of money.
> B. Yes. It is payable for a fixed amount of money, readily determinable when the house is sold.
> C. Yes. A court would interpret it as payable for the amount of one-third the value of the house.
> D. No. It is non-negotiable and thus invalid.
> E. No. It is conditional, payable only if the house is sold.

ANALYSIS. This question emphasizes that the amount of money payable must be determinable from the note (with narrow exceptions for things like variable interest rates). The promise certainly sounds like a definite promise to pay a certain amount of money. Bob promises "unconditionally" to pay one-third of the proceeds of the sale of a house. Such a promise has implicit contingencies, however: how much the house is sold for, whether it is sold at all, and what constitutes proceeds from the sale (e.g., gross proceeds or net proceeds). So this is not a fixed amount of money.

A is the best answer: It is not payable for a fixed amount of money.

B sounds plausible: "It is payable for a fixed amount of money, readily determinable when the house is sold." That means the amount will at some time be fixed, however, after a number of contingencies have been dealt with. Moreover, it is not clear the house will definitely be sold, nor that the amount of proceeds is "readily determinable." So **B** is a false friend.

C is again plausible: "A court would interpret it as payable for the amount of one-third the value of the house." Courts do that sort of thing when necessary. Here, however, that is not necessary. The question is not how much Noah owes but, rather, whether this is a negotiable promissory note. That question is readily answered: No. There is no need for the court to take on the job of guessing the value of the home. Contract law addresses such matters. Negotiable instrument law requires clearly defined financial obligations.

D is incorrect, because it repeats the misconception that an instrument is invalid if it is not negotiable. "Non-negotiable" just means that the instrument is not governed by the rules of UCC Article 3.

E is a good argument (even if it jumps ahead to later in the chapter). One could read the note as containing the implied condition that it is payable only if the house is sold. As we will see below, though, that would not succeed, because only express conditions make a note non-negotiable. It does, however, reinforce the policy issue here (the one that made **A** the correct answer). The amount payable is not fixed, because there are implicit conditions to figuring out the amount payable.

QUESTION 5. The fix is in. Totoro signs a promissory note, payable to the order of his neighbor, Satsuke, in the amount of "One thousand nine hundred and ninety-eight dollars, plus interest each year at the London Interbank Exchange Rate on Jan. 1, at the beginning of the year, with the principal due on Jan. 1, 2015." The note also provides that Totoro will pay any legal fees necessary to enforce the obligation. Satsuke sells the note to Mei. When Mei seeks to enforce it as a holder in due course, Totoro argues the note was not a negotiable instrument. Is the note negotiable?

A. No. It is not payable for a fixed amount of money, because the interest rate was not fixed.
B. Yes. It was not payable for a fixed amount of money, because the amount of fees payable was not fixed—indeed it had no limit.
C. Yes. The UCC provides that a note may be negotiable even if it uses a variable rate and/or provides for payment of fees.
D. Yes. All promissory notes are negotiable.

ANALYSIS.   When Totoro signed the note, the amount of the obligation was not set. He promised to pay $1,998, plus interest at a rate to be determined in the future, plus attorney's fees to be accrued in the future. The note, however, is still negotiable. The general requirement that the note be for "a fixed amount of money" has some relevant exceptions. Interest may be expressed as a "variable rate" and "may require reference to information not contained in the instrument." In addition, the definition of "negotiable instrument" permits it to be "with or without interest or other charges described in the promise or order." So the attorney's fees would be permitted as "other charges." These rules reflect a balance between two policies. The requirement that the instrument be for a "fixed amount of money" means that promises for unfixed amounts (e.g., one-half of the proceeds of the sale of a house, a salesperson's commission for three months, a fair price for a furniture set as determined by an appraiser) are not negotiable. Such promises are better governed by contract law, because they may require some factual determinations. They also interfere with negotiability, because the holder of the note needs to get facts from the underlying transaction. But a rigid rule barring variable interest rates or fees (like attorney's fees or other charges) would mean that many ordinary notes would be non-negotiable. Such provisions do not implicate the underlying transaction but, rather, are linked to the promise to pay money itself. So UCC Article 3 permits such provisions to appear on negotiable instruments.

A is not true. The interest rate is indeed variable, not fixed. But variable rates are permitted and may require reference to information not on the note (such as the LIBOR rate on this note, which happens to be a widely used reference rate).

B is likewise not true. The amount of fees is indeed not set in advance, or even limited by the note, but the definition of "negotiable instrument" permits that. Remember as a practice point, however, that the client should be aware of such a provision before signing and be given a chance to consider whether to agree.

C is true, as discussed above.

The statement in **D**, "All promissory notes are negotiable," goes too far. Many promissory notes are not negotiable. So **D** is not a good answer.

3. *Unconditionally (the "unconditional" condition)*

A negotiable instrument must be an *unconditional* promise or order. Once again, it should be something that whoever holds the note can look at and tell whether they are entitled to payment or not. If it says, "I promise to pay $100,000 provided that my business makes that much profit next year," that is not a negotiable instrument. If it says, "I promise to pay $100,000, provided I was delivered a boatload of lecterns that were made out of oak, and were brand new and were not defective," that is not negotiable either. Those notes specifically provide conditions, which are defenses to payment. We don't want to apply Article 3, because Article 3 says you can't raise your defenses against a holder in due course. The signer of a *negotiable* instrument promises to pay unconditionally. The signer should therefore not be surprised when the holder in due course shows up and expects to get paid no matter what has happened.

Section 3-106(a) provides a rule to determine if a promise or order is conditional:

> A promise or order is unconditional unless it states (i) an express condition to payment (ii) that the promise or order is subject to or governed by another record, or (iii) that rights or obligations with respect to the promise or order are stated in another record. A reference to another record does not of itself make the promise or order conditional.

Section 3-106 also permits the inclusion of certain conditions without destroying negotiability. Such conditions normally appear on promissory notes and do not implicate the merits of the underlying transaction: "I promise to put up collateral" or "I only have to pay if there is enough money in my bank account to cover it." Section 3-106(b) provides:

> A promise or order is not made conditional (i) by a reference to another record for a statement of rights with respect to collateral, prepayment, or acceleration, or (ii) because payment is limited to resort to a particular fund or source.

> **QUESTION 6. No strings attached?**   Elton, the owner of a piano bar, purchases a piano on credit from Piano Seller. He signs two pieces of paper and gives them to Piano Seller: (1) a sales contract, in which he promises to pay $4,000 for the piano, on the condition that the piano is not defective; and (2) a promissory note, which reads in full: "I promise to pay $4,000 on demand to the order of Piano Seller; dated Dec. 5; signed Elton." Is the note negotiable?
>
> A. Yes. All promissory notes are negotiable.
> B. Yes. It meets all the requirements.
> C. No. It is conditional, because Elton does not have to pay if the piano is defective, an express condition in the sales contract.
> D. No. It is conditional, because Elton does not have to pay if the piano is defective, an implied condition in the promissory note.

ANALYSIS.   A negotiable instrument is "an unconditional promise or order." That requirement applies to the promise or order itself, not to the overall transaction. Elton signed a sales contract, in which he promised to pay $4,000 on the condition that the piano was not defective. That sales contract has a condition, so it would not be a negotiable instrument; however, the promissory note Elton signed contained no condition: "I promise to pay $4,000 on demand to the order of Piano Seller; dated Dec. 5; signed Elton." In the note, Elton promises to pay $4,000, period. That is an unconditional promise and the note is negotiable. (It meets the other requirements for negotiability, which the reader could verify as an exercise after finishing this chapter.)

A again gives the right answer—"Yes"—but for the wrong reasons ("All promissory notes are negotiable," which is far from true), so it is not a good answer.

B is correct.

C is plausible, and indeed may reflect Elton's belief if he does not know negotiable instrument law. He may assume that if he buys a piano on credit, he does not have to pay if the piano is defective. That is the case if he only signs a sales contract. That is not the case if he signs a negotiable promissory note. As we will see in later chapters, if he signs the note and gets a defective piano, he will still have to pay the note if a holder in due course holds the note. That is a key risk of signing a negotiable instrument.

D is not correct. A note is conditional only if there is an express condition to payment.

Would it make any difference if Elton and Piano Seller made a clear oral agreement that Elton would pay only if the piano was not defective? No. Under § 3-106, a note is unconditional unless the condition is on the note itself: "A promise or order is unconditional unless it states (i) an express condition to payment, (ii) that the promise or order is subject to or governed by another record, or (iii) that rights or obligations with respect to the promise or order are stated in another record." If the note itself appears negotiable, a future transferee would not know about the oral condition. So the rule requires that a party who wishes to make a condition stick (against transferees of the instrument) put the condition in writing.

QUESTION 7. Terms and conditions.   Which of the following would render a note conditional, and thus non-negotiable?

A.   "Subject to conditions in bill of sale."
B.   "Maker is not liable in the event of loss of employment or other act of God."
C.   "This note was signed in connection with the contract for sale of a Steinway piano, and is payable only if such piano is timely delivered and meets all warranties."
D.   "Void after 60 days."
E.   All of the above.

ANALYSIS.   Section 3-106 specifically allows some provisions that might otherwise be deemed conditions: "A promise or order is not made conditional (i) by a reference to another record for a statement of rights with respect to collateral, prepayment, or acceleration, or (ii) because payment is limited to resort to a particular fund or source." None of these, however, falls within those safe harbors. **A** is a condition, rather than a mere reference to another writing. **B** is a condition, relieving Maker of liability if certain events occur. **C** refers to another writing (which is permissible) but then goes on to make the promise to pay conditional. **D** makes payment conditional on presenting the writing within 60 days. So, **E** is the best answer.

So none of the notes are negotiable, and therefore none are subject to Article 3 of the UCC. What law would apply to them? A court might apply contract law, which generally governs promises subject to conditions. If it were an issue about things like indorsement, presentment, or transfer, a court might apply the rules of Article 3 by analogy, reasoning that Article 3 provides a good set of rules governing such matters. But if it were a holder in due course issue, the court would not apply the holder in due course rule from Article 3. As we will see, the holder in due course rule says, in effect: Someone who signs a negotiable instrument promises unconditionally to pay it. But each of these promises are explicitly conditional, meaning it would make no sense to treat them as unconditional promises to pay. In short, the requirement that a negotiable instrument be unconditional serves to preserve the character of conditional promises.

> **QUESTION 8. Acceptable condition.** Bob the Builder agrees to help
> Noah renovate his old summer house at the beach. In return, Noah signs
> and delivers to Bob the following promissory note: "I hereby promise to
> pay to the order of Bob the Builder, $200,000, on the condition that such
> liability is limited to payment from the proceeds of the sale of my old
> summer house, not from my other assets. Signed, Noah."
>
> Is the note negotiable?
>
> A. No. It is not payable for a fixed amount of money.
> B. No. It is conditional, payable only if the house is sold.
> C. Yes. A note may still be negotiable even if payment limited to resort to
>   a particular source.
> D. Yes, but the limitation would not apply. Noah would be liable for
> $200,000 even if the house was sold for $100,000.

ANALYSIS.   This question illustrates that the obligation to pay may be limited.
The note here is a promise to pay $200,000, but only "on the condition that such
liability is limited to payment from the proceeds of the sale of my old summer
house, not from my other assets." That certainly looks like a condition to payment. But § 3-106 permits such a limitation to appear without destroying negotiability: "A promise or order is not made conditional . . . (ii) because payment
is limited to resort to a particular fund or source." So that limitation does not
render the note conditional (for the purposes of negotiability). The note meets
all the other requirements for negotiability, so it is a negotiable instrument.

At first, this seems to open a loophole in the "conditional" requirement.
Instead of using a condition to payment ("payable only if I sell my house"),
it simply characterizes the condition as a limitation to a particular source of
funds ("payable only from the proceeds of the sale of my house"). But most
conditions are not amenable to such drafting. A typical condition to a payor's
obligation ("payable only if the piano I'm buying is not defective") cannot be
readily converted into a limitation on source ("payable only from the rental
payments I get on the piano I'm buying" might work, but not if the piano is
bought for use other than renting it out). So the loophole is not broad.

It does create a limitation on payment that goes beyond the face of the
note, but as with things like variable interest rates, it is one closely linked to the
payment obligation. Such a note still fits well with all the rules of UCC Article
3, so it makes sense to make it negotiable.

A misdirects. The note is payable for a fixed amount of money, $200,000.
Whether that amount of money will be available from the sale of the house is
not yet determined. But whether a note has money available to pay it is always
a question. "I promise to pay $200,000" leaves open the question of whether I
will ever have $200,000 to pay.

B is incorrect. The note is conditional in the usual sense of the word, but not
in the special meaning spelled out by § 3-106, for the purposes of negotiability.

C is correct: "A note may still be negotiable even if payment limited to resort to a particular source." The note states a condition that is permitted.

D spells out the practical impact. The limitation does not make the note non-negotiable, but the limitation is still effective as a condition. Payment is limited to a particular source. If there is no money in the source, then the obligation to pay does not reach other assets. So, yes, but the limitation would not apply. Stating that Noah would be liable for $200,000 even if the house was sold for $100,000 is not accurate.

4. *Consumer credit sale notes: may be negotiable but must preserve defenses*

If a commercial party buys equipment on credit, it can bargain for better terms by agreeing to sign a negotiable note (i.e., making its promise to pay more credible by giving up the right to raise defenses against a future holder in due course). A typical consumer, however, probably does not know about the risks of the holder in due course doctrine and assumes that one would not have to pay if the promised goods are not delivered (or are defective), even if a promissory note was signed. So consumers probably do not bargain with the holder in due course doctrine in mind.

Federal regulations now insulate consumers from the holder in due course doctrine for some transactions. Federal Trade Commission (FTC) regulations require that all notes executed as part of consumer credit sales be conditional. If Consumer buys some furniture with a promissory note, FTC regulations require that the note contain language providing that Consumer retains all her defenses to payment. So her obligation to pay is conditional on Seller's meeting its obligations. UCC § 3-106 has a provision that allows such notes to be negotiable, even though they are conditional:

> (d) If a promise or order at the time it is issued or first comes into possession of a holder contains a statement, required by applicable statutory or administrative law, to the effect that the rights of a holder or transferee are subject to claims or defenses that the issuer could assert against the original payee, the promise or order is not thereby made conditional for the purposes of Section 3-104(a); but if the promise or order is an instrument, there cannot be a holder in due course of the instrument.

We will see more on consumer credit sale notes in the holder in due course chapters.

5. *Payable to bearer or to order (checks don't need the word "order")*

To be payable, a note must be payable to bearer or order. Section 3-109 fleshes out that requirement.

> **§ 3-109(a).**   A promise or order is payable to bearer if it:
> (1) States that it is payable to bearer or to the order of bearer or otherwise indicates that the person in possession of the promise or order is entitled to payment;
> (2) Does not state a payee; or

(3) States that it is payable to or to the order of cash or otherwise indicates that it is not payable to an identified person.

(b) A promise or order that is not payable to bearer is payable to order if it is payable (i) to the order of an identified person or (ii) to an identified person or order. A promise or order that is payable to order is payable to the identified person.

There are three possibilities for promissory notes.

1. **Payable to bearer.** "I promise to pay to the bearer of this instrument," or "I promise to pay cash," or "I promise to pay to whoever shows up with this thing." If I sign a promissory note and I make it out to bearer, I should expect it to be negotiated.

2. **Payable to order.** To use a magic word called "order" (e.g., "I promise to pay to the *order* of Granger") is potentially negotiable. It means that I will pay Granger or to whomever Granger transfers the promissory note. I will pay it as directed by Granger. I should expect him to transfer it to someone else.

3. **Personal promise — non-negotiable.** This makes a promissory note non-negotiable. "I promise to pay Granger $1,000" is a personal promise running to Granger and no one else, so it is not negotiable.

The "payable to bearer or order" requirement applies only to promissory notes, not to checks. UCC § 3-104(c). Everyone who deals with a check expects it to be negotiated (deposited and sent through the check collection process). So, § 3-104(c) provides that checks are negotiable, even if not made out to bearer or using that magic word "order." It would defeat the usual expectations for checks if someone could write a check that could only be presented by the payee of the check. Like notes, checks are always payable either to bearer or to an identified person or persons, but the check need not be written using the word "order."

QUESTION 9. Payable to bearer or order?   Which of the following could appear on a negotiable promissory note?

A. "Pay to the order of George Best."
B. "Pay George Best or order."
C. "Pay George Best or bearer."
D. "Pay George Best."
E. All of A-C above.

ANALYSIS.   This question gives us practice with § 3-109.

A, "Pay to the order of George Best," comes comfortably within § 3-109(b). A promise is "payable to order if it is payable (i) to the order of an identified person." Historically, this technically meant, "Pay this instrument as directed by George Best." Now it means that the instrument is payable to George Best and is negotiable (meaning George Best can transfer to someone else).

B is an example of the variation permitted by § 3-109(b). An instrument "is payable to order if it is payable (i) to the order of an identified person or

(ii) *to an identified person or order.*" (Emphasis added.) So, the wording in **B** has exactly the same effect as the wording in **A**: order paper.

C fits into the broad description of bearer paper. Any wording with the effect that the bearer is entitled to payment will qualify as payable to bearer. "Pay George Best or bearer" says, "Pay George or whoever shows up with this instrument." It is payable to bearer.

D finally gives us an instrument payable neither to bearer nor to order. It is specifically payable to George Best, so it is not payable to bearer. It is not payable "to the order of" George Best nor to George Best "or order," so it is not payable to order. If it is neither payable to bearer or order, then it is non-negotiable.

The best answer then, is **E**: "All of A-C above."

QUESTION 10. Negotiable?   Which of the following could appear on a negotiable promissory note?

A. "Pay to George Best."
B. "Pay to George Best or assignee."
C. "Pay per instructions of George Best."
D. "Pay to the order of George Best."
E. All of the above.

ANALYSIS.   This question emphasizes the magical quality of the word "order," when it comes to negotiability. To be payable to order, the instrument must be payable "(i) to the *order* of an identified person or (ii) to an identified person or *order*." (Emphasis added.)

A is payable specifically to George Best, so it is clearly not negotiable.

B sounds negotiable, because it is payable to George Best or to whomever he assigns his rights. However, it says "George Best or assignee," not "George Best or order," so it is not negotiable.

C likewise uses words indicating assignability but is not negotiable. "Pay per instructions of George Best" sounds like "Pay to the order of George Best," but UCC Article 3 is formalistic: only if the magic word "order" is used will the instrument be payable to order. So **C** is non-negotiable.

D uses the magic word: "Pay to the *order* of George Best." **D** is the best answer. The others are all non-negotiable.

The requirement of the word "order" is not a silly formality. In many areas of the law, courts will give effect to the parties' apparent intention, or to substance over form, but not here. If the instrument is negotiable, it is governed by the rules of UCC Article 3, including the holder in due course doctrine. Those rules are specially designed to apply only to negotiable instruments and could give odd results if applied to other sorts of promises. Parties should not wander into UCC Article 3 by accident but, rather, should invoke it by design. The requirement of the word "order" protects someone from inadvertently promising to pay a future holder in due course, even if they did not receive the promised performance. One might question how strong that protection is because often a negotiable instrument is drafted by someone other than the signer; it does, however, at least require some warning to the signer (and her attorney).

QUESTION 11. Reality check: anything goes. Which of the following could appear on a negotiable check?

A. "Pay to the order of George Best."
B. "Pay George Best or assignee."
C. "Pay George Best or bearer."
D. "Pay George Best."
E. All of the above.

ANALYSIS. A check is negotiable even if not made payable to bearer or "order," so **E** is the best answer.

6. *Payable on demand or at a definite time*

The instrument must be "payable on demand or at a definite time." For an instrument to be negotiable, a transferee should be able to look at the instrument itself and know when payment is due. If the time for payment can only be determined by factors beyond the note, then the promise is more appropriately governed by contract law.

§ 3-108. Payable on Demand or at Definite Time

(a) A promise or order is "payable on demand" if it (i) states that it is payable on demand or at sight, or otherwise indicates that it is payable at the will of the holder, or (ii) does not state any time of payment.

(b) A promise or order is "payable at a definite time" if it is payable on elapse of a definite period of time after sight or acceptance or at a fixed date or dates or at a time or times readily ascertainable at the time the promise or order is issued, subject to rights of (i) prepayment, (ii) acceleration, (iii) extension at the option of the holder, or (iv) extension to a further definite time at the option of the maker or acceptor or automatically upon or after a specified act or event.

QUESTION 12. Timely enough? A promissory note is payable to bearer in the amount of $10,000. Which of the following would make the note non-negotiable?

A. No time of payment is stated.
B. It reads: "I will pay upon being asked."
C. It reads: "Payable June 1, 2015, but the holder may extend the date of payment in the holder's discretion."
D. It reads: "Payable June 1, 2015, but I, the obligor, may extend the date of payment in my discretion."
E. It reads: "Payable June 1, 2015, but I, the obligor, may extend the date of payment to June 1, 2016, in my discretion."

ANALYSIS.   This question emphasizes that there are many ways to set the time for payment, but there are limits.

A shows a gap filler, one of many in UCC Article 3. The note does not state a time of payment. One might think that is therefore never due and so fails to be "payable on demand or at a definite time." UCC § 3-108 has it covered, however: A note is payable on demand if it "does not state any time of payment." If Dana signs a note promising to pay $1,000 to the holder of the note and no time of payment is stated, then it is payable on demand, which is whenever the holder demands payment.

The statement in **B**, "I will pay upon being asked," does not use the words "payable on demand." But § 3-108 does not require magic words. A note is payable on demand if it "states that it is payable on demand or at sight, or *otherwise indicates that it is payable at the will of the holder.*" (Emphasis added.) A promise to pay upon being asked indicates that the obligor will pay at the will of the holder.

C permits the holder to extend the due date: "Payable June 1, 2015, but the holder may extend the date of payment in the holder's discretion." One might argue that the note is not payable at a definite time, because the due date in the note can be changed. But § 3-108 expressly allows such a provision allowing "extension at the option of the holder." This does not undercut the policy of requiring the note to be payable on demand or at a definite time. Rather, it allows the holder, in effect, to convert a note due at a particular time to a demand note, by extending the due date.

D looks similar: "Payable June 1, 2015, but I, the obligor, may extend the date of payment in my discretion." The only difference is that the obligor, rather than the holder, has the right to extend the due date. This is not permitted by the statutory provision, however, which allows only an indefinite extension at the option of the *holder*. The distinction makes sense. If the obligor could always extend the due date, the note would never truly be due. It would, in effect, say, "I promise to pay when and if I choose to pay." That is not really a promise to pay. **D** is the best answer, because **D** is not negotiable.

E looks similar, but has a key distinction: "Payable June 1, 2015, but I, the obligor, may extend the date of payment to June 1, 2016 in my discretion." The obligor has the right to extend the due date, but that right is limited to extending the due date to June 1, 2016. So the note will definitely be due no later than June 1, 2016. Unlike **D**, **E** represents a real promise to pay that will definitely come due. So § 3-108 permits "extension to a further definite time at the option of the holder."

QUESTION 13. Back and forth.   Which of the following would be considered payable on demand or at a definite time?

A. "Payable when I start my first job after graduating from law school."
B. "Payable when I start my first job after graduating from law school, but the holder may demand payment on June 1, 2015."
C. "Payable on June 1, 2015, but the holder may accelerate the due date and demand payment if I graduate from law school before then."

> **D.** "Payable on June 1, 2015, but will be extended to June 1, 2016 if I
>   have not graduated by June 1, 2015."
> **E.** C and D.

ANALYSIS.   **A** is not payable at a definite time. The signer may have a definite time in mind for when she plans to start work, but that is subject to contingencies (e.g., graduating, getting the job, not being hit by a meteorite). This note is not negotiable. (Remember, as always, that "non-negotiable" does not mean "invalid." It could still be a perfectly valid promissory note).

B is not payable at a definite time, as set out in § 3-108. One could argue that it will be payable no later than June 1, 2015. It does not, however, fit into any of the categories permitted by § 3-108, which allow a note with a fixed date of payment to be subject to prepayment, acceleration, and certain extensions. Rather, this is a note with an indefinite time, subject to an optional definite time. **B** is also not payable on demand, because it is not payable "at the will of the holder." Rather, the holder has the option to make it payable not when she chooses, but on June 1, 2016. So **B** is not payable on demand or at a definite time.

Although **B** would not seem to defeat the underlying purpose of the rule (because the holder can require payment no later than June 1, 2016), § 3-108 does not allow it. Where the statute spells out in great detail which provisions are permitted, a court is less likely to permit one that does not fit.

C is negotiable. Section 3-108 permits a note to be payable at a definite time, subject to a right of acceleration: "Payable on June 1, 2015, but the holder may accelerate the due date and demand payment if I graduate from law school before then."

D is also negotiable. Section 3-108 permits a note to have a fixed date, subject to extension "automatically upon or after a specified act or event." **D** is such a note: "Payable on June 1, 2015, but will be extended to June 1, 2016 if I have not graduated by June 1, 2015." (One might unconvincingly quibble that this is subject to extension upon nonoccurrence of an event—i.e., not graduating.)

E is the best answer.

7. *No extra promises (does not state any other undertaking or instruction by the issuer)*

Section 3-104 provides that an instrument is not negotiable if it states, "any other undertaking or instruction by the person promising or ordering payment to do any act in addition to the payment of money." The rationale is that the instrument should just be a promise or order to pay money and not carry along extra promises, which would complicate the transaction.

The rule does allow some extra promises. Some promises typically appear on promissory notes, however, and would not interfere with the policy's underlying negotiability. A promise to put up collateral or to surrender in litigation would not interfere with the liquidity of the note but, if anything, would add to it. So § 3-104 provides that the "the promise or order may contain (i) an undertaking or power to give, maintain, or protect collateral to secure payment, (ii) an authorization or power to the holder to confess judgment or realize on or dispose of collateral, or (iii) a waiver of the benefit of any law intended for the advantage or protection of an obligor."

QUESTION 14. Promises, promises. Borrower signs a promissory note stating, "I promise to pay, on demand, $15,000 to the Order of Pitbull Bank. I also promise to seek all my future business loans from the Pitbull Bank or the holder of this note. Signed, Buyer." Is the note a negotiable instrument?

A. No. The extra promise destroys negotiability.
B. Yes. It has the necessary promise to pay money, so the additional promise to use Pitbull as future lender does not destroy negotiability.
C. Yes. There is an extra promise, but it runs to the holder of the note and so does not destroy negotiability.
D. No. Notes are not negotiable unless they are payable for more than $50,000.

ANALYSIS.   The note has a promise to pay money, but also has another promise. That promise is not one of the extra promises allowed (putting up collateral, confessing judgment, waiver of rights). The note is not negotiable. **A** is the best answer. The question also illustrates the reason for the rule. UCC Article 3 provides a set of rules designed to enforce promises to pay money. The promise to use Pitbull or holder for future loan service is a much different type of promise, best left to contract law. The rule forces parties to keep notes simple in order to use UCC Article 3's rules.

8. *The issuer may opt out of Article 3: "NON-NEGOTIABLE"*

Section 3-104 allows the issuer of a note to opt out of Article 3:

> "(d) A promise or order other than a check is not an instrument if, at the time it is issued or first comes into possession of a holder, it contains a conspicuous statement, however expressed, to the effect that the promise or order is not negotiable or is not an instrument governed by this Article."

Careful issuers put "NON-NEGOTIABLE" on things not intended to be treated as negotiable. Suppose School District hired Contractor to build a new computer lab. As part of the transaction, School District signs a promissory note for the contract price. But the agreement is that the payments are due only if certain construction deadlines are met. If the note is negotiable, School

District would be obliged unconditionally to pay it to a holder in due course. One could simply include the conditions in the note, making it conditional and therefore non-negotiable. But the conditions might be complex and might be phrased in a way that could be unclear as to whether it was conditional (when read out of context of the construction contract as a whole). To make things clear, School District can simply put "NON-NEGOTIABLE" on the note. The opt-out provision ensures that parties can avoid application of UCC Article 3's rules if they so agree.

Note that the rule does not apply to checks. So if a check otherwise meets the requirements for being negotiable, it will be negotiable even if it says "NON-NEGOTIABLE." Why? Checks are processed routinely and are normally negotiated from bank to bank. A party that signs a check can still make it non-negotiable by writing conditions to payment on the check.

QUESTION 15. Deem it negotiable?   Bernie the attorney drafts a long promissory note. After comparing its provisions to the detailed requirements of the UCC, Bernie is not quite sure whether the note is negotiable. He decides to clarify things by putting "NEGOTIABLE" front and center on the note. Will that ensure that the note is negotiable?

A. No. The note will only be negotiable if it meets all the requirements of § 3-104.
B. Yes. The parties can opt-in to Article 3.
C. Yes. The intention of the parties will govern, as if it were a contract.
D. No. Everything is negotiable, as they say.

ANALYSIS.   Putting "NEGOTIABLE" on a note will not make it negotiable (and therefore governed by all the rules of UCC Article 3), if other provisions of the note make it non-negotiable. For example, if there are conditions to payment, they would still be effective and could be raised as a defense against enforcement of the note, contrary to the holder in due course doctrine of Article 3. If Maker agrees to pay $3,000 on the express condition that certain goods are delivered, it would make no sense to treat that as an unconditional obligation. **A** is the best answer.

9. *Longevity of negotiability*

Negotiability plays a less central role than in earlier times. Professor Mann discusses several reasons why many notes are not negotiable, and why negotiability is less important to notes and checks. See Mann, *Payment Systems and Other Financial Transactions* (Aspen Publishers, 2008). FTC regulations, discussed previously, have made the holder in due course rule inapplicable to consumer credit sales. Certain tax advantages of bearer instruments no longer exist. Notes are not negotiable if they contain conditions or extra promises.

Lawyers find it very difficult to resist putting conditions and extra promises on documents, and a more complex commercial world often requires them. Parties that deal with notes and checks now often use ways to deal with risks that may not depend on negotiability (e.g., some securitization and contracts). Electronic items are not negotiable instruments, but many notes, and the vast majority of checks, are still negotiable instruments. UCC Article 3 governs them and provides a set of rules that often guide legal analysis of other items, so it still plays an important role in commercial law.

D.   The closer

> **QUESTION 16. IM Negotiable?**   Highly Solvent, a startup biotech company, sends the following e-mail to Angel, its principal investor: "Highly Solvent hereby promises to pay to the order of Angel one million dollars on demand. Signed, Highly Solvent." Highly Solvent signs the e-mail with its fancy digital signature authentication software. Is the e-mail a negotiable instrument?
>
> **A.** Yes. It is a signed promise to pay a fixed promise of money on demand.
> **B.** No. It is not a signed writing.
> **C.** No. It would be interpreted to be a corporate bond.
> **D.** Yes. An e-mail could be forwarded, so the promise is negotiable.

ANALYSIS.   This question goes to the scope of UCC Article 3, which applies only to writings—written promises or orders. An e-mail uses alphabetical characters, just as a note or check does. It is a written communication in a broad sense, similar in many ways to a writing on paper, just a lot faster. An e-mail does not, however, qualify as a "written instruction," because it is not a writing, which (as stated above) requires "printing, typewriting, or any other intentional reduction to tangible form." UCC § 1-201.

A is not correct. An e-mail is arguably "a signed promise to pay a fixed promise of money on demand." The definition of "promise," however, is "a *written* undertaking to pay money signed by the person undertaking to pay." (Emphasis added.) An e-mail is not a UCC Article 3 writing.

B is therefore correct.

C is a red herring. Whether the e-mail is a corporate bond is not determinative, or perhaps even relevant. The question is whether it is a UCC Article 3 "promise." Indeed, a corporate bond could be a UCC Article 3 promise, if it were a negotiable bond.

D is likewise misleading. An e-mail can indeed be forwarded. Negotiable instruments can be transferred from holder to holder, which is similar, but not everything that can be transferred is a negotiable instrument. To the contrary, negotiable instruments are a small subset of transferable assets. **D** also serves to show that barring things like e-mails from negotiable status is not simply formalism or anachronism. An e-mail can be forwarded. That usually leaves at least three copies of the e-mail: the one received, the one forwarded, and the one in the "sent" folder. Negotiable instruments should be unique, however, so only one person can enforce them. The rules of UCC Article 3 are designed to apply to a single piece of paper that is sent from person to person and can be enforced by the holder. If Mara signs a negotiable promissory note, she promises to pay the holder of the note. The holder must present the note to show she is the holder. When Mara pays, she can stamp "PAID" on the note and knows that her obligation is discharged. If there were other valid copies of the note floating around, that scheme would not work. Another holder could show up with his copy the next day. There could be multiple, simultaneous holders of the various copies of the e-mail. None of this is to say that electronic promissory notes are a bad idea or should not be enforceable, but another body of law (contracts, or a specialized e-commerce law) would govern them better.

The rule requiring a signed writing also yields the non-negotiability of the lowest tech promises: An oral promise to pay money is not negotiable, even though it can be passed on ("Dana promised to pay me $500. She can owe you."). There would likewise not be a single embodiment of the promise. Oral promises are better governed by contract law.

 ## McJohn's picks

1. Into the pit of despair?	E
2. When is a promise not a promise?	C
3. Which of the following would qualify as an "order"?	E
4. Promise to split	A
5. The fix is in	C
6. No strings attached	B
7. Terms and conditions	E
8. Acceptable condition	C
9. Payable to bearer or order?	E
10. Negotiable?	D
11. Reality check: Anything goes	E
12. Timely enough?	D
13. Back and forth	E
14. Promises, promises	A
15. Deem it negotiable?	A
16. IM negotiable?	B

3

Parties to the Instrument

~

Lulu lost her paycheck.
The thief is not a holder,
Unless—and this may scare her—
It's payable to bearer.

~

CHAPTER OVERVIEW
A. The characters and actions in the life of an instrument
B. Typical check
C. Typical note
D. To whom the instrument is initially payable
E. To whom the instrument becomes payable next
F. The closer
◈ McJohn's picks

A. The characters and actions in the life of an instrument

Dana writes a check to Patrick. How can Patrick make the check payable to Hilda? This chapter deals with the following question: As the instrument goes from person to person, who has the right to payment? This chapter also covers the stages of issuing, transferring, and presenting an instrument for payment. The key term introduced is *holder*. Someone is a holder if two things are true: (1) she is in possession of the instrument, and (2) it is payable to her. As we will see, the second condition depends on whether the note is payable to bearer (in which case it is payable to the possessor, who would then necessarily be the bearer) or payable to an identified person (in which case, we must ask whether the person in possession is the identified person).

First, some more terms. In the life of a check, there are several stages. If Dana (the *drawer*) writes a check on her account at Gringotts Bank (the *drawee* or *payor*) and gives it to Paula (the *payee*), it is *issued*. If Paula then delivers it to someone else to give them the right to collect (e.g., by depositing in a bank, cashing it at a check-cashing outlet, or giving it away as a donation), that's a *transfer*. When someone takes it to Gringotts and demands payment, that is a *presentment*. These categories are mutually exclusive: an issuance is not a transfer, a presentment is not a transfer, and an issuance is not a presentment. These categories are important because each triggers a different set of legal consequences.

The life of a note is a little different. A check is issued by the *drawer*; a note is issued by the *maker*. Like a check, a note is usually issued to the payee and may be transferred to others. Unlike a check, it is presented for payment to the issuer.

Each stage is defined in the Uniform Commercial Code (UCC):

> **§ 3-105.** (a) "Issue" means the first delivery of an instrument by the maker or drawer, whether to a holder or nonholder, for the purpose of giving rights on the instrument to any person. . . .

> **§ 3-203.** Transfer (a) An instrument is transferred when it is delivered by a person other than its issuer for the purpose of giving to the person receiving delivery the right to enforce the instrument.

Transfer is a key concept, because it triggers several consequences: The transferee receives whatever rights the transferor had. The transferor potentially makes warranties (that the instrument is not stolen, that the issuer is obliged to pay it, and that it has not been altered) to the transferee and subsequent parties (including a narrower warranty to the party to whom the instrument is presented).

"Presentment" is also defined.

> **§ 3-501.** (a) "Presentment" means a demand made by or on behalf of a person entitled to enforce an instrument (i) to pay the instrument made to the drawee or a party obliged to pay the instrument or, in the case of a note or accepted draft payable at a bank, to the bank, or (ii) to accept a draft made to the drawee.

QUESTION 1. Issue: "issued"?   Once a retired postal worker has been issued a pension check, it is too late to change pension plans. Murray, a recent retiree, contacts the pension office to change his plan to give his spouse rights of survivorship. The office informs him it is too late. Just that morning, they had cut and signed his first check and had it ready to send. If the court goes by the UCC definition, has the check been issued?

A. Yes. It was a negotiable instrument.
B. Yes. It was enforceable once signed.
C. Yes. Murray had rights in the check.
D. No. It had not been delivered yet.

ANALYSIS. The definition of "issue" is the "first delivery" of the instrument to someone for purpose of giving him rights on it. The check had not been delivered to Murray, so it had not been issued. The best answer is **D**. This is based on a real case, with a happy ending for the retiree and spouse.

QUESTION 2. Transference? Sigmund signs a promissory note in obtaining a mortgage loan from Jung Bank. Jung Bank signs an assignment, selling its rights in the note to Anna Bank. But Jung Bank does not deliver possession of the note to Anna Bank. After Sigmund fails to make payments on the note, Anna Bank seeks to enforce the note. Has the note been transferred to Anna Bank?

A. No. The note was not delivered to Anna Bank.
B. Yes. The assignment is effective to transfer rights in the note.
C. Yes. Anna is still obliged to pay the note.
D. No. The note was not indorsed.

ANALYSIS. The note was not transferred, because that requires delivery of the note. It would be sufficient if Jung Bank had assigned its rights *and* agreed to hold the note as Anna Bank's agent, but that did not occur here. The best answer is **A**. Some mortgage assignments and securitizations have failed to observe the requirements for properly transferring notes, meaning that the bank or investor that thought it had the right to enforce the note was unable to do so.

Contrary to **B**, the note itself must be delivered. Assigning the intangible rights is insufficient.

Anna is still obliged to pay. The question is: Who is entitled to enforce that obligation? As we will see, without a transfer, the right to enforce payment does not move. The question was not whether Anna was still obliged to pay. The question was whether the note has been transferred. **C** is off base.

D looks to an irrelevant factor. The definition of transfer, given above, requires only delivery with intent to give the party rights on the note. Indorsement is not required, so **D** is incorrect. We will see, however, that indorsement is a good idea, for a number of reasons.

QUESTION 3. Presenting presentment. Fordham Ford presents Lightning McQueen a big check for winning the Windy 500. McQueen gives the check to his friend Mater as a present. Mater ceremoniously deposits it at Local Bank, who sends it on to Zitibank, Ford's bank, for payment. Who has presented the check, as UCC Article 3 defines "presentment"?

A. Local Bank, who presented it for payment.
B. Ford, who presented it as the prize.
C. Lightning, who gave it as a present.
D. Mater, who presented it to his bank to get the money.
E. All of the above.

ANALYSIS.

Ford → McQueen → Mater → Local Bank → Zitibank

"Presentment," for the purposes of UCC Article 3, means a demand for payment from the party obliged to pay it (such as someone who signed it) or to the drawee of a check (Ford's bank, in this case). So only Local Bank presented the check. **A** is the best answer. Simply delivering it as a prize, as a present, or as a deposited item do not qulafiy, so the other answers are incorrect.

B.   Typical check

Drawer → Payee → Depositary Bank → Payor Bank (aka Drawee Bank)
Dana   Paula   BDA Bank   Bank of America
       Issued   Transfer   Presented

There could be many variations. Payee might never transfer the check, or simply present it directly to the Drawee. If the Drawee refuses to pay the check, it may then be presented to the indorsers or the drawer, who by signing guaranteed payment. Or the check might be lost, stolen, or destroyed anywhere along the way.

C.   Typical note

Maker   →   Payee   →   Transferee
Borrower   Bank   Finance Company
          Issue   Transfer

Transferee makes presentment to Maker.

The same terms apply with notes, but the practicalities are different. A typical note could be issued by Borrower to Bank. Bank might transfer the note to Finance Company. Finance Company could present the note when due directly to Borrower (as opposed to a check, which is not typically presented to the issuer). There could be many variations. Bank could simply hold the note until it was due, and present it to Borrower for payment. Or, Bank might transfer it to Finance Company, who might transfer it to Gyro Company, who might transfer it to Holding Company.

As with checks, if the note is presented and not paid, the holder may present it to others who signed (e.g., indorsers).

D.   To whom the instrument is initially payable

When written, the instrument is either payable to bearer (whoever is in possession of the instrument) or to an identified person or persons. What if the issuer does not write the name quite right? The Uniform Commercial Code (UCC) takes a functional rather than formalistic approach. The instrument is payable to whomever the issuer, intended to pay, whether they got the name right or not. If Drawer intends to write a check to Lisa Murkowski, the check is payable to her, even if Drawer writes "Lisa Muchoughski" or even "Alice Nagurski." As § 3-110 puts it:

§ 3-110. Identification of Person to Whom Instrument Is Payable
(a) The person to whom an instrument is initially payable is determined by the intent of the person, whether or not authorized, signing as, or in the name or behalf of, the issuer of the instrument.

UCC Article 3 § 110 also resolves such issues as, what if a check is made payable to "Peter, Paul, and Mary"? "It is payable to all of them and may be negotiated, discharged, or enforced only by all of them." UCC § 3-110(d). To "Peter, Paul, or Mary"? "It is payable to any of them and may be negotiated, discharged, or enforced by any or all of them in possession of the instrument." Id. Section 3-110 further addresses such issues as an instrument made payable to a trust, to an account number, and to an organization that has not been legally created (like an informal club). In short, § 3-110 is the place to look first to figure out who the payee is.

QUESTION 4. As you wish. Debtor owes $5,000 to her local bank, AAA Banking. To pay, she sends a check, payable to "AAA." To whom is the check payable?

A. Any entity with AAA in its name, including AAA Banking.
B. Any entity with AAA as its complete name.
C. No one, because she did not correctly name the payee.
D. Any bearer, because she did not correctly name the payee.
E. To AAA Banking, because that is whom Debtor intended.

ANALYSIS. This question shows the practical approach taken in deciding to whom the instrument is payable. Section 3-110 looks to the intent of the signer of the instrument. Debtor intended to pay AAA Banking, so the check is payable to AAA Banking, even though she did not specifically write that. A more formalistic approach would be to look simply to the face of the instrument, but that is not the rule.

A might be correct if the face of the instrument governed. The check says "AAA," so anyone with AAA in its name would qualify.

B might be the rule under a very formalistic regime. Such a rule would say, "To make it payable to AAA Banking, you have to write AAA Banking." That is not the approach of UCC Article 3 and would impose considerable costs on people to write their checks exactly correctly — and would frustrate the purpose of those that did not "dot every 'I' and cross every 'T.'" Sometimes the

UCC is that demanding. An Article 9 financing statement must state the debtor's name accurately, or it will mislead those people searching the records.

C likewise would be the result under a punctilious rule but is not the result under the rule of UCC Article 3, which seeks to give effect to the intent, even if the payee is not perfectly named (or, in fact, even if grossly misnamed).

D would be another possible result but goes too far.

E is the best answer.

QUESTION 5. Who done it?   Daffy writes a check to Polly, on Daffy's account at Sedna Bank. Polly deposits the check with a teller at her bank, Banco Wacko. Polly did not indorse the check. Banco Wacko sends a messenger with the check over to Sedna Bank, and Sedna Bank gives the amount of the check to the messenger. Sedna Bank sends the check back to Daffy along with her monthly statement. Who transferred the check?

A. Daffy, Polly, Banco Wacko, the messenger, and Sedna Bank.
B. Daffy, Polly, and Banco Wacko.
D. Polly.
E. No one, because the check was not properly indorsed.

ANALYSIS.

Daffy → Polly → Banco Wacko → Messenger → Sedna Bank → back to Daffy
    Issued   Transfer   Presented

This question drives home the definition of "transfer": "An instrument is transferred when it is delivered by a person other than its issuer for the purpose of giving to the person receiving delivery the right to enforce the instrument." Daffy did not *transfer* the instrument, for UCC Article 3 purposes. She gave the instrument itself to Daffy, but that is not a UCC Article 3 transfer ("delivered by a person other than its issuer"). So Daffy did not transfer the instrument. This may seem like a formality here, but later we will see how sensible the distinction is. A transfer has several effects (transfers rights, creates a transfer warranty, creates a presentment warranty) that should not apply to the issuer.

Polly transferred the check to Banco Wacko.

Banco Wacko did not transfer the instrument to the messenger. Banco Wacko delivered the instrument to the messenger, but not for the purpose of giving her the right to enforce the instrument. Rather, Banco Wacko delivered the instrument to the messenger for the purpose of transporting the instrument to Sedna Bank.

Banco Wacko (via the messenger) did not transfer the instrument to Sedna Bank. Banco Wacko delivered the instrument to Sedna Bank, but not for the purpose of giving Sedna the rights to enforce the instrument. Rather, the purpose was to have Sedna Bank pay the instrument. So Banco Wacko presented (not transferred) the instrument to Sedna Bank. A presentment is not a transfer.

Sedna Bank delivered the check back to Daffy. This was again not a transfer. The purpose was not to give Daffy the right to enforce the instrument. The purpose was to return the paid check to Daffy.

The best answer is **C**.

E. To whom the instrument becomes payable next

The key term is *holder*. Someone is a holder if two things are true: (1) she is in possession of the instrument, and (2) it is payable to her. If Delia writes a check payable to Paul and gives it to him, Paul is the holder. He is in possession and the check is payable to him. Likewise, if it was payable to bearer, Paul would be the holder. He is in possession and it is payable to bearer, the person in possession.

How does Paul now make it payable to Helen? It depends on whether the instrument is bearer paper or payable to an identified person. Bearer paper is payable to whoever has it, so simply handing the instrument over makes it payable to the recipient. If Paul hands Helen a bearer instrument, it is now payable to Helen, the person in possession.

If the instrument is payable to an identified person, it is a little more complicated. If the check is payable to Paul, he can use an indorsement to make it payable to Helen. There are two ways to do this. If the check is payable to Paul, he can just sign his name. That is a blank indorsement and makes the check into bearer paper. Now it is payable to whoever has it. This is risky, because maybe he intends to give it to Helen, but by endorsing it ahead of time, if he sends it to her and it is lost, or if he sticks it in his pocket intending to give it to her and it is stolen, it will be payable to whomever finds or receives it. Paul has actually increased the risk associated with the instrument. The safer thing to do would be to make the check payable only to Helen. Paul can do this with a special indorsement by writing, "pay Helen, signed Paul." Now the check is payable only to Helen, rather than creating the risk of having bearer paper.

As the UCC puts it:

§ 3-205. (a) If an indorsement is made by the holder of an instrument, whether payable to an identified person or payable to bearer, and the indorsement identifies a person to whom it makes the instrument payable, it is a "special indorsement." When specially indorsed, an instrument becomes payable to the identified person and may be negotiated only by the indorsement of that person. The principles stated in Section 3-110 apply to special indorsements.

(b) If an indorsement is made by the holder of an instrument and it is not a special indorsement, it is a "blank indorsement." When indorsed in blank, an instrument becomes payable to bearer and may be negotiated by transfer of possession alone until specially indorsed."

The definition of indorsement does not require any special form:

§ 3-204. (a) "Indorsement" means a signature, other than that of a signer as maker, drawer, or acceptor, that alone or accompanied by other words is made on an instrument for the purpose of (i) negotiating the instrument, (ii) restricting payment of the instrument, or (iii) incurring indorser's liability on the instrument, but regardless of the intent of the signer, a signature and its accompanying words is an indorsement unless the accompanying words, terms of the instrument, place of the signature, or other circumstances unambiguously indicate that the signature was made for a purpose other than indorsement. For the purpose of determining whether a signature is made on an instrument, a paper affixed to the instrument is a part of the instrument.

In addition, Paul can give Helen the right to payment simply by transferring the check to her.

§3-203. (b) Transfer of an instrument vests in the transferee any right of the transferor to enforce the instrument.

Normally, of course, a party does both (indorses the instrument and transfers it), making the recipient a holder.

QUESTION 6. Transference.   After a big plant sale, Bonnie has a stack of checks written to her by happy customers. Bonnie does not feel like individually signing the checks before transferring them to Casher, who buys her checks at 90 cents on the dollar. Bonnie writes, "I hereby indorse all these checks payable to Casher, Bonnie" on a piece of paper with her letterhead, and folds the paper around the stack of checks. She delivers the checks to Casher. What is the legal effect of her actions?

A. Casher is the holder of the checks. It is in possession and the checks are payable to Casher, because Bonnie indorsed them to Casher.
B. The signature is not an indorsement, so the checks are still payable to Bonnie.
C. No one has rights of a holder. Bonnie is not in possession, and the checks are not payable to Casher. In effect, Bonnie has accidentally voided the checks.
D. Casher has received Bonnie's rights as a holder.

ANALYSIS.
Customer → Bonnie → Casher

This question covers two concepts: indorsement and transfer. Bonnie can give Casher the right to enforce the checks either by indorsing them to Casher or by transferring them to Casher (or by both indorsing and transferring, as is commonly done). Bonnie's intent was to indorse the checks over to Casher, so a rule turning purely on intent would give effect to her writing. The definition of indorsement also follows another key UCC Article 3 policy, however:

putting the necessary information on the instrument itself. An indorsement must be "made on an instrument." That has some flexibility: "a paper affixed to the instrument is a part of the instrument." Bonnie did not affix the paper to the checks, however; rather, she wrapped the paper around the checks. Therefore, Bonnie did not indorse the checks.

She did, however, transfer the checks to Casher. She delivered them to Casher, intending Casher to have the right to enforce them. So, under the transfer rule, Bonnie's rights pass to Casher, even though she did not indorse the checks.

A is not quite true. **A** states that Casher is the holder because Bonnie indorsed them to Casher. First, the premise is not true, because Bonnie did not indorse them. Second, Casher is not a holder, technically. Casher has the rights of a holder. Usually that would be a distinction without a difference, as it is in this case. When it comes to becoming a holder in due course, however, it can make a difference.

B states, "The signature is not an indorsement, so the checks are still payable to Bonnie." The signature is indeed not an indorsement; however, Bonnie transferred the checks, and her rights in them, to Casher. So **B** is not true.

C stands for "Cassandra" here. The check on its face is payable to Bonnie, but Casher has it, so maybe no one is a holder and the check is effectively void. If this were the rule, then checks would be quite risky to deal with, because a forgotten or ill-made indorsement could easily invalidate them. Things are not so dire, however. The transfer is sufficient to give Casher the rights of a holder.

D succinctly states it: Casher has Bonnie's rights as a holder. Bonnie transferred the checks to Casher, even if Bonnie did not indorse them.

Note that the definition of "indorsement" includes the three reasons to make indorsements:

1. To negotiate the instrument. For Paul to make the check payable to Helen, he indorsed it over to her.
2. To restrict payment. If Paul had a bearer check, payable to anyone in possession, he could use a special indorsement to restrict payment (making it less risky). He could indorse it to Helen ("Pay Helen, Paul") or even himself ("Pay Paul, Paul"). The UCC also permits a "restrictive indorsement" (e.g., "For Deposit Only, Paul"), after which only a bank can be a holder. It also permits a holder to convert someone else's blank indorsement to a special indorsement. If Paul had merely signed "Paul" and given the check to Helen, it would be bearer paper. Helen could restrict payment to her by writing "Pay Helen" over Paul's signature.
3. To indorse an instrument is to incur indorser's liability—in other words, to promise to pay if the instrument is not paid. In general, anyone who signs a negotiable instrument promises to pay it. By signing, an indorser becomes a guarantor.

Often, an indorsement will have all three effects. When Paul indorses the check, "Pay Helen, Paul," he makes it payable to Helen to negotiate it to her, he restricts payment to her (rather than making it bearer paper by just signing

"Paul"), and he promises to pay the holder if the check is not paid by the drawee bank. He may not realize all that, but that's the effect of that simple indorsement.

QUESTION 7. Alternatives.   Dana writes a check to Patrick, for some auto supplies. How can Patrick give Leah the rights of a holder?

A. Sign "Patrick" and hand her the check.
B. Sign "Pay Leah, Patrick" and hand her the check.
C. Hand her the check, intending to make her entitled to payment.
D. All of the above.

ANALYSIS.   This question reviews the ways the holder can give rights on the instrument to someone else. If Patrick indorses in blank ("Patrick"), the check becomes bearer paper, payable to whoever possesses it. If Patrick transfers the check to Leah, she is the bearer, and so the holder. **A** works.

If Patrick writes "Pay Leah, Patrick," he has made the check payable to Leah, using a special indorsement. If he delivers the check to Leah, she is the holder (she is in possession and it is payable to her). **B** works.

It works even without an indorsement. If Patrick hands her the check intending to make her entitled to payment, then that is a transfer. When an instrument is transferred, all the rights of the transferor pass to the transferee. Patrick was the holder, now Leah has the rights of a holder. **C** works.

D is the best answer: all of the above.

QUESTION 8. Oops?   Under what sequence of events would a check issued by Dana to Patrick become payable to Thief?

A. Patrick signs "Patrick" and hands Leah the check. Thief steals it from her wallet.
B. Patrick signs "Pay Leah, Patrick" and hands Leah the check. Thief steals it from her wallet.
C. Patrick hands Leah the check, intending to make her entitled to payment. Thief then steals it from her wallet.
D. All of the above.

ANALYSIS.   This question, like many to come, emphasizes how risky bearer paper is (as well as illustrating the difference between bearer and order paper, and the mechanics of transferring rights for both).

In **A**, Patrick signs "Patrick" to a check payable to him. That blank indorsement converts the check into bearer paper, payable to whoever is in possession. Patrick hands Leah the check. She is now the holder, but only until Thief steals it from her wallet. Thief is now in possession of bearer paper, so the check is payable to Thief. **A** is the correct answer. Note that Thief is also the holder.

In **B**, Patrick signs "Pay Leah, Patrick." The check becomes payable to Leah. Patrick hands Leah the check, making her the holder. Thief steals it from her wallet. Leah did not indorse it to Thief and did not transfer it to Thief, so the check is still payable to Leah, not Thief.

In **C**, Patrick hands Leah the check, intending to make her entitled to payment. That is a transfer, so Leah receives Patrick's rights. The check is now payable to Leah. Thief then steals it from her wallet. Again, Leah has not transferred it to Thief or indorsed it, so it is still payable to her, not Thief.

This may seem a little odd. Patrick saves the day once by being careful (using a special indorsement, "Pay Leah") and once by being careless (forgetting to indorse the check at all). This just shows that to make it possible to make Thief the holder, Patrick has to affirmatively do something needlessly risky: indorse the check in blank, converting it into bearer paper.

It may sound worse than it is. In **A**, Thief is the holder of the check, and it is payable to Thief. The check still belongs to Leah, however, as upcoming chapters discuss, and she has the right to retrieve the check from Thief. If the bank pays Thief on a bearer instrument, it will have paid the check properly, and so Patrick or Leah will take the loss. If a bank pays improperly (e.g., pays Thief in situation **B** or **C**, where the check is payable to Leah), the bank will take the loss first. All that is a preview of later chapters.

B and **C** do not make the check payable to Thief, so **D** is not true.

QUESTION 9. Make it safe. Dana writes a check to Patrick. Patrick signs "Patrick" and hands Leah the check. She realizes that it is bearer paper, payable to whoever has it. She wishes to make it less risky. She would indorse it to her bank but cannot remember the bank's present name. It had been Bay Bank, then Fleet Bank, then Bank of Boston, then Bank of America. . . .

How can Leah reduce the risk?

A. Write "Pay Leah, Leah."
B. Write "Pay Leah" over Patrick's signature.
C. Write "For Deposit Only, Leah."
D. All of the above.

ANALYSIS.
Dana → Patrick (signs "Patrick") → Leah

This question emphasizes how easy it is to avoid walking around with bearer paper. Leah has a bearer check, payable to anyone in possession. She wants to restrict payment. She has three easy options. One is to make a special indorsement to herself: "Pay Leah, Leah." **A** works.

B looks like forgery. In **B**, Leah writes "Pay Leah" over Patrick's signature. Any lawyer jumps at the mention of someone altering a document signed by somebody else. Leah could not write herself into her deceased grandmother's will, or retroactively and unilaterally triple the salary in her employment contract. But UCC Article 3 specifically permits her to change an existing blank indorsement into a special indorsement. This does Patrick no harm. He made the check into bearer paper and then gave ownership of the check to Leah. We have already seen she can make it payable to herself. This simply allows her to do so more quickly—and more importantly, without signing the check herself. Leah avoids signing as an indorser, and it does not increase Patrick's responsibility as an indorser. **B** works.

C, "For Deposit Only," is another way to avoid a thief becoming a holder. After that restrictive indorsement, only a bank can be a holder. **C** works.

D, "All of the above," is the best answer.

What about a forged signature? The forged signature doesn't count. Rather, it counts as a signature of the forger, as though the forger had indorsed it in their own name. UCC § 3-403. If Ike steals a check payable to Paul, and Ike writes Paul's name on the back of it, it doesn't count as Paul's signature. It counts as Ike's signature. It does not change the fact that the check is payable to Paul.

QUESTION 10. Holder or hold-up?   Dana writes a check payable to Patrick. Thief steals the check and forges Patrick's signature. Thief, pretending to be Patrick, cashes the check at Check Casher. Check Casher then indorses the check, "Pay to Binko Bank, Check Casher," and transfers the check to Binko Bank. Is Binko Bank a holder?

A. Yes. Check Casher indorsed the check to Binko Bank.
B. Yes. Check Casher indorsed the check to Binko Bank, who took it in good faith, for value, and without notice of the theft.
C. Yes. Check Casher transferred the check to Binko Bank, so Binko Bank received the right to payment under the transfer rule.
D. No. The check was payable to Patrick. Patrick never transferred the check or indorsed it, so it is still payable only to him.

ANALYSIS.

Dana → Patrick → Thief → Check Casher → Binko Bank

This question practices applying the definition of "holder." To be a holder, a person must be (1) in possession (2) of a check payable to the person (or payable to bearer, which would be payable to anyone in possession). Binko is in possession, but the check was payable to Patrick. Patrick never indorsed it or transferred it, so it is still payable only to Patrick. Binko is therefore not a holder.
A is not correct. Check Casher did indorse the check to Binko, but that does not make the check payable to Binko. Only a holder can make the check payable to someone else by endorsing it.

B is a long red herring. It is true that "Check Casher indorsed the check to Binko Bank, who took it in good faith, for value, and without notice of the theft." Binko's state of mind is irrelevant as to whether Binko is a holder, however.

In **C**, Check Casher did indeed transfer the check to Binko, so Binko receives Check Casher's rights; however, Check Casher did not have rights of a holder. Check Casher got the check from Thief. Thief was not transferred the check by Patrick, so Thief had no rights of a holder. Check Casher got only Thief's rights.

D avoids the fallacies of **A**, **B**, and **C**. To figure out if Binko is a holder, the easiest way is not to start with Binko. Start with the issuance: "The check was payable to Patrick. Patrick never transferred the check or indorsed it, so it is still payable only to him." It is not necessary to ask how Binko got it or whether Check Casher indorsed the check. In general, to figure out to whom an instrument is payable, we start at the beginning and follow the chain of transfers and valid indorsements, if any (here, there were none).

QUESTION 11. What about Patrick?   In the scenario described in Question 7, is Patrick a holder?

A. Yes. The check was payable to Patrick. Patrick never transferred the check or indorsed it, so it is still payable only to him.

B. Yes. He was the holder and Thief stole it, so the check is still his property.

C. No. Binko Bank is the holder, because Thief indorsed the check to Binko Bank and Binko Bank is in possession.

D. No. Patrick is not the holder because he is not in possession. No one is the holder.

ANALYSIS.   "Holder" is simply a technical, UCC Article 3 term used in applying many of the rules discussed in later chapters. Holder does not mean owner, or good faith transferee, or anything other than "holder" as defined in UCC § 1-201: In possession of a check payable to you.

The check was stolen from Patrick, so Patrick still owns it. Patrick is not in possession, however, so he is not the holder. No tragedy: as we will see, Patrick still has the right to be paid on the check. As to the specific question—Is Patrick the holder?—the answer is no.

A answers the wrong question. A good question: after the check is stolen, is Patrick still entitled to enforce it? Later chapters will show that he is. It is fully true that "Patrick never transferred the check or indorsed it, so it is still payable only to him." But Patrick is not in possession, so one requirement of being a holder is not met.

B likewise answers a different question. Thief has possession, but the check still belongs to Patrick. Patrick owns the check but does not possess it, so he cannot be a holder.

C misdirects. Patrick is not the holder, as we have figured out. So, who is? Binko has the check, so maybe Binko is the holder. The check is not payable to Binko, however, so Binko does not meet the other requirement to qualify as holder.

D correctly states it: "No one is the holder."

F.   The closer

QUESTION 12. Bearer variation.   Dana writes a check payable to bearer and issues it to Patrick. Thief steals the check and forges Patrick's signature. Thief, pretending to be Patrick, cashes the check at Check Casher. Check Casher then indorses the check, "Pay to Binko Bank, Check Casher," and transfers the check to Binko Bank. Is Binko Bank a holder?

A. Yes. Check Casher indorsed the check to Binko Bank.
B. Yes. Binko Bank took it in good faith, for value, and without notice of the theft.
C. No. The check was stolen, and no one but the owner can be the holder of a stolen check.
D. No. The check was payable to Patrick. Patrick never transferred the check or indorsed it, so it is still payable only to him.

ANALYSIS.

Dana writes bearer check → Patrick → Thief → Check Casher → Binko Bank

Bearer paper is payable to the bearer. So anyone in possession of bearer paper is the holder. Patrick was the holder when he had it. Thief had it next, albeit wrongfully, so Thief became the holder. Thief transferred possession to Check Casher, who became the holder. As holder, Check Casher could convert the check from bearer paper to order paper, by specially endorsing it to Binko Bank. Check Casher then transferred possession to Binko. To see if Binko is a holder, we ask two questions: Is Binko in possession? Yes. Is the check payable to Binko? Yes. So Binko is a holder.

A is therefore true, and so **A** is the best answer.

B gives the right bottom line ("Yes") but for the wrong reasons. Whether Binko took it in good faith, or for value, or without notice of the theft are all irrelevant. They would be relevant if the question were (as discussed in later chapters) whether Binko is a holder in due course. **B** is therefore not as good an answer as **A** but is useful as a preview of the holder in due course doctrine. **C** is not true. Anyone in possession of bearer paper—stolen or not—is the holder.

D is not true. The check was not payable specifically to Patrick; it was bearer paper. So neither a transfer by Patrick nor an indorsement by Patrick were necessary to make the check payable to someone else.

 # McJohn's picks

1.	Issue: "issued"?	**D**
2.	Transference?	**A**
3.	Presenting presentment	**A**
4.	As you wish	**E**
5.	Who done it?	**C**
6.	Transference	**D**
7.	Alternatives	**D**
8.	Oops?	**A**
9.	Make it safe	**D**
10.	Holder or hold-up?	**D**
11.	What about Patrick?	**D**
12.	Bearer variation	**A**

4

The Underlying Transaction (and "Paid in Full")

If a check says, "Paid in full,"
Cash it and that ends the duel.

CHAPTER OVERVIEW
A. Effect of taking instrument in a transaction
B. "Payment in full"
C. The closer
✦ McJohn's picks

A. Effect of taking instrument in a transaction

If an obligee (someone who is owed money) takes a note or ordinary check, the obligation is suspended. The obligation is then discharged if the check is paid, or reinstated if the check is dishonored. If the obligee takes a cashier's check, the obligation is discharged.

Deirdre buys some lecterns from Paula and gives her a check for $1,000. Has Deirdre paid Paula? The next day, can Paula say, "Deirdre owes me $1,000; she gave me a check for $1,000, but that is just a piece of paper. I haven't actually been paid yet. She breached the contract. She hasn't paid me. I'll sue her." The answer, of course, is no. But what if the check is not paid when presented? Has Deirdre nevertheless paid Paula, because she took the check as payment? The answer is again no. Deirdre has not failed to pay, and has not paid. Hmm.

§ 3-310. Effect of Instrument on Obligation for Which Taken

(a) Unless otherwise agreed, if a certified check, cashier's check, or teller's check is taken for an obligation, the obligation is discharged to the same extent discharge would result if an amount of money equal to the amount of the instrument were taken in payment of the obligation. Discharge of the obligation does not affect any liability that the obligor may have as an indorser of the instrument.

(b) Unless otherwise agreed and except as provided in subsection (a), if a note or an uncertified check is taken for an obligation, the obligation is suspended to the same extent the obligation would be discharged if an amount of money equal to the amount of the instrument were taken, and the following rules apply:

(1) In the case of an uncertified check, suspension of the obligation continues until dishonor of the check or until it is paid or certified. Payment or certification of the check results in discharge of the obligation to the extent of the amount of the check.

(2) In the case of a note, suspension of the obligation continues until dishonor of the note or until it is paid. Payment of the note results in discharge of the obligation to the extent of the payment.

If someone takes an ordinary check or note for an obligation, that suspends the obligation but it doesn't discharge it. If Paula took a check from Deirdre, she shouldn't be able to turn around and sue her for not paying at this time. But if the check is dishonored, all bets are off. The obligation is no longer suspended. Now Paula can sue Deirdre on the check or she can sue Deirdre for the underlying sales contract. She can say, "You wrote a check, signed it, and gave it to me; I am entitled to enforce it against you." Alternatively, she can say, "You have a contract to pay me $1,000. You didn't pay, because you wrote me a check that wasn't honored. Therefore, you are still liable under that contract."

If the instrument is dishonored and is now in the hands of someone other than Paula, however, Paula may not sue Deirdre on the underlying obligation, because that would expose Deirdre to double liability. Suppose Paula sold the check to Check Casher, who now has the dishonored check. If Paula could collect from Deirdre on the sales contract and Check Casher could collect from Deirdre on the check, then that would make Deirdre pay twice. Rather, by giving up her rights on the check, Paula also gives up her rights on the underlying obligation.

The hazard of double payment also arises if the obligee takes the check and then it is lost or stolen or destroyed. The obligee is still entitled to enforce its rights on the check, but cannot sue on the underlying obligation. Otherwise, the check could show up in the hands of a holder in due course.

There is a different rule if Paula takes a cashier's check (or certified check, or teller's check) from Deirdre. If Deirdre offers a cashier's check in payment and Paula takes it, then that discharges the obligation to pay. Deirdre is discharged, even if the bank has become insolvent and does not pay the cashier's check. Paula cannot recover from Deirdre, even though Paula winds up with $0 in exchange for those $1,000 worth of lecterns.

Here is the rationale: This isn't going to give Deirdre a windfall. Normally, to procure a cashier's check, the customer must pay the bank in advance. Deirdre paid $1,000 to the bank; the bank gave Deirdre the cashier's check. Deirdre then offered it to Paula. Paula then took it. When she did that, she gave up her rights against Deirdre in exchange for rights against the bank on the cashier's check. Banks normally are much more credit worthy than the average business (even after the 2008 financial crisis). Every now and then, however, a bank goes insolvent. If a party chooses to take on the credit risk of a bank by accepting a cashier's check, then they take the loss if the bank goes insolvent.

QUESTION 1. Lost in transit.   Harper, a publisher, owes author Clemens $50,000 for royalties. Harper sends a check for $50,000 via first-class mail. The check is lost in the mail. Clemens sues for the $50,000. Harper defends on the grounds that the debt is suspended, at least until the mystery of the missing check is cleared up. Otherwise, if the check shows up in the hands of a holder in due course, Harper will have to pay twice. Can Clemens sue for the unpaid royalties?

A. No. The obligation to pay was suspended when Harper sent the check.

B. Clemens cannot collect on the obligation to pay, because that was discharged by sending the check. Clemens can, however, collect from Harper as the owner of the lost check.

C. Yes. The obligation to pay was not suspended, because Clemens did not receive the check.

D. Yes. An obligation to pay is only suspended or discharged when the money actually changes hands, not just pieces of paper.

ANALYSIS.   An obligation is suspended if and when the obligee takes an instrument for the obligation. If Clemens took a check for the unpaid royalties, then that would suspend the obligation to pay until the check was paid (which would discharge the obligation) or dishonored (which would revive the obligation); however, the check was lost before Clemens had a chance to take it.

A is incorrect, because the obligation is suspended only if Clemens takes the check for the obligation, which he never had a chance to do.

B likewise overstates the effect of sending the check. Putting a check in the mail does not discharge the obligation to pay. **B** also gives a little inaccurate preview. A holder that loses a check can still enforce it; Clemens was never the holder, so he has no right to enforce the check.

C is correct.

D overstates things in the other direction from **A** and **B**. Actual transfer of money is not required for the obligation to be suspended. Rather, the obligation would have been suspended if Clemens had taken the check. After that, it would have been discharged if and when the check was paid. That would not require money being physically transferred. Often, payment involves crediting an account.

QUESTION 2. Do-over. Harper sends a royalty check to Thompson, another of its authors. Thompson sells the check to Check Casher, in exchange for a promise of $10,000. Check Casher gets the Harper check paid in full but does not pay Thompson the promised $10,000. Can Thompson, who has not received a penny, sue Harper for the "unpaid" royalties?

A. No. Harper's obligation to pay was discharged when the check was paid.

B. Not right away. Harper's obligation to pay was suspended when Thompson took the check. If Thompson is not able to enforce the debt against Check Casher, then the suspension will be lifted and Thompson can recover from Harper.

C. Yes. Thompson has a contractual right to be paid, not just to receive paper.

D. Yes. Harper must pay Thompson and retrieve the wrongful payment from Check Casher.

ANALYSIS.

Harper → Thompson → Check Casher → Drawee pays
Check Casher gets $, but doesn't pay Thompson

Thompson has not been paid. She has a right to payment—but no longer a right to payment from Harper. When Thompson took the check, the obligation was suspended. When the check was paid, the obligation was discharged. Harper is no longer liable, nor should he be, because Harper has not gotten a free ride. Rather, the promised money has been taken from Harper's account. Thompson, in effect, gave up her rights on the check in exchange for a promise of money from Check Casher.

A correctly states that "Harper's obligation to pay was discharged when the check was paid."

B is incorrect, by stating that Harper's obligation will be reinstated if Thompson cannot collect from Check Casher. The obligation is not just suspended, it has been discharged.

Contrary to **C**, a right to payment can be discharged without receipt of money. Thompson had a contractual right to payment. That right, however, has been discharged. It was suspended when Thompson took the check, and was discharged when the check was paid.

A rule like **D** would greatly undercut negotiability. The holder is entitled to payment, not the obligee on the original transaction. The whole point of negotiability is to separate the right to payment from the rights on the underlying transaction.

QUESTION 3. A deal is a deal. Tobbs lends $25,000 to Burton, taking a negotiable promissory note signed by Burton, with payment due in five years. A year later, Tobbs learns that Burton is in dire financial straits. Concerned that Tobbs may go into bankruptcy; Tobbs would like to sue for the debt. May she sue for the unpaid debt, or must she impatiently sit while the funds to repay her go down the bankruptcy tubes?

A. Tobbs may sue for the unpaid debt and disregard the note, because there has been a change of circumstances.
B. The debt was suspended when Tobbs took the note, and remains suspended until the note is dishonored or paid.
C. The debt was not suspended because Tobbs did not transfer the note to anyone else. She may immediately sue on the debt.
D. The debt was not suspended because Tobbs did not take the note for the debt. Rather, the note simply reflected the existence of the debt.

ANALYSIS.

Burton → Tobbs, note not yet due

Tobbs cannot sue for the unpaid debt. The right to collect the debt was suspended when Tobbs took the note. Until the note is paid or dishonored, the debt remains suspended. It was not paid and cannot be dishonored until it becomes due.

A is incorrect. No other circumstances are relevant.

B is correct.

C does not help Tobbs. The obligation is suspended, whether the note has been transferred or not. The rule does not serve simply to protect negotiability. It also protects the issuer, by preventing the payee from taking an instrument and then attempting to rewrite the bargain between the parties.

D invents a rule. A negotiable note must be a promise to pay. A mere acknowledgement of debt is not an instrument.

Tobbs is limited to her rights on the instrument, until it is paid or dishonored. Having reached that conclusion, Tobbs still may have a chance to sue without waiting. She should examine the note and see if it provides for a right of acceleration, which would be triggered by Burton's financial distress.

QUESTION 4. Rent. Sara sends a check for her monthly rent to Caspar. Caspar puts the check in his wallet and loses it. Can Caspar sue Sara for the rent? For the check? Or both?

A. Sara has not paid any money and so is still liable for the rent. She is not liable for the check, because Caspar lost it.
B. Sara is liable only on the check.

C. Caspar has rights to the rent or as the owner of the lost check. He
    may sue Sara on either theory but is entitled only to one payment.
D. Caspar has no rights to payment. He took the check and lost it, so he
    took the risk of nonpayment. Sara was not at fault.

ANALYSIS.

Sara → Caspar, loses check

Uniform Commercial Code (UCC) § 3-310 provides that when the obligee takes an instrument, the obligation is suspended until the instrument is
paid or dishonored. If the instrument is lost, the obligee is limited to her rights
on the instrument to avoid the risk of double payment.

A states it backward. Caspar cannot enforce the rent obligation, but he
may enforce the check.

B is correct. Sara is liable only on the check.

C gives Caspar too many options. Unlike someone in possession of a dishonored check, Caspar may sue only on the check. If Caspar could recover for
the rent, that would leave open the possibility of a holder in due course showing up with the check.

D is too dire. Caspar does not lose all rights along with the check; that
would be a windfall to Sara. Rather, Caspar can enforce the check, subject to
safeguards against Sara paying twice.

QUESTION 5. To take or not to take?   Roxanne has a contract to
sell some real estate to Pumpkin. At the closing, Roxanne takes a cashier's
check for the purchase price, issued by Beryl Bank. Roxanne signs the
deed and pockets the check. She deposits it that night—and soon learns
that Beryl Bank has gone into insolvency proceedings and has dishonored
the cashier's check. Can Roxanne sue Pumpkin for the unpaid price of the
real estate?

A. Yes. The obligation to pay was suspended when Roxanne took the
    check but is reinstated because the check was dishonored.
B. Yes. The obligation was not even suspended, because Pumpkin ten-
    dered a check written not by him but by someone else.
C. No. When Roxanne took the cashier's check, the obligation to pay
    was not merely suspended, it was discharged.
D. It depends on whether Pumpkin paid in advance for the cashier's
    check.

ANALYSIS.

Beryl Bank → Pumpkin → Roxanne—presents fruitlessly to Beryl Bank

When Roxanne took the cashier's check, she gave up her rights against
Pumpkin in exchange for the right to recover from Beryl Bank. When a cashier's

check is taken for an obligation, the obligation is discharged, not merely suspended. Even if the cashier's check is subsequently dishonored, the obligation is not reinstated.

A states the rule for ordinary checks, not cashier's checks.

B invents a requirement not in the UCC. Section 3-310 applies when an instrument is taken for an obligation. It has no requirement that the instrument be issued by the obligor. This does not open the door for shady dealing, because the obligee is not obliged to take the instrument.

C states the rule correctly for cashier's checks: If the obligee takes the cashier's check, the obligation is discharged. The rationale is that, to procure the cashier's check, the customer typically has to pay the bank the amount of the check. Pumpkin has therefore presumably paid once. If Pumpkin had to pay again, that would be double payment. Rather, Roxanne is given the choice between relying on the bank or relying on Pumpkin for payment.

D is not the rule, although the rationale would support it. If in this particular case Pumpkin had not paid for the cashier's check, Pumpkin would be getting a windfall; however, that would considerably complicate a rather clear rule.

The rule does require a choice by someone in Roxanne's position: Should she take the cashier's check, thereby giving up her rights against Pumpkin, or reject the cashier's check, thereby giving up a promise of payment from a bank (and messing up the transaction with Pumpkin)? In real transactions, this can be dealt with in the contract. The contract could provide for a cashier's check from a specified trusted bank, a guaranty of payment, or a different means of payment, such as a wire transfer.

B.   "Payment in full"

UCC Article 3 provides a simple mechanism for parties in a dispute to settle it, by an accord and satisfaction. "Payment in full" (or similar words) written on a note or check will be given effect — if the recipient cashes the check — if the check is offered in good faith to settle a bona fide dispute, and the words are written *CONSPICUOUSLY*. There are some safeguards to protect the recipient, which § 3-311 spells out in detail.

> **§ 3-311. Accord and Satisfaction by Use of Instrument**
>
> (a) If a person against whom a claim is asserted proves that (i) that person in good faith tendered an instrument to the claimant as full satisfaction of the claim, (ii) the amount of the claim was unliquidated or subject to a bona fide dispute, and (iii) the claimant obtained payment of the instrument, the following subsections apply.
>
> (b) Unless subsection (c) applies, the claim is discharged if the person against whom the claim is asserted proves that the instrument or an accompanying written communication contained a conspicuous statement to the effect that the instrument was tendered as full satisfaction of the claim.

(c) Subject to subsection (d), a claim is not discharged under subsection (b) if either of the following applies:

(1) The claimant, if an organization, proves that (i) within a reasonable time before the tender, the claimant sent a conspicuous statement to the person against whom the claim is asserted that communications concerning disputed debts, including an instrument tendered as full satisfaction of a debt, are to be sent to a designated person, office, or place, and (ii) the instrument or accompanying communication was not received by that designated person, office, or place.

(2) The claimant, whether or not an organization, proves that within 90 days after payment of the instrument, the claimant tendered repayment of the amount of the instrument to the person against whom the claim is asserted. This paragraph does not apply if the claimant is an organization that sent a statement complying with paragraph (1)(i).

(d) A claim is discharged if the person against whom the claim is asserted proves that within a reasonable time before collection of the instrument was initiated, the claimant, or an agent of the claimant having direct responsibility with respect to the disputed obligation, knew that the instrument was tendered in full satisfaction of the claim.

This one is sometimes a surprise. Paula ships the lecterns to Deirdre. Deirdre opens them up. She believes they are not what she was promised. The contract price is $10,000, but Deirdre believes these lecterns are worth only $5,000. Paula responds that she had to change the dimensions because one of her suppliers was late. Paula contends that it was a perfectly reasonable adjustment to the contract and that Deirdre owes her $10,000. Deirdre sends her a check for $7,500. In big, bold letters it says, "payment in full for my obligation on the lectern contract." Paula thinks that Deirdre can't unilaterally tell her how much she owes. Paula deposits the $7,500 check (which is paid) and then sues Deirdre for the remaining $2,500.

Paula will lose that lawsuit. UCC Article 3 gives effect to an accord and satisfaction offered on a check. From Paula's point of view, it may look as though Deirdre was able to unilaterally say, "You think I owe you $10,000, but I think I owe you $7,500. All I will pay is $7,500." The drafters of Article 3 look at it another way. Deirdre was offering to settle a bona fide dispute between the two. The two can sit down and negotiate the dispute; they can litigate the dispute, which is costly; or, they can just agree to settle it. If they agree to settle it, then that is effective. Article 3 allows a very efficient way to settle the dispute: One party can write on the check, "payment in full of the debt," and then it is up to the other party to decide whether to accept the settlement amount offered. If they cash the check, then that is deemed to be acceptance of the offer.

One key requirement is that the writing has to be *CONSPICUOUS*.

§ 1-201(10). "Conspicuous," with reference to a term, means so written, displayed, or presented that a reasonable person against which it is to operate ought to have noticed it. Whether a term is "conspicuous" or not is a decision for the court. Conspicuous terms include the following: (A) a heading in capitals equal to or greater in size than the surrounding text, or in contrasting type, font, or color to the surrounding text of the same or lesser size; and (B) language in the body of a record or display in larger type than the surrounding text, or in contrasting type, font, or color to the surrounding text of the same size, or set off from surrounding text of the same size by symbols or other marks that call attention to the language.

A party can't just write it in small letters and try to avoid the full debt that way.

The other key safeguard is that proffering the check or note with PAID IN FULL must be a good faith attempt to settle a bona fide dispute. Good faith is "honesty in fact and the observance of reasonable commercial standards of fair dealing." UCC § 3-103. A party cannot use a dishonest or unfair approach (e.g., directing attention away from the relevant language). There must be a bona fide dispute about the amount of the debt, so § 3-311 will not apply where the parties agree about how much is owed.

QUESTION 6. Fin.   Jacob leased a gas station from Emily. The two parties had genuine disagreements about whether Emily provided the promised amenities and whether Jacob owed the full amount of the lease payments, $50,000. Jacob sent a check to Emily for $30,000, with "PAYMENT IN FULL OF ALL LEASE PAYMENTS" prominently written on the top of the check. Emily huffed and promptly deposited the check, and it was paid. The next week, Emily sued Jacob for the remaining $20,000, on the theory that a court, not Jacob, decides the rights between the parties. Can she pursue her claim?

A. Yes. Jacob cannot unilaterally arbitrate the dispute.

B. Yes. Emily did not agree to Jacob's offer to settle the dispute. He might as well ask her to signal agreement by continuing to breathe.

C. No. Jacob tendered an instrument conspicuously stating that it was tendered as full payment, there was a bona fide dispute about the amount owed, and Emily obtained payment.

D. Yes. She can still pursue her claim, provided that she returns the money to Jacob.

ANALYSIS.

Jacob ("PAYMENT IN FULL") → Emily → Depositary Bank → Drawee pays

Emily's claim is discharged. For the rule to apply, three initial requirements are as follows: (i) that the person in good faith tendered an instrument to the claimant as full satisfaction of the claim, (ii) the amount of the claim was not liquidated or subject to a bona fide dispute, and (iii) the claimant obtained payment of the instrument. Jacob met all three: (i) He tendered a check in payment in full, (ii) the amount of the claim was subject to a bona fide dispute, and (iii) Emily obtained payment of the check. As long as those three requirements are met, then "the claim is discharged if the person against whom the claim is asserted proves that the instrument or an accompanying written communication contained a conspicuous statement to the effect that the instrument was tendered as full satisfaction of the claim." Jacob's check indeed contained the required conspicuous statement ("PAYMENT IN FULL OF ALL LEASE PAYMENTS") prominently written on the top of the check. Emily's claim is therefore discharged.

The statement in **A** is true in that "Jacob cannot unilaterally arbitrate the dispute," but he did not attempt to do that. He offered to settle, and Emily accepted.

B is incorrect because Emily did not expressly agree to any offer. Rather, as Emily views it, she cashed a check for a portion of the money owed to her. But § 3-311, in effect, treats Jacob's tender of the check marked "PAYMENT IN FULL" as an offer to settle. If Emily cashes the check bearing that conspicuous statement, § 3-311 treats it as implicit acceptance, and Emily is bound by it.

C is the best answer.

D is incorrect. Emily cannot return the $30,000 and pursue her claim for the full $50,000. Subsection c of § 3-311 does allow parties to do that in general, but subsection d provides a big limitation. The party cannot refund and sue if they were aware of the language on the instrument before collecting payment. Emily was "huffily" aware.

QUESTION 7. No tricks. Jacob owes $60,000 to Multi Bank for inventory financing. Jacob decides to try a little sly UCC usage. He visits a branch of Multi Bank (carefully picking one where he is not known) and hands a teller a check for $1,000 and a payment slip. On the check, Jacob has written "payment in full of inventory financing debt" in tiny letters. Jacob explains that the payment is just his regular payment on his bank loan, and the teller sends it to accounting, which unwittingly sends the check on for payment and credits a $1,000 payment to Jacob. Has Jacob managed to erase the entire $60,000 debt?

A. No. Jacob did not act in good faith.
B. No. There was no bona fide dispute about the amount of the debt.
C. No. The statement was not *conspicuous*.
D. A, B, and C are all correct.
E. Yes. By obtaining payment, Multi Bank accepted his offer to settle the debt. Multi Bank should train its staff not to cash checks with suspicious language on them.
F. It depends on whether Multi Bank returns the money to Jacob within 90 days.

ANALYSIS.

Jacob ("payment in full") → Multi Bank → Drawee pays

Section 3-311 does not provide a slick way to cut down on debt. It provides only a mechanism for parties to offer to settle bona fide disputes, in good faith. Jacob fails on several counts.

A is correct, that Jacob did not act in good faith. Rather, he acted deceptively, picking a branch where he was not known, informing the teller that it was just a regular payment, and writing the statement in microscopic letters. For these reasons, § 3-311 would not provide for discharge.

B is also correct. Section 3-311 applies only where the debt is not liquidated or there is a bona fide dispute. Jacob owes the money, without any genuine dispute about the claim or its amount, so he cannot invoke § 3-311.

C is also correct. As a safeguard, the statement must be *CONSPICUOUS*, but Jacob wrote the statement in tiny letters.

D is the best answer.

E is not correct, because Jacob did not meet the requirements of § 3-311.

F is incorrect. When a claim is potentially discharged, the claimant may have the right to give the money back and pursue the claim. Multi Bank does not need to do that here, because the claim is not discharged.

QUESTION 8. Strike that.   Sterling and Luca have a bitter dispute about Luca's failure to pay for a shipment of wine, which Sterling invoiced at $4,500. Luca, who believes the wine was substandard, finally sends a check for $2,000. Sterling deposits the check without noticing that Luca had written "PAYMENT IN SATISFACTION OF ALL AMOUNTS DUE FOR WINE SHIPMENT" in big letters on the check. When Sterling e-mails him a few weeks later about the remainder, Luca says, "I've paid all that was due. Look at the check. Copy attached." Sterling looks at the cancelled check, and discovers what Luca had written. Is the debt finally settled?

A. Yes. By obtaining payment, Sterling unknowingly and irrevocably agreed to settle the dispute.

B. No. The rule only applies between organizations, not individuals.

C. No. There was bad blood between the parties, so the tender could not be made in good faith.

D. No. The debt could be discharged, but Sterling can prevent discharge by tendering repayment of the $2,000 within 90 days of payment of the check.

ANALYSIS.

Luca ("PAYMENT IN FULL") → Sterling → Depositary Bank → Drawee pays

Section 3-311 does give some parties a second chance. A claim is not discharged if "within 90 days after payment of the instrument, the claimant tendered repayment of the amount of the instrument to the person against whom the claim is asserted." This does not apply if the recipient knew before collecting on the check that it was tendered in full satisfaction (as with Jacob above), but Sterling did not know. So, if he tenders repayment within 90 days, he can seek full payment of $4,500. Note what he cannot do: keep the $2,000 and still seek the remaining $2,500.

A is incorrect. Because Sterling acted without knowing of the tender in satisfaction, the discharge is revocable, along with the payment.

B is a red herring. Other provisions in § 3-311 apply only to organizations, but not this one.

C raises a paradox. How can parties act in good faith if they would like to strangle each other? Good faith does not require forgiveness, just "honesty in fact and the observance of reasonable commercial standards of fair dealing." UCC § 3-103. Luca could act in good faith, in trying to settle a bitter dispute.

D states things correctly. If Sterling tenders repayment within 90 days, the claim is not discharged. If he keeps the money, the claim is discharged.

QUESTION 9. Fine print.   Maricel has a long-running dispute with Shun, stemming from a disastrous joint venture investment. Maricel sends Shun a check for $1,100, accompanied by a lengthy letter. One of its many paragraphs states in passing, "The enclosed check represents full satisfaction of all claims owed to you arising out of the joint venture." Shun cashes the check without reading the letter. Are his claims discharged?

A. Yes. Shun was negligent in not reading the accompanying letter.
B. No. The language is only effective if written on the check itself.
C. No. The language is only effective if conspicuous, and this statement was buried.

ANALYSIS.

Maricel ("payment in full") → Shun → Depositary Bank → Drawee Bank pays

The statement must be *conspicuous*. A statement buried in one of many paragraphs of a lengthy letter is not conspicuous.

A relies on a standard that does not exist. The recipient of an instrument is under no duty of care to examine all relevant documents for tenders in satisfaction. Much time would be wasted if every time a check was sent, everything in sight had to be carefully perused to avoid losing rights.

B also invents a rule. Section 3-311 applies if "*the instrument or an accompanying written communication* contained a conspicuous statement to the effect that the instrument was tendered as full satisfaction of the claim." (Emphasis added.) Requiring all statements to be on the check itself would be unnecessarily formalistic. It is not necessary for purposes of negotiability. The accord and satisfaction applies only between those two parties, not subsequent holders of the check. It would also require, in some cases, difficult drafting. The statement would have to be so brief that it could be written conspicuously on a check, which might be difficult for a complicated transaction, requiring reference to various documents, transactions, and other matters.

C is the best answer.

The key safeguard is that the statement must be **CONSPICUOUS**.

QUESTION 10. Misdirected? Kilroy Construction Co. includes the following *conspicuous* provision in all of its contracts: "All communications concerning disputed debts, including an instrument tendered as full satisfaction of a debt, are to be sent to the Kilroy Legal Department, Attn: Tomas Terminator." One of Kilroy's disgruntled customers attempts to settle a dispute about contract payments due by sending a check to the accounting department (the usual place for payment) with the conspicuous legend: "PAYMENT IN COMPLETE AND UTTER SATISFACTION OF ALL CONTRACT LIABILITY WITH KILROY." A bewildered clerk brings it to the chief contract administrator, who smiles and orders deposit of the check. Kilroy takes the position that the claim is not discharged, due to the failure to send it to the correct person. Is the claim discharged?

A. No. Section 3-311(c)(1) allows an organization to require that any attempted tender of full satisfaction be sent to a designated person, office, or place. The tender is not effective unless received as designated.

B. No. Failure to send the check to the right place renders it bad faith.

C. No, provided Kilroy returns the funds within 90 days.

D. Yes. The claim is discharged, because the check was deposited after the chief contract administrator became aware of the attempt to tender payment in full satisfaction.

ANALYSIS.

Customer $\rightarrow$ Kilroy smiles, deposits $\rightarrow$ Depo $\rightarrow$ Drawee pays ("PAYMENT IN FULL")

Section 3-311 provides a safeguard for organizations. An organization might have checks handled by workers with no particular knowledge about the underlying transactions or the various legal issues. It would be hazardous if a clerk in the payments department could unknowingly give up rights simply by cashing a check. So, § 3-311 provides that an organization may require transmittal of "a conspicuous statement . . . that communications concerning disputed debts, including an instrument tendered as full satisfaction of a debt, are to be sent to a designated person, office, or place." If a tender in satisfaction is not sent to the correct office, it is not effective. As with the 90-day refund rule, however, this bar is not effective if the recipient knows the check is sent as tender in satisfaction and still cashes it.

A states the general rule but omits the limitation.

B relies on nonexistent facts. There could be several reasons to send the check to the wrong office. Here, the customer simply sent the check to the usual place. We do not have facts showing bad faith.

C is incorrect. Unfortunately, the 90-day rule is not available where, as in **C**, Kilroy (through its chief contract administrator), knew the check was tendered in full satisfaction.

D, which puts it that the check is discharged, is correct. This is because the check was deposited after the chief contract administrator became aware of the attempt to tender payment in full satisfaction. Neither the 90-day rule nor the mail-it-to-this-office rule for organizations bars discharge. All of the elements are met (bona fide dispute, good faith attempt to settle, conspicuous statement), so the claim is discharged.

C.   The closer

> **QUESTION 11. Expunged.**   Wallace claims Grommit owes $1 million for patent royalties. Wallace grumbles, but takes a check from Grommit for $500,000, with "PAID IN FULL" prominently penciled on its perimeter. The check bounces unpaid back to Wallace. Can he recover from Grommit?
>
> **A.** Yes. He can seek to recover $500,000 on the check or $1 million on the debt.
> **B.** Yes, but he can only seek to recover $500,000 on the check, having settled his claim for $1 million.
> **C.** No. He gave up all rights to sue clever Grommit by taking the check.
> **D.** No. He is not entitled to recover on the $1 million claim and the $500,000 check.

ANALYSIS.

Wallace → Grommitt grumbles but deposits → Depo → Drawee dishonors ("PAID IN FULL")

This question emphasizes the practical approach of the satisfaction and accord provision, § 3-311. A party may tender an instrument in good faith to offer to settle a bona fide dispute. The offer is accepted not just if the other party takes the instrument, but if they obtain payment. The check was not paid, so the dispute is not settled. Wallace may sue on the original dispute, or sue as the holder of the dishonored check. **A** is the best answer.

McJohn's picks

1. Lost in transit	**C**
2. Do-over	**A**
3. A deal is a deal	**B**
4. Rent	**B**
5. To take or not to take?	**C**
6. Fin	**C**
7. No tricks	**D**
8. Strike that	**D**
9. Fine print	**C**
10. Misdirected?	**D**
11. Expunged	**A**

5

Enforcement of a Lost, Stolen, or Destroyed Instrument—and the PEEI

~

Should a check apparate
Don't get in a state.
All will be fine—
Cite 309.

~

CHAPTER OVERVIEW
A. Enforcement of lost, destroyed, or stolen instrument
B. The person entitled to enforce the instrument (the "PEEI")
C. The closer
✦ McJohn's picks

A. Enforcement of lost, destroyed, or stolen instrument

If an instrument is lost or stolen or destroyed, the owner can still enforce it. The court may require the owner to provide security to the person paying, to guard against the risk of paying twice, if a holder in due course shows up with the instrument.

The big check arrives — and then is lost or stolen. Still pay the payee? Aye. Section 3-309 states the rule

§ 3-309. Enforcement of Lost, Destroyed, or Stolen Instrument

(a) A person not in possession of an instrument is entitled to enforce the instrument if:

(1) the person seeking to enforce the instrument

(A) was entitled to enforce the instrument when loss of possession occurred, or

(B) has directly or indirectly acquired ownership of the instrument from a person who was entitled to enforce the instrument when loss of possession occurred;

(2) the loss of possession was not the result of a transfer by the person or a lawful seizure; and

(3) the person cannot reasonably obtain possession of the instrument because the instrument was destroyed, its whereabouts cannot be determined, or it is in the wrongful possession of an unknown person or a person that cannot be found or is not amenable to service of process.

(b) A person seeking enforcement of an instrument under subsection (a) must prove the terms of the instrument and the person's right to enforce the instrument. If that proof is made, Section 3-308 applies to the case as if the person seeking enforcement had produced the instrument. The court may not enter judgment in favor of the person seeking enforcement unless it finds that the person required to pay the instrument is adequately protected against loss that might occur by reason of a claim by another person to enforce the instrument. Adequate protection may be provided by any reasonable means.

Dan writes a check to Purvi for $1,000. It is stolen, lost, or destroyed. That does not mean that Purvi has lost her right to the $1,000. If an instrument is lost, stolen, or destroyed, the owner can still enforce it. Purvi can say to Dan, "You wrote me a check for $1,000, meaning you promised to pay me $1,000 and you must perform that promise." Otherwise, Dan would get a windfall. Purvi must prove the terms of the note and her rights in the note.

There is, however, a possible hazard. Suppose that Dan wrote the check for cash and gave it to Purvi. Then she lost it. Now it shows up in the hands of a holder, because it was payable to bearer. If the holder took it for value, in good faith, and without notice of Purvi's claim to the instrument, Dan has to pay that holder in due course (as later chapters will discuss). It would be unfair if Dan also had to pay Purvi. So, for Purvi to get paid, she has to protect Dan against the risk of a holder in due course popping up with the instrument. What she has to do depends on the particular case. The court has discretion to fashion an appropriate means to provide "adequate protection" to Dan. If Dan had written a check for cash to Purvi and all Purvi can say is, "I have no idea where it is," then the court might require Purvi to post a bond or a letter of credit or sign an indemnity agreement. In another case, suppose that Dan wrote a check not to cash, but to Purvi. Purvi has several people who can testify that that check fell into the furnace and was incinerated along with the trash. It is pretty unlikely that a holder in due course is going to appear out of nowhere with that check, so the court may require less stringent protection.

Note that the rule only applies if the instrument is lost, stolen, or destroyed. It does not apply if the holder has transferred the instrument to someone else (even if they did not get what they were promised for the instrument). Nor does it apply if the instrument is the subject of a "lawful seizure." It also only applies when there has been a loss of possession. So if an instrument is lost in the mail on the way to payee, payee has no rights under § 3-309. Of course payee still has the right to collect whatever debt the instrument was intended to pay.

QUESTION 1. Stray note. Morgana Bank seeks to enforce an alleged note against Denise. Morgana can show that $100,000 was paid to her five years ago. Morgana alleges that it was a loan, and that Denise signed a promissory note to repay the loan, with interest, after four years. Denise denies it all, arguing the money was received for other purposes. Morgana cannot produce the note, nor anyone who can testify what the terms of the note were. Can Morgana recover from Denise on the note?

A. No. To enforce a lost note, the payee must prove the terms of the note.
B. No. To enforce a note, Morgana must have the note.
C. Yes. Morgana can enforce the debt.
D. Yes. Denise is responsible for keeping track of the note.

ANALYSIS. As **A**, the best answer, succinctly states, a party seeking to enforce a lost note must prove the terms of the note. This has been a hindrance to enforcement of some mortgages, where banks have been lax about keeping track of the relevant promissory notes. In such cases, banks may be able to produce some evidence about the terms of the note, because many terms were relatively standard and might be reflected in other documentation. But the basic principle remains: A party wishing to have rights on a note must ensure that it has the note or can prove its terms.

QUESTION 2. Checked out. Darius writes a check payable to Persia. The check is stolen by persons unknown. Can Persia enforce the check against Darius?

A. Yes. She can enforce it, but under § 3-309 the court will assess what protection is necessary to protect Darius against the possibility that the check will show up in the hands of a holder in due course.
B. Yes. She can enforce the check. No safeguards are necessary, because Darius can simply tell his bank not to pay the check should it show up.
C. No. Persia is not the holder, because she does not have the check.
D. No. Persia was negligent with the check.

ANALYSIS.

Darius → Persia → Thief

A states the rule quite correctly.

B is inaccurate. Darius can tell his bank not to pay the check, but there is still a risk that a holder in due course could appear with the check, and Darius would be required to pay the holder in due course.

Contrary to the statement in **C**, the whole point of § 3-309 is that one need not be in possession to enforce a lost, stolen, or destroyed instrument.

Contrary to the statement in **D**, § 3-309 does not depend on whether the former holder was at fault in losing the instrument.

QUESTION 3. Lawful Caesar? Darius writes a check payable to Persia, as payment for Maltese Falcon. The check is confiscated by the authorities, as proceeds of an illegal antiquities sale. Can Persia enforce the check against Darius?

A. Yes. She can enforce it, but under § 3-309 the court will assess what protection is necessary to protect Darius against the possibility that the check will show up in the hands of a holder in due course.

B. Yes. She can enforce the check. No safeguards are necessary, because we know where it is—in custody of law enforcement authorities.

C. No. Persia is not the holder, because she does not have the check.

D. No. Persia was negligent with the check.

ANALYSIS.

Darius → Persia → Feds

The check has not been lost, stolen, or destroyed. Rather, it was the subject of a lawful seizure, and so Persia cannot enforce it. Therefore, the best answer is **B**. The rule stated in **A** is not applicable here. **C** and **D** are off-point for the same reasons.

B. The person entitled to enforce the instrument (the "PEEI")

The key phrase "person entitled to enforce the instrument" (PEEI) is used frequently in later chapters and means

Holder, or

Transferee from a holder, or

Owner of lost, stolen, or destroyed instrument, who retains right to enforce it.

We now have three ways in which someone can say, "I'm the person who is entitled to enforce that instrument." First, they can qualify as a holder (in possession of an instrument payable to them). Second, they can qualify if it was payable to someone who transferred it to them. Third, they can qualify if it used to be payable to them and it was lost or stolen or destroyed.

§ 3-301. Person Entitled to Enforce Instrument

"Person entitled to enforce" an instrument means (i) the holder of the instrument, (ii) a nonholder in possession of the instrument who has the rights of a holder, or (iii) a person not in possession of the instrument who is entitled to enforce the instrument pursuant to Section 3-309 or 3-418(d). A person may be a person entitled to enforce the instrument even though the person is not the owner of the instrument or is in wrongful possession of the instrument.

We will see that the main theories of liability with respect to instruments invoke the PEEI.

Underlying obligation: Obligor may enforce, if PEEI.

Contract liability: Signers of the instrument promise to pay the PEEI.

Warranty liability: Persons that transfer or present the instrument give warranty that they are the PEEI.

Claim to instrument: PEEI may recover from wrongful possessor.

Conversion: Someone who takes or pays the instrument from a non-PEEI is liable to the PEEI.

Properly payable and wrongful dishonor: Bank must pay check that is properly payable, only to the PEEI.

In addition, the validation rules sometimes serve to make someone the PEEI even where there has been a forgery or other misdeed, where appropriate, in order to shift the loss (to one that was negligent, or gave a check to an impostor, or hired a forger or embezzler). With that said, PEEI is a term to know well.

QUESTION 4. PEEI?   Under which of the following facts would Pedro be a PEEI?

A. Darius writes a check payable to Petra, who indorses it to Pedro and hands it to Pedro.

B. Darius writes a check payable to Petra, who hands it to Pedro but forgets to indorse it.

C. Darius writes a check to Pedro and gives it to him. Lief steals the check from Pedro.

D. Darius writes a check payable to Pedro, and hands it to Pedro.

E. All of the above.

ANALYSIS.

Darius → Petra → Pedro

There are three ways to be a PEEI. This question illustrates each.

In **A**, the check is first payable to Petra. She makes it payable to Pedro and hands it to him. Pedro is in possession of an instrument payable to him, the very definition of "(i) the holder of the instrument."

In **B**, the second variation, Petra hands the check to Pedro. Petra forgets to indorse the check; it is not payable to Pedro, so he is not a holder. Under the transfer rule, however, Pedro still gets whatever rights Petra has. Petra was the holder, so Pedro now has the rights of a holder. He qualifies as a PEEI: "a nonholder in possession of the instrument who has the rights of a holder."

In **C**, Pedro starts as a holder but loses possession to a thief. Pedro is no longer a holder (not in possession) or a nonholder in possession with rights of a holder (again, not in possession). He is, however, still a PEEI: "(iii) a person not in possession of the instrument who is entitled to enforce the instrument pursuant to Section 3-309 or 3-418(d)." When an instrument is stolen, the ex-holder still has the right to payment. The thief gets physical possession, but not the rights of the owner. So, the definition of PEEI includes someone who no longer has physical possession but still has the right to payment.

D is simply a reminder that the payee is usually a holder, and therefore a PEEI.

E, "All of the above," is the best answer.

QUESTION 5. PEEI this time?   Last month, Tashi purchased an earthmover from Jack, issuing a negotiable promissory note payable in one year. Tashi soon finds out the earthmover is defective. Jack meanwhile has negotiated the note to Chintus, who innocently pays good money for the note without knowledge of the problem. Is Chintus a PEEI?

A. Yes. Chintus has the note and it was indorsed to Chintus.
B. Yes. Chintus took the note in good faith, for value, and without notice of Jack's defense.
C. No. Chintus cannot be entitled to enforce the note, because Jack has a defense of breach of contract.
D. No. The note was issued to Jack, so only Jack can be a PEEI.

ANALYSIS.

Tashi → Jack → Chintus

This question offers several misdirections. PEEI is a technical term, useful in applying many rules of UCC Article 3. Whether someone qualifies as a PEEI depends only on whether they fall into one of the three categories as described in § 3-301. Tashi issues a note to Jack, who negotiates the note to Chintus. Chintus is the holder of the note. A holder is a PEEI.

A is therefore correct.

B states the correct conclusion but for the wrong reason. Whether Chintus took the note in good faith, for value, or without notice of Jack's defense are all irrelevant to PEEI status. They would all be relevant for holder in due course status, so are mentioned here to distinguish the concepts.

C is incorrect. Chintus is the PEEI. We will see that the PEEI may not necessarily succeed in getting paid. Jack may be able to raise his defense against Chintus. But, as with holder in due course, that is another matter.

D is a real red herring. If a note is negotiable, that means that potentially anyone could be a PEEI. They just need a transfer from a holder.

QUESTION 6. Still got it.   Milo writes a check payable to Humbug, who sticks it in his wallet. The check is stolen by Lief. Who is a PEEI?

A. No one.
B. Humbug.
C. Lief.
D. Humbug and Lief.
E. All of the above.

ANALYSIS.
Milo → Humbug → Lief

To be a PEEI, one must be a holder; a transferee from a holder; or the owner of a lost, stolen, or destroyed instrument. Milo wrote the check payable to Humbug. Humbug was in possession and the check was payable to him, so Humbug was a holder. The check was stolen by Lief, but Humbug neither indorsed it nor transferred it, so it could be payable to no one else. Humbug is still entitled to enforce it—not as a holder, but as the owner of a stolen check.

A is incorrect. It is possible to have no PEEI, but this is not the case here.
B is correct. Humbug is a PEEI.
C is incorrect because Lief is not a holder—the check is not payable to Lief.
D is also incorrect.
E is logically impossible.

QUESTION 7. PEEI and evil twin.   Milo writes a check to Humbug, who signs "Humbug" on the back. The check is stolen by Lief. Who is a PEEI?

A. No one.
B. Humbug.
C. Lief.
D. Humbug and Lief.

ANALYSIS.
Milo → Humbug → Lief

This question reminds us, not for the first time, of the hazards of bearer paper.

A is incorrect, there is a PEEI.

B is also incorrect. Milo wrote a check to Humbug. Humbug, the holder, indorsed in blank, making the check payable to bearer.

C is not the correct answer, either. When Lief stole the check, Lief became the holder. Humbug became the owner of a stolen check. So Lief is a PEEI (as holder), and Humbug is a PEEI (as someone entitled to enforce a stolen check).

D is the best answer.

How can two people be entitled to enforce one check, especially where one owns the check (but does not have it) and the other has the check (but does not own it)? Because PEEI is just a technical term, for someone with standing to sue on the check, as we will see. It certainly does not mean the person will win the lawsuit. Here, Humbug would win and Lief would lose. But if Lief negotiated the check to a holder in due course, we will see, the holder in due course would have rights in the check superior to Humbug, the owner of the check. Injustice? Humbug was the one who made it into bearer paper.

QUESTION 8. Something smells fishy. Junie B. writes a check to May to pay her for some sports equipment. May signs her name on the back and slips the check into a deposit envelope, intending to drop it in the ATM. She gets into a conversation with Walter and mislays the envelope. Unable to locate the check, May seeks to enforce it against Junie B. Junie B. contends that she cannot be required to pay, because she would have to pay twice if the check, now bearer paper, showed up in the hands of a third party. Will the court make Junie B. pay May?

A. No. May is not a holder, because she is not in possession of the check.
B. No. May is not the PEEI, because whoever is in possession of the check is the holder and, therefore, the PEEI.
C. Yes. Junie B. signed and she must pay.
D. Yes. Junie B. is liable, but the court will require May to protect Junie B. against the risk of paying twice.

ANALYSIS.

Junie B. → May lost check after making it bearer paper

This one gives us an example of permitting someone to enforce a missing check. Under § 3-309, May can enforce the check against Junie B., even though May no longer has it. The court, however, will order adequate protection for Junie B. against the risk of paying twice. Junie B. can stop payment on the check, but someone could find the check, which is now bearer paper. If it is negotiated to a holder in due course, then the holder in due course could enforce it against Junie B. (as we will see in more detail later). The court will assess the likelihood that the lost check could show up and be negotiated to someone who takes it in good faith, for value, and without notice of it being lost. The court can then order whatever safeguards are reasonable (e.g., having May post a bond or sign an indemnity). The best answer is **D**.

C.   The closer

> **QUESTION 9. The elevator to nowhere.**   Heinlein writes LeGuin a healthy check in exchange for a robot. Clarke offers LeGuin a space elevator. LeGuin signs over the check from Heinlein, only later to learn that the elevator is a pipe dream. Clarke signs the check over to Checks Galore. LeGuin contends that she can still enforce the check—because it was stolen by Clarke's fraud. Is LeGuin a PEEI?
>
> A. No. A PEEI must be in possession.
> B. No. A PEEI must be the holder.
> C. Yes. The check still belongs to LeGuin, because she never received the elevator.
> D. No. LeGuin has no right to enforce the check.

ANALYSIS.
Heinlein → LeGuin → Clarke → Checks Galore

LeGuin is not a PEEI—yet. To be a PEEI, one must be

- A holder
- A non-holder in possession with the rights of a holder (i.e., a transferee from a holder that did not indorse)
- Someone who can enforce a lost, stolen, or destroyed instrument under § 3-309

D is the best answer. LeGuin is not in possession, so she does not qualify under the first two possibilities. Nor was the instrument lost, stolen, or destroyed. She willingly transferred it (even if due to deception). Checks Galore is the only PEEI. Section 3-309 does not apply if the check has been transferred or lawfully seized, only if the check is lost, stolen, or destroyed. A PEEI in the third category need not be in possession, so **A** and **B** are incorrect. The check may belong to LeGuin, under contract and property law, but that was not the question, so **C** is inappropriate. Having said that, LeGuin may have the right to get the check back from Checks Galore and become the PEEI. That would depend on whether Checks Galore is a holder in due course—but we will get to that later in the book.

McJohn's picks

1.	Stray note	**A**
2.	Checked out	**A**
3.	Lawful Caesar	**B**
4.	PEEI?	**E**
5.	PEEI this time?	**A**
6.	Still got it	**B**
7.	PEEI and evil twin	**D**
8.	Something smells fishy	**D**
9.	The elevator to nowhere	**D**

6

Liability on the Instrument (Signers Promise to Pay the PEEI)

She that signs a check or note
promises to float a groat
to the holder of the chit.
Indorsement? Enforcement, to wit.

CHAPTER OVERVIEW
A. Sign the instrument, promise to pay it
B. Obligation of issuer of note or cashier's check
C. Obligation of drawer
D. Obligation of indorser
E. Drawee bank
F. What counts as a signature?
G. Have presentment and dishonor occurred?
H. Joint and several liability
I. The closer
 McJohn's picks

A.   Sign the instrument, promise to pay it

One that signs an instrument may be liable to pay the person entitled to enforce the instrument (PEEI). Signers include the issuer (drawer of check, maker of note, bank that issues cashier's check), indorsers, and acceptor (a drawee bank that certifies a check).

Drawee Bank, unless it has signed the check, is not liable on the instrument to the PEEI.

Almost anyone who signs a negotiable instrument promises to pay it. "Almost," because Siggi does not promise to pay if she makes clear that it is not a promise to pay: She makes clear on the instrument that she signs for another purpose, such as a receipt, as a witness to someone else's signature, or as an indorsement "without recourse."

Suppose Darth writes a check to Pearl. He issues it to Pearl. Pearl indorses it and negotiates it to Depot Bank. Depot presents it to the drawee bank but is not paid. Depot is the person entitled to enforce it because it is the holder. Depot can enforce it against anyone that signed it. Depot can sue Pearl, because she indorsed the instrument. Depot can also skip over Pearl and seek to recover from Darth. Note that the drawee bank did not sign it, and therefore is not liable to pay it.

Now, suppose Marvin issues a promissory note to Patsy, who indorses it to Finance. Finance is entitled to payment from Marvin. If Marvin refuses to pay, Finance can recover from Marvin, or from Patsy.

Those that are liable have different responsibilities, depending on whether they signed as a maker of a note, drawer of a check, indorser, or drawee that signs a check (i.e., certifies payment), not to mention issuers of cashier's checks, traveler's checks, and teller's checks.

The simplest liability is maker's liability. If Marvin issues a note, he is liable. His liability depends on the terms of the note, such as the amount and the due date. Likewise, if Bank issues a cashier's check, it is liable to pay the instrument according to its terms.

B.   Obligation of issuer of note or cashier's check

The maker of a negotiable promissory note is liable, according to the terms of the note as issued or completed. Who must they pay? Our friend, the PEEI (introduced earlier: a holder, ex-holder of stolen instrument, or transferee from a holder). Or, if the note has already been paid by an indorser, then the maker must reimburse the indorser.

The issuer of a cashier's check is similarly simple.

§ 3-412. Obligation of Issuer of Note or Cashier's Check
The issuer of a note or cashier's check or other draft drawn on the drawer is obliged to pay the instrument (i) according to its terms at the time it was

issued or, if not issued, at the time it first came into possession of a holder, or (ii) if the issuer signed an incomplete instrument, according to its terms when completed, to the extent stated in Sections 3-115 and 3-407. The obligation is owed to a person entitled to enforce the instrument or to an indorser who paid the instrument under Section 3-415.

In short, Marvin (in the example above) is liable to the PEEI, according to the terms of the note when he signed it (or as completed, if Marvin unwisely signed with key terms blank).

A bank that certifies a check similarly is liable on the check.

QUESTION 1. You're fired. Kiln, impersonating Donald Trump, manages to receive a big loan from Manhattan Bank. The staff at Manhattan diligently check new customers' identity and assets but are fooled by Kiln's expertly forged documents and uncanny resemblance to the mogul. Kiln signs "Donald Trump" perfectly to a promissory note and disappears with the funds in a southerly direction. Is Trump liable to pay the note?

A. No. He did not sign the note.

B. Yes. His signature is on the note, even if it was done by someone else.

C. It would depend. Manhattan can collect if it took the note in good faith, for value, and without notice of the forgery.

D. Yes. Deep pockets are always liable.

ANALYSIS.

Kiln forges Trump's signature as maker → Manhattan Bank

A is the best answer. Someone who signs a negotiable instrument promises to pay it. A person is liable on an instrument if and only she or her representative signs it. UCC § 3-401. Something identical to Trump's signature is on the instrument, but Trump did not sign it. Kiln signed without authority from Trump. Trump is not liable on the instrument. We will see that one need not personally sign the instrument to be liable. One can authorize others to sign. Even a forged signature may count against one who is deemed negligent. None of those are at issue here, however. Trump did not sign, so he is not liable.

B misdirects. Trump's signature is a symbol done by him or with his authority. A symbol identical to the one he makes does not count as his signature.

C looks to irrelevant facts. It does not matter what Manhattan did. Nothing Manhattan did or did not do can make Trump liable, if he did not sign the note.

D does seem like the rule, sometimes, but invokes no rule of law.

QUESTION 2. Secondary liability. Candlestick issues a promissory note to Paula, who indorses it over to Hestia. When the note is due, Candlestick refuses to pay Hestia. Hestia recovers from Paula as an indorser. Paula then seeks recovery from Candlestick, who refuses:

"I promised to pay the holder. Nice of you to pay for me, but I did not promise to pay you." Is Candlestick liable?

A. Candlestick was liable to the holder Hestia, but Paula got him off the hook.
B. Paula is entitled to restitution from Hestia, who will then be entitled to recover from Candlestick.
C. Candlestick is liable to Paula, as an indorser who paid the instrument.
D. Candlestick is liable to Paula for fraud, because he deceptively promised to pay the instrument when he signed it.

ANALYSIS.

Candlestick → Paula → Hestia

Those that sign are liable. To whom are they liable? To the PEEI or to a subsequent indorser that paid. An indorser promises to pay the instrument. If she pays, she can recover from those that signed before her. In effect, an indorser guarantees the promises of those whose signatures are on the instrument and may recover from them if she has to pay in their place. So if Paula has to pay as indorser, she can recover from the issuer, Candlestick.

A is not correct. Candlestick is still liable if Hestia gets paid by Paula. Candlestick is no longer liable to Hestia, but is liable to Paula.

B is not correct. Paula has no rights against Hestia.

C states things correctly.

D overstates things. We have no facts indicating that Candlestick defrauded Paula, nor is fraud necessary. Simply by signing as issuer, Candlestick promised to pay any indorser that paid the instrument.

QUESTION 3. Moving the goalposts.   Macher signs a promissory note for $10,000 getting a loan from Romance Finance. Romance alters the note artfully to $100,000 and sells it to innocent Cody Collections. Macher objects to paying Cody the raised amount. Cody responds that the note is unconditional, so Macher must pay it according to its terms. Is Macher obliged to pay Cody anything?

A. Yes. Macher is obliged to pay Cody $10,000.
B. Yes. Macher is obliged to pay Cody $100,000.
C. No, Cody cannot enforce a fraudulent note.
D. No. The note was no longer negotiable because it was not for a fixed amount of money.

ANALYSIS.

Macher → Romance Finance alters amount → Cody Collections

A is the best answer. The maker is liable to pay the note "according to its terms at the time it was issued." Likewise, we will see that parties that sign promise to pay the instrument as it was when they signed it (which makes sense). If we were liable for the alterations of others, we would be ill-advised ever to sign an instrument. There are exceptions we will see. If someone signs a blank instrument, they are liable to pay it according to how others complete it (so never sign a blank check or note). If someone is negligent and that causes an alteration, they are liable to pay according to the altered amount. But neither is the case here.

C.   Obligation of drawer

Drawer liability is slightly more complicated. If Dana writes a check, she does not expect the holder to come to her for payment. The holder should present the check to the drawee bank for payment. If the drawee bank declines to pay the check, however, then Dana is liable. If a check is dishonored, the drawer is liable to pay the PEEI according to its terms as issued (or as completed, if drawer unwisely signed a blank check).

> § 3-414(b). If an unaccepted draft is dishonored, the drawer is obliged to pay the draft (i) according to its terms at the time it was issued or, if not issued, at the time it first came into possession of a holder, or (ii) if the drawer signed an incomplete instrument, according to its terms when completed, to the extent stated in Sections 3-115 and 3-407. The obligation is owed to a person entitled to enforce the draft or to an indorser who paid the draft under Section 3-415.

D.   Obligation of indorser

An indorser, like the drawer of a check, is liable if the instrument is dishonored. Remember an indorser could indorse a check or a note. Indorsers also have other protection. An indorser will not be liable unless they receive proper notice of dishonor and (if a check) if it is not presented or deposited within 30 days of the indorsement. In addition, an indorser is not liable if they indorse a note "without recourse." That allows someone to negotiate a note without becoming liable on it.

Which signatures are indorsements? Any signature not done for some other purpose, such as issuing the note, or signing a receipt for payment:

> § 3-204. "**Indorsement**" means a signature, other than that of a signer as maker, drawer, or acceptor, that alone or accompanied by other words is made on an instrument for the purpose of (i) negotiating the instrument, (ii) restricting payment of the instrument, or (iii) incurring indorser's liability on the instrument, but regardless of the intent of the signer, a signature and its accompanying words is an indorsement unless the accompanying words, terms of the instrument, place of the signature, or other circumstances unambiguously indicate that the signature was made for a purpose

other than indorsement. For the purpose of determining whether a signature is made on an instrument, a paper affixed to the instrument is a part of the instrument.

QUESTION 4. As you wish.   Buttercup signs as "Witness," attesting to the authenticity of Humperdinck's signature on a promissory note. When Humperdinck fails to pay, is Buttercup liable as an indorser?

A. No. She unambiguously did not sign as an indorser.

B. Yes. She is an indorser, because there is no other role for her. Humperdinck is the maker, and she is not the holder. That leaves only indorser.

C. Yes. Everyone who signs a negotiable instrument is liable on the instrument.

D. No, not unless she received the loan.

ANALYSIS.   There are many reasons to sign an instrument, other than to indorse it or issue it. One might sign as a witness (like Buttercup), as a receipt, to show chain of custody, as an acknowledgment, and so on. Section 3-204 provides that such signatures will not be treated as indorsements, provided that (as with Buttercup), it is clear that the signature was not made as an indorsement. Therefore, **A** is the best answer.

For indorsers, there are quite a few conditions to liability:

§ 3-415. Obligation of Indorser

(a) Subject to subsections (b), (c), and (d) and to Section 3-419(d), if an instrument is dishonored, an indorser is obliged to pay the amount due on the instrument (i) according to the terms of the instrument at the time it was indorsed, or (ii) if the indorser indorsed an incomplete instrument, according to its terms when completed, to the extent stated in Sections 3-115 and 3-407. The obligation of the indorser is owed to a person entitled to enforce the instrument or to a subsequent indorser who paid the instrument under this section.

(b) If an indorsement states that it is made "without recourse" or otherwise disclaims liability of the indorser, the indorser is not liable under subsection (a) to pay the instrument.

(c) If notice of dishonor of an instrument is required by Section 3-503 and notice of dishonor complying with that section is not given to an indorser, the liability of the indorser under subsection (a) is discharged.

(d) If a draft is accepted by a bank after an indorsement is made, the liability of the indorser under subsection (a) is discharged.

(e) If an indorser of a check is liable under subsection (a) and the check is not presented for payment, or given to a depositary bank for collection, within 30 days after the day the indorsement was made, the liability of the indorser under subsection (a) is discharged.

An indorser promises to pay, if the instrument is dishonored. An indorser is not liable, however, if she signs "without recourse" (this enables us to separate the functions of indorsing to guaranty payment from the function of indorsing to negotiate the instrument), if the indorser does not get proper notice of dishonor, or if a check is not presented within 30 days of the indorsement. The indorser is treated differently from the drawer. The drawer signs a check and expects ultimately to pay—either by reimbursing the drawee bank after it pays, or paying the holder if the bank dishonors the check. So, the drawer of a check cannot effectively sign "without recourse," or get off the hook because notice of dishonor does not come (the drawer can tell if the check has been paid or not by checking her account) or because the holder waited more than 30 days to present (because there was presumably a debt to pay with the check). The drawer is discharged in the unlikely event that the check is presented more than 30 days after issuance and the bank has meanwhile gone insolvent. The drawer, like an indorser, is discharged if the bank certifies the check (i.e., promises to pay it).

QUESTION 5. Unliable.   Indigo indorses a check. Which of the following would ensure that Indigo will not be liable as an indorser?

A. Indigo indorses "without recourse"
B. The check is paid.
C. The check is not presented for payment within 30 days of Indigo's indorsement
D. Indigo is not given the necessary notice of dishonor.
E. All of the above.

ANALYSIS.   The indorser is given several protections that are not given to the issuer of an instrument. The issuer promises to ultimately pay the instrument. An indorser is only a fallback, who normally signs the instrument simply to pass it along and expects never to see it again. So the indorser liability is limited by several conditions listed above. Therefore, **E** is the best answer.

E.   Drawee bank

A drawee bank normally does not sign the check, so it is not liable on the instrument. UCC § 3-408.

> **§ 3-408. Drawee Not Liable on Unaccepted Draft**
> A check or other draft does not of itself operate as an assignment of funds in the hands of the drawee available for its payment, and the drawee is not liable on the instrument until the drawee accepts it.

If the drawee signs the check (known as certifying or "accepting" the check), however, it is obliged to pay the check. UCC § 3-409.

QUESTION 6. **Entitled?**   Zeus writes a check to Athena on his account at Olympus Bank. Athena indorses the check to Poseidon, who presents it to Olympus Bank for payment. There is plenty of money in Zeus' account to cover the amount of the check, and Poseidon has proof of identification entirely satisfactory to Olympus Bank. The Bank, however, arbitrarily refuses to pay the check. What is the Bank's liability to Poseidon?

A. The Bank is liable to Poseidon, because he is the PEEI.
B. It depends on whether the Bank reasonably refused to pay.
C. The Bank is not liable to Poseidon, because the Bank did not sign the check.
D. The Bank is only obliged to pay if the original payee Athena presents the check for payment.

ANALYSIS.

Zeus → Athena indorses → Poseidon presents → Olympus Bank

This question emphasizes an important practical point. With an ordinary check, the drawee bank does not sign it. The drawee bank is therefore not liable on the instrument. UCC § 3-408. The PEEI has no rights against the drawee bank. The drawee bank's name might appear on the preprinted check form, but that is not a signature.

A is incorrect. Poseidon is indeed entitled to enforce the instrument, but only against people that signed.

B is also incorrect. Whether the Bank was reasonable or not is irrelevant. It has no obligation to Poseidon.

C is correct. The Bank is not liable to Poseidon, even though its customer ordered it to pay the holder of the instrument, and there was plenty of money in the account to pay.

D is also incorrect. Even Athena, whose name was on the check, has no rights against the Bank (or anyone else that did not sign the check). Bank might reasonably have questioned whether Athena's indorsement was authentic.

QUESTION 7. **Time heals all wounds.**   Achilles purchases a used chariot from Odysseus, paying with a check drawn on Achilles' account at Spartan Savings and certified by Spartan Savings. When Odysseus presents the check for payment at Spartan the next day, Spartan refuses to pay. Is Spartan liable to Odysseus?

A. Yes, because Odysseus is the original payee named on the check itself by Spartan's customer, Achilles.
B. Yes, because Spartan signed the check.
C. No. The drawee bank is not liable on the check, only the drawer and indorsers are.
D. No. By certifying the check, Spartan discharged all parties, including itself.

ANALYSIS.

Achilles signs, Spartan Savings certifies → Odysseus presents → Spartan Savings

This question has one key difference from the last question. In each, the question was whether the bank was liable to the holder of the check; however, the previous question involved an ordinary check. This question involves a certified check—a check signed by the bank. A bank that signs the check promises to pay it. UCC § 3-409. So Spartan is liable.

A is not a good answer. Spartan is liable, but not simply because Odysseus was the payee on the check.

B states the better reason: Spartan is liable because it signed the check.

C is wrong. The drawee bank is normally not liable on a check. But this is not a normal check; it is a certified check, signed by the bank.

D is a silly answer, included simply to remind us that when Spartan certified the check, it did discharge the liability of Achilles to pay the check.

———————————

To sum up:

Maker of note—liable, according to terms of note as issued or completed
Issuer of cashier's check—liable
Drawer of check—liable if check dishonored
Indorser—liable if instrument dishonored, receives proper notice of dishonor, did not indorse (without recourse), and (if a check) presented or deposited within 30 days
Drawee bank—not liable, unless it signed the check

Note: We will see in later chapters that a party may be able to raise defenses to payment. The drawer of a check, for example, may be able to defend by showing she did not receive the promised goods. If a holder in due course has the instrument, the right to raise defenses is severely limited.

F.   What counts as a signature?

A person is not liable unless they signed the instrument (themselves, or through a representative). A signature can be any symbol intended to authenticate a writing. A forged signature does not count as the person's signature (subject to validation rules discussed in later chapters).

Who signed?

§ 3-401. Signature

(a) A person is not liable on an instrument unless (i) the person signed the instrument, or (ii) the person is represented by an agent or representative who signed the instrument and the signature is binding on the represented person under Section 3-402.

(b) A signature may be made (i) manually or by means of a device or machine, and (ii) by the use of any name, including a trade or assumed name, or by a word, mark, or symbol executed or adopted by a person with present intention to authenticate a writing.

What if a signature is forged?

§ 3-403. Unauthorized Signature

(a) Unless otherwise provided in this Article or Article 4, an unauthorized signature is ineffective except as the signature of the unauthorized signer in favor of a person who in good faith pays the instrument or takes it for value. An unauthorized signature may be ratified for all purposes of this Article.

When is a signature by an agent effective to bind the principal? To bind the agent?

§ 3-402. Signature by Representative

(a) If a person acting, or purporting to act, as a representative signs an instrument by signing either the name of the represented person or the name of the signer, the represented person is bound by the signature to the same extent the represented person would be bound if the signature were on a simple contract. If the represented person is bound, the signature of the representative is the "authorized signature of the represented person" and the represented person is liable on the instrument, whether or not identified in the instrument.

(b) If a representative signs the name of the representative to an instrument and the signature is an authorized signature of the represented person, the following rules apply:

(1) If the form of the signature shows unambiguously that the signature is made on behalf of the represented person who is identified in the instrument, the representative is not liable on the instrument.

(2) Subject to subsection (c), if (i) the form of the signature does not show unambiguously that the signature is made in a representative capacity or (ii) the represented person is not identified in the instrument, the representative is liable on the instrument to a holder in due course that took the instrument without notice that the representative was not intended to be liable on the instrument. With respect to any other person, the representative is liable on the instrument unless the representative proves that the original parties did not intend the representative to be liable on the instrument.

(c) If a representative signs the name of the representative as drawer of a check without indication of the representative status and the check is payable from an account of the represented person who is identified on the check, the signer is not liable on the check if the signature is an authorized signature of the represented person.

So an agent may sign on behalf of a principal (e.g., a treasurer may be authorized to sign checks on behalf of the company). Section 3-402 also sets out how the treasurer can ensure that the company is liable, but not the treasurer. The treasurer signs, but not on her own behalf, and should make that clear on the check—to make sure she does not end up paying it herself.

QUESTION 8. **All in a day's work**.   Coriolis Corp. is in dire financial straits. Sam, the treasurer, signs several corporate checks payable to suppliers. She signs her own name. The checks have Coriolis Corp. imprinted on them and are payable from a Coriolis account. Unfortunately, there is no money in that account. After the checks bounce, the suppliers sue Sam, because she signed the checks (and Coriolis has no assets to go after). Is Sam liable on the instruments?

A. No. She signed merely as a representative, and that capacity was made clear on the check.
B. Yes. She signed the instrument, and so promised to pay it.
C. No, not unless she now personally owned the goods the suppliers delivered.
D. Yes, as a corporate officer she is liable for all corporate debts.

ANALYSIS.   The general rule is that a representative is not liable, provided that it is clear from the instrument and surrounding circumstances that the person signed as a representative. For checks, there is a bright line rule applicable here. If the check has the name of the represented person (Coriolis) and is payable from that person's account, then the representative is not liable. **A** is the best answer, contrary to **B**. **C** and **D** invent spurious rules.

QUESTION 9. **Signature variations.**   Pauli issues a $300,000 promissory note to Alpher, who indorses it and sells it to Bethe, who indorses it and sells it to Gamow, who likewise indorses it and sells it to Teller. When Teller presents the note when due to Pauli, he refuses to pay. Teller sues Alpher on his indorsement liability. Is Alpher liable on the instrument to Teller?

A. No. Alpher would only be liable to the person to whom he indorsed it, Bethe.
B. No. Pauli is the maker and is primarily liable, so Alpher becomes liable only if Pauli is proved unable to pay.
C. Yes. Alpher is liable but is entitled to recover $100,000 each from the other two indorsers, Bethe and Gamow.
D. Yes. Alpher is liable. He cannot recover from the other indorsers but is entitled to recover from Pauli.

ANALYSIS.
Pauli → Alpher indorses → Bethe indorses → Gamow indorses → Teller

If an instrument is dishonored, any indorser is liable to the PEEI. Any indorser that pays is entitled to collect from previous indorsers.

A is too narrow. Alpher, by indorsing, guaranteed payment not only to Bethe, but to any subsequent PEEI or indorser.

B is likewise too narrow. It states a guaranty of solvency, where a guarantor agrees to pay if the primary obligor is unable to pay. An indorsement is not so limited. An indorser promises to pay if the instrument is dishonored.

C is incorrect. Parties that sign in the same capacity are jointly and severally liable, with a right of contribution. If Alpher, Bethe, and Gamow signed as co-makers, the one that paid would have a right to contribution from the others. Here, they did not sign in the same capacity. They did not sign as joint indorsers; rather, they were people that indorsed the check. An indorser that pays is entitled to recover from previous indorsers, not subsequent indorsers. So Alpher would not be entitled to collect anything from Bethe and Gamow. When Alpher signed, Bethe and Gamow had not signed, so Alpher had no reason to rely on them. Nor did they have an agreement to sign as guarantors.

D correctly states Alpher's rights and obligations. He is liable but can recover from Pauli.

QUESTION 10. I wash my hands of this check.   Frege writes a check to Russell. Russell deposits it, indorsing it as follows: "Pay Bank of Boston, Without Recourse, Russell." Bank of Boston makes the funds available right away, and Russell takes the money. Bank of Boston then presents the check to Frege's bank, which dishonors it. When Bank of Boston seeks the money back from Russell, he points to his indorsement and states that only Frege is liable. Can Bank of Boston recover from Russell?

A. Yes. "Without recourse" has no effect. Anyone who indorses a check is liable as an indorser.
B. Probably. Russell is not liable as an indorser, but Bank of Boston no doubt is protected by a clause in the deposit contract.
C. No. Russell indorsed the check "without recourse," so Bank of Boston has no recourse against Russell. QED.
D. No. Bank of Boston assumed the risk by making the funds available before assuring themselves of payment.

ANALYSIS.   Indorser liability is not the only liability one gets when transferring an instrument. An indorser may indorse "without recourse" and avoid any liability as an indorser; however, it is not a blanket protection from all liability. Russell indorsed while depositing the check with his bank, Bank of Boston. Bank of Boston advanced him the funds. Russell indorsed "without recourse," meaning that Russell had no indorser liability. When the check was dishonored, Russell was not liable as an indorser. He probably does not get to keep the money, with Bank of Boston going after Frege for drawer's liability. Without doubt, Russell's deposit contract with Bank of Boston provides that if a check is dishonored, then the customer (Russell) is liable to Bank of Boston for any amounts advanced on the check (and perhaps a little fee as well).

A is incorrect. "Without recourse" does eliminate liability as an indorser, but it leaves other theories available.

B states things correctly. We do not have the contract, but banks routinely include such a clause.

C has been disposed of in the discussion above.

D has things backward. As an accommodation to customers, banks advance funds provisionally, pending payment. So the risk banks assume is the customer not paying for checks that are deposited and then not honored.

QUESTION 11. Off the hook?   Charles writes a check to Peirce to pay for some books. Peirce indorses the check over to Sanders, to pay a long-standing debt. Sanders leaves the check sitting in her safe for several months. When she finally deposits it, the check is dishonored for lack of funds. She seeks reimbursement from Peirce and Charles, but they contend that Sanders caused the loss by delaying. Are Peirce and/or Charles liable?

A. Yes. They both signed the check, promising to pay it, so they are both liable.
B. No. Neither is liable, because of Sanders' delay.
C. Perhaps. It depends on whether Charles had enough money in the account to pay the check when written (and for the 30 days after).
D. Peirce is not liable, but Charles is.

ANALYSIS.   A delay in seeking payment will discharge an indorser, but normally not the drawer of the check:

§ 3-414(f). If (i) a check is not presented for payment or given to a depositary bank for collection within 30 days after its date, (ii) the drawee suspends payments after expiration of the 30-day period without paying the check, and (iii) because of the suspension of payments, the drawer is deprived of funds maintained with the drawee to cover payment of the check, the drawer to the extent deprived of funds may discharge its obligation to pay the check by assigning to the person entitled to enforce the check the rights of the drawer against the drawee with respect to the funds.

Only if Charles' bank had gone down the tubes, taking Charles' money with it, after 30 days, would the delay discharge Charles' liability. So, **D** is the best answer.

QUESTION 12. Blue Tuesday.   Tuesday pays Sontag with a check for help with a screenplay. Sontag indorses the check over to Marty. Marty deposits it in her bank, but it comes back stamped "Not Sufficient Funds." Marty puts it aside, then after a couple of months complains to Sontag and Tuesday. Are they liable?

A. Yes. They both signed the check, promising to pay it, so they are both liable.
B. No. Neither is liable, because of Marty's delay.

> **C.** Perhaps. It depends on whether Sontag had enough money in the account to pay the check when written (and for the 30 days after).
> **D.** Sontag is not liable, but Tuesday is.

Tuesday → Sontag → Marty → Drawee dishonors

An indorser of a check is entitled to timely notice of dishonor, but a drawer is generally not. So, **D** is the best answer.

G.   Have presentment and dishonor occurred?

A drawer or indorser is not liable until the instrument is properly presented and dishonored (unless those are excused, such as where an instrument is lost or is known to be unpayable).

The drawer and indorsers become liable if the instrument is dishonored. Dishonor occurs if the instrument is properly presented after it becomes due and the party refuses to pay. UCC § 3-502. Under § 3-501, presentment is a demand for payment by the PEEI. Presentment "may be made by any commercially reasonable means, including an oral, written, or electronic communication." The party presenting must "(i) exhibit the instrument, (ii) give reasonable identification and, if presentment is made on behalf of another person, reasonable evidence of authority to do so, and (iii) sign a receipt on the instrument for any payment made or surrender the instrument if full payment is made."

Dana writes a check and her bank refuses to pay it, or Marvin issues a note and then refuses to pay when the holder demands payment on the due date. So, dishonor requires a proper presentment. To present the instrument, the PEEI must demand payment (or certification of a check) from the obligee or drawee. Presentment must be made in a reasonable manner, at a reasonable time. The PEEI must exhibit the instrument, give identification, and sign receipt on the instrument. If the PEEI does not make a proper presentment, there is no dishonor and the liability of the drawer and indorsers is not triggered.

Presentment, along with notice of dishonor, may be excused.

§ 3-504. Excused Presentment and Notice of Dishonor

(a) Presentment for payment or acceptance of an instrument is excused if (i) the person entitled to present the instrument cannot with reasonable diligence make presentment, (ii) the maker or acceptor has repudiated an obligation to pay the instrument or is dead or in insolvency proceedings, (iii) by the terms of the instrument presentment is not necessary to enforce the obligation of indorsers or the drawer, (iv) the drawer or indorser whose obligation is being enforced has waived presentment or otherwise has no reason to expect or right to require that the instrument be paid or accepted, or (v) the drawer instructed the drawee not to pay or accept the draft or the drawee was not obligated to the drawer to pay the draft.

(b) Notice of dishonor is excused if (i) by the terms of the instrument notice of dishonor is not necessary to enforce the obligation of a party to pay the instrument, or (ii) the party whose obligation is being enforced waived notice of dishonor. A waiver of presentment is also a waiver of notice of dishonor.

(c) Delay in giving notice of dishonor is excused if the delay was caused by circumstances beyond the control of the person giving the notice and the person giving the notice exercised reasonable diligence after the cause of the delay ceased to operate.

QUESTION 13. Offline. Marco gets airplane tickets to Nunavut from Aurora Travel, paying by indorsing over his paycheck. The check is soon dishonored, Marco's employer having gone bankrupt. Aurora tries diligently for months to locate Marco. When he shows up in town after six months, Aurora gives notice and sues him as indorser. Is Marco off the hook, because Aurora did not give him notice of dishonor until six months after the fact?

A. No. The failure to give notice of dishonor is excused.
B. No. He signed, he must pay. Period. That is what indorsement means.
C. Yes. Indorsers must get notice of dishonor within 30 days.
D. He is off the hook anyway. Marco cannot be faulted because his employer did not pay the check.

ANALYSIS. Failure to give notice of dishonor is excused "if the delay was caused by circumstances beyond the control of the person giving the notice and the person giving the notice exercised reasonable diligence after the cause of the delay ceased to operate." So, the best answer is **A**.

H.   Joint and several liability

Parties that sign as co-parties may have rights of contribution, but each is liable for the full amount to the holder.

§ 3-116. Joint and Several Liability; Contribution.
(a) Except as otherwise provided in the instrument, two or more persons who have the same liability on an instrument as makers, drawers, acceptors, indorsers who indorse as joint payees, or anomalous indorsers are jointly and severally liable in the capacity in which they sign.

(b) Except as provided in Section 3-419(e) or by agreement of the affected parties, a party having joint and several liability who pays the instrument is entitled to receive from any party having the same joint and several liability contribution in accordance with applicable law.

QUESTION 14. With a little preview.   Alpher, Bethe, and Gamow sign, as makers, a promissory note for $300,000, as part of a real estate investment. The property turns out to be a black hole, and a holder in due course seeks to enforce the note against Gamow. What is Gamow's liability?

A. Gamow is liable only if Alpher and Bethe are also sued.

B. Gamow is liable for $100,000.

C. Gamow is liable to the holder for $300,000 but may recover $100,000 each from Bethe and Gamow.

D. Gamow is liable to the holder for $300,000, and Gamow has no right to collect from Alpher or Bethe.

E. Gamow is not liable, because he did not receive the profits expected from the investment.

ANALYSIS.   If parties sign in the same capacity, they are jointly and severally liable. Alpher, Bethe, and Gamow signed in the same capacity, as makers of a promissory note for $300,000, so they were jointly and severally liable. A holder of the note could sue them together (jointly) or separately (severally). Each would be liable for the full amount, with a right of contribution against the others after paying.

A is not correct. The holder can choose to sue one, two, or three of them.

B is not correct. Gamow might think he is only liable for one-third, but he is liable for the full amount.

C states things correctly: Gamow is liable to the holder for $300,000, but may recover $100,000 each from Bethe and Gamow.

D is too dire. Gamow must pay the whole amount but has the right to contribution from the others.

E shows the risks of signing a negotiable instrument. Gamow promised to pay unconditionally. He is liable unconditionally.

I.   The closer

QUESTION 15. Sophomoric.   Facile writes a check to Ziggy, who indorses it to Dutiful in exchange for cash. Dutiful presents the check to Washou Bank (Facile's bank), who declines to pay it. Dutiful seeks the money from Facile, who argues: "No one is liable for that check. A drawer or indorser is liable only if the check is dishonored. Washow declined to pay, but they had no obligation to pay it, because they did not sign it. So, nobody is obliged to pay. Sorry!" Is Facile liable?

A. Yes. The check was dishonored.

B. No. The check was not dishonored.

> **C.** No, not until Ziggy refuses to pay.
> **D.** Yes. The drawer is liable as soon as she signs the check.

ANALYSIS.

Facile → Ziggy → Dutiful → Washou Bank

This question emphasizes the roles and duties of the parties. Washou Bank, the drawee bank, did not sign the check and so has no obligation to the holder of the check. The drawer, Facile, signed the check (an order to Washou to pay) and becomes liable if the check is presented and dishonored. So, **A** is the best answer.

B is incorrect. The check was dishonored. Washou refused to pay, after a proper presentment.

C is incorrect. Facile becomes liable upon dishonor, not after all other parties are asked to pay.

D jumps the gun. The drawer is liable, but not until the check is dishonored.

 # McJohn's picks

1.	You're fired	A
2.	Secondary liability	C
3.	Moving the goalposts	A
4.	As you wish	A
5.	Unliable	E
6.	Entitled?	C
7.	Time heals all wounds	B
8.	All in a day's work	A
9.	Signature variations	D
10.	I wash my hands of this check	B
11.	Off the hook?	D
12.	Blue Tuesday	D
13.	Offline	A
14.	With a little preview	C
15.	Sophomoric	A

Defenses, Discharge, and Claims to the Instrument

She that signs a check or note
Promises to pay the goat
That holds the paper;
Only, though,
If she acquires the quid pro quo.

CHAPTER OVERVIEW

A. When a holder enforces the instrument, the signer may raise any defense to payment she has (but we will see, not against a holder in due course, the super-plaintiff)
   1. Any defense provided by UCC Article 3
   2. Any defense that would be available in a contract case
   3. Claim in recoupment (a setoff arising out of the transaction)
   4. Discharge
   5. Any claim to the instrument
B. No defenses or claims? Not unusual
C. The closer
◈ McJohn's picks

A.   When a holder enforces the instrument, the signer may raise any defense to payment she has (but we will see, not against a holder in due course, the super-plaintiff)

Buyer signs a promissory note (or a check) when purchasing a new car. Buyer believes she has a reason not to pay the instrument. The car was defective, or misrepresentations were made to her, or there is a breach of warranty. If sued on her liability on the note, can she raise such defenses? Yes—her promise to pay is subject to any defenses she has (unless, as we will see in later chapters, the note or check is in the hands of a holder in due course).

The right to enforce an instrument is subject to

Defenses provided by Uniform Commercial Code (UCC) Article 3
Defenses available in a contract action
Claims to the instrument
Claims in recoupment (a setoff arising out of the transaction)
Discharge

A person entitled to enforce the instrument (PEEI), other than a holder in due course, who is only subject to some defenses, is subject to all of the above.

Someone who signs a negotiable instrument promises to pay it, whether they sign as an issuer (e.g., maker of a note, drawer of a check, a bank that issues a cashier's check), an indorser, or a bank that certifies a check. That promise may not be enforceable if the signer has a defense to raise or if the instrument is subject to a claim or is discharged.

Anthony → Cleopatra → Julius

Anthony signs a negotiable promissory note, purchasing some buggy Web software from Cleopatra. The software's failures cause Anthony to breach several client contracts. Cleopatra meanwhile sells the note to Julius, not before mentioning that Anthony may resist paying. Is Julius' right to collect subject to Anthony's defenses? Yes.

A mere holder of an instrument is subject to

- any defense or discharge provided by UCC Article 3 (meaning that Anthony could raise defenses of breach of promise under § 3-303),
- any defense that would be available in a contract case (meaning Anthony can raise such defenses of breach of contract, breach of warranty, and misrepresentation), and
- any claim to recoupment arising out of the transaction (meaning Anthony could raise his claim to damages for breach of contract), any claim to the instrument (meaning Anthony could raise a claim to rescind the transaction and get the note back).

In addition, a mere holder is subject to discharge of the instrument (such as if the note had been paid, or intentionally ripped up), but discharge is not an issue in this example.

1. Any defense provided by UCC Article 3

The obligation to pay is subject to "a defense of the obligor stated in another section of this Article." UCC § 3-305(a)(2). Article 3 of the UCC provides a number of defenses.

Section 3-303(b) provides: "The drawer or maker of an instrument has a defense if the instrument is issued without consideration. If an instrument is issued for a promise of performance, the issuer has a defense to the extent performance of the promise is due and the promise has not been performed." Suppose Roosevelt is considering buying a fountain from Cherrie Imports. Roosevelt writes a check for the fountain but does not reach agreement on the contract terms. If sued on the check, Roosevelt could raise the defense of lack of consideration. If the parties agreed to a contract, but Cherrie never delivered the fountain, or delivered one that did not live up to the promises made by Cherrie, Roosevelt would have the defense of nonperformance of promise.

Section 3-105 provides the defenses of nonissuance and conditional issuance. It would apply if Roosevelt wrote a check to Cherrie, but held onto the check, intending to hand it over only when the fountain was delivered. If Roosevelt lost the check, or it was stolen, Roosevelt would have the defense of nonissuance. If he handed the check to Cherrie, with the agreement that Cherrie would only cash the check after delivery, but Cherrie cashed the check without delivering the fountain, Roosevelt would have the defense of conditional issuance. Similarly, suppose that Roosevelt and Cherrie signed a separate contract, which stated that the check was only payable if the fountain was delivered (but it was not). Then Roosevelt could raise the defense, under § 3-117, of "other agreements affecting instrument."

Article 3 has a number of more specific defenses, such as payment in violation of an indorsement (§ 3-206) and failure to countersign traveler's check (§ 3-106). So, before paying, a signatory may search through Article 3 to see if there is a specific rule that relieves liability.

QUESTION 1. No quid, no pro quo. Ivan purchases a tractor for his farm, issuing a negotiable note to the seller for $19,170. The seller, however, fails to deliver the tractor. The seller next sues Ivan for payment of the note, pointing out that Ivan promised to pay, with no conditions to that obligation. Is Ivan liable?

A. No. Ivan has the defense of nonperformance.
B. Yes. Ivan promised to pay, period.
C. It would depend if the note was payable on demand.
D. It would depend if the note was secured by collateral.

ANALYSIS.   This question illustrates that a signer may raise defenses, even though the instrument on its face is unconditional. One such defense provided by Article 3 is failure to perform the promise for which the instrument was issued. **A** is the best answer. **B** misstates the law. **C** and **D** are red herrings.

2. *Any defense that would be available in a contract case*

In addition to any UCC Article 3 defenses, someone who signs may raise any defense "that would be available if the person entitled to enforce the instrument were enforcing a right to payment under a simple contract." UCC § 3-305(a)(2). Signing an instrument is a promise to pay the instrument. Contract law often relieves the liability to perform, for breach of contract, fraud, or mutual mistake, or any of the many available defenses. So if Buyer signs a note to buy a truck, and the truck is never delivered (or is delivered late, or is defective, etc.), then Buyer can raise the defense of breach of contract if the holder of the note sues Buyer for payment (unless—we'll repeat the big exception that future chapters will address—the holder is a holder in due course, who can enforce the note and not be subject to any such defenses, meaning Buyer would have to pay the note Buyer issued in exchange for a truck that never arrived, or was defective . . .).

QUESTION 2. Unconditional love.   Kristen issues a negotiable promissory note to Cedar, as part of a real estate investment (a popular source of payment systems litigation). Sure enough, the project does not proceed as planned. Cedar attempts to enforce the note against Kristen. She pleads the defense of breach of contract, arguing that Cedar did not perform various chores required under the contract. Cedar responds by reminding the court that a negotiable instrument must contain an unconditional promise to pay. Kristen promised to pay, period. Can she raise the defense of breach of contract?

A. No. Unconditional means unconditional. The very nature of a negotiable note is an unconditional promise to pay.
B. No, unless the note specifically preserves her right to raise defenses.
C. Yes. Kristen can raise any defense in the action on the note that she could have raised in a contract case.
D. No. She can only raise defenses that go to the note itself, such as claims that she was defrauded into signing the note.

ANALYSIS.
Kristen → Cedar

Someone who has signed an instrument may raise any defense provided by UCC Article 3 or any defense they could raise in a contract case. A mere holder's right to enforce the instrument is subject to "a defense of the obligor stated in another section of this Article or a defense of the obligor that would be available if the person entitled to enforce the instrument were enforcing a right to payment under a simple contract." A negotiable instrument must indeed contain an unconditional promise or order to pay, but the UCC makes it subject to implicit conditions. So, Kristen can raise her defense of breach of contract.

A takes the unconditional language too literally. As with contracts generally, the enforcement of promises to pay notes is subject to defenses the signer has.

B sets too high a standard. The note need not specifically preserve her right to raise defenses, such as through the statement, "I promise to pay $10,000, provided I receive the promised quality investment." Indeed, such language would make the note non-negotiable, because it would state an express condition.

C is the best answer.

D is too narrow. The signer is not limited to defenses going to the note itself but rather may raise any defense provided by UCC Article 3 or that would be available in a contract case.

A standard disclaimer for the whole chapter: As we will see, things are different if the person enforcing the instrument is a holder in due course. If Cedar had negotiated the note to Harvey, a holder in due course, then Harvey would not be subject to Kristen's defense of breach of contract.

QUESTION 3. False start.   Milo has tentatively agreed to buy a plot of land from Tock, without signing a binding contract. The parties draw up all the necessary documents, including a negotiable note payable to Tock for the purchase price. Milo signs the note but instructs his attorney not to hand it over. The note is in a folder in a conference room where the parties hope to close the transaction. Despite hours of negotiation, several issues remain open, and they break for the day. Tock lingers, however, and takes the note. He then tells Milo, "I have your note, and am ready to sign over the property. So you have no defenses to raise against me." Is Milo liable to Tock on the note?

A. No. Milo has a defense of nonissuance.
B. The note is fully enforceable, so it will depend on whether Milo has a defense to enforcement of the underlying transaction.
C. Yes. Milo promised to pay by signing the note.
D. Yes. Milo issued the note by bringing it to the closing.

ANALYSIS.

Milo → Tock takes

Milo can raise any defense provided by UCC Article 3. One such defense is the defense of nonissuance, as **A** states.

B overstates the rights of the PEEI. Tock is indeed the PEEI, but the PEEI is subject to any defense Milo has.

C again places too much weight on the unconditional promise to pay. D is contrary to the definition of issue.

QUESTION 4. Shields up.   In exchange for a combine harvester sold by Butterfly, Raven signs a sales contract and a negotiable note. Raven is not satisfied with the combine, and refuses to pay the note when due. Which of the following defenses could Raven raise if sued by Butterfly on the note?

A. Breach of contract: failure to deliver the goods required by the contract.
B. Breach of warranty: failure to meet contract specifications.
C. Misrepresentation: intentional or negligent incorrect description of the goods and their qualities.
D. Mistake: parties did not form an enforceable contract, because they each had different models of the combine in mind.
E. All of the above, and more.

ANALYSIS.
Raven → Butterfly

A holder of a note (as opposed to a holder in due course, in the next chapter) is subject to any defense the signer has. So, Raven could raise breach of contract (**A**), breach of warranty (**B**), misrepresentation (**C**), mistake (**D**), or any other defense that Raven could raise in a contract case. **E** is therefore the best answer.

This is not to say that Raven will succeed on all those defenses. Answering that question requires fuller examination of the facts and relevant contract law, all beyond the scope of UCC Article 3. The only issue that UCC Article 3 addresses is which issues the signer may raise when sued on the instrument.

QUESTION 5. Shields up again.   Assume the same facts as in the previous question, but suppose this time that Butterfly had indorsed the note over to Frogger for a nice sum, after warning Frogger that Raven might be unhappy because of Raven's complaints about the combine. Which of the following defenses could Raven raise if sued by Frogger on the note?

A. Breach of contract: failure to deliver the goods required by the contract.
B. Breach of warranty: failure to meet contract specifications.
C. Misrepresentation: intentional or negligent incorrect description of the goods and their qualities.
D. Mistake: parties did not form an enforceable contract, because they each had different models of the combine in mind.
E. All of the above, and more.

ANALYSIS.

Raven → Butterfly → Frogger

Frogger might think that Raven's defenses can only be raised against Butterfly. Butterfly sold the combine, not Frogger. If Raven has a problem with the combine, she must litigate with Butterfly, not use it to resist paying on the unconditional promise she made—right? Unfortunately for Frogger, Raven can raise her defenses against any mere PEEI: "the right to enforce the obligation of a party to pay an instrument" is subject to her defenses. So, the correct answer is **E**

QUESTION 6. Ball and chain. Credible signs a note for $200,000, receiving a mortgage from Shark Bank. Shark Bank sells the note to Investor Bank. Shark Bank transfers the note to Investor Bank but does not indorse the note. Credible soon comes to believe that Shark Bank made many fraudulent misrepresentations about the transaction. Can Credible raise those defenses against Investor Bank?

A. Yes. Credible may raise any defense that Credible wishes to raise.
B. Credible does not even need to raise defenses. Shark Bank did not indorse the note over to Investor Bank, so Investor Bank cannot enforce it.
C. No. Only Shark Bank is responsible for Shark Bank's fraud (if any).
D. No. Investor Bank took the note in good faith, for value, and without notice of the alleged fraud, so is not subject to that defense.

ANALYSIS.

Credible signs note → Shark transfers with indorsing → Investor Bank

Shark Bank transferred the note to Investor Bank, so Shark Bank transferred the right to enforce the note, even though Shark Bank did not indorse it. A transfer of an instrument transfers all the transferee's rights in the instrument. So **B** is incorrect. But Credible may raise any defense it has against whoever enforces the instrument (standard disclaimer: except a holder in due course). Therefore, **A** is the best answer.

Whoever takes a note or check (unless they qualify as a holder in due course, we repeat once again), takes it subject to whatever defenses to payment or claims to the instrument exist, so **C** is not correct. But wait (here's a little preview of the holder in due course rule): Why isn't Investor Bank a holder in due course? It did indeed take the note in good faith, for value, and without notice of the defense (fraud, in this case). Those are three of the requirements to be a holder in due course, as we will see. But Investor Bank, because the note was not indorsed to it, was not a holder. It was a transferee with the rights of the previous holder, Shark Bank, who took in bad faith with notice of the fraud, if there was fraud. So **D** is incorrect.

This question has real practical significance. Under the practice of securitization, notes taken in mortgage transactions were often locked in vaults. Rights to the notes were sold to banks or investors, without the notes themselves being indorsed. Likewise, even if notes were not securitized, mortgage practices often included selling rights to notes without bothering to indorse them. So many banks and investors had rights to enforce notes (as transferees), but did not qualify as holders in due course. This means they remain subject to any defenses that the borrowers wished to raise arising from the original transaction. Especially where borrowers ran into trouble, they might claim many defenses—predatory lending, misrepresentation, bad faith failure to arrange suitable terms—and such banks or investors could not use the holder in due course doctrine to insulate themselves from the original transaction.

3. *Claim in recoupment (a setoff arising out of the transaction)*

The right to enforce the instrument is also subject to "a claim in recoupment of the obligor against the original payee of the instrument if the claim arose from the transaction that gave rise to the instrument; but the claim of the obligor may be asserted against a transferee of the instrument only to reduce the amount owing on the instrument at the time the action is brought." UCC § 3-305(a)(3). Note that the setoff is limited to the amount owing, so the holder would not be liable to pay additional amounts to the signer.

4. *Discharge*

A signer's liability may be discharged in several ways. Under § 3-601(a), "The obligation of a party to pay the instrument is discharged as stated in this Article or by an act or agreement with the party which would discharge an obligation to pay money under a simple contract." As with defenses, discharge may be provided by Article 3 or by facts that would discharge the obligation to perform a promise under contract law.

Article 3 provides several modes of discharge.

§ 3-602. Payment

  (a) Subject to subsection (b), an instrument is paid to the extent payment is made (i) by or on behalf of a party obliged to pay the instrument, and (ii) to a person entitled to enforce the instrument. To the extent of the payment, the obligation of the party obliged to pay the instrument is discharged even though payment is made with knowledge of a claim to the instrument under Section 3-306 by another person.

Similar to payment, the drawer and indorsers are discharged if a bank certifies a check.

The most recent version of the UCC also deals with the following issue: What if the issuer pays the payee after an instrument has been transferred? Suppose Mac issues a note to Pam, who sells the note to Hal, but Pam duplicitously collects on the note from Mac. Where payment is made to a former PEEI, there is discharge effective against the real PEEI, even a holder in due course, unless the PEEI has given notice of the transfer to the obligor. UCC § 3-602(b)(d). In other words, when Hal buys the note from Pam, Hal should give notice to Mac. Then, if Mac is so foolish as to pay Pam, that will not give a discharge effective against Mac.

QUESTION 7. Discharged or pay again?   Trusty borrows $100,000 from Shady Finance, signing a note for $100,000 plus interest. Shady soon sells the note to Oak Street Bank. When the note comes due, Shady demands payment in full from Trusty, gets it, and disappears with the funds. Then Oak Street appears and demands payment from Trusty. Trusty responds that the note was discharged by payment. Was it?

A. Yes. Trusty paid the note in full. Payment to anyone gives discharge.
B. Yes, unless Trusty is held negligent.
C. No. The note is not discharged because Trusty paid the wrong person.
D. Yes. Trusty had no notice of the transfer and thus was entitled to pay the person Trusty believed was entitled to payment.

ANALYSIS.
Trusty → Shady Finance (gets paid by Trusty after selling note) → Oak Street

Under the most recent version of the UCC, payment to the payee will discharge the note, unless the transferee gives notice to the obligor of the transfer. Oak Street did not notify Trusty of the transfer, so payment to Shady discharged Trusty's liability. Therefore, **D** is the best answer.

QUESTION 8. Unpaid.   Mia writes a check payable to Local Bookie (Mia's favorite bookstore). The check is stolen from the bookkeeper's desk by Digits. Digits convinces Mia subsequently that the check was given to Digits. Mia pays Digits. Then Local Bookie demands payment. Was Mia's liability discharged when she paid Digits?

A. Yes. Mia paid the check in full and is discharged.
B. Yes, unless Mia is held negligent.
C. No. The liability is not discharged because Mia paid the wrong person.
D. Yes. Mia had no notice of the theft.

ANALYSIS.
Mia → Local Bookie → Digits, gets paid by Mia

Here, unlike the previous question, Mia paid someone who was never entitled to payment. Therefore, the issue of notice does not arise. Mia paid the wrong person and therefore gets no discharge. Therefore, **C** is the best answer.

The PEEI can choose to discharge the signer's liability.

§ 3-604. Discharge by Cancellation or Renunciation

(a) A person entitled to enforce an instrument, with or without consideration, may discharge the obligation of a party to pay the instrument (i) by an intentional voluntary act, such as surrender of the instrument to the party, destruction, mutilation, or cancellation of the instrument, cancellation or striking out of the party's signature, or the addition of words to the instrument indicating discharge, or (ii) by agreeing not to sue or otherwise renouncing rights against the party by a signed record.

(b) Cancellation or striking out of an indorsement pursuant to subsection (a) does not affect the status and rights of a party derived from the indorsement.

(c) As used in this section, "signed," with respect to a record that is not a writing, includes the attachment to or logical association with the record of an electronic symbol, sound, or process to or with the record with the present intent to adopt or accept the record.

In addition, miscellaneous discharge provisions include alteration of the instrument (which gives limited discharge, because the signer is still liable for the original terms of the instrument) under § 3-407; cancellation of indorsements by a holder who reacquires an instrument, under § 3-207; and acceptance varying the terms of a draft.

QUESTION 9. Up in shreds?   Conrad, to guard against identity theft, puts things like credit card solicitations, paid bills, and bank statements through his Patsy 2000 Shredder. One day, he looks up to see his dividend check from MegaMark Company disappearing into the spinning teeth. MegaMark is not sympathetic, telling him that they consider the debt to be discharged by Conrad's destruction of the check. Is MegaMark's liability on the check discharged?

A. Yes. Conrad discharged the liability by destruction of the check.

B. Yes. Conrad discharged the liability by mutilation of the check.

C. No. Conrad did not destroy the check; the shredder destroyed the check.

D. No. Conrad did not intend to discharge the debt.

ANALYSIS.

MegaMark → Conrad accidentally shreds check

Conrad did not discharge MegaMark's obligation to pay. A PEEI "may discharge the obligation of a party to pay the instrument (i) by an intentional voluntary act, such as surrender of the instrument to the party, destruction, mutilation, or cancellation of the instrument, cancellation or striking out of the party's signature, or the addition of words to the instrument indicating discharge." UCC § 3-604. Conrad destroyed the check, but he did not intend to discharge MegaMark. One might argue that Conrad performed an action, shredding the check, which qualified as discharge. The statute clearly covers acts intended to discharge liability, however, like crossing out the party's signature or writing "DISCHARGED" on the instrument.

A places too much weight on the inadvertent destruction of the check.

B likewise relies on a word taken out of context.

C goes too far in the other direction. If Conrad had intentionally run the check through the shredder, intending to discharge MegaMark, that would have been sufficient.

D is the best answer.

QUESTION 10. Discharge by disgruntled? Lear writes a promissory note to Metabolite, reflecting Lear's debt for inventory financing. The check is stolen from Metabolite's office by Quest, a disgruntled former employee. Quest realizes that Lear will not pay him, so he burns the note, taking satisfaction that Metabolite will not get the money. Is Lear's liability on the note discharged?

A. Yes. Quest destroyed the note with the intention of discharging Lear's liability.

B. No. Quest did not intend to discharge Lear's liability.

C. No. Quest did not have the capacity to discharge Lear's liability.

D. Yes. Metabolite cannot enforce a note that no longer exists.

ANALYSIS.

Lear → Metabolite → Quest steals and burns note

The holder has power to discharge, but someone who has no interest in the note does not. So, there would be no discharge. **C** is the best answer.

5. Any claim to the instrument

Someone who has possession of an instrument may be subject to another's claim to the instrument (as where the instrument is stolen, or came from a transaction that is rescinded).

> § 3-306. Claims to an Instrument
> A person taking an instrument, other than a person having rights of a holder in due course, is subject to a claim of a property or possessory right in the instrument or its proceeds, including a claim to rescind a negotiation and to recover the instrument or its proceeds. A person having rights of a holder in due course takes free of the claim to the instrument.

QUESTION 11. "Holder" ≠ "owner." Lief sneaks into Benitez Auto and purloins a number of checks payable to Benitez Auto from customers. The bookkeeper, who has authority to sign for Benitez Auto, had stamped the checks to indorse them "Benitez Auto" and put them into a deposit envelope to take to the ATM. When Benitez Auto seeks the checks back, Lief brazenly defends with the theory that, because the checks had been converted to bearer instruments, Lief is now a holder. Can Lief retain the checks?

A. Yes. Lief is the holder, due to the bookkeeper's carelessness.
B. No. Benitez Auto has a claim to the checks.
C. Yes. Lief can keep the checks, but it will not help Lief. Benitez Auto can still enforce the checks against the drawers, who in turn will stop payment on the checks.
D. No. The theft invalidates the indorsement, so Lief is not a holder.

ANALYSIS.

Drawers → Benitez Auto made bearer paper → Lief

The checks were payable to Benitez Auto. The bookkeeper indorsed the checks in blank, by stamping them "Benitez Auto." The blank indorsements made the checks into bearer paper, payable to whoever was in possession of them. When Lief stole the checks, Lief did indeed become the holder of the checks; however, a holder is subject to a claim to the instrument. Benitez Auto has a claim to the instruments: Benitez Auto is the owner of the instruments. Had Lief negotiated them to a holder in due course, the story would not have a happy ending. A holder in due course is not subject to any claim to the instrument (even the claim of the owner of the instrument!).

A places too much weight on holder status. Lief is the holder. Lief is the PEEI. Lief is, however, subject to the claim of Benitez Auto.

B accurately punctures Lief's argument and, therefore, is correct.

C is partly true. Benitez could ask the various owners to stop payment on the checks. Benitez does have the right to enforce the stolen checks. But Benitez also has the right to get the checks back from Lief.

D offers a hopeful but inaccurate theory. The theft does not invalidate the indorsement. The bookkeeper did indeed make the checks into bearer paper, and the theft does not change that. Luckily, the checks were tracked down before they wound up in the hands of a holder in due course.

QUESTION 12. Good faith alone is not a shield. Assume the same facts as the previous question, but now suppose that by the time Benitez Auto had located Lief, he had given the checks as a gift to his innocent uncle. The uncle had presented the checks and received payment. Would the uncle be liable to Benitez Auto?

A. No. Benitez has a claim to the checks, but the uncle does not have the checks.

B. No. The uncle cannot be liable, because he took in good faith without knowledge of the theft.

C. Maybe. If the uncle indorsed the checks, he would be liable as an indorser.

D. Yes. Benitez Auto has a claim to the checks or their proceeds.

ANALYSIS.

Drawers → Benitez Auto made bearer paper → Lief → Innocent Uncle

"A person taking an instrument, other than a person having rights of a holder in due course is subject to a claim of a property or possessory right in the instrument *or its proceeds*." UCC § 3-306 (emphasis added). The uncle was subject to Benitez Auto's claim to the check or its proceeds. The uncle received the proceeds of the checks and so is liable to Benitez Auto. This is an example of the general rule that a holder is subject to all defenses or claims to the instrument, whether the holder knew about the defenses or not.

A understates the power of a claim to the instrument. Benitez Auto need not locate the checks themselves before payment. Benitez Auto, the owner of the checks, has a claim to the checks or their proceeds.

B previews the holder in due course doctrine, but insufficiently. If the uncle had taken for value, without notice and in good faith, he would be a holder in due course. A holder in due course is not subject to a claim to the instrument or its proceeds. The uncle got the checks as a gift, however, so would not qualify as a holder in due course (did not give value).

C raises irrelevant theories. Benitez Auto is not trying to enforce the check against the uncle; Benitez Auto is bringing a claim to the proceeds of the check.

D is the best answer.

B.   No defenses or claims? Not unusual

The holder of an instrument, we have now seen, can be subject to defenses in UCC Article 3 or from contract law, to discharge, and to claims to the instrument and claims in recoupment. It is worth mentioning that the typical note or check has none of those. If Borrower signs a note and gets a loan (and there are no legal problems, such as usurious interest rate, an illegal transaction, or fraud, for example), then Borrower is liable to pay the note and has no defenses to raise against the holder of the note. If Buyer writes a check for some equipment and gets what she was promised, she likely has no claims or defenses and is liable for the money.

C.   The closer

> **QUESTION 13. A bearer is a bearer.**   Assuming the same facts as Question 8, would Mia be discharged if she had issued a bearer check to Local Bookie and then paid Digits, who stole the bearer check?
>
> **A.** No. She is only discharged if she pays the owner of the check.
> **B.** No. She would be negligent to pay anyone but Local Bookie.
> **C.** Yes. If she paid the bearer of a bearer instrument, she would be discharged.
> **D.** Yes, but. . . . She would be discharged on the check but would still be liable on the underlying debt to pay for the books.

ANALYSIS.

Mia → The Local Bookie → Digits steals, gets paid by Mia

Once again, we see the risks of bearer instruments. Mia paid a thief, but she paid the person entitled to enforce the instrument. She would be discharged. Local Bookie would no longer be able to collect, because Mia would have a discharge. Local Bookie could have avoided this by converting the check to order paper—such as by indorsing it, "Pay to Local Bookie, Signed Local Bookie." Then, if Mia paid a thief, she would not have paid the PEEI and would not be discharged. Local Bookie could have enforced it under § 3-309. Therefore, **C** is the best answer.

A is incorrect, because discharge depends on paying the PEEI, not necessarily the owner.

B is incorrect, because Mia is entitled to pay the holder of bearer paper.

D is incorrect, because the underlying debt is discharged.

 ## McJohn's picks

1. No quid, no pro quo	**A**
2. Unconditional love	**C**
3. False start	**A**
4. Shields up	**E**
5. Shields up again	**E**
6. Ball and chain	**A**
7. Discharged or pay again?	**D**
8. Unpaid	**C**
9. Up in shreds	**D**
10. Discharge by disgruntled	**C**
11. "Holder" ≠ "owner"	**B**
12. Good faith alone is not a shield	**D**
13. A bearer is a bearer	**C**

8

The Holder in Due Course

A typical holder in due course,
Arrives on a llama or blue horse,
Asks for the money
And if something's funny
Says, "Pay me. There's no other recourse."

CHAPTER OVERVIEW
A. The holder in due course
B. Becoming a holder in due course
    1. Holder
    2. Value
    3. No notice
    4. Good faith
    5. Shelter rule
C. The holder in due course doctrine does not apply to consumer credit sale notes
D. The closer
 McJohn's picks

A.   The holder in due course

If you ask a lawyer to think back to her commercial paper class in law school, she will probably mention the holder in due course (HIDC) doctrine. If there is a commercial paper question on the bar exam, it is likely an HIDC question. It is a central concept in commercial law, even if declining slowly in commercial importance.

Sasha Furniture → Kofi → Trusty Finance, an HIDC

Suppose that Kofi breaches completely, but Sasha Furniture must still pay Trusty Finance.

Sasha Furniture agrees to borrow $10,000 from Kofi and signs a note promising to pay $10,000 plus interest at 10 percent. Kofi, however, never delivers the money. Sasha Furniture puts the failed transaction out of mind. Years later, when the note comes due, Trusty Finance informs Sasha that Trusty Finance holds the note. Trusty Finance bought the note in good faith from Kofi, unaware that the loan was never made. Must Sasha Furniture pay, even though it never got a penny? Yes. In contract law, such a material breach will make a promise unenforceable. In negotiable instrument law, however, the result can be quite different.

An HIDC may enforce a negotiable instrument without being subject to most defenses or claims to the instrument. The HIDC doctrine gives a much different set of rights to the parties to a transaction than contract law usually does. Suppose that Buyer signed a sales contract with Seller to purchase a truckload of lecterns for $10,000. Seller assigned the sales contract to Bank, in exchange for a payment of $8,000. In the meantime, Seller has failed to deliver the promised lecterns. Bank then seeks to enforce Buyer's obligation to pay the contract price. Buyer, under contract law, could easily defend. If Seller has not performed (because Seller did not deliver the lecterns), then Buyer would not have to pay. Seller assigned Seller's contract rights to Bank, so Bank had the right to collect the price subject to the conditions of the contract. In short, Buyer did not get the lecterns, so Buyer does not have to pay.

If a negotiable instrument is involved, the HIDC doctrine can give a different result. This time, suppose that Buyer signs a sales contract (agreeing to pay $10,000 in exchange for a truckload of lecterns) and also signs a $10,000 negotiable promissory note. Seller negotiates the note for $8,000 to Bank, who becomes an HIDC of the note. Seller again does not deliver the lecterns. Bank seeks to enforce the note against Buyer. Bank wins. Because Bank is an HIDC, Buyer cannot raise the defense of breach of contract. Buyer has to pay Bank, even though Buyer never received the lecterns. Buyer's only chance is to sue Seller for breach of contract and hope that Seller is not judgment proof.

The same result would obtain for most defenses a party has to payment of a negotiable instrument. Even if Seller had defrauded Buyer, or it was an unconscionable contract, or there was a mistake that made the sales contract unenforceable, or Seller had delivered completely defective lecterns, Buyer could not raise those defenses against an HIDC. There are a few defenses that someone can raise, but there are precious few that go to the very heart of taking a legal obligation (along the lines of, "There was a gun to my head when I signed that promissory note" or "I was only 12 years old when I signed)."

The HIDC doctrine serves to make negotiable instruments more freely negotiable. An HIDC can acquire a negotiable instrument without worrying whether it is subject to defenses, because the HIDC will take free of those defenses. So, the HIDC doctrine makes negotiable instruments more valuable.

In effect, someone who signs a negotiable instrument agrees to pay an HIDC, even if the signer has a valid defense to payment. When Buyer signed the promissory note and handed it to Seller, Buyer had obliged herself to pay any HIDC of the note, even if Buyer never received the lecterns. Is that horribly unfair? Not if Buyer knowingly accepts that risk as part of the terms of a commercial transaction. As we will see in later chapters, payment systems often work that way. If Buyer paid Seller with cash, which Seller had spent, Buyer could not get the actual cash back from the innocent party that now has it. If Buyer pays with a debit card or wire transfer and does not get what she is promised, then Buyer cannot get the money back from her bank but, rather, must seek to recover from Seller. Credit cards and letters of credit, on the other hand, do offer considerable protection to buyers.

Why would anyone sign a negotiable instrument, giving up their potential defenses? Presumably, it would be in exchange for other aspects of the transaction. Seller may offer the lecterns at a cash price of $9,000, or for a $10,000 negotiable promissory note, or for $11,000 in installment payments. If Buyer chooses the negotiable instrument option, then she takes on the risks of dealing with an HIDC. So, Buyer should consider the trustworthiness of Seller, the risks of the other options, and other ways to reduce her risk (such as signing the note only after picking up the lecterns). The HIDC doctrine allows Buyer to make her promise to pay more valuable by saying, "I promise to pay, no matter what." If the promise is more valuable, then Buyer can use it to get more in exchange. In short, the HIDC doctrine is one of many ways commercial law allows the parties to a transaction to allocate risk. It is like warranties with goods. Buyer may agree to buy the goods without a warranty ("as is"), taking on the risk of a defect in exchange for a more favorable price or for some other term.

As with warranties in sales law, the HIDC doctrine has been limited with respect to consumers. If a consumer bought some furniture on credit and signed a promissory note, the consumer would likely assume that if the furniture never arrived or was defective, the consumer would not have to pay. Most consumers would not use negotiability as a bargaining chip to get a more favorable price. More likely, a consumer would never have heard of the HIDC doctrine. Federal law, recognizing this, has effectively abolished the HIDC doctrine with respect to consumer credit sales.

QUESTION 1. Vulnerable. Meercat is a holder of a negotiable promissory note issued by Badger. Meercat is not an HIDC but is merely a holder. The original payee, Otter, had given the note as a gift to Meercat. Which of the following defenses could Badger raise, if sued by Meercat on the note?

A. Breach of contract (alleging that Otter had breached the sales contract, because the painting was not what Otter had warranted).

B. Unfair competition violation (alleging that due to Otter's misrepresentations, a local unfair competition statute provided a defense against enforcement of the contract).

C. Fraud (alleging that Otter had tricked Badger, getting the note in exchange for a forged Pollock painting).

D. All of the above.

E. None of the above.

ANALYSIS.

Badger → Otter gave as gift to → Meercat

This question illustrates the rule that applies when someone suing on a note or check is not an HIDC. The general rule is that a promise to pay is subject to any defenses the promissor had. If someone signs a negotiable instrument, she promises to pay it. But when that promise is enforced, she may raise any defense that she could raise in a contract action. In common sense terms, you do not have to pay if the other party did not perform (unless the note is held by an HIDC, as we will see).

When someone is sued on a note by someone who is not an HIDC, she can raise any defense that she could raise in a contract case, provided the defense arises out of same transaction. So, if Badger was sued by Meercat, a non-HIDC, Badger can raise any defense that she could have raised against Otter. Badger can raise fraud, breach of contract, consumer protection violation, or any other defense she wishes to raise.

A is correct, because breach of contract can be raised as a defense. Signing an instrument is a promise to pay it, but breach by the other party may make the promise unenforceable.

B is also correct. Any defense that could be raised in a contract case may be raised against a mere holder (i.e., not an HIDC). If a local consumer protection statute provides a defense, then that may be raised against an HIDC.

C is likewise correct. If the signer alleges the transaction was fraudulent, then that may be raised as a defense to payment.

Because **A**, **B**, and **C** are all correct, the best answer is **D**, "All of the above."

E is incorrect.

> **QUESTION 2. Invulnerable.**   Suppose that Meercat does not sue Badger on the note. Rather, Meercat negotiates the note to Mighty Mouse, who takes the note for value, in good faith, and without notice of any defenses or other problems concerning the note. Mighty Mouse qualifies as an HIDC. As discussed below, Mighty Mouse meets the four requirements (holder, value, good faith, no notice). Which of the following defenses could Badger raise, if sued by Mighty Mouse on the note?
>
> A. Breach of contract (alleging that Otter had breached the sales contract, because the painting was not what Otter had warranted).
> B. Unfair competition violation (alleging that due to Otter's misrepresentations, a local unfair competition statute provided a defense against enforcement of the contract).
> C. Fraud (alleging that Otter had tricked Badger, getting the note in exchange for a forged Pollock painting).
> D. All of the above.
> E. None of the above.

ANALYSIS.

Badger → Otter gave as gift to → Meercat → Mighty Mouse, HIDC

This question shows the stark difference when an HIDC is the plaintiff. Most of the defenses that could be raised in a contract case cannot be raised against an HIDC. For that reason, an HIDC is sometimes called a "super-plaintiff," as though HIDC status confers immunity against defenses. Hence, Mighty Mouse is subject to none of the listed defenses and the correct answer is **E**, "None of the above."

A is not correct. Breach of contract is probably the most common defense raised in commercial litigation: "Seller did not perform, so I do not have to pay." However, it is not one of the defenses that can be raised against an HIDC.

B is not correct. A party sued on a debt is likely to try to find some statute that protects her payment, be it unfair competition, usury, regulations of business practices, and so on. But such a defense may not be raised, unless it fits into one of the defenses on the very short list of defenses that can be raised against a holder in due course.

C is not correct. Even if the promise to pay was induced by fraud, the promise may be enforced. This is quite different from many areas of the law, where fraud receives special treatment and victims of fraud are able to rescind transactions. The HIDC rule is thus a strict one: she who signs a negotiable instrument agrees to pay, even if she has been defrauded. As discussed in the next chapter, one rare category of fraud may be raised as a defense (essentially, something along the lines of "They tricked me into signing what I thought was an application to law school, but it was really a promissory note"), but the most common types of fraud may not be.

B.   Becoming a holder in due course

An HIDC is often called a "super-plaintiff." Because the plaintiff cannot raise most defenses against an HIDC, the HIDC is likely to win the lawsuit. But that does not mean that every holder who sues on an instrument will win. Rather, the hard part is for the holder to prove that she is an HIDC. The UCC strikes a balance between the rights of an HIDC and the set of parties that have those special rights. An HIDC can enforce a negotiable instrument without being subject to most defenses or claims. But not everyone that gets hold of a negotiable instrument gets those special rights. Rather, to be an HIDC, the person in question must meet four requirements: holder, value, good faith, and no notice.

1. Holder

To be an HIDC, one must be a holder. To be a holder, recalling earlier chapters, requires two things. First, the person must be in possession of the instrument. Second, the instrument must be payable to that person. If it is bearer paper, then it is payable to whoever is in possession. Whoever has it is therefore a holder. If it is order paper, then any necessary indorsements must be on the instrument or be deemed to be there, under one of the validation rules (negligence, impostor rule, fictitious payee rule, employee forger rule).

> **QUESTION 3. The "H" in HIDC.**   Ash Inc. writes a check payable to Sweeps for some chimney supplies. Unhappy with the supplies, Ash stops payment on the check. In the meantime, Sweeps cashes the check at QuikiMart, a convenience store, who gives $500 for the check in good faith, with no notice of any problems with the supplies. Sweeps does not indorse the check. If QuikiMart sues Ash on the check, may Ash raise the defense of breach of contract?
>
> **A.** Of course. Someone that signs a negotiable instrument (be it a check or note) can always raise the defense that they did not get what they were promised.
> **B.** Of course not. QuikiMart is an HIDC, because it took in good faith, for value, with no notice of any problems. QuikiMart is not subject to a defense of breach of contract.
> **C.** Yes. QuikiMart is not a holder, because the check was not made payable to QuikiMart. If not a holder, QuikiMart cannot be an HIDC.
> **D.** No. Sweeps did not indorse the check, but did transfer it to QuikiMart. So QuikiMart is entitled to enforce it.

ANALYSIS.
Ash Inc. → Sweeps does not indorse → QuikiMart

Not a holder; therefore not an HIDC (a *holder* in due course).

A is incorrect, because it denies the very HIDC doctrine. If the plaintiff is an HIDC, then the defendant that signed the instrument is indeed unable to raise most defenses. That does not help QuikiMart, because QuikiMart is not even a holder, meaning . . . .

B is incorrect. QuikiMart is not an HIDC. QuikiMart took in good faith, for value, with no notice of any problems. The check was payable to Sweeps, however, and was not made payable to QuikiMart. QuikiMart is in possession of the note but is not a holder, because the note is not payable to QuikiMart. To be an HIDC, one must be a holder, and QuikiMart is not. So **C** is correct.

Note that depositary banks have a rule that helps them avoid this problem. Recall that if a customer is the holder of an instrument and deposits it in the customer's account, the bank automatically becomes a holder, whether the customer indorses the instrument or not.

D is a bit of a red herring. The check was payable to Sweeps. Sweeps transferred it to QuikiMart, but that does not make QuikiMart a holder. QuikiMart is indeed the person entitled to enforce it — but remains subject to defenses against enforcement.

Note that QuikiMart has the rights of a holder (because it received a transfer from a holder, Sweeps) but does not qualify as holder in its own right, because the instrument was not enforced. Nor could it use its rights from Sweeps to qualify as an HIDC. Sweeps was a holder, but as seller of the supplies would have notice of any problem with them. If there is a defense arising out of the original transaction, the payee would normally have notice of that defense, being the one whose conduct created the defense. So QuikiMart gets Sweep's rights — the rights of a holder who took with notice, and therefore was not an HIDC.

2. *Value*

Someone does not get the special rights of an HIDC unless they have given up something substantial. UCC § 3-303 lists several ways value can be given.

- 1. A promise of performance, to the extent the promise has been performed;
- 2., 3. instrument is payment or collateral for an debt, even if pre-existing;
- 4. exchange for another instrument;
- 5. incurring an irrevocable obligation to a third party.

The value requirement has real bite to it. Making a promise does not constitute giving value. Making a promise and performing is value, under option 1. If the promise has not yet been performed, then HIDC status is unnecessary, because the promissor can simply refuse to perform. Suppose that Shady Merchant sells a batch of defective paint to Paint Co., in exchange for a negotiable promissory note. Shady sells the note to Bank for a promise of $10,000. If Bank has paid the $10,000, then Bank has given value and can be an HIDC. If Bank has not paid, Bank has not yet given value and so is not an HIDC.

Bank will be unable to collect from Paint Co.—but that does not harm Bank, who can in turn refuse to pay Shady. But suppose Bank has promised to pay someone else, such as by issuing an irrevocable letter of credit. Bank cannot get out of this promise, so Bank is deemed to have given value and can thus be an HIDC, under option 5.

Similarly, if Bank gave another Shady note in exchange, then Bank has likely given up something substantial, so option 4 makes that count as value. If Bank handed over a worthless note in exchange, then Bank would likely fail to meet the good faith requirement, discussed below.

Options 2 and 3 address the situation where Bank takes the note from Shady as payment or collateral for an existing debt. Bank may not hand over any new money (if the debt was already in place). Viewing the loan transaction overall, however, Bank extended credit in reliance on the note (either by loaning or by refraining from collecting the debt), which is giving something substantial.

QUESTION 4. Value?   Finbar signs a $10,000 promissory note, as part of a transaction in which it purchases the assets of Dingle Drapes. Dingle Drapes negotiates the note to Belfry Bank. In which of the following would Belfry Bank be deemed to have given value for purpose of becoming an HIDC?

A. Belfry Bank agrees to pay $10,000 for the note and indeed hands over $10,000 cash two days later.

B. Belfry Bank agrees to pay $5,000 for the note and indeed hands over $5,000 cash two days later.

C. Belfry Bank gives Dingle Drapes a check originally issued by another party, Dell, to Belfry Bank.

D. Belfry Bank agrees to pay $10,000 for the note, a year later, when the note is due with interest.

E. A–C.

ANALYSIS.

Finbar → Dingle Drapes → Belfry Bank

This question illustrates that the value requirement can be met several ways, but something substantial must be given up. The only scenario in which Belfry Bank does not qualify is **D**. In **D**, Belfry made a promise but did not perform it yet, so Belfry Bank has not given value.

In **A**, Belfry Bank promises to pay $10,000 and has performed, so Belfry Bank has given value. Likewise, in **B**, Belfry Bank has promised and fully performed. Note that Belfry Bank has completely met the value requirement, even though it paid only $5,000 cash for a face value $10,000 note, because its promise was to pay $5,000. Had Belfry Bank promised $10,000 and paid $5,000, then it would have met the value requirement to the extent of performance, meaning Belfry Bank could be an HIDC for one-half the amount of the note, or $5,000.

In **C**, Belfry Bank has not handed over any money, so one might reason that, as in **D**, Belfry Bank has not met the value requirement. But Belfry Bank has given up its rights in the check from Dingle Drapes, as opposed to merely making a promise to pay. That is sufficient to constitute value.

So, the best answer is **E**.

Note that Belfry Bank could also have met the value requirement by taking the note as collateral for a debt. Likewise, Belfry Bank would give value by making an irrevocable obligation to a third party, such as if it issued a cashier's check to Margo, who holds the mortgage on Dingle Drape's real estate.

QUESTION 5. Collateral value. Cesario presses Olivia for payment on a debt she owes him. Olivia persuades him to hold off collection proceedings and take as collateral a promissory note issued by Viola. Unbeknowst to Cesario, Viola claims a defense to payment on the grounds that Olivia made certain misrepresentations about the original transactions. If Cesario is an HIDC, he will not be subject to such defenses. But Viola contends Cesario is not an HIDC. He may be a holder that took in good faith without notice of the defense, but he did not give value. Did Cesario give value?

A. No. He just took the note as collateral for an existing debt. He did not buy the note or give anything in exchange for it.
B. Yes. He took the note as collateral for an existing debt.
C. No. He has not performed any promises.
D. Yes. He gave value long ago, when he gave the loan to Olivia.

ANALYSIS.
Viola → Olivia gives as collateral for existing loan from → Cesario

Under § 3-303, a taker gives value if they take the instrument as payment or collateral for a debt, even if pre-existing. So Cesario gave value, by taking the note as collateral for the loan. The theory behind the rule (illustrated in this question) is that the taker really is giving value by taking the collateral rather than enforcing the loan. More commonly, a party will make a loan with collateral to include instruments that the borrower receives in the future. So the lender relied on those future instruments in making the loan and so gave value for them. Therefore, **B** is the best answer.

3. No notice

The HIDC can enforce the instrument without being subject to most defenses or claims. She can make Buyer pay, even if the promised lecterns were never delivered, as discussed in section A. An HIDC that holds a stolen check need not return it to its owner. The "no notice" requirement prevents someone from becoming an HIDC if they had notice of the claim or defense, or of facts that should have raised questions about the instrument. If, before taking the promissory note, Bank knew that Buyer had not received the promised lecterns, then Bank will not qualify as an HIDC. To qualify as an HIDC, one must take the instrument

> (iii) without notice that the instrument is overdue or has been dishonored or that there is an uncured default with respect to payment of another instrument issued as part of the same series, (iv) without notice that the instrument contains an unauthorized signature or has been altered, (v) without notice of any claim to the instrument described in Section 3-306, and (vi) without notice that any party has a defense or claim in recoupment described in Section 3-305(a).

Someone has notice of a fact when she knows or should know it. UCC § 1-201. Under (v) and (vi), a holder will not be an HIDC if it had notice of a claim or defense. If Harriet takes the note knowing that the signer was defrauded, or simply did not receive the promised exchange for the note, or that the transaction ran afoul of a business practices law, Harriet will not be an HIDC. Just as she must give value to be an HIDC and cut away claims and defenses, so she will not be able to be an HIDC if she took the note knowing about a claim or defense.

Under (iii), she will not qualify as an HIDC if she took the instrument knowing of facts that indicate that there may be a defense or claim to the instrument. If the note is overdue or the signer refused to pay, the reason may be that the signer has a defense to payment. If Harriet takes it knowing that it was overdue, she will be subject to that defense. Likewise, if she takes with notice that the instrument was altered or bears a forged signature, she will not be an HIDC. Likewise, under § 3-303(a), she will not be an HIDC if the instrument bears such "apparent evidence of forgery or alteration or is not otherwise so irregular or incomplete as to call into question its authenticity."

The notice requirement means that the payee will rarely be an HIDC in a case where it matters. Suppose that Pirate Paragliders sells a defective machine to Falling Waters, in exchange for a promissory note. Falling Waters crashes and refuses to pay the note. Pirate Paragliders, the payee, will not qualify as an HIDC, because it had notice of the defense of breach of contract. It knew or should have known the machine was defective. In short, if the signer has a claim or defense, it usually arises out of the payee's conduct, so the payee will have notice and will not qualify as an HIDC. Nor should it — Pirate Paragliders, who sold the defective machine, should not be able to use the HIDC doctrine to collect on the note.

Courts sometimes extend this to a party closely associated with the payee. Suppose that Pirate Paragliders signed the note over to Pirate Finance, a separate corporation owned and controlled by the same crew that runs Pirate Paragliders. A court may well treat Pirate Paragliders and Pirate Finance as the same entity for the purpose of notice.

QUESTION 6. On notice, without noticing.   Smullyan Finance
sells Gardner a promissory note issued by Tiger Trucking. When Gardner
seeks to enforce the note, Tiger Trucking raises the defense of breach
of contract, on the grounds that the truck purchased with the note had
faulty logic in its operating software. Tiger Trucking further contends that
Gardner cannot be an HIDC (who would be insulated from the defense),
because Gardner took the note several weeks after it was due. Gardner
credibly contends he did not notice that the note was overdue and therefore took without notice of that fact. Can Gardner qualify as an HIDC?

A. No. He should have known the note was overdue, so he took with
notice.
B. Yes. If he did not know the note was due, he did not take with notice.
C. It does not matter. The note is overdue, so it is no longer payable.
D. Yes. If he gave value and acted in good faith, it does not matter if he
was on notice.

ANALYSIS.

Tiger Trucking $\rightarrow$ Truck Seller $\rightarrow$ Smullyan Finance $\rightarrow$ Gardner

Someone has notice of a fact when she knows or should know it. UCC
§ 1-201. When a note is due is such a key fact that a party taking a note should
always know when it is due. So the taker will be on notice, whether they actually know the due date or not. Therefore, **A** is the best answer.

Actual knowledge is not required to have notice, contrary to the statement
in **B**.

C corrects a common misunderstanding. If a note is "overdue," that means
it simply has not been paid on time. It still is payable.

To be a holder in due course, one must meet all four requirements: 1) holder
that 2) takes in good faith, 3) without notice, 4) for value. **D** is too forgiving.

QUESTION 7. Notice, but no problem. Larry lends Ishy $20,000. Ishy
gives him a note for $20,000 plus interest at 10 percent. The transac-
tion complies fully with applicable lending law. Ishy nevertheless refuses
to pay the note on its due date, a year later. Larry later sells the note to
Harriet for $12,000. When Harriet seeks payment, Ishy laughs and says,
"You took the note with notice that it was overdue. The due date is right
on top of the first page. You are no HIDC and I do not have to pay you."
Who will win, Harriet or Larry?

A. Larry. Harriet knew or should have known the note was overdue. She
is therefore not an HIDC.
B. Larry. Harriet not only had notice the note was overdue, but she
should have known that Larry had dishonored it. She is doubly dis-
qualified from HIDC status.

> **C.** Harriet. She is indeed not an HIDC, because she took with notice that the note was overdue. But she can still enforce the note.
> **D.** Harriet. She qualifies as an HIDC. She is a holder and took the note in good faith and for value.

ANALYSIS.

Ishy → Larry sells note after due date → Harriet

This problem demonstrates the interplay between the notice requirement, defenses, and enforceability of an instrument. Someone who takes with notice of a claim or defense will not be an HIDC. In addition, someone who takes with notice of a problem (the note is overdue, dishonored, or has obvious alterations) will not be an HIDC. The problem should make them aware that there may be a defense to the note. It may have been dishonored or become overdue because the signer did not get the promised exchange, or there may be no underlying defense, as here. The note was overdue, but not because Ishy had a defense. Rather, he simply refused to meet his legal obligation to pay. He is still obliged to pay the person entitled to enforce the instrument, HIDC or not.

D is wrong. Harriet is not an HIDC. She took with notice that the note was overdue (and perhaps should have known that it was dishonored, because she probably should have asked Larry why it was overdue). As we saw previously, however, HIDC status makes no difference where the defendant has no defense to raise. If Ishy had a defense (Larry never delivered the money, or charged an illegal rate of interest) he could raise it against Harriet, a non-HIDC. Here, Ishy has no defense. He has no legal reason not to pay the note.

A and **B** are not good answers. Rather, they both err in concluding that Larry will win if Harriet is not an HIDC.

C is correct. Harriet, as the holder of the note, is entitled to enforce it against Ishy. Ishy has no defense to raise, and so Harriet will win the lawsuit. Of course, maybe Ishy refused to pay because he has no assets. If so, Harriet will still win the lawsuit, but will end up only with a judgment that is not worth much.

4. *Good faith*

One cannot be an HIDC if she does not take the instrument in good faith. Good faith is "honesty in fact and the observance of reasonable commercial standards of fair dealing." UCC § 1-201. The good faith requirement is a more general version of the no notice requirement. If a holder took the instrument knowing of a specific problem with the instrument or the underlying transaction, she would not meet the no notice requirement. If Bank knew Seller had failed to deliver the lecterns, Bank would not meet the no notice requirement. Or, Bank might not know that Seller failed to deliver the lecterns, but Bank might know that Seller often fails to deliver. Bank would not take the note in good faith, meaning Bank would not be an HIDC and would be subject to Buyer's defense of breach of contract.

Two classic examples of good faith cases follow.

QUESTION 8. Accomplices.   Potter, a professional Quidditch player, bought a phony Nimbus 2000 broom from Slytherin Sports, signing a $1,000 negotiable promissory note. Slytherin sells the note to Malfoy. Malfoy knows full well that many of Slytherin's brooms are inauthentic, defective, or stolen. Malfoy nevertheless buys Slytherin's notes, because Slytherin prices them very attractively. Malfoy has laughingly told Slytherin, "Don't tell me about problems with your sales. What I don't know can help me become an HIDC, because I do not have notice." When Malfoy sues Potter on the note, may Potter raise the defense of breach of contract?

A. No. Malfoy may have known that Slytherin Sports was sleazy, but Malfoy did not have notice that the note was subject to a defense.

B. Yes. Malfoy had notice of the defense, because he knew that many of the brooms that Slytherin Sports sold were defective. Slytherin Sports took with notice and therefore is not an HIDC.

C. Yes. Malfoy acted in bad faith, because he purchased the note from someone he knew often received notes by defrauding its customers and he intentionally avoided notice of problems.

D. No. Potter signed a negotiable instrument. He must pay, period.

ANALYSIS.

Potter → Slytherin Sports → Malfoy buys at discount,
                    knowing Slytherin Sports is shady

This problem is an example of a situation in which courts typically find lack of good faith. Malfoy knows Slytherin Sports cheats its customers to get promissory notes. Malfoy still buys those notes; that alone is bad faith. Moreover, Malfoy has intentionally cut off Slytherin Sports from giving information, exactly because Malfoy knows there is plenty of bad information to be had. That also is bad faith. Buyers of notes generally have no duty to inquire into the underlying transaction; however, if the surrounding facts suggest likely defense, they act in bad faith if they purchase the notes without investigation. So, the correct answer is **C**.

QUESTION 9. Good faith discount.   Knopler Co. is in dire financial straits. Floyd Astronomicals holds a $100,000 note that Knopfler had signed in exchange for a shipment of inventory. Floyd Astronomicals sells the note to Zep Bank for $25,000 cash. Before buying the note, Zep Bank had made extensive inquiries and reasonably believed that Knopfler Co.

had received the inventory as promised and that Knopfler Co. would be able to pay some of the money due, although likely not all. Hoping to get around $35,000 for the note, Zep Bank bought it. Sued, Knopfler Co. refuses to pay the note, claiming the equipment was faulty. Is Zep Bank an HIDC, not subject to such a defense?

A. No. Zep Bank knew there were problems with the transaction, so it acted in bad faith.

B. No. Zep Bank paid $25,000 for a $100,000 note, so it acted in bad faith.

C. Yes. Zep Bank took the note for value, in good faith, and without notice. It paid only $25,000, but that could be a good faith price for a $100,000 debt from a distressed company.

D. Yes, but Zep Bank is an HIDC only up to its good faith payment of $25,000.

ANALYSIS.

Knopfler Co. → Floyd Astronomicals → Zep Bank, buys at discount knowing
Knopler Co. not flush

A court would likely hold that Zep Bank took in good faith. It paid only one-fourth the face value of the note. That seems to be a fair price, however, given that the issuer has such financial problems that it will probably make partial payment on the note. The note was not discounted because there was a likely underlying defense or because it was purchased from a dubious payee. Good faith requires honesty and reasonable commercial fairness, and that would be met here. The best answer is **C**.

QUESTION 10. Sharky.   Check Casher is a business that cashes checks for a 5 percent fee. Check Casher normally handles paychecks, insurance checks, government benefit checks, and other checks, taking them from people with no bank account. Sharky has a $20,000 mutual fund check payable to Rabbit, indorsed to Sharky. Sharky explains that he is an investment adviser, cashing the check for Rabbit in order to invest it on Rabbit's behalf. Check Casher takes the check and gives Sharky $19,000. Sharky indorses the check to Check Casher. It turns out that Sharky had defrauded Rabbit (with a story about a great diamond investment) and absconded with the $19,000 cash. Rabbit seeks to bring a claim to the check, but the claim cannot be raised if Check Casher is an HIDC. Is it?

A. No. Check Casher did not act in good faith.

B. Yes. Check Casher was perfectly honest and paid out good money, minus a reasonable fee.

C. No. Check Casher did not give value.

D. Yes. To be an HIDC, Check Casher must be in possession of an instrument payable to it, and it was.

ANALYSIS.

Check Casher did not act in good faith. The transaction was highly dubious. Sharky claimed to be an investment adviser but was willing to give up $1,000 to cash the check. A normal investment adviser would simply deposit the check in an account and pay no fee. The check was much different from the sort of checks that are honestly presented to Check Casher and should have raised a red flag. Check Casher did nothing to verify the transaction. Because Check Casher did not act in good faith, it is not an HIDC. Therefore, **A** is the best answer.

D is a red herring. Check Casher is a holder—but not a holder in due course.

5. *Shelter rule*

No one can become an HIDC unless they take in good faith, for value, and without notice. That sentence is technically true, but HIDC rights are not limited to such deserving parties. Recall that when an instrument is transferred, the transferee automatically gets the rights of the transferor. This includes HIDC rights. So, if an HIDC transfers an instrument, the transferee gets the rights of the HIDC—even if the transferee does not give value, or takes in bad faith, or has notice of a problem. Transfer of HIDC rights are only barred if the transferee was "engaged in fraud or illegality affecting the instrument." UCC § 3-203(b).

The rationale is twofold. Once someone becomes an HIDC, anyone who signs the instrument is on the hook to pay. Whether they pay the HIDC or the transferee does not really matter. More importantly, the shelter rule protects negotiability, by telling HIDCs they can transfer their rights.

The shelter rule can be confusing, because it requires us to keep track of two sets of rights. If transferee takes an instrument, she gets the rights of the transferor. In addition, she has whatever rights she has in her own right. So, she may get HIDC rights as a transferee, or by qualifying as an HIDC (by being a holder that took for value, in good faith, without notice).

QUESTION 11. Life is unfair.   Hopeful signs a promissory note, as part of a real estate investment. The payee, Dreamstoke Realty, sells and negotiates the note to Conflict Averse Finance, who takes for value, in good faith, and without notice of the fact that Dreamstoke Realty has made numerous misrepresentations about the real estate and availability of various tax benefits. When Conflict Averse Finance seeks to enforce the note, Hopeful strenuously objects. Conflict Averse Finance, rather than suing, sells the note at a discount to Hardhead Collections. Conflict Averse Finance first advises Hardhead Collections of Hopeful's objections to payment. Hardhead Collections does not pay cash for the note, but rather promises to pay the agreed price in one year, with interest. Can Hardhead Collections have the rights of an HIDC?

A. No. It took with notice of the defenses, because Conflict Averse Finance disclosed them before selling the note.

B. No. It took in bad faith, because it took a note knowing the party that signed it claimed fraud.

C. No. It did not give value, because it had not paid for the note, rather only promised to pay later.

D. All of the above.

E. Yes. Hardhead Collections took a transfer from an HIDC.

ANALYSIS.

Hopeful → defrauded by Dreamstoke → Conflict Averse → Hardhead
                                                              not a holder takes with notice,
                                                              not for value, possibly in
                                                              bad faith

This question emphasizes that under the shelter rule, a transferee from an HIDC has the rights of an HIDC, even if they do not meet the four requirements for HIDC status, or any of them.

Conflict Averse Finance was an HIDC. It was a holder, because Dreamstoke Realty "negotiated" the note to Conflict Averse Finance. This is a reminder that a "negotiation" is a transfer that makes the recipient a holder. So Conflict Averse Finance is a holder, and Dreamstoke Realty must have made any necessary indorsement. Conflict Averse Finance also took in good faith, without notice, and for value. So Conflict Averse Finance met all four requirements to be an HIDC. Conflict Averse Finance transferred the note to Hardhead Collections, so Hardhead Collections has the rights of an HIDC. **E** is the best answer.

Hardhead Collections was definitely not a holder in due course, for the reasons given in **A**, **B**, and **C**. *But* the note was transferred to Hardhead Collections by an HIDC, so under the shelter rule, the HIDC rights also transfer to Hardhead Collections. So Hardhead Collections can collect from Hopeful and not be subject to Hopeful's defenses. As stated above, the rationale is that once Conflict Averse Finance became an HIDC, Hopeful lost its rights to raise defenses. So rather than forcing Confict Averse Finance to recover, we allow the HIDC to transfer the instrument along with HIDC rights, which keeps negotiable instruments negotiable.

C. The holder in due course doctrine does not apply to consumer credit sale notes

The best rationale for the HIDC doctrine is that it allows someone to increase the value of her promise to pay by giving up her defenses to payment. That rationale does not apply if the signer does not appreciate the risks she is taking on. Business people may appreciate the risks and benefits of negotiable instruments, but most consumers do not. It would be a rare consumer who bargained for a better price by offering to sign a negotiable promissory note, as opposed to a non-negotiable promissory note. The HIDC doctrine is tough enough for lawyers to appreciate, let alone people shopping for consumer goods.

Federal regulators have effectively abolished the HIDC doctrine with respect to consumer credit sales. Any note signed by a consumer buying goods or services on credit is required to bear the language that provides that the rights of the holder are subject to any claims or defenses that the consumer had against the seller. Here is the required provision:

> NOTICE
> ANY HOLDER OF THIS CONSUMER CREDIT CONTRACT IS SUBJECT TO ALL CLAIMS AND DEFENSES WHICH THE DEBTOR COULD ASSERT AGAINST THE SELLER OF GOODS OR SERVICES OBTAINED WITH THE PROCEEDS HEREOF. RECOVERY HEREUNDER BY THE DEBTOR SHALL NOT EXCEED AMOUNTS PAID BY THE DEBTOR HEREUNDER.

16 CFR 433.2(a). Even if the required language is omitted, the UCC deems it to be on the promissory note. UCC § 3-305(e). The UCC provides that such notes are negotiable (despite the condition to payment), but no one can become an HIDC of such a note, whether the required provision is included or not.

So, a consumer who signs a promissory note in a credit sale transaction retains her defenses. If the goods are not delivered or are defective, or she has any other defense, she can raise that defense against any holder of the note.

This rule does not make consumers completely immune to the HIDC doctrine. It applies to promissory notes signed in connection with consumer credit sales. It therefore does not apply to checks, and consumers sign plenty of those. It also does not apply to transactions other than consumer credit sales. So it does not apply, for example, to promissory notes signed in connection with loans of money. Those sorts of transactions trigger the HIDC doctrine less frequently. Banks infrequently rely on the HIDC doctrine to get money on checks, relying rather on their rights to get the money from their customer's account. With respect to loans, consumers usually would have no defense to raise. If the consumer gets the money, she usually has no defense to payment. Money is not like furniture or cars, which may not be delivered or may be defective. In addition, there are consumer protection laws beyond the UCC that would likely apply. There are certainly some cases, however, in which the HIDC doctrine may be used against a consumer.

QUESTION 12. Consumers conserve defenses. Potter, an amateur Quidditch player, bought a phony Nimbus 2000 broom from Slytherin Sports, signing a $1,000 negotiable promissory note. Although it is a consumer credit sale, the note lacks the federally mandated language that any holder of the note is subject to the consumer's defenses. Rather, on its face it looks like the sort of note a consumer might sign when getting a loan of money. Potter discovers that the broom is defective. Meanwhile, Slytherin Sports sells the note to McGonagall. McGonagall becomes a holder without knowledge of Potter's defense. Could McGonagall successfully enforce the note against Potter?

A. Yes. She is an HIDC, not subject to his defense.
B. It depends on whether she is deemed to take in good faith and without notice (because she met all the other requirements for HIDC status—value and holder). A court might hold that she should have asked more questions.
C. No. A consumer credit sale note is deemed to be subject to the buyer's defenses, whether it says so or not on the note.
D. No. McGonagall lacks privity, because she did not deal with Potter.

ANALYSIS.

Potter → Slytherin Sports → McGonagall: HIDC?

This question illustrates the strong protection for consumers in credit sale transactions. The UCC deems all such notes to be subject to the buyer's defenses. In other words, federal law requires such a clause to be on the note, and state UCC law says that even if you omit it, the note will be treated as subject to defenses. So the correct answer is **C**. **A** and **B** are incorrect, because no one can exercise HIDC rights against the consumer. **D** is a red herring—out of left field, just to remind us that of course negotiable instruments are enforced by people who are not in privity—that's the whole point of negotiability.

QUESTION 13. Consumer loan note.   Solo gets a loan from Consumer Kredit, to fund a vacation to Germany. Can anyone become a holder in due course of the note she signs?

A. Yes, if they are a holder that takes for value, in good faith, and without notice.
B. No. Consumers are not subject to the HIDC doctrine and may always raise any defenses they have.
C. No. The note should have language on it that preserves the signer's defenses.
D. Yes, provided they meet a heightened standard of good faith.

ANALYSIS.

Solo → Consumer Kredit → HIDC?

Consumer credit sale notes are not subject to the HIDC rule. But this consumer note is not from a credit sale transaction; it is from a loan. This question reminds us that consumers are still subject to the HIDC doctrine in transactions other than credit sales. Therefore, **A** is the best answer.

D.   The closer

QUESTION 14. **Vulnerable but winning.**   Dobby gets a $10,000 loan from Lucas and signs a negotiable promissory note. The loan transaction is perfectly legal and fully enforceable. Lucas negotiates the note to Draco, as a gift. Draco did not give value, so Draco is not an HIDC. Dobby learns this and celebrates. Will Draco, not being an HIDC, be unable to enforce the note against Dobby?

A. Yes. Because Draco is not an HIDC, Draco cannot enforce the note.
B. It depends. If Lucas qualified as an HIDC, his rights will transfer to Draco, who will then have the necessary HIDC rights to enforce the note.
C. No. It does not matter whether Draco qualifies as an HIDC. As a mere holder, Draco can successfully enforce the note against Dobby.
D. No. The HIDC doctrine applies only to notes signed in connection with sales of goods transactions.

ANALYSIS.
Dobby → Lucas gives as gift to → Draco

This question highlights where the HIDC doctrine fits in. The benefit of becoming an HIDC is that an HIDC is not subject to most defenses to enforcement of the instrument. Even if the defendant has a defense (breach of contract, unconscionability, mistake, and so on), the defendant still has to pay. In a case like this, however, in which the defendant has no defense to raise, HIDC status is irrelevant. Draco is the holder of the note and can enforce it against Dobby. Dobby has no defense (the loan transaction was perfectly legal and enforceable), and so Dobby will have to pay Draco.

A is wrong, because Draco can enforce the note. **B** is wrong, because Draco does not need HIDC rights. **D** is wrong (it's simply a red herring). The correct answer is **C**. In a case in which the defendant has no defense to raise, the plaintiff does not need to establish HIDC status to win. Rather, as long as the plaintiff is the person entitled to enforce the instrument, she can recover.

The three problems above illustrate the effect of the HIDC doctrine. Now we will spell out the details: how to become an HIDC. The next chapter will discuss in detail the rights of an HIDC, including what defenses may be raised against one.

McJohn's picks

1.	Vulnerable	**D**
2.	Invulnerable	**E**
3.	The "H" in HIDC	**C**
4.	Value?	**E**
5.	Collateral value	**B**
6.	On notice, without noticing	**A**
7.	Notice, but no problem	**C**
8.	Accomplices	**C**
9.	Good faith discount	**C**
10.	Shaky	**A**
11.	Life is unfair	**E**
12.	Consumers deserve defenses	**C**
13.	Consumer loan note	**A**
14.	Vulnerable but winning	**C**

9

The Rights of a Holder in Due Course (It's Good to Be One)

Sued by a holder in due
Reason to be pretty blue
A fight where the pug on one side
Has both hands behind the back, tied.

CHAPTER OVERVIEW
A. A holder in due course is subject only to a small set of defenses, known as the real defenses
B. The real defenses
   1. Infancy
   2. Duress
   3. Lack of legal capacity
   4. Illegality
   5. Fraud in the making
   6. Bankruptcy discharge
   7. An HOIC is not subject to *any* claim to an instrument
C. A holder in due course is also subject to
   1. Discharge by payment or other means
   2. Consumer's defenses in a credit sale transaction
D. Shelter rule

E. Often, holder in due course status does not matter
F. The closer
✦ McJohn's picks

A. A holder in due course is subject only to a small set of defenses, known as the real defenses

Buyer signs negotiable instrument → Merchant → Finance Company

If Finance Company qualifies as a holder in due course (HIDC), Buyer must pay Finance Company, even if Buyer was defrauded by Merchant, did not get the promised goods, or has some other personal defense.

Buyer buys a shipload of goods from Merchant and hands over a negotiable promissory note or check. Merchant negotiates the instrument to Finance Company. Finance Company is entitled to enforce the instrument against Buyer (and Merchant, if Buyer refuses to pay). If Finance Company is a mere holder, we have seen that it is subject to any defense to the instrument. So, Buyer could raise defenses like breach of contract, mistake, unconscionability, fraud in the inducement ("They made knowingly deceptive statements to get me sign that thing to make me promise to pay that money") or any other defense you can raise in a contract action.

Likewise, a mere holder is subject to any claim to an instrument. Suppose that Trader negotiates a check to Check Casher, who becomes a mere holder. A mere holder is subject to any claim to the check ("I want to rescind my negotiation to Trader, because Trader tricked me" or "That check was stolen from me and sold to Trader").

An HIDC, however, is subject only to a small set of defenses, known as the "real defenses." Someone sued by an HIDC may only raise the following defenses:

§ 3-305(A)(2):
a defense of the obligor based on (i) infancy of the obligor to the extent it is a defense to a simple contract, (ii) duress, lack of legal capacity, or illegality of the transaction which, under other law, nullifies the obligation of the obligor, (iii) fraud that induced the obligor to sign the instrument with neither knowledge nor reasonable opportunity to learn of its character or its essential terms, or (iv) discharge of the obligor in insolvency proceedings.

In effect, the only defenses that can be raised against a holder in due course are:

When I signed the note or check,

(i) I was a minor.
(ii) There was a gun to my head
    I was mentally incompetent (for a human) or did not exist (for a corporation)

It was for a gambling debt or other illegal transaction, or

(iii) I had no idea what I was signing—and I was reasonable in not knowing.

Or, after I signed the note or check,

(iv) That debt was discharged in bankruptcy.

That is a small set of possible defenses, none of which come up in the vast majority of transactions. To remember them for bar examination purposes, use a visual mnemonic: an incompetent baby holding a gun and gambling, while signing a note without looking, sitting on a broken bench ("bankruptcy" is said to be from "bancus ruptus," Latin for broken bench, a sign that the business has been shut down).

B.   The real defenses

1. Infancy

In an infancy defense, the signer claims that they were an infant when they signed the promissory note. Remember that in the law, "infant" does not mean a baby; instead, it means someone who in that jurisdiction is not old enough to make a binding legal obligation.

QUESTION 1. Non-binding.   Huck, age 17, signs a negotiable note to purchase a boat from Tom, to start a Mississippi River excursion business. Tom negotiates the note to McCoy, who takes in good faith, for value, and without notice. If the boat is faulty, does Huck have any defenses he can raise against McCoy?

A. Breach of contract. A buyer need not pay if the goods are defective.
B. Infancy, depending on the rules in Huck's jurisdiction.
C. Yes, any defense Huck has. The note is a consumer credit note, so no one can be an HIDC.
D. No. The note is negotiable, so Huck promised unconditionally to pay.

ANALYSIS.
Huck, 17, signs note to buy boat for business → Tom → McCoy (H, GF, NN, Val)

McCoy is an HIDC, only subject to the real defenses. Breach of contract is not in the small set of defenses, so cannot be raised. Therefore, **A** is out.

An HIDC is subject to "infancy of the obligor to the extent it is a defense to a simple contract." So Huck would be able to raise the defense of infancy, if a 17-year-old can do so in Huck's jurisdiction. **B** is the best answer.

Huck bought the boat for business reasons, and so it is not a consumer credit sale. That means it is not excluded from the HIDC rule. In real life, most purchases by young people are consumer credit sales, and so not subject to the HIDC rule, even if the buyer is old enough to make a binding contract. **C** is out.

Contrary to **D**, remember that, although negotiable instruments are unconditional on their face, they remain subject to whatever defenses the signer is permitted to raise under Article 3.

2. Duress

A duress defense requires a fairly high standard. Essentially, it means something like, "There was a gun to my head to get me to sign that promissory note." It does not mean, "I really needed the loan for my struggling business."

QUESTION 2. Need. Solo's creditors are circling like vultures. To make her various payments, she borrows money from Last Chance Finance. Last Chance Finance extracts high fees, hefty interest rates, and a security interest in Solo's remaining personal property. Last Chance Finance negotiates the note to Good Faith Bank, an HIDC. Can Solo raise the defense of duress against Good Faith Bank, on the grounds that Solo desperately needed the loan?

A. No. Urgent need for funds does not constitute duress.
B. Yes. Last Chance Bank took advantage of Solo's weak bargaining position.
C. No. Unless Solo was a minor, she cannot raise any defenses against an HIDC.
D. Yes. Good Faith Bank can have no greater rights to collect than the party that transferred it the note.

ANALYSIS.
Solo → Last Chance Finance → Good Faith Bank

If Good Faith Bank qualifies as an HIDC, then it is subject to only the real defenses. Duress is a real defense, but the facts here do not show duress. As **A** accurately states, urgent need for funds does not constitute duress. People and businesses often borrow money because they really need it. If that were duress, then the HIDC rule would have a gigantic loophole. **A** is the best answer, and **B** is not.

C misstates the rule. Infancy is only one of the defenses that can be raised against an HIDC.

D radically misstates things. The whole point of the HIDC rule is that an HIDC is not subject to defenses that could have been raised against the payee.

Having said that, if this were a real case, we could look for facts to help Solo. If the terms of the loan from Last Chance Bank were truly heinous, then Solo might have such defenses as unconscionability, violation of consumer protection law, or usury. Those are not listed among the real defenses, so they could not be raised against an HIDC. The question has us assume that Good Faith Bank is an HIDC. But if we looked into things, that might change. How could Good Faith Bank have acquired the note in good faith if it was really so culpable? If Good Faith Bank knew or should have known the unconscionable nature of the transaction or of Last Chance Bank's (presumed) ill business tactics, then Good Faith Bank would not be an HIDC. This reminds us that in HIDC cases, the real issue is usually not whether one of the real defenses applies, but rather whether the plaintiff qualifies as an HIDC.

Even if Good Faith is an HIDC, Solo may not have to pay. If her financial condition is indeed so dour, then bankruptcy may be the best option. It can be expensive, stressful, and costly, but could get her discharge of her debts and exempt some of her property from her creditors. But we will leave detailed discussion of bankruptcy to other books.

3. *Lack of legal capacity*

A lack of legal capacity defense is based on a statement like, "I signed that promissory note but I lacked the mental capacity to make a binding legal obligation." Another example is, "I'm a corporation now, but I wasn't a corporation when my president signed this thing, so I didn't exist legally. I didn't have the legal capacity to make a binding legal obligation."

4. *Illegality*

The classic example for an illegality defense is a gambling debt. If in that jurisdiction gambling is illegal, then gambling debts are void. A promissory note for gambling cannot be enforced, even by an HIDC. Courts differ on whether the rule requires that the debt be void or also specifically that instruments issued for the debt be void. This is a pretty high threshold, depending on the jurisdiction.

QUESTION 3. Know when to fold 'em.   Springs, an inveterate gambler, writes a check to cover a $50,000 debt to Bookie. In that state, gambling is illegal, gambling debts are not enforceable, and instruments written to pay them are void. The check bounces. The Depositary Bank, unable to get back the funds it had made available to Bookie, seeks to enforce the check against Springs. Assume the depositary bank qualifies as an HIDC. Can the bank successfully enforce the check?

A. Yes. Springs promised to pay, and his own illegality cannot protect him.

B. Yes. Springs does not have a defense he could raise against an HIDC.

C. No. Springs can raise the defense of illegality.

D. Yes. The bank was not a party to the illegal activity, so Springs cannot raise the defense against the bank.

ANALYSIS.

Springs → Bookie → Depositary Banks

Sometimes even an HIDC loses. Some defenses can be raised against an HIDC, and illegality is one such a defense.

A is contrary to the law, as stated in the question. In this state, checks written to pay gambling debts are not enforceable.

B is incorrect for the same reason that **C** is the best answer.

D overstates the rights of an HIDC, not to mention a holder. A defense can be raised against enforcement of the instrument, not just against the person to whom the instrument was issued.

QUESTION 4. Out of bounds. Litigant hires Attorney to defend him in a property dispute, involving sound traveling through Litigant's thin ceilings. Litigant is ordered to pay a judgment of $23,000. In addition to that, Attorney sends a bill of $2,300. Litigant sends her a check for $2,300; then, Litigant learns that Attorney was not licensed to practice law in that state. Under local law, the obligation is voidable, which relieves Litigant of the obligation to pay fees. Litigant stops payment on the check. The Litigant gets a demand for payment from Good Faith Bank, an HIDC of the check. Can Litigant raise his defense against Good Faith?

A. Yes. Litigant can raise any defense related to breach of the contract to perform legal services.
B. Yes. Litigant can raise the defense of illegality.
C. No. Litigant does not have a defense he can raise against an HIDC.
D. No. If Attorney rendered services, Litigant is liable to pay for them.

ANALYSIS.

Litigant → Attorney → Good Faith Bank

A signer can raise against an HIDC a defense based on "illegality of the transaction which, under other law, nullifies the obligation of the obligor." Litigant's defense here does not quite rise to the level required. Litigant's obligation was not void from the outset; rather, it was voidable. Only the sort of illegality, like gambling debts in the last question, that makes the obligation null from the outset can be raised against an HIDC. A broader reading of illegality would swallow up large parts of the HIDC doctrine.

A is way off base. Breach of contract definitely cannot be raised against an HIDC.

B is correct in stating that illegality can be raised against an HIDC but is wrong because the illegality here is not sufficient.

C is the best answer—although we should stress that jurisdictions vary in how high they set the bar for illegality to qualify as a real defense.

D treats this as a contract law question, but UCC Article 3 supersedes contract law for negotiable instruments.

5. *Fraud in the making*

Most defenses of fraud cannot be raised against an HIDC. Suppose that Lectern Seller deceitfully says, "These are solid oak lecterns made in 1850 by noted lectern crafter Draco." Buyer happily signs a promissory note and receives vintage-1995, mass-produced pine lecterns. Buyer was egregiously defrauded but does not have a defense if Lectern Seller has negotiated the note to an HIDC. The only fraud that can be raised against an HIDC is "fraud that induced the obligor to sign the instrument with neither knowledge nor reasonable opportunity to learn of its character or its essential terms." That would be fraud where the person signing didn't know they were signing a promissory note, and also didn't have a reasonable opportunity to figure out what they were signing.

Courts have routinely denied relief here. The most famous case involves a farmer. He was out in the field, and some bankers approached him and said they were just checking the documentation on his account and that he had to sign this paper to keep things up to date. The farmer wanted to read it, but his glasses were in the farmhouse. He didn't know what he was signing; it turns out that he was being induced by the fraudulent misrepresentation of the bank. The court held, and this is now the rule in the Uniform Commercial Code (UCC), that it has to be fraud where one does not know what one is signing and also does not have a reasonable opportunity to learn what it is before signing. This is the equivalent of saying, "Yes, farmer, you didn't have your glasses to read it, but before you sign something, at least in Kansas, you should figure out what you are signing. You shouldn't have just signed it. You should have walked over to the farmhouse and gotten your glasses, and then you would have known that it was a promissory note." It is hard to see a realistic situation in which someone could sign something and not have an opportunity to know what it is, so this defense will rarely apply.

QUESTION 5. **Going, going, gone.** At a going out of business sale, Esquire acquires a Persian rug for her law offices, signing a negotiable promissory note. The seller fraudulently assures Esquire of the rug's authenticity and promises to hold the note until Esquire has had time to verify the rug with an expert. Despite that, Seller immediately negotiates the note to Hannah, an HIDC. Esquire assumes that she need not pay a note when she discovers she has been defrauded. Must she pay Hannah?

A. No. A promise induced by fraud is not enforceable.

B. No. The policy against fraud would outweigh the policy in favor of making notes freely transferable.

C. Yes. She does not have a defense that she can raise against Hannah.

D. Yes. Her promise to pay was unconditional.

ANALYSIS.

Esquire → Seller → Hannah

If Seller had sued Esquire on the note, Esquire would win easily with her defense of fraud (not to mention various breaches of contract). But if Hannah is a "super-plaintiff," she is an HIDC. Fraudulent inducement, breach of contract, conditional issuance—none are among the real defenses, so none can be raised against an HIDC.

Isn't fraud a real defense, though? Yes, but the only fraud good against an HIDC is "fraud that induced the obligor to sign the instrument with neither knowledge nor reasonable opportunity to learn of its character or its essential terms." The fraud here is the more common type of fraud: fraudulent inducement.

A is not correct. A promise induced by fraud is enforceable by an HIDC, because the signer cannot raise that defense against enforcement of a negotiable instrument.

B is off point. Policy issues do not arise here, where the statute has quite clearly stated the rule and implemented a policy favoring negotiability.

C is the best answer.

D gives the wrong reason. Hannah did make an unconditional promise, but when that promise is enforced, she can raise any defenses she has—except against an HIDC like Hannah.

QUESTION 6. Autograph please. When he purchases an office building, Mole signs numerous documents at the closing. Toad slips a promissory note (meeting all the requirements for negotiability except for a maker's signature) in with the closing documents. Mole unwittingly signs it, between the Acknowledgement of Warning of Earthquake Zone and the Agreement to Abide by Mall Rules. Toad sells the now-negotiable note to Badger, an HIDC. In Badger's suit against Mole, can Mole raise the defense of fraud?

A. Yes. Fraud can always be raised, even against an HIDC.
B. Yes. This was fraud in the making, which voids the note and is a defense to which an HIDC is subject.
C. No. This fraud does not fall in the narrow category of fraud that can be raised against an HIDC.
D. No. Negotiable instruments are unconditional.
E. Yes. The instrument was never issued.

ANALYSIS.

Mole → Toad → Badger

Mole has at least two great defenses: nonissuance and fraud. They don't do any good, however, if he cannot raise them. He can raise only a real defense, one of the select few. Nonissuance is not on the list. The issue here is whether the fraud is the rare type of fraud that can be raised against an HIDC: "fraud that induced the obligor to sign the instrument with neither knowledge nor reasonable opportunity to learn of its character or its essential terms." UCC § 3-305(a)(2)(iii). Mole did not have knowledge of the character or the terms of the instrument, but he did have "reasonable opportunity to learn of its character or its essential terms." Mole was at a closing, signing legal documents. Before signing, he had the document in his hand. He could have not signed until he read it. If a farmer in a field without his glasses does not qualify for the defense, then Mole would not either.

A misstates the law. Fraud cannot always be raised. Most fraud cannot be raised against an HIDC. Cases showing the type of fraud that can be raised are rare indeed.

B gets the issue right, but the conclusion wrong. This would not qualify as fraud in the making, under the sparse authority defining the bounds.

C is the best answer.

D repeats a fallacy we have heard before.

Mole does have a defense of nonissuance, but that is not a defense that can be raised against an HIDC. This illustrates just how strong the rights of an HIDC are. Once a negotiable instrument is signed, the signer is on the hook. This risk arises upon signing the instrument, even without giving it to anyone.

QUESTION 7. Definancing. Patton signs a promissory note, as part of refinancing his mortgage. The mortgage broker, however, has grievously deceived Patton. The terms of the new mortgage are far worse (high fees, high and variable interest rate, along with various onerous default provisions). Patton does not realize that he has given up a nice, long-term, low rate mortgage for a new loan that will soon become unbearable. Patton, a retired schoolteacher with little business acumen, trustingly signed everything put before him. In a couple of years, if sued by an HIDC of the note, will Patton be able to raise the defense of fraud?

A. No. This was not "fraud that induced the obligor to sign the instrument with neither knowledge nor reasonable opportunity to learn of its character or its essential terms."

B. Yes. Such heinous fraud voids the obligation.

C. Yes. The transaction was unconscionable.

D. No. A holder is never responsible for the acts of others.

ANALYSIS. This case emphasizes how narrow is the category of fraud that can be raised against an HIDC. Even though this fraud was likely criminal, Patton cannot raise it as a defense against an HIDC. Patton could have sought advice or read the documents, but he did not. **A** is the best answer (in terms of the existing law; whether that's a good rule is a question about which there is some disagreement).

6. *Bankruptcy discharge*

Bankruptcy discharge has a different rationale. If I sign a promissory note and get a discharge in federal bankruptcy, then even if the HIDC shows up with it, I don't have to pay her. The drafters of UCC Article 3 included that one because they didn't have any choice. Bankruptcy law is federal law. If federal bankruptcy court discharges that debt, it is discharged. You cannot enforce the debt under your state-law rights. The law is drafted broadly enough so that it is applied to state law in solvency proceedings as well.

> **QUESTION 8. Absolved.**   Prudence impulsively borrows $500,000 to start a monorail company, signing a note to Friendly Lendly, who negotiates it to Buck Stops Finance. Things do not work for Prudence's venture. She files bankruptcy, and her meager assets are parceled out among her creditors, save her exempt assets (tools of the trade, clothing, furniture, homestead allowance, and some value of her vehicle). The bankruptcy court discharges all her pre-bankruptcy debt. Subsequently, Buck Stops Finance sues Prudence on the unpaid note. If Buck Stops Finance is an HIDC, must Prudence pay them?
>
> **A.** No. The debt was discharged, and discharge in insolvency proceedings may be raised against an HIDC.
> **B.** Yes. There is no reason to shield her from this debt. Prudence took a known risk. She was not defrauded, a minor, or mentally incompetent.
> **C.** It would depend on her ability to pay.
> **D.** Yes. The note was not discharged, because it was not paid.

ANALYSIS.

Prudence → Friendly Lendly → Buck Stops Finance

A states matter accurately. The debt was discharged, and discharge in insolvency proceedings may be raised against an HIDC. Prudence can raise the defense of discharge and will be successful. The UCC yields to a discharge in insolvency proceedings.

B is inaccurate. Most of the real defenses allow a party to raise a defense where the debt was void from the start: infancy, incapacity, duress, or fraud in the making. But the insolvency defense is different. The UCC simply defers to insolvency discharges, even if the debt was from a completely legitimate transaction.

C is incorrect. Bankrupcty discharge eliminates the debt, even if the debtor later makes money—the "fresh start." Otherwise, insolvent people would lose incentive to earn.

Contrary to **D**, payment is only one of several ways to discharge an instrument.

7. A holder in due course is not subject to any claim to an instrument

An HIDC is not subject to any claim to the instrument. As § 3-306 puts it: "A person having rights of a holder in due course takes free of the claim to the instrument." If an HIDC has an instrument that belongs to someone else, or comes from a transaction that will be rescinded, or otherwise is claimed by someone, the HIDC keeps the instrument nonetheless.

QUESTION 9. Force field.   Abdul receives a check payable to cash in exchange for one of his paintings. A thief steals the check. Check Casher buys the check from the thief, taking in good faith, for value, without notice of the theft. Abdul somehow tracks down the check and claims it, based on blatant illegality. Will Abdul's claim succeed against Check Casher?

A. Yes. Even an HIDC is subject to a claim or defense of illegality.
B. Yes. Abdul is the owner of the check.
C. No. Check Casher is the holder, because it has possession of a bearer instrument.
D. No. An HIDC is not subject to any claim to the instrument.

ANALYSIS.
Buyer → Abdul → Thief → Check Casher

Theft looks like something that could be raised against an HIDC — something that would be so illegal that it would fall in the small set of real defenses. Here we are not talking about defenses, though, we are talking about claims to the instrument. Abdul is the owner of the check and therefore has a claim to the check or its proceeds. An HIDC is not subject to any claims to the instrument, however, so Abdul's claim against Check Casher will not succeed.

A misdirects, speaking of defenses. An HIDC is subject to the real defenses but is not subject to any claims to the instrument.

B places too much weight on property rights. Ownership is subject to various limitations. The common law of property does not govern here, rather the law of negotiable instruments governs.

C gives the correct answer ("No") but for an insufficient reason. Being a holder alone is not enough to defeat a claim to the instrument. The thief was a holder but would be subject to a claim to the instrument or its proceeds. **C** reminds us not to place too much weight on the risks of bearer instruments.

D is the best answer.

QUESTION 10. No take back. Shirley, a child star, receives a check for her latest movie work. She signs the check over to her agent, who sells it to an HIDC. When Shirley's parents learn of this, they attempt to have the check returned, on the basis that Shirley, as a minor, lacked legal capacity to transfer the check. Must the HIDC return the check?

A. No. An HIDC is not subject to any claim on the instrument.
B. Yes. An HIDC is immune to most claims and defenses, but this is based on infancy, because Shirley was a minor.
C. No. Negotiation may not be rescinded.
D. No. The check was not stolen, so Shirley has no claim to it.

ANALYSIS.
Shirley → Agent → HIDC

An HIDC is immune to most defenses, but subject to the real defenses, such as infancy. An HIDC is subject to no claims, however, regardless of the basis. So the HIDC keeps the check. **A** is the best answer, and **B** is inaccurate.

Claims can be based on theft, but also on any other reason to claim an instrument, such as rescinding a transaction, so **C** and **D** are incorrect.

C. An HIDC is also subject to

1. Discharge by payment or other means

An HIDC is subject to discharge if the HIDC takes the instrument with notice of the discharge. UCC § 3-302(b). So, if the HIDC takes an $8,000 note with notice that $5,000 has been paid, the HIDC would be entitled to collect only the remaining $3,000. It is worth repeating the following: The most recent version of the UCC also deals with the issue of what happens if the issuer pays the payee after an instrument has been transferred? Suppose Mac issues a note to Pam, who sells the note to Hal—but Pam duplicitously collects on the note from Mac. Where payment is made to a former person entitled to enforce the instrument (PEEI), there is discharge effective against the real PEEI, even an HIDC, unless the PEEI has given notice of the transfer to the obligor. UCC § 3-602(b)(d). In other words, when Hal buys the note from Pam, Hal should give notice to Mac. Then, if Mac is so foolish as to pay Pam, that will not give a discharge effective against Mac.

QUESTION 11. Pagan? Trusty borrows $100,000 from Shady Finance, signing a note for $100,000 plus interest. Shady soon sells the note to Oak Street Bank. When the note comes due, Shady demands payment in full from Trusty, gets it, and disappears with the funds. Then Oak Street

Bank appears and demands payment from Trusty. Trusty responds that the note was discharged by payment. Is Trusty protected?

A. Yes. Trusty paid the note in full to the holder and the note is discharged.

B. Yes, unless Trusty is held negligent.

C. No. The note is not discharged because Trusty paid the wrong person.

D. Yes. Trusty had no notice of the transfer, and thus was entitled to pay the person Trusty believed was entitled to payment.

ANALYSIS.

Trusty → Shady Finance → Oak Street Bank

Even an HIDC is subject to discharge by payment to a former PEEI (unless the real PEEI has given notice of the transfer). UCC § 3-602. Trusty need not pay again. This is true even where the note has been transferred, where Trusty paid the wrong person, because Trusty was not given notice of the transfer. So, the best answer is **D**. The result would be different only if Oak Street Bank had, as it should, given notice of the transfer to Trusty before payment by Trusty.

An important practical point: This is the rule under the present version of the UCC. In a jurisdiction that has not yet adopted that revision, the former rule would govern, under which there is discharge only if payment is made to the PEEI. Under that rule, Trusty paid the wrong person (Shady) and is therefore still liable to the right person (Oak Street Bank)! Before paying, Trusty would have been well advised to require presentment of the note.

Upon paying, Trusty (under either rule) should require the note be stamped "PAID" to prevent liability to any future HIDC. As a practical matter, that may be tricky, especially if the note calls for regular payments.

2. Consumer's defenses in a credit sale transaction

The HIDC doctrine doesn't apply to promissory notes in consumer credit sales. Here is the rationale: It makes sense for businesses to be able to sign a promissory note and give up their defenses. That is a risk that a business can knowingly evaluate and agree to take on in exchange for other favorable terms. The rationale is weaker with consumers, however. Consumers are unlikely to know of the HIDC doctrine or its potential effects on the transaction, and they are unlikely to bargain to get a benefit from it. The Federal Trade Commission (FTC) has promulgated regulations that require that a promissory note in a consumer credit sale must state that whoever holds the note is subject to any defenses that the consumer has.

That doesn't mean that consumers are never subject to the HIDC doctrine, however. The rule applies only to promissory notes, so checks can be subject to the HIDC doctrine. Note that the rule also doesn't apply to promissory notes signed by consumers for loans of money.

D.   Shelter rule

The shelter rule contradicts some of the things that lie behind the HIDC doctrine. Suppose Buyer buys the defective lecterns, signs a promissory note, and gives it to Merchant. Merchant transfers the note to Bank, an HIDC. Bank transfers the note to Sheltered, who isn't an HIDC (Sheltered didn't give value, acted in bad faith, or had notice of buyer's defense). Sheltered still has the rights of the HIDC. It sounds unfair, because Sheltered says, "Ha, ha Buyer, I bought this promissory note and I knew that you had been defrauded in signing it and I can still enforce it against you. You can't raise that defense against me." The rationale is that once Bank became an HIDC, Buyer is going to have to pay—either Bank or somebody else. In addition, without the shelter rule, once someone becomes an HIDC, he can't transfer the instrument. Anyone the note was transferred to in good faith would have to be told, "Well, you should know that this is subject to a defense." That person would then say, "I won't take it if I can't enforce it." The only narrow exception to the shelter rule is if the transferee was involved in an underlying fraud in the transaction.

E.   Often, holder in due course status does not matter

Borrower → Lender → Factor

Borrower gets a loan from Lender and signs a note, which Lender sells to Factor. There are no legal problems. Borrower got the money, the interest rate was not usurious, the transaction was fully legal, and there was no fraud or misrepresentation. So, Borrower has no defenses to payment, and there is no claim or discharge. In that case, it does not matter if Factor qualifies as an HIDC. As long as Factor qualifies as a PEEI (i.e., Lender transferred the note to Factor), Factor is entitled to payment from Borrower. If Factor has not given value, has not acted in good faith, or has notice of a fact that would bar HIDC status (e.g., took the note knowing that it was overdue), Factor would not be an HIDC but would still win the lawsuit against Borrower. Likewise, if Buyer writes a check for some equipment and gets what she was promised, she likely has no claims or defenses and is liable for the money. So failure to qualify as an HIDC often does not mean the party is not entitled to collect. Only if a defense, claim, or discharge is raised will HIDC status be an issue.

QUESTION 12. **No means no.**   Snopes Drilling signs a negotiable promissory note, intending to purchase a heavy-duty truck from Faulkner Auto. Faulkner negotiates it to Halcomb, who takes for value, without notice of any problems, and in good faith. Which of the following defenses could Snopes raise if sued by Halcomb?

A. Lack of consideration (§ 3-303).
B. Failure to perform promise (§ 3-303).
C. Discharge by destroying the instrument (although it would be hard to become an HIDC without notice of the discharge, because note would be destroyed or have "PAID" written on it) (§ 3-604).
D. Discharge by agreeing to give up rights (§ 3-604).
E. Separate agreement (§ 3-117).
F. Nonissuance (the deal never closed and Faulkner stole the note) (§ 3-105)
G. Conditional issuance (Faulkner promised not to seek payment unless the truck was delivered) (§ 3-105).
H. Breach of contract.
I. Breach of warranty.
J. Misrepresentation.
K. Fraudulent inducement.
L. Mistake.
M. Impossibility.
N. No contract was formed.
O. Parol evidence.
P. Risk of loss (truck destroyed by lightning and Faulkner assumed that risk).
Q. Modification.
R. Unconscionability.
S. Claim in recoupment (Snopes has a counterclaim for damages, arising out of late delivery).
T. Anticipatory repudiation (Faulkner has given notice that he will not perform promised service on truck).
U. Estoppel.
V. Statute of frauds.
W. Incompleteness.
X. Conditions to payment not met.
Y. All of the above.
Z. None of the above.

ANALYSIS.
Snopes → Faulkner → Halcomb

The best answer is **Z.** An HIDC is immune to most defenses and is subject only to the small set of defenses known as the real defenses. None of the defenses listed above are real defenses, so none of them could be raised against an HIDC.

It would be quite different if Halcomb were not an HIDC. A mere holder is subject to any defense provided by Article 3 (such as **A–G** above) and any defense that the defendant could raise in a contract case (such as **H–X**). So the answer in that instance would be **Y**.

QUESTION 13. Silly trick question. Wilmer holds a negotiable promissory note issued by her granddaughter, Gladys, in exchange for funds to pay for music school. Wilmer decides to forgive the note, and writes "CANCELLED" on it. The note later winds up in the hands of Hank, a holder who takes in good faith for value. If Hank sues Gladys on the note, can she raise the defense of discharge?

A. No. An HIDC is not subject to discharge.
B. No. If she did not repay the loan, she remains liable to pay it.
C. Yes. Hank cannot be an HIDC!
D. Yes. Even an HIDC cannot enforce a discharged note.

ANALYSIS.
Gladys → Wilmer → Hank

Hank is not an HIDC. Hank gave value and acted in good faith but was on notice of the discharge. The note had "CANCELLED" written on it. So, **C** is the best answer.

QUESTION 14. Seat of learning. With a check, Consomme purchases a couch for her restaurant from Flora Furniture. Consomme does not know it, but Flora has long practiced fraudulent business practices. The couch is not an imported designer piece, as represented, but instead is a cheap knockoff. Consomme's head waiter alerts her, and she calls her bank and tells them not to pay the check. The check is in the hands of Currency Exchange, who processes all of Flora Furniture's checks. Currency Exchange had no information about the underlying transaction. Currency Exchange often returns to Flora Furniture checks that have not been paid owing to stop payment orders by dissatisfied customers. Currency Exchange has learned that Flora Furniture had an extraordinarily high level of customer dissatisfaction and Better Business Bureau complaints. If Currency Exchange sues Consomme on its drawer's liability, can Consomme raise its defenses of fraud and breach of contract?

A. No. Neither is a defense that can be raised against an HIDC.
B. No. If anything, Consomme is acting fraudulently by writing a check and then stopping payment.

C. Yes. Currency Exchange is not an HIDC, so it is subject to any defense Consomme has to raise.

D. Yes. Currency Exchange is an HIDC, but it is subject to the defense of fraud here.

ANALYSIS.

Consomme → Flora Furniture → Currency Exchange

The key issue in HIDC cases is often the threshold issue—whether the plaintiff qualifies as an HIDC. Consomme has a number of defenses to raise: fraud, breach of contract, and breach of warranty. None of them are real defenses, so Consomme cannot raise them against an HIDC. Currency Exchange would not qualify as an HIDC, however. Currency Exchange took the check from Flora, knowing from experience of Flora Furniture's apparently shoddy sales practices. Currency Exchange would be deemed not to be taking the checks in good faith. So, even though it was a holder that gave value and had no notice of the particular breach, it would not qualify as an HIDC. Note that this is a risk that Currency Exchange took upon itself.

A correctly states that Consomme has no defense it can raise against an HIDC, but Currency Exchange is not an HIDC.

B focuses on the wrong issue. The question is whether Consomme can raise the defense, not whether Consomme will win. Having said that, Consomme did not write the check intending to stop payment, so there was no fraud by Consomme.

C is the best answer.

D is wrong on two counts: Currency Exchange would not qualify as an HIDC, nor would an HIDC be subject to a fraud defense here. An HIDC is only subject to the sort of fraud where someone signs an instrument, not knowing its terms or character and without an opportunity to learn them. Consomme knew she was signing a check.

F.   The closer

QUESTION 15. Consumer protection. Consumer buys a couch for her home from Flora Furniture. As in the previous question, Flora Furniture makes numerous misrepresentations and breaches of warranty. Consumer signs a simple negotiable promissory note drafted by Flora Furniture. Flora Furniture omits the language that any taker of the note is subject to the maker's defenses, even though FTC rules require such a clause in a note from a consumer credit sale such as this. Flora Furniture negotiates the note to Shrub Fund, with a made-up story that it

> represents a note for a loan of money. Shrub Fund takes the note in good faith, for value, without notice of the breach of contract. Can Consumer raise her defenses against Shrub?
>
> A. Yes. Shrub is subject to any defense Consumer has, whether the required language is on the note or not.
> B. No. If the language is not on the note, Consumer cannot raise the defenses against an HIDC.
> C. Yes. Consumers can always raise fraud even against an HIDC.
> D. No. Consumer's only recourse is a breach of contract action against Flora Furniture.

ANALYSIS.

Consumer → Flora Furniture → Shrub Fund

Promissory notes given in consumer credit sales are not subject to the HIDC doctrine (even if they omit the FTC-required language). As **A** states correctly, Shrub is subject to any defense Consumer has, whether the required language is on the note or not.

The FTC rule requires the note to say that any holder is subject to any defenses the consumer has. The UCC further provides that even if the language is omitted, the holder of such a note is subject to all defenses of the consumer. So, **B** is not correct.

C overstates the protection given to consumers. The rule protecting consumers from the HIDC doctrine applies only to notes given in consumer credit sales. It does not apply to other notes (such as notes given in exchange for a loan of money) or to checks.

D would be correct only if Consumer was subject to the HIDC rule, but that is not the case here.

Note well: Consumers are protected by the FTC rule against the HIDC doctrine for promissory notes signed in consumer credit sales — but not with respect to notes signed in other transactions, or with respect to checks.

 # McJohn's picks

1.	Non-binding	**B**
2.	Need	**A**
3.	Know when to fold 'em	**C**
4.	Out of bounds	**C**
5.	Going, going, gone	**C**
6.	Autograph please	**C**
7.	Definancing	**A**

8. Absolved   **A**
9. Force field   **D**
10. No take back   **A**
11. Pagan?   **D**
12. No means no   **Z**
13. Silly trick question **C**
14. Seat of learning   **C**
15. Consumer protection **A**

10

Theft, Forgery, Alteration — Warranties

He that passes on a check
With juridical defect,
Though he knew it not a speck,
Pays the pal whose
Pay was wrecked.

A. Theft, forgery, alterations: Who bears the loss?

Front:

Pay Trunchbull $5,000
Five thousand dollars
Matilda

Back:

```
Pay Quentin

                    Trunchbull
```

Matilda issues? → Trunchbull indorses? → Quentin sells to → Roald

Q uentin sells Roald a check. The check appears to be written by Matilda to Trunchbull for $5,000, indorsed by Trunchbull to Quentin. Roald expects to be paid $5,000 by Matilda's bank. Failing that, Roald could enforce the check against anyone who signed it, but there could be problems. Quentin could have stolen the check and forged Trunchbull's indorsement. Trunchbull could have stolen Matilda's checkbook and forged Matilda's drawer's signature. The signatures could be valid, but Quentin or Trunchbull could have altered the amount, changing a $5 check to a $5,000 check. "Quentin" could actually be his evil twin, Quantum. Finally, the check itself could be fine (no forgeries, no alterations, not stolen), but Matilda could have a defense to payment (Trunchbull failed to deliver the promised books). This chapter deals with the way that Uniform Commercial Code (UCC) Article 3 generally allocates such risks.

We've seen two ways that somebody can get the rights to be paid on the instrument: if it's indorsed to them, or if it's transferred to them by the person who used to be entitled to the payment. If the instrument was stolen, then the possessor is not the person entitled to enforce the instrument (PEEI) (unless it is bearer paper, enforceable by whoever has it). The holder did not indorse the check (the indorsement was forged and was thus ineffective) and did not transfer it (it was stolen). So, whoever has the instrument does not have the right to enforce it. If they present the instrument for payment, they are not entitled to receive payment. If it is a check and the bank pays it, the bank is not entitled to reimbursement from its customer, because the check was not properly payable.

Likewise, an altered instrument is not properly payable or enforceable (or is enforceable only according to its original terms). Someone who signs an instrument promises to pay it, but only according to the terms of the instrument at the time they sign it. If a check or note has been altered, that does not increase the liability of those who have already signed it. If Matilda writes a $5 check, she is liable for only $5, even if Trunchbull changes it to $5,000.

In addition, the signers may have defenses to enforcement (breach of contract, etc.).

B.   The transfer warranty

A transferor for consideration warrants there is no legal reason why the instrument would not be paid (transferor is PEEI, instrument not stolen, no forgeries, not altered, no defenses to payment, no claims to instrument); the warranty runs to the transferee and (if indorsed by warrantor) to subsequent transferees. The transfer warranty also gives a very weak warranty about financial collectibility.

When a check or note is transferred, the transferee gets a broad warranty that amounts to this: "There's no legal reason for you not to get paid on this check. All of the signatures on it are authentic. There are no problems with the underlying transaction. It is not stolen. It hasn't been altered and was signed by the person who should have signed it. You should be able to turn around, present this check, and get paid. And, if the bank doesn't pay it, all the signatures you see on it are authentic, and you can recover from any of those people who signed it. There's no legal problem with this check." So the transfer warranty is breached if there is any legal reason why a transferee cannot collect. Note that it covers legal defects. The transferee warranty does not warrant that the persons obliged to pay actually have the money to pay. It is not a financial warranty, or a warranty of collectability—with one weak exception. The transferor warrants that they have no actual knowledge that the issuer is in insolvency proceedings.

Section 3-416 states the rule in detail:

§ 3-416. Transfer Warranties

(a) A person who transfers an instrument for consideration warrants to the transferee and, if the transfer is by indorsement, to any subsequent transferee that:

(1) the warrantor is a person entitled to enforce the instrument;

(2) all signatures on the instrument are authentic and authorized;

(3) the instrument has not been altered;

(4) the instrument is not subject to a defense or claim in recoupment of any party which can be asserted against the warrantor; and

(5) the warrantor has no knowledge of any insolvency proceeding commenced with respect to the maker or acceptor or, in the case of an unaccepted draft, the drawer; and

(6) with respect to a remotely-created consumer item, that the person on whose account the item is drawn authorized the issuance of the item in the amount for which the item is drawn.

(b) A person to whom the warranties under subsection (a) are made and who took the instrument in good faith may recover from the warrantor as damages for breach of warranty an amount equal to the loss suffered as a result of the breach, but not more than the amount of the instrument plus expenses and loss of interest incurred as a result of the breach.

(c) The warranties stated in subsection (a) cannot be disclaimed with respect to checks. Unless notice of a claim for breach of warranty is given to the warrantor within 30 days after the claimant has reason to know of the breach and the identity of the warrantor, the liability of the warrantor under subsection (b) is discharged to the extent of any loss caused by the delay in giving notice of the claim.

QUESTION 1. Breach. Quentin sells Roald a check, which appears to be issued by Matilda and indorsed by Trunchbull. Which of the following would breach the transfer warranty?

A. Matilda's signature is forged.
B. Trunchbull's indorsement is forged.
C. Matilda has a defense to payment: Trunchbull never delivered her the promised books.
D. The amount of the check has been altered.
E. The check was stolen from Trunchbull, who has a claim to the check.
F. Any or all of the above.

ANALYSIS.

Matilda issues $5,000 check? → Trunchbull indorses? → Quentin sells to → Roald

Any of these would breach the transfer warranty. If there is any legal reason why Roald may not be able to collect the check, that would breach the transfer warranty. Therefore, **F** is the best answer.

QUESTION 2. At the time . . . Abacus writes a check for $500 to Bacchus, who indorses the check and sells it to Calculus. Calculus alters the amount to $5,000, sells it to Check Casher for $4,750, and disappears with the money. The check is not paid. Who is liable for Check Casher's breach of transfer warranty?

A. Only Calculus. Bacchus made no warranty to Check Casher, because Bacchus never dealt with Check Casher.
B. Only Calculus. Bacchus did not breach the transfer warranty, because the check had not been altered when Bacchus transferred it.
C. Abacus, Bacchus, and Calculus.
D. All of the above.

ANALYSIS.

Abacus → Bacchus → Calculus alters → Check Casher

Bacchus transferred the check for consideration, so he made a transfer warranty. He indorsed the check, so he makes the warranty to all future transferees, contrary to **A**. But the warranty applies to the check as of the time of that transfer. Bacchus transferred a check that had not been altered (and had no other legal problem, such as forgery or defense to payment), so Bacchus did not breach the warranty. Calculus transferred an altered check (for consideration), so Calculus breached the transfer warranty to Check Casher. Therefore, **B** is the best answer.

Abacus issued the check and so makes no transfer warranty. The issue simply promises to pay the check as she issued it. So **C** is not correct. **D** is logically impossible.

QUESTION 3. Musical chairs. Able writes a check to Baker. Cain steals it, forges Baker's indorsement, and sells the check to Demure, who innocently indorses and sells the check to Eric. Able stops payment, so the check is dishonored when Eric presents it. Who is liable to Eric for breach of transfer warranty?

A. Demure, who transferred the check to Eric.
B. No one. Demure had no knowledge of the theft and forgery.
C. Cain, the only one with knowledge of the theft and forgery.
D. Cain and Demure.
E. Baker, Cain, and Demure.

ANALYSIS.

Able → Baker → Cain steals → Demure → Eric → Drawee dishonors

This question is an example of how the warranties allocate the risk of stolen checks. Anyone that transfers the check for consideration makes a transfer warranty. Able issued the check, so Able did not transfer it. The check was stolen from Baker, so Baker did not transfer it. Cain transferred it to Demure for money, so Cain made a transfer warranty (and because Cain indorsed it, Cain makes the warranty to all future transferees). Demure transferred the check to Eric for money, so Demure also made a transfer warranty.

The transfer warranty was breached on multiple grounds: there was a forged indorsement, the transferors were not the PEEI, and Baker had a claim to the check. So, Cain and Demure breached the transfer warranty to Eric, and Cain breached the transfer warranty to Demure.

Eric can put the loss back onto Demure and Demure can put the loss back onto Cain. Cain is probably judgment proof (cannot be located or has no assets to go after), so the loss would likely fall on Demure, the person that took the stolen check from the thief. In practical terms, when Demure transfers the check to Eric, Demure warrants "there is no legal reason why this check will not be paid." That warranty is not true, so Demure has to pay.

A is only partially correct. Demure is liable, but Cain is also liable.

B offers false hope to Demure. It is true that Demure had no knowledge of the theft and forgery. But Demure still makes and breaches the transfer warranty. Warranty liability is strict liability. If Demure transfers a stolen check, Demure is liable, even if Demure acted completely innocently.

For the same reason, **C** is only partially correct. Cain is liable, but so is the innocent Demure.

D is the best answer.

E goes too far. Baker did not transfer the check and so is not liable for transfer warranty.

> **QUESTION 4. Never promised you a rose garden.** Insolvent Ike writes a bearer check to Merchant, who sells it to Check World without indorsing it. Unknown to Merchant, Ike is broke. Ike's bank does not pay the check, for lack of funds in Ike's account. Is Merchant liable to Check World?
>
> **A.** Yes, for breach of warranty—for transferring a worthless check.
> **B.** Yes, as an indorser. Even though Merchant did not sign the check, it is deemed to indorse it.
> **C.** No. Merchant did not make a transfer warranty.
> **D.** No. Merchant made a transfer warranty but did not breach it. Merchant did not indorse the check and so is also not liable as an indorser.

ANALYSIS.

Insolvent Ike → Merchant → Check World → Ike's bank dishonors

The transfer warranty promises there is no legal reason why the check is not enforceable. It does not warrant that the signers have money to pay their obligations. Merchant made a transfer warranty to Check World. Merchant did not breach the transfer warranty. Merchant was the PEEI, the check was not stolen, all signatures were authentic and authorized, there were no defenses to payment, and there were no claims to the instrument. In sum, there was no legal obstacle to enforcing the check, so the transfer warranty was not breached.

A overstates the transfer warranty. It was indeed a worthless check, but Merchant did not guaranty payment.

Merchant did not indorse the check. Warranty liability cannot be disclaimed on checks, but indorser liability can (either by not indorsing, or by indorsing without recourse), so **B** is incorrect.

C gives the wrong reason. Merchant made a transfer warranty but did not breach it.

All of this makes **D** the best answer.

Note that if Merchant had indorsed the check, Merchant would be liable to pay the check. Signers promise to pay the instrument. That is why banks, check cashers, and anyone else that takes a check or note is well advised to have the transferor indorse the instrument, even if that is not necessary to transfer it. An indorsement is a guaranty of payment. Of course, if the indorser is also out of funds, that does not solve the problem.

> **QUESTION 5. A difficult one.** Baba sells a load of defective baseball bats to Woodsy, taking a note. Woodsy refuses to pay the note on its due date. Baba discounts the note to Bucks for Notes, who takes in good faith, with no inkling of Woodsy's complaint. Bucks for Notes,

in turn, sells the note to Credit Enforcer. When Woodsy refuses to pay Credit Enforcer because of Baba's breach, Credit Enforcer seeks to recover for breach of warranty from Bucks for Notes (who had not indorsed the note). Is Bucks for Notes liable to Credit Enforcer for breach of transfer warranty?

A. Yes, for transferring an overdue note.

B. Yes, for transferring a note that was later not paid.

C. Yes, for transferring a note subject to a defense.

D. No. Bucks for Notes did not know that the note was subject to a defense and so did not breach the transfer warranty.

E. No. Bucks for Notes did not indorse the note and so did not make a transfer warranty.

ANALYSIS.

Woodsy → Baba → Bucks for Notes → Credit Enforcer

Understanding this question requires understanding pretty much everything in the book up to this point. Bucks warrants to Credit that there is no legal reason that Credit could not enforce the note against everyone who signed it (no forged signatures, no alterations, no defenses that would prevent enforcement). Woodsy has a defense: breach of contract. Could Woodsy raise it against Credit Enforcer? That depends on whether Credit Enforcer has the rights of a holder in due course (HIDC).

To qualify as an HIDC, the party must be a holder that takes in good faith, for value, and with no notice of any problem regarding the instrument. The note was past its due date when Bucks for Notes took it. So, neither Bucks for Notes nor Credit Enforcer would qualify as an HIDC, because each took it with notice it was overdue. Bucks for Notes transferred an instrument subject to a defense, so Bucks for Notes is liable to Credit Enforcer for breach of transfer warranty. Therefore, **C** is the best answer.

QUESTION 6. Who warrants?   Aaron writes a check for $755 to Bonds to pay for some debentures. Bonds indorses the check and sells it to Cedeno. Cedeno artfully alters the amount to $7,550, signs it, and cashes it with DP. DP presents it for payment, but the teller at the bank looks at the check suspiciously and refuses to pay. Who is liable to DP for breach of transfer warranty?

A. No one.

B. Aaron, Bonds, and Cedeno, each of whom transferred the check.

C. Bonds and Cedeno, who both transferred the check.

D. Cedeno.

ANALYSIS.

Aaron → Bonds → Cedeno → DP → Drawee bank dishonors
$750 check   alters to $7,550

An alteration breaches the transfer warranty. So, from whom can DP collect? Aaron issued the check, not transferred it, so he made no transfer warranty. Bonds transferred the check, so he made a transfer warranty, and indorsed it, so the warranty flows to any future transferee. DP therefore gets a transfer warranty from Bonds. Bonds did not breach the transfer warranty, however. When Bonds transferred the check, it had not been altered. Cedeno breached the transfer warranty made to DP.

A is too narrow.

B is too broad. Not everyone that makes a transfer warranty is liable; they are liable only if they breached the transfer warranty. Aaron, moreover, did not even make a warranty.

C is too broad. Bond and Cedeno both made the warranty, but only Cedeno breached it.

D is the best answer.

Suppose Cedeno is not to be found. Does DP have any theory against Bonds? Bonds is not liable for breach of warranty, but Bonds did indorse the check, promising to pay it if it was dishonored. So, DP can recover from Bonds on his indorser liability. *But,* like warranty liability, indorser liability looks to the time the indorsement is made. Bonds indorsed a $750 check, so he is liable to DP only for $750. DP would take the loss on the remaining $6,800.

C.   Presentment warranty

A payor gets a warranty from the presenter and earlier transferors that the warrantor was the PEEI and (if a check) that the check was not altered. The warranty can also be violated for "telephone checks" (also known as "remotely-created consumer items"), if not authorized by the customer or for any instrument if the warrantor knew of the forgery.

When an instrument is presented, a party that pays gets a somewhat narrower warranty than the presentment warranty. For checks, it is "I am the PEEI and this check has not been altered." For ordinary checks, the presentment warranty is this:

> § 3-417(a). If an unaccepted draft is presented to the drawee for payment or acceptance and the drawee pays or accepts the draft, (i) the person obtaining payment or acceptance, at the time of presentment, and (ii) a previous transferor of the draft, at the time of transfer, warrant to the drawee making payment or accepting the draft in good faith that:
>
> (1) the warrantor is, or was, at the time the warrantor transferred the draft, a person entitled to enforce the draft or authorized to obtain payment or acceptance of the draft on behalf of a person entitled to enforce the draft;

(2) the draft has not been altered;

(3) the warrantor has no knowledge that the signature of the drawer of the draft is unauthorized;

(4) with respect to any remotely-created consumer item, that the person on whose account the item is drawn authorized the issuance of the item in the amount for which the item is drawn.

(c) The warranties stated in subsections (a) and (d) cannot be disclaimed with respect to checks. Unless notice of a claim for breach of warranty is given to the warrantor within 30 days after the claimant has reason to know of the breach and the identity of the warrantor, the liability of the warrantor under subsection (b) or (d) is discharged to the extent of any loss caused by the delay in giving notice of the claim.

The bank that pays a check is entitled to reimbursement if the check is properly payable. If it pays an authorized check (signed by its customer, no stop payments or post-dating in effect) to the right person (i.e., necessary indorsements are not forged) for the right amount (no alterations), the drawee is entitled to reimbursement. The presentment warranty covers some of those risks. The drawee bank gets a presentment warranty, from the presenter and previous transferors, that amounts to, "I am the PEEI" (meaning necessary indorsements are not forged) and "The check has not been altered." Note that the warranty does not cover stop payment orders, post-dating, or forged drawer's signatures. The drawee bank is in a better position than the presenting bank on those matters. It has received the stop payment order or the notice of post-dating.

The more surprising rule is that the drawee gets no warranty about the authenticity of the drawer's signature (unless the warrantor actually knows about the forgery). The underlying theory is that the drawee bank has its customer's signature on file and so can check it before paying. That is undercut by modern banking practices, in which banks do not have personal relationships with their customers and generally do not verify signatures before paying checks. They can, however, do other things to guard against paying forged checks. They could, like credit and debit card issuers, use software to detect patterns of fraud. They can use "positive pay" systems, with which a customer sends an electronic notice each time a check is written, meaning that if a check shows up without such a notice, the bank should not pay it. At any rate, UCC Article 3 still does not give the drawee bank a warranty as to the authenticity of the drawer's signature, with one exception: for a "remotely-created consumer item" (i.e., a check created by a telephone or online marketer, with representation that customer authorized the check to be drawn on customer's account), the drawee bank gets a warranty "that the person on whose account the item is drawn authorized the issuance of the item in the amount for which the item is drawn."

For promissory notes, the presentment warranty is even narrower. The warrantor simply warrants that she is the PEEI. The warranty does not cover alterations, on the theory that if the note has been altered since the maker signed it, the maker would be able to know that.

> **QUESTION 7. Presenting the presentment warranty.** Haystack Bank pays a check written by its customer, Lana, to Philo. The check was stolen by Olga and then was deposited with Frost Bank, who then presented it to Haystack Bank. Can Haystack Bank recover from Frost Bank?
>
> A. Yes, but only if Frost Bank indorsed the check.
> B. Yes, for breach of transfer warranty.
> C. Yes, for breach of presentment warranty.
> D. No. Frost Bank did not breach the presentment warranty. It was in no better position than Haystack Bank to know that Olga had stolen the check.

ANALYSIS.

Lana → Philo → stolen by Olga → Frost Bank presents → Haystack Bank pays

We now move to the presentment warranty. When the check is presented and paid, Haystack Bank gets a presentment warranty from the presenter and all previous transferors. The presentment warranty on checks warrants that the person is the PEEI and that the check has not been altered. The check was payable to Philo, who never indorsed or transferred the check. So, only Philo is a PEEI, and no one else. Olga and Frost Bank both breached the presentment warranty to Haystack Bank. The possible answers sort out some common mistakes about presentment warranties.

A is incorrect, because a presenter or transferor makes the presentment warranty whether she indorses or not.

B names the wrong warranty. A transferee gets the broad transfer warranty; someone that pays the instrument gets only the narrow presentment warranty. Here, however, even the narrow presentment warranty is breached.

C is the best answer.

Contrary to **D**, presentment warranty does not rest on fault or knowledge. It is strict liability, like the transfer warranty. So, even if Frost Bank acted in good faith and reasonably and without knowledge, it would still be liable for breach of presentment warranty.

> **QUESTION 8. Altered states.** Haystack Bank also pays a check for $10,000 written by Lana to Harmon. It turns out that Lana had written a check only for $100, however, which Harmon altered before depositing with Stratton Bank. Is Stratton Bank liable to Haystack Bank?
>
> A. Yes, for breach of presentment warranty.
> B. Yes, if Stratton Bank had any reason to know of the alteration.
> C. No, not if Stratton Bank took for value, in good faith, and without notice of the alteration.
> D. No, Haystack Bank assumed the risk by paying the check.

ANALYSIS.
Lana $100 $\rightarrow$ Harmon alters to $1,000 $\rightarrow$ Stratton Bank $\rightarrow$ Haystack Bank pays
$$\$1,000$$

The narrow presentment warranty says, "I am the PEEI and the check has not been altered." Stratton Bank breached the second part, because the check had been altered. So, Stratton Bank is liable for $900.

A is the best answer.

Contrary to **B**, warranty liability does not rest on fault or knowledge.

C talks about the requirements for HIDC status, which are irrelevant for the reason just given. An HIDC is a super-plaintiff in enforcing the instrument and a super-defendant in resisting claims to the instrument but can still be liable for breach of warranty.

D states the allocation of risk policy backward. A bank can pay a check, knowing that it does not assume the risks of forged indorsements or alterations, because those are covered by the presentment warranty. A bank that pays a check does take other risks: that its customer does not have funds to reimburse the bank, that it is failing to follow a stop payment order, or, key to the scope of the presentment warranty, that its customer did not sign the check (as later questions show).

QUESTION 9. Risk of forged drawer's signature. Prospector steals Quechee's checkbook and signs Quechee's name to a check to Texas for a fountain. Texas deposits the check with Rocky Bank. Rocky presents the check through a local clearinghouse to Quechee's bank, Overlook Bank. Overlook Bank pays the check without a glance at any of the signatures. Can Overlook Bank recover for breach of warranty?

A. Yes, it can recover for breach of transfer warranty by Prospector, Texas, and Rocky Bank.

B. Yes, it can recover for breach of presentment warranty by Prospector, Texas, and Rocky Bank.

C. It cannot recover for breach of warranty, because it did not rely on the signature.

D. It cannot recover from Texas or Rocky Bank, because the forged drawer's signature does not breach the presentment warranty.

ANALYSIS.
Prospector forges "Quechee" $\rightarrow$ Texas $\rightarrow$ Rocky Bank $\rightarrow$ Overlook Bank

Rocky Bank (along with previous transferors) warrants that the check hasn't been altered. Rocky Bank also warrants that it's the person who is entitled to get paid on the check. Rocky Bank doesn't, however, warrant that the drawer's signature is authentic. The underlying reasoning, which made a lot more sense when banks had personal relationships with their customers, was this: "Overlook Bank knows their customer. They've got Quechee's signature on file. Before they pay a check on the account, they can look and compare the check against Quechee's signature and see if it's authentic. If it isn't, or if it looks shaky, they don't have to pay it. They can call Quechee and ask if they should pay it. Rocky Bank can't do that. Rocky Bank doesn't know who Quechee is; they are just processing a check apparently written by Pam. So, as between Rocky Bank and Overlook Bank, Overlook Bank is in a better position to handle Quechee's the risk of the forged drawer's signature. Therefore, we don't have Rocky Bank warrant the authenticity of the drawer signature."

Today, when banks have thousands upon thousands of customers, that particular rationale might be a little bit questionable. A bank doesn't know its customers' signatures. Banking practice isn't to compare signatures before they pay checks. Checks are handled in large volume, in largely mechanized and electronic fashion. Nevertheless, the rule is still the rule under the most recent version of the UCC. As discussed, one could argue that the drawee bank is in the best position to reduce fraud, by introducing positive payment systems or using fraud detection software. At any rate, **D** is the best answer.

Note the misleaders: A forged drawer's signature does breach the *transfer* warranty. The drawee bank gets the narrow presentment warranty, however, not the broad transfer warranty, so **A** is incorrect. Reliance is not necessary for warranty liability, so **C** gives the right answer (No) for the wrong reason.

QUESTION 10. Bearer: Beware. Ascutney writes a bearer check and gives it to Lincoln to repay a loan. Worth steals the check, forges Lincoln's signature, and sells it to Check Bazaar, who gets payment from the drawee, Skylight Bank. Ascutney meanwhile has written another check to Lincoln and complains mightily that his bank has paid a stolen check. Skylight Bank turns back to Check Bazaar and demands reimbursement. Is Skylight Bank entitled to the money back for breach of warranty?

A. Yes. Check Bazaar presented a stolen check.
B. Yes. Check Bazaar presented a check with a forged indorsement.
C. It would depend on whether Check Bazaar qualified as a holder in due course.
D. No. There was no breach of the presentment warranty.

ANALYSIS.
Ascutney → Lincoln → Worth steals → Check Bazaar → Skylight

Bearer paper is payable to whoever has it! The check was properly payable, and there was no breach of presentment warranty, so Lincoln will take loss. Therefore, **D** is the best answer. Note that the forged indorsement does not matter, because it was not a *necessary* indorsement. So **B** relies on an irrelevant fact.

D.   The closer

QUESTION 11. **One fine point.**   Townshend, a real wheeler and dealer, signs a $10,000 note in one of her many transactions. The note is altered by the payee, Parvati, to $100,000, and sold for $90,000 to Antone. Townshend pays Antone $100,000 when the note is presented. Not long after, she realizes the note had been altered and she over-paid by $90,000. She sues Antone for breach of presentment warranty. Who wins?

A. Townshend, because Antone presented a fraudulently altered note.
B. Townshend, because Antone was not the person entitled to enforce the instrument.
C. Antone, because Antone did not breach the presentment warranty.
D. Antone. Townshend has no damages, because Townshend has the right to recover from the original payee.

ANALYSIS.

Townshend $10,000 → Parvati alters to $100,000 → Antone presents to → Townshend

The presentment warranty is even narrower for notes. When Antone presents the note and Townshend pays it, Antone makes a presentment warranty. For checks, that is "I am the PEEI and it has not been altered." For notes, it is "I am the PEEI." A check is written by the customer and presented to the drawee bank. The drawee bank has no way of knowing whether the check has been altered. A note is written by the maker and presented to the maker. If it has been altered, the maker could recognize it, as she issued the instrument. For example, in this case, Townshend signed a $10,000 note. Antone bought it from Parvati, thinking it to be a $100,000 note. Townshend then paid $100,000 on a note she herself had written for $10,000. She was in a better position than Antone to recognize that there had been an alteration. Townshend should have remembered the amount of the note she signed, or at least referred to her records (which should include a copy of the note) before paying. As between the two, it makes little sense for Antone to warrant whether the note has been altered.

A would be correct only if the presentment warranty for notes covered alterations.

B is incorrect, because Antone is the PEEI. The note has been altered, but it is still payable to Antone (for $10,000, not $100,000).

C is the best answer.

D gives an unnecessary theory. There was no breach of warranty, so damages are not an issue.

This question emphasizes the role of the warranties. A transferor warrants that there is no legal defect, so the transferee can enforce the instrument. For checks, the presentment warranty includes the warranty that the check was not altered. For notes, the instrument is being presented to the person who issued it. They could recognize if it had been altered since they signed it (unlike the drawee bank, who would never have seen the check), so they get only the warranty that the warrantor is the PEEI.

 # McJohn's picks

1. Breach	**F**
2. At the time ...	**B**
3. Musical chairs	**D**
4. Never promised you a rose garden	**D**
5. A difficult one	**C**
6. Who warrants?	**D**
7. Presenting the presentment warranty	**C**
8. Altered states	**A**
9. Risk of forged drawer's signature	**D**
10. Bearer: Beware	**D**
11. One fine point	**C**

The Validation Rules: Beware the Bookkeeper, the Impostor, and Yourself

~

Embezzler's trusting boss
Takes the loss.

~

CHAPTER OVERVIEW
A. The validation rules
B. Negligence rule
C. The impostor rule
D. The fictitious payee rule
E. Employee indorsement rule
F. Comparative negligence applies
G. The closer
 McJohn's picks

A.   The validation rules

Customer	→	Health Services	→	Thief	→	Check Casher	→	Depot	→	Drawee
issues		receives		steals, indorses		cashes		presents		pays

Some rules provide validation of forgery or alteration, to put the loss on the one in the best position to have avoided it (e.g., one that was negligent, or issued a check to impostor, or hired a forger or embezzler).

Warranties, discussed in the last chapter, usually put the loss from forgery, alteration, or theft on the person who took the instrument from the bad actor (or the drawee bank that paid over a forged drawer's signature). Example: Customer writes a check to Health Services. The check is stolen by Thief, who forges Health Services' indorsement and sells the check to Check Casher. Check Casher deposits the check in its account at Depot Bank. Depot presents it to Drawee Bank, who pays it. Where Drawee Bank pays over a forged indorsement, it isn't entitled to reimbursement from its customer, because it paid the wrong person. The check was payable to Health Services; Health Services never indorsed it or transferred it, so it's still payable to them. Health Services would be entitled to collect, by enforcing the stolen check against Customer. Meanwhile, Drawee can recover from the Depot Bank for breach of the presentment warranty. Depot Bank can in turn recover from Check Casher, for breach of the transfer warranty. So, Check Casher takes the loss, unless they can locate and collect from Thief. The rationale is that of the innocent people—Customer, Health Services, Check Casher, Depot Bank, and Drawee Bank—the one in the best position to avoid the loss was Check Casher, who took the check from the forger over the forged indorsement. They dealt directly with the forger, so they take the loss for a forged indorsement.

However, the validation rules can change that. Sometimes, someone else is in a better position to avoid the loss. The validation rules fine-tune the risk allocation for particular situations. Some of them apply to indorsements, some apply to alterations, and some apply to drawer signatures.

Suppose that Health Services had been negligent and caused the loss. They knew that Thief had a long record of theft and forgery, and nevertheless allowed Thief easy access to the drawer where the check was kept. The negligence rule would make the forged indorsement effective for some purposes, which would change the result of the case above. If the forged indorsement was effective, then Drawee would have paid a properly payable check, meaning Drawee would be entitled to reimbursement from Customer, who in turn would no longer be obliged to pay Health Services. So, in this scenario, Health Services, the negligent party, would take the loss.

B. Negligence rule

§ 3-406. Negligence Contributing to Forged Signature or Alteration of Instrument

(a) A person whose failure to exercise ordinary care substantially contributes to an alteration of an instrument or to the making of a forged signature on an instrument is precluded from asserting the alteration or the forgery against a person who, in good faith, pays the instrument or takes it for value or for collection.

The *negligence rule* is a nice all-around rule that shifts the loss where one of the parties was negligent. It provides an incentive to act with due care. Where there's a loss, it provides a mechanism to put the loss on the negligent party. If someone's negligence causes a forgery or alteration to be made, the forgery or alteration counts as valid with respect to that person. For example, a party that entrusted their checkbook to someone known to be dishonest would be negligent. That would validate the forged signature on the checks written by the dishonest person. Because the signatures counted as valid, the drawee bank would be entitled to reimbursement for paying the checks. Rather than the drawee taking the loss (because it paid over a forged drawer's signature), the negligent customer would take the loss (because the check would be properly payable). Likewise, if a payee negligently left a valuable check where it would likely be stolen, that would validate the forged indorsement. The payee would then be unable to bring a claim if the check ended up in the hands of a holder in due course or was paid to the wrong person.

There must be negligence that substantially contributes to the making of the forgery or alteration. In a notable case, the drawer wrote a check for $250.00. The holder of the check changed that amount by skillfully erasing the period after "250," putting in a comma, adding another zero, putting in a period, and adding two more zeros. On the line where the amount was written in words, the holder wrote "two fifty" and managed to squeeze in "thoud," an abbreviation of the word "thousand." So now, it was a $250,000.00 check. It was deposited and paid.

The drawee bank argued that its customer was negligent for writing the check in such a way that it could be altered. The court, however, held there was no negligence. The customer had not left a gaping space, inviting alteration, or written the check in easily erased pencil. Rather, they left a small space after the words where the bad actor could barely squeeze in "thoud," and couldn't even get in the whole word "thousand." They also left a space after the numbers, but people always leave a space after the numbers.

QUESTION 1. Oops.   The office at Sam's Store always looks like a tornado just went through. Because Sam is so messy, his secretary leaves Sam's checkbook on the customer service counter. The checkbook is away from the mess and available to write checks for deliveries but is sitting in a spot accessible to the public. One day, Opportunist grabs a few checks, makes them out to Cash, and signs Sam's name. Sam's bank pays the checks. Is the drawee bank entitled to reimbursement from Sam?

A. No. Sam did not sign the checks, so they were properly payable.

B. Yes. Sam's negligence validates the forged signatures, so they count as valid against Sam.

C. Yes. The checks were payable to cash, so they were payable to any-
    one. Sam's signature does not matter.
D. No. Sam was not the bad actor—Opportunist was.

ANALYSIS.

Opportunist writes checks on Sam's account → Sam's Bank pays the checks

Normally, if a bank pays checks that its customer did not authorize, the
bank is not entitled to reimbursement, because the checks are not properly
payable. But Sam's negligence causes the forged signatures to be validated.
B is the best answer. **A** cites the general rule, but the negligence rule creates
an exception in cases like this.

C places too much reliance on the bearer nature of the checks. To be properly payable, a check must be paid to the right persons and be authorized by
the customer.

Opportunist was the most culpable party. But the issue is, as between
innocent Sam and innocent drawee bank, who should take the loss? So **D** is off
base. The UCC puts the loss on the negligent party.

QUESTION 2. Open door policy.   The account manager at Boring
Bank allows Whitey (a known embezzler and check kiter) to open an
account under the name of California Catering. Before long, Whitey
uses the account to process a number of checks stolen from California
Catering. When the drawer seeks to use comparative negligence against
Boring Bank, it argues that the negligence did not contribute to the
making of the forgeries. Rather, the bank argued, the checks were
already forged by the time the bank dealt with them. Should the bank
bear some of the loss under comparative negligence?

A. Yes. Its negligence in opening the account helped the overall scheme
    and therefore contributed to the making of the forgeries.
B. Yes. Banks should always bear the loss, because they have deep
    pockets.
C. No. The bank received the checks after the indorsements were forged.
    Causation cannot go back in time.
D. No. All parties should have access to banking services.

ANALYSIS.   The bank's negligence here did enable the scheme to go forward,
and therefore the bank's negligence contributed to the forgery. Therefore, **A** is
the best answer. It might be different if the opening of the account and the forgery were less directly related, such as if the account had been opened years ago.
But where the events were so close, there would be a sufficient contribution.

The negligence rule is handy, but not always predictable. Any time rules use terms like "reasonable," "substantial," "material," or "adequate," the fact finder must consider all relevant factors in that particular case to come to a determination. Sometimes the law likes more cut and dried rules, which are easier to apply. In tort law, there is a general negligence standard (what would the reasonable person do?) and per se negligence rules (if the person violated a law related to safety, she is deemed negligent). Uniform Commercial Code (UCC) Article 3 likewise provides a set of specific validation rules. They apply in particular situations where somebody is, in effect, deemed to be negligent. The first is the *impostor rule.*

C.   The impostor rule

Dana writes check to Unicef → Impostor → Drawee pays

Impostor rings Dana's doorbell and says, "I'm from Unicef." Dana writes a check for $250.00. One could argue about whether that constitutes negligence. Maybe a reasonable person should have checked identification, or maybe for a $250.00 charitable contribution that's not a reasonable precaution. The impostor rule says, "Let's not worry about negligence. If you issue an instrument to an impostor, the rule makes the forged indorsement effective." When Impostor indorses it as "Unicef," it is effective for the purpose of negotiating or paying that instrument. So, when that check is paid, Dana can no longer argue, "I wrote that to the Unicef. You didn't pay the Unicef or anyone that transferred it to, so the check was not properly payable." Dana, who dealt directly with Impostor and handed her a check, intending her to be paid (even though misinformed about her identity), was in a better position to avoid the loss than the innocent other parties.

As the UCC puts it:

> § 3-404(a). If an impostor, by use of the mails or otherwise, induces the issuer of an instrument to issue the instrument to the impostor, or to a person acting in concert with the impostor, by impersonating the payee of the instrument or a person authorized to act for the payee, an indorsement of the instrument by any person in the name of the payee is effective as the indorsement of the payee in favor of a person who, in good faith, pays the instrument or takes it for value or for collection.

QUESTION 3. Postal impostor. Lucienne receives a heart-tugging solicitation in the mail, purportedly from Doctors Without Borders. Lucienne writes out a check and mails it to the address provided, which is actually the home of Donald without conscience. Donald signs "Doctors Without Borders" and deposits it with Marie Bank, who gets payment from the drawee, Glynnis Bank. Who takes the loss, if Donald is judgment proof (i.e., has no assets to get)?

> **A.** Lucienne
> **B.** Marie Bank
> **C.** Glynnis Bank
> **D.** Doctors Without Borders

ANALYSIS.

Lucienne → Donald as "Doctors" → Marie Bank presents → Glynnis Bank pays

Without the validation rules, Marie Bank would take the loss. Glynnis paid the wrong person and so would not be entitled to reimbursement from Lucienne; however, Glynnis could use presentment warranty to put the loss on Marie.

The impostor rule makes Donald's forged indorsement of "Doctors Without Borders" effective. One might think that the impostor rule did not apply, because Donald did not meet with Lucienne, pretending to be with Doctors Without Borders. But the impostor rule applies where an impostor acts "by use of the mails or otherwise." Donald's forgery is effective as Doctors Without Borders' signature, so Marie is the person entitled to enforce the instrument (PEEI), the check is properly payable, and Glynnis is entitled to reimbursement from Lucienne, so Lucienne takes the loss.

A is the best answer.

Marie Bank took from the thief, but still qualifies as a PEEI, contrary to **B**.

Glynnis Bank paid the check properly, contrary to **C**.

Doctors Without Borders did nothing here and so could not be liable on any theory. Note that the signature is effective as the indorsement of Doctors Without Borders for the purpose of making subsequent parties the PEEI, but does not make Doctors Without Borders liable as an indorser. Therefore, **D** is incorrect.

One could also potentially apply the general negligence rule, but where one of the more specific rules applies, that is unnecessary. To apply the negligence rule, we would have to discuss whether, under the facts of this particular case, Lucienne was negligent. That would involve a discussion of all relevant facts, not to mention custom among individuals and charities. The impostor rule simplifies things: Lucienne wrote a check to an impostor, so the forged indorsement is effective.

QUESTION 4. Stop stitchin'. Imelda, pretending to be Peggy, visits Peggy's Aunt Doris. Doris, taken in by Imelda's ruse, writes a check payable to Peggy for $500 and hands the check to Imelda. Imelda indorses the check in Peggy's name and transfers the check to Depo Bank, which gives Imelda $500. Depo Bank acts in good faith, with no notice of any irregularity. In the meantime, Doris has stopped payment on the check and it is dishonored when presented to the drawee. Can Depo Bank enforce the check against Aunt Doris?

A. No. The impostor rule is not applicable because Doris intended the payee to get the money.
B. No, because Doris had stopped payment on the instrument.
C. No, because Depo Bank did not give value to the person entitled to enforce the instrument.
D. Yes, because the forged signature is effective in this case.
E. No. Aunt Doris did not sign the check.

ANALYSIS.
Aunt Doris → Imelda as "Peggy" → Depo Bank → Drawee dishonors

This question shows how the validation rules can apply in a holder in due course case. Depo has a check signed by Aunt Doris. To enforce it, Depo Bank has to be the PEEI. The check was written to Peggy, who did not indorse the check or transfer it. The impostor rule makes the forged indorsement effective. An impostor induced Aunt Doris to issue the check, so the forged indorsement is effective. Depo Bank is the PEEI and can enforce the check. Moreover, Depo Bank took in good faith, for value, and without notice, so Depo Bank qualifies as a holder in due course, immune to Aunt Doris's defense of fraud.

A confuses the fictitious payee rule with the impostor rule. The drawee always intends the payee to get the money in an impostor situation.

B raises a common misconception. A stop payment order affects only the drawee bank's right to pay the check. The check can still be enforced against any signer, if dishonored.

Depo Bank gave value to the wrong person, but the impostor rule still makes Depo Bank the holder, able to qualify as a holder in due course. Sorry, C.

D is the best answer.

E tries to confuse the facts. Aunt Doris did sign the check.

QUESTION 5. How valid is that signature? Assuming the same facts as in the previous question, could Depo Bank enforce the check against Peggy?

A. No. The impostor rule is not applicable because Doris intended the payee to get the money.
B. No, because Doris had stopped payment on the instrument.
C. No, because Depo Bank did not give value to the person entitled to enforce the instrument.
D. Yes, because the forged signature is effective in this case.
E. No, because Peggy did not sign the check.

ANALYSIS. The forged signature is effective, but not for all purposes. It is effective as Peggy's indorsement for the purpose of making Depo Bank the holder and imposing liability on Doris, who issued the check to the impostor. It does not, however, impose liability on Peggy, a complete stranger to the story. So, **E** is the best answer.

D. The fictitious payee rule

The *fictitious payee rule* often applies where an embezzler is padding the payroll or writing checks to creditors and then pocketing them. If the person writing the check intends to take the proceeds (rather than sending the check to the named payee), the forged indorsement counts—meaning that the party that let the embezzler write checks will take the loss.

> **§ 3-404(b).** If (i) a person whose intent determines to whom an instrument is payable (Section 3-110(a) or (b)) does not intend the person identified as payee to have any interest in the instrument, or (ii) the person identified as payee of an instrument is a fictitious person, the following rules apply until the instrument is negotiated by special indorsement:
>
> (1) Any person in possession of the instrument is its holder.
>
> (2) An indorsement by any person in the name of the payee stated in the instrument is effective as the indorsement of the payee in favor of a person who, in good faith, pays the instrument or takes it for value or for collection.

Bookkeeper prepares checks for Employer with fictitious payees → Employer's
bank pays

Suppose the bookkeeper makes up a list of checks to be paid that month, but puts fictitious people on that list. So, the employer cuts checks to non-existent people. Then, instead of sending them out, the bookkeeper deposits them in her account. That's an example of the fictitious payee rule. Because the check was made to a fictitious person, the forged indorsement is effective, which means that check is properly payable, and the money can come out of the employer's account. Again, as between the Depot Bank and Drawee Bank, and the employer that issued a check to a non-existent person, there's an argument that the employer was in the best position to avoid that loss.

The fictitious payee rule includes checks made to non-existent people, and checks where the person signing it didn't intend the payee to receive a benefit. If the bookkeeper was allowed to issue checks and issued checks to people, intending to steal the check, the forged indorsements will be effective.

QUESTION 6. Embezzlers' employers' headaches. Bart, the comptroller at Leaky Ink, has authority to write checks. Bart prepares and signs a batch of checks to pay suppliers, but Bart sends the checks to his confederate, Millhouse. After the checks are deposited and paid, and Bart and Millhouse head for an island haven, where will the loss fall when the litigation music stops?

A. Leaky Ink.

B. The depositary bank.

C. The drawee bank.

D. The unlucky suppliers.

ANALYSIS.

Leaky Ink → Millhouse → depositary bank → drawee bank pays

The fictitious payee rule makes the forged indorsements effective, even though the payees are real (or real in this fictional case). The fictitious payee rule applies where the person writing the check does not intend the payee to have any interest in the instrument.

Leaky Ink takes the loss, because the checks are properly payable and Leaky Ink must reimburse the drawee bank. Therefore, **A** is the best answer.

The depositary bank did not breach the presentment warranty, because the forged indorsements are effective, making the depositary bank a PEEI. So **B** is not to be.

The drawee bank paid, but is entitled to reimbursement because of the validation. **C** is out.

The suppliers did not get their money, but they are still owed the money. The checks never reached them, so the debts to them were not suspended. So, contrary to **D,** they do not take the loss here.

The employee indorsement rule, discussed next, would also apply in this case.

E. Employee indorsement rule

The *employee indorsement rule* is the validation rule that is applied most often. If someone employs an individual, and the individual (or somebody working with him) makes a fraudulent indorsement, the fraudulent indorsement is effective. This can apply in two types of situations: where the employer writes the check, and where the employer receives the check. For example, if our bookkeeper has the employer cut some supplier checks, then steals those checks and forges the supplier's indorsements, then the indorsements are effective. Or, if the checks come in payable to the employer, and the bookkeeper steals those checks and forges the employer's indorsement, likewise, the employee indorsement rule makes the indorsements effective, shifting the loss from the depositary bank to the employer.

Here's § 3-405 in all its splendor:

§ 3-405. Employer's Responsibility for Fraudulent Indorsement by Employee.

(a) In this section:

(1) "Employee" includes an independent contractor and employee of an independent contractor retained by the employer.

(2) "Fraudulent indorsement" means (i) in the case of an instrument payable to the employer, a forged indorsement purporting to be that of the employer, or (ii) in the case of an instrument with respect to which the employer is the issuer, a forged indorsement purporting to be that of the person identified as payee.

(3) "Responsibility" with respect to instruments means authority (i) to sign or indorse instruments on behalf of the employer, (ii) to process instruments received by the employer for bookkeeping purposes, for deposit to an account, or for other disposition, (iii) to prepare or process instruments for issue in the name of the employer, (iv) to supply information determining the names or addresses of payees of instruments to be issued in the name of the employer, (v) to control the disposition of instruments to be issued in the name of the employer, or (vi) to act otherwise with respect to instruments in a responsible capacity. "Responsibility" does not include authority that merely allows an employee to have access to instruments or blank or incomplete instrument forms that are being stored or transported or are part of incoming or outgoing mail, or similar access.

(b) For the purpose of determining the rights and liabilities of a person who, in good faith, pays an instrument or takes it for value or for collection, if an employer entrusted an employee with responsibility with respect to the instrument and the employee or a person acting in concert with the employee makes a fraudulent indorsement of the instrument, the indorsement is effective as the indorsement of the person to whom the instrument is payable if it is made in the name of that person. If the person paying the instrument or taking it for value or for collection fails to exercise ordinary care in paying or taking the instrument and that failure substantially contributes to loss resulting from the fraud, the person bearing the loss may recover from the person failing to exercise ordinary care to the extent the failure to exercise ordinary care contributed to the loss.

QUESTION 7. A classic.   Dozens of happy customers mail checks each month to Adair Supplements, to pay for vitamin and mineral pills. Waverly, a bookkeeper at Adair, has the job of recording the payments and then taking the checks to the company treasurer. Waverly pockets a good number of checks one week, forges Adair's signature, and deposits them with Philippa Bank, who gets payment from Clementine Bank. Who takes the loss?

A. The customers, who will have to write checks again.
B. Adair, who employed Waverly.
C. Philippa Bank, who took the checks over Waverly's forgery.

D. Clementine Bank, who paid checks to the wrong person.

E. All of the above.

ANALYSIS.

Customer → Adair → Waverly → Phillippa Bank → Clementine Bank

steals, forges indorsement

This is a typical example of how the validation rules operate. It may be the most common example, because employee forgers account for a large percentage of check theft. Employees often have access and opportunity with respect to lots of money in checks.

Without the validation rules, Philippa Bank would take the loss, as the entity who took the check from the bad actor (unless Philippa Bank could recover from Waverly). The check was payable to Adair, who never indorsed or transferred the check. Philippa would not be the person entitled to enforce the instrument (PEEI). Philippa would be liable to Clementine for breach of presentment warranty. Adair could enforce the check (as PEEI of a lost or stolen instrument) against Customer. Customer would pay only once, because the check was not properly payable. Alternatively, Adair could recover directly from Philippa Bank for conversion, because Philippa Bank took from a non-PEEI.

When we add the validation rules, things change. The employee indorsement rules apply here, because an employee with responsibility for checks made a forged indorsement. So, Waverly's indorsement is as effective as Adair's indorsement. That means Philippa Bank was the PEEI. Philippa Bank therefore does not breach the presentment warranty (the warranty that it was the PEEI is true) and is not liable for conversion (it took from the PEEI). The check is properly payable, so Clementine Bank is entitled to reimbursement from Customer. That means Adair cannot enforce the stolen check, because § 3-309 does not require Customer to pay twice on one check. So, Adair takes the loss. As a matter of risk allocation, that makes sense. Adair, who controlled Waverly and the check, was in a better position to avoid the loss than Philippa Bank, which simply took deposit of a check.

A is not correct. The check will be properly payable, so the Customer will have to reimburse Clementine Bank. But that is what Customer expected when writing the check, so Customer is not taking a loss.

B is the best answer.

C would be the result if not for the validation rules, which change the allocation of loss in several categories of cases, like this one.

The validation of the forgery makes the check properly payable, so Clementine Bank is entitled to reimbursement from Customer. Without validation, Clementine Bank would have a breach of presentment warranty recovery from Philippa Bank. So, **D** is off on both counts.

They cannot all take the loss, so **E** is off.

QUESTION 8. Filching and forging.   Dov and Akiva work at Sander Corp. One payday, Dov and Akiva go out for dinner after work. Dov skillfully steals his colleague's paycheck from his wallet, writes "Akiva" on the back, and deposits it in Yannick Bank. Guillame Bank pays the check. Dov of course absconds with the proceeds. Who takes the loss?

A. Akiva, who negligently failed to go straight to the ATM with his paycheck.

B. Sander Corp. The check is properly payable, because the impostor rule makes the forgery effective.

C. Sander Corp. The check is properly payable, because the employee indorsement rule makes the forged signature effective.

D. Yannick Bank. It is liable for breach of presentment warranty.

ANALYSIS.

Sander → Akiva → Dov forges → Yannick Bank presents → Guillame Bank pays

This one looks like an employee indorsement situation, but it is not. Indeed, none of the validation rules apply. Sander Corp. did employ Dov, but it did not give him responsibility with respect to checks. So, this does not fall within the scope of the employee indorsement rule. It is not an impostor or fictitious payee case either, so we then ask if the general negligence rule would apply. Akiva was not negligent with the check. He simply stuck it in his pocket, which would not be deemed negligence. (It might be different if the check were for a stupendous amount, as opposed to being his paycheck.)

A gives a feeble argument for negligence. No court would hold that one should proceed immediately to the nearest ATM upon receiving a check.

Contrary to **B**, an impostor did not induce Sander Corp. to issue the check. Sander Corp. issued the check to Akiva. Not every forgery triggers the impostor rule.

C applies the employee indorsement rule too broadly. It might apply if, say, Sander Corp. gave Dov responsibity for checks and Dov stole a check payable to Sander Corp. or forged Sander Corp.'s signature to a check.

D is the best answer.

To sum up: Where a check has a forged indorsement or alteration, the loss is likely to fall on the party that took the check from the bad actor. If there is a forged drawer's signature, the loss will fall on the drawer bank if it pays the check. However, if one of the validation rules applies, the loss will be shifted to the party deemed to be at fault.

F.   Comparative negligence applies

To add one more twist: Each of these validation rules is subject to *comparative negligence.* In other words, if the bank is using the impostor rule, the employee indorsement rule, the fictitious payee rule, or the negligence rule, the customer can argue comparative negligence. If the court finds that another party was negligent, it can allocate the loss accordingly. It can split the loss between the two, according to respective fault.

QUESTION 9. Old leaf. Finnegan runs a thriving architectural firm. His brother asks him to hire Florian, the "bad news" member of the family. Florian has a long history of check forgery and theft, but has recently shaped up, attending night classes and helping out the relatives with various tasks. Finnegan puts Florian to work in the office. Florian's jobs have nothing to do with check but he has free access to everything, including Finnegan's checkbook and bank statements. One rainy Monday, Florian signs Finnegan's name to a big check payable to Florian and deposits it with Zev Bank. Becket Bank pays the check. Florian flees. Who pays?

A. Finnegan, under the employee indorsement rule.
B. Zev Bank, who got payment for Florian.
C. Becket Bank, who paid, despite the forgery of their customer's signature.
D. Finnegan, under the negligence rule.

ANALYSIS.

"Finnegan" forged by Florian → Florian → Zev Bank presents → Becket Bank pays

This question illustrates how to pick which validation rule, if any, applies. Without the validation rules, Becket Bank would take the loss. Becket Bank paid the check but is not entitled to reimbursement from Finnegan, because Finnegan did not sign the check. Finnegan's signature was forged. Becket Bank cannot put the loss back onto the depositary bank, Zev Bank, because the presentment warranty does not cover forged drawer's signatures. The presentment warranty covers alterations and forged indorsements — in effect saying, "I am the PEEI and this check has not been altered."

The validation rules can change that, however, if there is one that will make the forged drawer's signature effective, so that it is as effective as Finnegan's signature. We cannot use the impostor rule, the employee indorsement rule, or the fictitious payee rule. They all apply only to forged indorsements, not forged drawer's signatures. However, the negligence rule can apply to any forged signature (as well as alterations), and there was negligence here: Finnegan gave a known forger free access to his checkbook and bank statements.

A cites to the wrong rule.

B makes up a rule. There is no rule, as such, against obtaining payment for the wrong person.

C would be the case, but for the negligence rule validating the forgery.

D is the best answer.

> **QUESTION 10. Selecting the applicable rule.**   India, a graphic designer at Leaky Ink, wanders into the accounting department. She takes an unattended company checkbook and writes a check to her friend, Laputa Labs. As soon as the next checking statement comes, Leaky Ink complains to its bank. Which rule, if any, will make the forged drawer's signature by India effective?
>
> **A.** Impostor rule
> **B.** Employee indorsement rule
> **C.** Fictitious payee rule
> **D.** Bank statement rule
> **E.** Negligence rule

ANALYSIS.
India as "Leaky Ink" → Laputa Labs → depositary bank → drawee bank

This question helps understand how to choose the applicable validation rule. Look at it this way:

RULE	May apply to:
a. Negligence rule	Alterations and any forged signature
b. Impostor rule	Forged indorsements
c. employee indorsement rule	Forged indorsements
d. fictitious payee rule	Forged indorsements
e. bank statement rule	Alterations and forged drawer's signatures (and rarely to forged indorsements) (Discussed in Properly Payable chapter)

India forged the drawer's signature of Leaky Ink. From the above table, we are reminded that only the bank statement rule and the negligence rule can make drawer's signatures effective. The bank statement rule is not at issue, because Leaky Ink did not delay in reporting the problem after getting the statement. So, the only potentially applicable rule is the negligence rule. Therefore, **E** is the best answer. Note that even though there may be an employee forger, and hints of an impostor or suspicious payee, those rules apply only when an indorsement is at issue.

G.   The closer

> **QUESTION 11. Employee indorsement.**   India, now working processing checks, stole a check, written by Stationery Canary payable to Leaky Ink, and forged Leaky Ink's indorsement before depositing it with Dijon Bank. Fortunately, the staff at the payor bank noticed something

suspicious. After a few quick phone calls, Stationery Canary told the payor bank not to pay the check. Dijon Bank now has the check back but has already advanced the funds to India, who is no longer to be found. Which rule, if any, may apply to the forged indorsement by India?

A. Impostor rule
B. Employee indorsement rule
C. Fictitious payee rule
D. Bank statement rule
E. Negligence rule
F. Both B and E

ANALYSIS.

Stationery Canary → Leaky Ink → India steals → Dijon Bank → Payor bank
dishonors

This time a forged indorsement is at issue, so all the validation rules are on the table. The check was not induced by an impostor, so the impostor rule does not apply. Leaky's indorsement was forged by an employee with responsibility for instruments, so the employee indorsement rule does apply. The check was not written to a fictitious person or with fictitious intent, so the fictitious payee rule does not apply. There are no issues about slow monitoring of the bank statement, so the bank statement rule does not apply. The negligence rule is always potentially applicable when one of the more specific rules applies. So, the best answer is **F**—both the employee indorsement rule and the negligence rule potentially apply here. Of course, there is no need to apply the more fact-specific negligence analysis, because the employee indorsement rule clearly makes the indorsement effective.

 # McJohn's picks

1.	Oops	B
2.	Open door policy	A
3.	Postal imposter	A
4.	Stop stitchin'	D
5.	How valid is that signature?	E
6.	Embezzlers' employers' headaches	A
7.	A classic	B
8.	Filching and forging	D
9.	Old leaf	D
10.	Selecting the applicable rule	E
11.	Employee indorsement	F

12

Conversion (Took from or Paid to a Non-PEEI)

If checks are subject to diversion
Or other financial perversion
The thief may be bankrupt
But don't give the ghost up
Just sue the banks for conversion.

CHAPTER OVERVIEW
A. Conversion
B. Conversion defined
C. Who can bring a conversion action?
D. Safe harbor
E. The closer
✦ McJohn's picks

A. Conversion

Employer → Paula → Robin steals → Depo Bank → Drawee Bank pays

Robin, Depo Bank, and Drawee Bank are all liable to Robin for conversion.

If Robin steals Paula's paycheck, Robin is liable to Paula for conversion. The common law tort of conversion is the unauthorized use of someone's property, to their detriment. Your Torts class may have skipped conversion (along with other lesser-known torts, like defamation of vegetables, a tort in some agricultural jurisdictions). Conversion is an intentional tort, meaning that someone would be liable for conversion only if they knew that the property was not theirs to use. The Uniform Commercial Code (UCC) provides an expanded definition of conversion, however, imposing liability on anyone who takes an instrument from the someone not entitled to enforce it (i.e., a non-PEEI [person entitled to enforce the instrument]), or pays a non-PEEI.

B.   Conversion defined

One that steals an instrument is liable for conversion. In addition, one that takes an instrument from a non-PEEI, or pays a non-PEEI, is liable for conversion.

§ 3-420. Conversion of Instrument
        (a) The law applicable to conversion of personal property applies to instruments. An instrument is also converted if it is taken by transfer, other than a negotiation, from a person not entitled to enforce the instrument or a bank makes or obtains payment with respect to the instrument for a person not entitled to enforce the instrument or receive payment.

Robin steals Paula's paycheck and deposits in Robin's account at Depo Bank. Depo Bank gets payment from Drawee Bank. Paula could recover in conversion from Robin (for theft), from Depo Bank (for taking from a non-PEEI), or from Drawee Bank (for paying a non-PEEI). Just as warranty imposes liability on someone passing on a stolen instrument, so conversion imposes liability on someone taking a stolen instrument.

Suppose that Paula's employer had issued a second check to replace the stolen one. Could Paula still recover in conversion from the banks, getting a windfall? No. Section 3-420 limits Paula's recovery to her actual damages.

        (b) In an action under subsection (a), the measure of liability is presumed to be the amount payable on the instrument, but recovery may not exceed the amount of the plaintiff's interest in the instrument.

QUESTION 1. Converters?   Entropy Corp. hands a paycheck to Parallax. Lefe steals the check, forges Parallax's indorsement, and deposits it with Diffraction Bank, who obtains payment from Poly Bank, the drawee. Who is liable for conversion to Parallax, the payee?

A. Lefe.
B. Diffraction Bank.
C. Poly Bank.
D. All of the above.

ANALYSIS.

Entropy Corp. → Parallax　　→　Lefe　→　Diffraction Bank → Poly Bank
　　　　　　　　　　steals, forges indorsement　　　　　　　　pays

　　Lefe stole the check, so Lefe is liable for conversion. In addition, and with deeper pockets, Diffraction Bank took from a non-PEEI and Poly Bank paid a non-PEEI, so they are each liable to the PEEI, Parallax, for conversion. So, the best answer is **D**, all of the above.

　　This illustrates the typical role of conversion. After an instrument is stolen, the person the instrument is payable to may go after the thief and anyone who takes from the thief, directly or indirectly. Note that conversion does not depend on fault. Diffraction Bank and Poly Bank are liable, even if they took the check innocently.

> **QUESTION 2. No double dipping.**   Assuming the same facts as in the previous question, suppose Parallax seeks to recover from Poly Bank. Poly Bank defends by arguing, "I paid Diffraction Bank. I also have to refund the money I took to cover the check from Entropy Corp.'s account, because the check was not properly payable. If I also have to pay Parallax, that means I am triply liable, even though I was innocent. That cannot be the result." Is Poly Bank liable to Parallax?
>
> **A.** No. Poly Bank can only be liable once for its innocent wrongdoing.
> **B.** No. Poly Bank did not convert the check, because the drawee bank does not claim ownership of the check.
> **C.** Yes. Triple damages is appropriate, to encourage care in processing checks.
> **D.** Yes. Poly Bank is liable to Parallax for conversion, but Parallax can avoid loss on the overall case.

ANALYSIS.

Entropy Corp.→Parallax→Lefe, thief→Diffraction Bank→Poly Bank

　　Poly Bank is liable to Parallax for conversion, because Poly Bank paid a non-PEEI. If Poly Bank had to pay three times without any way to get it back, that would be unfair. Poly Bank can recover the money, however.

　　The check was payable to Parallax, who did not transfer or indorse it. So, only Parallax qualified as a PEEI. Poly Bank is liable to Parallax for conversion. Poly Bank has already paid Diffraction Bank, but Poly Bank can recover that money. Diffraction Bank was not the PEEI, so Diffraction Bank is liable to Poly Bank for breach of presentment warranty. In addition, when Poly Bank pays Parallax, Poly Bank will be paying the PEEI. Poly Bank will be properly paying the check that Entropy Corp. wrote, so Poly Bank will be entitled to reimbursement from Entropy Corp. So, Poly Bank ends up even, and Diffraction Bank takes the loss—because Diffraction Bank took the check from the bad actor. If Entropy Corp. or Diffraction Bank is insolvent, of course, Poly Bank will take the loss. Not for legal reasons, but financial reasons (bad credit).

A, we have seen, is incorrect. Parallax can be liable more than once. If Parallax has rights against others to balance things out, it will not end up paying more than once.

B views conversion far too narrowly. The UCC has a broad definition of conversion.

C is a red herring, drawn from other areas of the law.

D is the best answer.

Note that if Parallax had already been paid (Entropy Corp. issued another check, Diffraction Bank paid up for conversion, or, miraculously, Lefe the thief paid up), then Poly Bank would have no liability for conversion. Damages are limited to the plaintiff's interest in the check.

QUESTION 3. Miraculous conversion. Leaf picks Proto's pocket, steals Proto's paycheck issued by Entropy Corp., forges Proto's indorsement, and deposits it with DeVries Bank. Planet Bank, the drawee, pays the check. Proto learns the facts. At first angry, Proto then joyfully realizes: "I can recover from Leaf, DeVries Bank, and Planet Bank for conversion, and I can still recover from the Entropy Corp. on its drawer's signature. I get paid quadruple this month." Has Proto hit the theft quadrifecta?

A. Yes. Each of the parties is liable, and cannot excuse their own fault by another's liability.

B. No. Proto can collect a total of zero.

C. No. Proto, regardless of whom Proto sues, is entitled to collect only once.

D. Yes. Each of the parties must pay Proto and then seek to recover from the party before. Leaf can thus end up paying four times, which is appropriate for intentional wrongdoing.

ANALYSIS.

Entropy Corp. → Proto → Leaf → DeVries Bank → Planet Bank
steals and deposits   presents   pays

Proto is entitled to recover from Entropy Corp. (Entropy Corp. signed the check, Proto is the PEEI) or Leaf (conversion, for stealing) or DeVries Bank (conversion, took from non-PEEI) or Planet Bank (conversion, paid non-PEEI). However, Proto is not entitled to recover from Entropy Corp. *and* Leaf *and* DeVries Bank *and* Planet Bank. Under § 3-309, Proto is entitled to enforce the check against Entropy Corp., but Proto must protect Entropy Corp. from paying twice. If Proto also recovered from Planet Bank, Planet Bank would be entitled to reimbursement from Entropy Corp. for paying the PEEI, Proto. In a similar vein, Proto is entitled to recover in conversion from Leaf, DeVries Bank, or Planet Bank. The measure of liability for conversion is the party's damages and is limited to the party's interest in the check. If Proto has gotten paid once, Proto would have zero damages to recover.

A overstates Proto's rights. The point of liability (except for Leaf) is to compensate, not to punish.

B understates. Proto is not like Zeno's donkey, unable to choose between two carrots.

C is the best answer, summing up the general rule that the rules will not operate to overcompensate a party.

D confabulates a flimsy rationale for a rule that would triply compensate Proto. If nothing else, the rule is rather unrealistic. Getting a thief to pay once is tricky, let alone three times.

QUESTION 4. Chain of events.   Pandora scoots down to the ATM with her paycheck. She is in a rush to deposit it, because she needs the money soon to make her monthly car payment. Rushed, she unknowingly drops the check and deposits an empty envelope. Snopes finds the check and deposits it in his account at Credulous Bank, who obtains payment from Automatic Bank. Credulous Bank and Automatic Bank are liable in conversion to Pandora. Are they liable for the amount of the check only, or also for her consequential damages (her car was repossessed, causing the sudden demise of her weekend catering business, and she was arrested for writing bad checks)?

A. No. Conversion liability is limited to the amount of the instrument.
B. Yes. A party is liable for the natural consequence of their actions.
C. No. The banks did not repossess her car.
D. No. The banks did not sign the check.

ANALYSIS.   UCC Article 3 expands the normal definition of conversion. Conversion liability usually requires knowingly using someone's property without authority to their detriment. For checks and notes, however, under UCC Article 3, a party that innocently takes a check or note from the wrong person is liable for conversion. UCC Article 3 tempers it, however, by providing that liability is limited to the amount of the instrument. Therefore, **A** is the best answer.

The thief, who would be liable for good old common law conversion, could be liable for consequential damages (although it might be difficult to show causation — once Pandora lost the check, the chain of events including repossession and arrest may already have been in motion).

QUESTION 5. Hazardous paper.   Plutonium gets a check in the mail from a rich uncle. Plutonium signs his name on the back of the check and strolls toward the bank. He fills out a deposit envelope and drops it in the old-fashioned ATM. However, he inadvertently leaves the check on the counter. Oort, another customer, deposits the check in his own account. The check is presented by Doppler Bank and paid by Probable Bank. Oort disappears in a cloud of hasty purchases. Who is liable to Plutonium for conversion?

A. Oort.

B. Oort and Doppler Bank.

C. Oort, Doppler Bank, and Probable Bank.

D. No one, because of Plutonium's ill-chosen indorsement.

ANALYSIS.

Uncle → Plutonium, → Oort, → Doppler Bank → Probable Bank
       makes bearer paper   steals

Here is another question that stresses the risks of bearer paper. When Plutonium indorsed the check in blank (by simply signing her name), she made the check bearer paper, payable to whoever had it. When Oort picked it up, Oort became a holder and, hence, the PEEI. Oort did not own the check. Oort was subject to a claim to the check by Plutonium. Oort is liable for conversion for stealing the check, but Oort was the PEEI. So, Doppler Bank took the check from a PEEI and is not liable for conversion. Probable Bank paid a PEEI and is not liable for conversion (and the rich uncle is obliged to reimburse Probable and is therefore not liable to Plutonium, having paid once).

Plutonium is not without someone to sue, though. Plutonium is entitled to recover from Oort, for conversion. In the likely event that Plutonium cannot locate Oort or Oort's assets, Plutonium will take the loss. If only she had indorsed the check "For Deposit Only."

A is the best answer.

B is incorrect because Doppler paid the PEEI and so is not liable for conversion.

C is doubly incorrect because Probable paid the PEEI, so there is no conversion liability.

D is a little too pessimistic, because Oort is liable.

Note potentially perplexing polysemy: Plutonium "converted" the check to bearer paper, meaning that the innocent parties that dealt with it later were not liable for "conversion."

QUESTION 6. Render unto me.   Delia writes a check to Paul, to pay for some horses. Paul takes the check down to Delia's bank, Damascus Bank, and presents it over the counter for payment. The misguided teller tries to save Delia some money. The teller informs Paul, "We are not going to pay the check, and you can't sue us. We are not liable on the check, because we did not sign the check. We are not liable for conversion, because we did not take from a non-PEEI. We took from you, the PEEI. Have a nice day." The teller also refuses to return the check to Paul. Can Paul recover from Damascus Bank?

> **A.** No. Paul is limited to his rights against Delia.
> **B.** No. Paul has no damages to recover, because Paul is still entitled to collect from Delia.
> **C.** Yes. Damascus Bank implicitly promised to pay the check by accepting it over the counter.
> **D.** Yes. Damascus Bank is liable for conversion.

ANALYSIS.

Delia → Paul presents → Damascus Bank dishonors but keeps

This question reminds us that anytime someone wrongfully exercises possession over an instrument, they may be liable for conversion.

Damascus Bank did "take" the check from the PEEI. Damascus Bank is still liable, however, because § 3-420 also includes common law conversion. Just like the thieves in the previous questions, Damascus Bank has taken property belonging to another. So, **D** is the best answer.

A is incorrect. Paul also has rights against Delia, but he also has the right to recover from Damascus Bank.

B overstates the rule limiting damages. If **B** were correct, then a payee would normally not be able to recover in conversion with respect to a stolen check.

C overstates the effect of taking possession of the check. "Accepting" a check means that the drawee signs it (i.e., certifies it), promising to pay it. Damascus Bank did not do that.

C.   Who can bring a conversion action?

Buyer → Thief → Depo → Drawee

Sends check to Seller, Thief Intercepts

Buyer sends a check to Seller, but it is intercepted by a thief. Seller cannot bring a conversion action (versus Thief, Depo, or Drawee)—but can still recover from Buyer. Buyer does not have to reimburse Drawee (check who paid the wrong person). Drawee can recover from Depo, who can recover from Thief (in the unlikely event Thief is to be found and has identifiable assets).

Section 3-420(a) limits the standing of certain parties to bring a conversion action:

> An action for conversion of an instrument may not be brought by (i) the issuer or acceptor of the instrument or (ii) a payee or indorsee who did not receive delivery of the instrument either directly or through delivery to an agent or a co-payee.

The theory of conversion is interference with the owner's rights. The issuer of an instrument no longer owns it. A payee that never received the instrument was never the holder (and is entitled to enforce the underlying debt, because the payee did not take the instrument). So, such parties are barred from bringing a conversion action if the instrument is stolen, on the theory that they already have more direct rights (the issuer is not obliged to pay, if a non-PEEI has the check, and the payee still has the right to payment for which the errant check was issued).

The statute does not state who can bring a conversion action. Presumably, the payee of a stolen check can bring an action for conversion. Likewise, the owner of a stolen bearer instrument could bring an action for conversion. Trickier questions arise where someone claiming an interest in the instrument is not the named payee. The Seventh Circuit held that a party claiming an equitable interest in the check was not entitled to bring a conversion action. See *ANICO v. Citibank*, 543 F.3d 907 (7th Cir. 2008). ANICO had hired Underwriters to manage an insurance pool. Checks would come in payable to Underwriters. An Underwriters employee stole the checks and obtained payment for himself. The court held that only the named payee, Underwriters, was entitled to bring a conversion action — not the party entitled to the underlying funds, ANICO. The court reasoned:

> ANICO seems oblivious to the burden that its theory would put on every bank that was presented with a check for negotiation. Instead of being able to look at the payee line and to verify that the person presenting the check was indeed entitled to do so, banks in ANICO's world would need to conduct a full-blown investigation every time to make sure that a party with an equitable interest in the check was not lurking in the background. Such a system would bring commercial transactions to a grinding halt.

That reasoning might go too far. The question in the case was not whether the bank was liable. It was liable to Underwriters but had settled. The question was, who was entitled to enforce that liability? It remains for other courts to fill in the statutory blank, when someone who is not the named payee is entitled to sue for conversion. Another close case would be a transferee, where there was no indorsement. The transferee would be the PEEI but would not be named on the check.

QUESTION 7. Impossible plaintiff. Entropy Corp. mails a paycheck to Parallax. Lefe steals it before it reaches Parallax's mailbox. Lefe deposits it with Diffraction Bank, who obtains payment from Poly Bank, the drawee. Who is liable for conversion to Parallax, the payee?

A. Lefe.
B. Lefe and Diffraction Bank.
C. Poly Bank.
D. All of the above.
E. None of the above.

ANALYSIS.

Entropy Corp. → Lefe (bypassing Parallax) → Diffraction Bank → Poly Bank

Parallax may well feel that the check belongs to her, and that anyone treating it otherwise is liable to her for conversion: Lefe as the thief, Diffraction Bank for taking it from Lefe, and Poly Bank for paying the wrong person. However, UCC § 3-420 states that a payee that never received the check may not bring a conversion action. So, the best answer is **E**, none of the above.

This does not leave Parallax out in the cold. Entropy Corp. mailed her paycheck, but it never reached Parallax. The underlying debt was therefore never suspended, let alone discharged. Parallax is still owed her pay. The policy of the UCC in these situations is to take the simplest approach. The payee cannot sue, but rather, is left in an unchanged position.

UCC § 3-420 also states that the issuer cannot bring a conversion action. So, Entropy Corp. could not have recovered in conversion from Lefe, Diffraction Bank, or Poly Bank, even though they were handling, without authority, a check written by Entropy Corp. That should be okay, however, because Entropy Corp. is not liable to reimburse Poly Bank (who paid a non-PEEI).

QUESTION 8. I am not the plaintiff you are looking for. Paul owes Orbison a bundle. Paul promises to pay as Paul's big royalty check from Music Co. arrives. The check arrives, but is stolen and cashed by Martha. Can Orbison recover from Martha for conversion?

A. No. Martha did not convert Orbison's property or pass on a check payable to Orbison.

B. Yes. Martha interfered with Orbison's right to payment from Paul.

C. No. Martha had no debt to Orbison.

D. Yes. Orbison was the person with the ultimate right to the money that was taken.

ANALYSIS.

Music Co. → Paul → Martha steals

Orbison did not have a property right in the check, nor was it payable to Orbison. Martha is indeed liable for conversion, but not to Orbison. Rather, she is liable in conversion to Paul. The best answer is **A**.

D.   Safe harbor

UCC § 320 provides protection against conversion liability for intermediary banks.

(c) A representative, other than a depositary bank, who has in good faith dealt with an instrument or its proceeds on behalf of one who was not the person entitled to enforce the instrument is not liable in conversion to that person beyond the amount of any proceeds that it has not paid out.

Suppose that Lefe deposits a stolen check at Depo, who sends it on for collection through Inter Bank, who sends it on to the Drawee, who pays the check. Depo and Drawee would be liable for conversion, but not Inter Bank (unless it actually still had the money to hand over). The same would apply if an innocent agent dealt with an instrument.

E.   The closer

QUESTION 9. **If a check falls in the woods . . .**   Could the holder of an instrument be liable for conversion?

A. No, because the instrument must be payable to the holder, in order for that person to be the holder.
B. Yes, if the holder had forged an indorsement.
C. No, because the holder must have acted in good faith to qualify as the holder.
D. Yes, if the holder had stolen a bearer instrument.

ANALYSIS.   Yes, this is similar to Question 5—the situation involving the thief Oort and Plutonium's check. This question emphasizes that "holder" has a limited meaning: a person in possession of an instrument payable to them. A holder need not own the instrument; take it in good faith, for value, or without notice of problems; receive the instrument through a transfer; or even get it rightfully. Holder just means holder.

So could a holder be liable for conversion? Conversion liability arises in three ways: common law conversion, usually meaning theft; taking the instrument from a non-PEEI; and paying a non-PEEI. Taking the last two together: someone who paid a non-PEEI or took from a non-PEEI would hardly be a likely holder. If the last person with the instrument was not a holder, how could they make the present possessor a holder? It might be possible, but let us consider the first category, the thief. If a thief stole bearer paper, as we have seen several times by now, the thief would be a holder—and liable for conversion, as a thief.

A is incorrect, because we have seen it is possible.

B states the wrong basis for conversion. Forgery alone will not create conversion liability.

C is incorrect because "no" is wrong, and also because good faith is not necessary for holder status (as opposed to holder in due course status).

D is the best answer.

McJohn's picks

1.	Converters?	**D**
2.	No double dipping	**D**
3.	Miraculous conversion	**C**
4.	Chain of events	**A**
5.	Hazardous paper	**A**
6.	Render unto me	**D**
7.	Impossible plaintiff	**E**
8.	I am not the plaintiff you are looking for	**A**
9.	If a check falls in the woods . . .	**D**

13

Guarantors, a.k.a. Accommodation Parties

~

Could you co-sign this little loan?
The bank will just leave you alone.
You won't be asked to pay it off.
My business could not hit a trough.

~

CHAPTER OVERVIEW
A. Introduction
B. When a signer is an "accommodation party"
C. The right to reimbursement
D. Defenses and discharge of accommodation party
E. Waivers
F. Scope of guaranty
G. The closer
✦ McJohn's picks

A. Introduction

This chapter discusses the rights and obligations of a guarantor, called an "accommodation party." If someone signs an instrument to incur liability on the instrument without being a direct beneficiary of the value given for the instrument (or, in simpler terms, co-signs the loan), they are an accommodation party. They are liable on the instrument but have some special rights. If they are required to pay, they are entitled to reimbursement from the principal obligor (the "accommodated party"). In addition, if the creditor does something to increase the risk on the guaranty (e.g., loses the collateral, lets the principal obligor off the hook), the accommodation party may have a defense to payment (one of the "surety defenses"). In many transactions, however, the accommodation party waives their defenses as part of the overall deal.

Lenders sell money, taking promises as payment. Borrowers buy money, paying with promises to repay. The more valuable Borrower's promise to pay, the better the deal that Borrower can negotiate with Lender. Suppose Lender is considering lending $100,000 each to Solid Borrower (perfect credit record, solid financial condition, collateral to offer) and Risky Borrower (spotty record, shaky finances, no collateral). Risky Borrower's promise to repay the $100,000 loan is less valuable (more risky), so Lender will charge Risky Borrower more (more fees, a higher interest rate, more restrictive terms). Maybe Lender will lend to Solid Borrower at 6 percent interest, and to Risky Borrower at 12 percent interest — or not lend at all.

Risky Borrower can increase the value of its promise to repay (make a more credible commitment) by decreasing the chance that the loan will not be repaid: Risky can find collateral to put up or get a third party to guaranty payment. If Moneybags will guaranty repayment of the loan, perhaps Lender will lend to Risky at 6 percent.

A guaranty helps the Lender in two ways.[1] First, it gives Lender another, deeper pocket from which to seek payment. Second, it aligns the accommodation party's interests with Lender's. Suppose that Moneybags is the president and sole shareholder of Risky (a common setting for guaranty loans). Sometime after the loan is made, Risky starts doing very badly, perhaps heading for bankruptcy. As a shareholder, Moneybags might simply walk away, figuring the shares were likely worth nothing, and that there were more valuable uses for her time, expertise, and energy. If Moneybags is a guarantor, however, she has reason to try to stick with Risky and put resources into helping Risky survive and pay its debt. The more of its debt Risky can pay off, the less exposure Moneybags has on the guaranty. In addition, Moneybags may influence Risky in choosing which creditors to pay. If Risky has limited assets and cannot pay all creditors, Moneybags may have Risky pay off Lender ahead of other creditors.

Moneybags can guaranty the debt by signing a separate guaranty agreement with Lender. Parties often do this because it allows them to have various clauses setting out their respective rights and liabilities. A simpler method is for Moneybags simply to sign the promissory note (as a co-maker or indorser). If Moneybags signs the note itself, then that makes her liable on the note, as what Uniform Commercial Code (UCC) Article 3 calls an "accommodation party." UCC Article 3 gives Moneybags two sets of rights:

---

1. See the Guarantor chapter in Mann, *Payment Systems* (4th edition, Aspen Publishers, 2008).

(1) Right to reimbursement: If Moneybags has to pay Lender, Moneybags is entitled to reimbursement from the primary obligor, Risky.

(2) Defenses and discharge: If Risky had a defense to payment, Moneybags may be able to raise that defense Lender. In addition, if Lender unilaterally increases the risk on Moneybags' guaranty (e.g., gives Risky more time to pay, releases Risky, loses the collateral that Risky put up), that *may* discharge Moneybags.

B. When a signer is an "accommodation party"

Section 3-419(a) defines when a party qualifies as an accommodation party, meaning they will have rights to potential discharge if the Lender increases their risk, and rights to reimbursement if they have to pay:

> (a) If an instrument is issued for value given for the benefit of a party to the instrument ("accommodated party") and another party to the instrument ("accommodation party") signs the instrument for the purpose of incurring liability on the instrument without being a direct beneficiary of the value given for the instrument, the instrument is signed by the accommodation party "for accommodation."

If Moneybags co-signs a note with Risky to get a loan from Bank to Risky, Moneybags is an accommodation party. The note was issued for value given for the benefit of Risky (the "accommodated party"). Moneybags signed it for the purpose of incurring liability. Moneybags was not a direct beneficiary of the value. Note that Moneybags may have received an indirect benefit (as part owner of the party that got the money) but still is an accommodation party.

An accommodation party may sign in any capacity (maker, drawer, acceptor, indorser) and is liable in that capacity. UCC § 3-419(b). The accommodation party is liable even if it does not get consideration. Id.

Section 3-419 sets out the rule for determining when someone is treated as an accommodation party.

> (c) A person signing an instrument is presumed to be an accommodation party and there is notice that the instrument is signed for accommodation if the signature is an anomalous indorsement or is accompanied by words indicating that the signer is acting as surety or guarantor with respect to the obligation of another party to the instrument.

In a well-drafted transaction, the documents will make clear if someone signs as an accommodation party, such as by putting "Guarantor" by Moneybags' signature. UCC § 3-419(c). If the documents are unclear, then it becomes a question of fact: Did this party sign as a guarantor, or for some other reason? Courts may look to various factors, such as who received the money, or the negotiations among the parties. If the signature was an anomalous indorsement (i.e., an indorsement that was not necessary to nego-tiate the instrument), there is a presumption of accommodation status. UCC § 3-419(c). There was no other apparent reason to sign, so the indorser must have signed as a guarantor.

An accommodation party, like Moneybags, can make a more limited guaranty, by explicitly signing "Collection Guaranteed," or other words show-ing that it is not guarantying payment of the note, but rather is guarantying collection of any judgment against the primary obligor, Risky.

> (d) If the signature of a party to an instrument is accompanied by words indicating unambiguously that the party is guaranteeing collection rather than payment of the obligation of another party to the instrument, the signer is obliged to pay the amount due on the instrument to a person entitled to enforce the instrument only if (i) execution of judgment against the other party has been returned unsatisfied, (ii) the other party is insolvent or in an insolvency proceeding, (iii) the other party cannot be served with process, or (iv) it is otherwise apparent that payment cannot be obtained from the other party.

QUESTION 1. Spot the accommodation party.   Python Bank makes a loan to Bright Side. Bright Side signs as maker to the promissory note payable to Python Bank. Bright Side's president, Comma, indorses the note. Bright Side delivers the note to Python Bank, who indorses it and sells it to Holding Investments. Who is an accommodation party?

A. Everyone who signed it, because they all promised to pay: Bright Side, Comma, and Python Bank.
B. Bright Side and Comma, because an indorser indorses (i.e., guaranties payment).
C. Comma, who made an anomalous indorsement.
D. No one.

ANALYSIS.
Bright Side → Comma indorses → Python Bank indorses → Holding
                                                              Investments

The only accommodation party is Comma. An accommodation party "signs the instrument for the purpose of incurring liability on the instrument without being a direct beneficiary of the value given for the instrument." UCC § 3-419(c). Bright Side signed it but received the direct benefit of the value for issuance of the instrument. Comma signed as an indorser but did not receive the direct benefit (although Comma likely got an indirect benefit). Comma also signed for the purpose of incurring liability, and not for any other reason. Comma's indorsement was not necessary to issue or negotiate the instrument, and did not restrict payment.

So, Comma signed as a guarantor, meaning Comma is liable but has the rights of an accommodation party. Therefore, **C** is the best answer.

Not everyone who signs is a guarantor, so **A** is incorrect.

With many instruments there is no accommodation party, but there was one here: Comma. So, **D** is incorrect.

B mixes up indorsers and guarantors. Python Bank also indorsed the instrument, guarantying payment, but Python did not simply sign for the purpose of incurring liability. Python Bank's signature was necessary to make the note payable to Holding Investments. More importantly, Python Bank did receive direct benefit of the value for the instrument. Python Bank did not get the initial value (rather, it advanced a loan to Bright Side). Python Bank did, however, receive the value from Holding Investments. Python Bank is not a third-party guarantor; it is a primary obligor.

C.   The right to reimbursement

If Moneybags pays, Moneybags is entitled to collect from Risky.

> **§ 3-419(f).** An accommodation party who pays the instrument is entitled to reimbursement from the accommodated party and is entitled to enforce the instrument against the accommodated party.

The right to reimbursement may not be worth much. The reason Moneybags had to pay may be that Risky could not come up with the money.

The reverse is not true. If the accommodated party, Risky, pays first, it is not entitled to reimbursement from the accommodation party, Moneybags.

QUESTION 2. All for one, one for all.   Hansel gets a $20,000 loan from Spiderwick Bank, only by getting Gretel to co-sign as maker, next to the word "Guarantor." Sure enough, Hansel declines to pay when the note comes due. Gretel pays $20,000 plus interest, then seeks reimbursement from Hansel. He offers $10,000, arguing that as co-makers they are jointly and severally liable, with a right of contribution (meaning Hansel must contribute his share, $10,000). Is Hansel liable to Gretel?

A. No. He has no liability, because Gretel did not give him any consideration. Rather, she acted as a guarantor for Spiderwick Bank's direct benefit.

B. Yes. Hansel is liable for his share, $10,000.

C. Yes. Hansel is liable for the entire amount, $20,000.

D. No. Hansel is not liable, because Gretel was not liable. She did not get the loan, so she was not obliged to repay it.

ANALYSIS.   Parties that sign in the same capacity are jointly and severally liable, with a right of contribution. That does not apply to accommodation parties, however, who are subject to the more specific rule of § 3-419. Under that rule, an accommodation party that pays is entitled to full reimbursement from the accommodated party. So, **C** is the best answer.

Section 3-419 makes Hansel liable, irrespective of whether he received consideration from Gretel, so **A** is incorrect.

Contrary to **B**, Hansel's liability is not limited to a share. He is liable for the full amount.

D is also contrary to § 3-419. An accommodation party is liable, even if it does not receive consideration.

D.   Defenses and discharge of accommodation party

If Risky had a defense against Lender, Moneybags may raise that against Lender.

> **§ 3-305(d).** In an action to enforce the obligation of an accommodation party to pay an instrument, the accommodation party may assert against the person entitled to enforce the instrument any defense or claim in recoupment under subsection (a) that the accommodated party could assert against the person entitled to enforce the instrument, except the defenses of discharge in insolvency proceedings, infancy, and lack of legal capacity.

If Lender never delivered the funds (meaning Risky had a defense of lack of performance), Moneybags may raise that defense. The same would hold if the note was for a shipment of goods on credit, and the goods never arrived or were defective. The guarantor could raise the buyer's defenses, like breach of contract, against the holder of the note. Moneybags, however, cannot raise defenses based on Risky's discharge in insolvency proceedings, infancy, or lack of legal capacity. Those are defenses that are personal to Risky and cannot be raised for the benefit of Lender. In other words, if Moneybags guaranteed the debt of a minor, a bankrupt, or a nonexistent corporation, Moneybags will have to pay. Note also that Moneybags can raise only the defenses that Risky could have raised. If the plaintiff is a holder in due course, that will cut away defenses.

If Bank releases Risky without retaining rights against Moneybags, Moneybags is released. UCC § 3-605(a). In addition, under § 3-605(b), Moneybags *may* be discharged if Lender does something that increases the risk to Moneybags. Here are the provisions in gory detail (a summary follows):

> (b) If a person entitled to enforce an instrument grants a principal obligor an extension of the time at which one or more payments are due on the instrument and another party to the instrument is a secondary obligor with respect to the obligation of that principal obligor, the following rules apply:
>   (1) Any obligations of the principal obligor to the secondary obligor with respect to any previous payment by the secondary obligor are not

affected. Unless the terms of the extension preserve the secondary obligor's recourse, the extension correspondingly extends the time for performance of any other duties owed to the secondary obligor by the principal obligor under this article.

(2) The secondary obligor is discharged to the extent that the extension would otherwise cause the secondary obligor a loss.

(3) To the extent that the secondary obligor is not discharged under paragraph (2), the secondary obligor may perform its obligations to a person entitled to enforce the instrument as if the time for payment had not been extended or, unless the terms of the extension provide that the person entitled to enforce the instrument retains the right to enforce the instrument against the secondary obligor as if the time for payment had not been extended, treat the time for performance of its obligations as having been extended correspondingly.

(c) If a person entitled to enforce an instrument agrees, with or without consideration, to a modification of the obligation of a principal obligor other than a complete or partial release or an extension of the due date and another party to the instrument is a secondary obligor with respect to the obligation of that principal obligor, the following rules apply:

(1) Any obligations of the principal obligor to the secondary obligor with respect to any previous payment by the secondary obligor are not affected. The modification correspondingly modifies any other duties owed to the secondary obligor by the principal obligor under this article.

(2) The secondary obligor is discharged from any unperformed portion of its obligation to the extent that the modification would otherwise cause the secondary obligor a loss.

(3) To the extent that the secondary obligor is not discharged under paragraph (2), the secondary obligor may satisfy its obligation on the instrument as if the modification had not occurred, or treat its obligation on the instrument as having been modified correspondingly.

(d) If the obligation of a principal obligor is secured by an interest in collateral, another party to the instrument is a secondary obligor with respect to that obligation, and a person entitled to enforce the instrument impairs the value of the interest in collateral, the obligation of the secondary obligor is discharged to the extent of the impairment. The value of an interest in collateral is impaired to the extent the value of the interest is reduced to an amount less than the amount of the recourse of the secondary obligor, or the reduction in value of the interest causes an increase in the amount by which the amount of the recourse exceeds the value of the interest. For purposes of this subsection, impairing the value of an interest in collateral includes failure to obtain or maintain perfection or recordation of the interest in collateral, release of collateral without substitution of collateral of equal value or equivalent reduction of the underlying obligation, failure to perform a duty to preserve the value of collateral owed, under Article 9 or other law, to a debtor or other person secondarily liable, and failure to comply with applicable law in disposing of or otherwise enforcing the interest in collateral.

In plain English: If Lender releases Risky from liability, that releases Moneybags, unless the release specifically reserves rights against Moneybags; if Moneybags had indorsed a check, she is discharged even despite contrary terms in the release. UCC § 3-605(a).

If Lender gives Risky extra time to pay, that discharges Moneybags if she can show that it will cause her a loss. If not discharged, Moneybags gets the extra time (unless Lender specifically excludes Moneybags from the extension). UCC § 3-605(b)(2). The tricky part for Moneybags may be showing that the extension caused a loss to Moneybags. If Risky could not have paid on time, or if the extension improved Risky's ability to pay, then there was no loss to Moneybags. If Moneybags can show, however, that Risky could have paid on time, then was circling into a financial drain by the time the extended due date arrived, then Moneybags would be discharged.

Similarly, if Lender modifies the terms of the debt by agreement with Risky, that discharges Moneybags if it causes her a loss. UCC § 3-605(c)(2). If not discharged, Moneybags may choose to go by the terms of the modification.

Finally, if Lender impairs the value of any collateral (e.g., Lender loses the gold coins Risky put up as collateral), that discharges Moneybags to the extent of the lost value. UCC § 3-605(d).

Note that Moneybags has these protections only if the person enforcing the instrument has notice that Moneybags was acting as a guarantor:

> (e) A secondary obligor is not discharged under subsection (a)(3), (b), (c), or (d) unless the person entitled to enforce the instrument knows that the person is a secondary obligor or has notice under Section 3-419(c) that the instrument was signed for accommodation.

So, a guarantor should be sure to sign with words like "Guarantor" by her name if she wishes to have those protections available. (As discussed below, guarantors often waive those rights—not because they want to, but in order to get the loan made.)

QUESTION 3. Standby.   Lili purchases an airplane from Wright on credit. To get the deal, Geiger co-signs the promissory note with Lili, listed as "Guarantor." Wright delivers a plane that will fly only for short distances, and only on windy days. Lili refuses to pay, so Wright seeks the money from Geiger. Geiger likewise refuses to pay, because of the defective plane. Wright responds: "You are a Guarantor, someone who guarantees the debt will be paid. You got what you were promised. You signed so I would agree to the transaction. If Lili has complaints about the plane, that's between her and me." Can Geiger raise Lili's defense against enforcement?

A. No. A party can only raise their own defenses.

B. No. A guaranty is an unconditional promise to pay. That's what "guaranty" means.

C. Yes. An accommodation party may raise the defenses of the accommodated party.

D. Yes. Lili and Geiger are legally identical.

ANALYSIS. Normally, a party can only raise their own defenses. If that were always true, **A** would be correct. Section 3-419 allows an accommodation party to raise defenses of the accommodated party, however, so **C** is the best answer.

B overstates the obligation of an accommodation party (or guarantor). The accommodation party promises to pay but may raise defense to enforcement of the promise—its own defenses or those of the accommodated party.

D overstates things in a different way. The accommodation party may use some of the accommodated party's rights, but the two have other rights and liabilities that are distinct.

QUESTION 4. Parental consent. Pip, an entrepreneurial preteen, gets a loan from Bleak House for her web-development business. Gargery, Pip's father, co-signs as guarantor. Pip discovers she is not obliged to pay, because in that jurisdiction, Pip was too young to make an enforceable promise to pay. Sued by Bleak House, Gargery seeks to raise Pip's defense of infancy. Gargery argues that an unenforceable obligation cannot be enforced against the obligor or the guarantor. Bleak House responds, "You are a Guarantor, someone who guarantees the debt will be paid. You got what you were promised. You signed so I would agree to the transaction. If Pip has complaints about the repayment, that's between her and me. You are far too old to raise the defense of infancy." Can Gargery raise Pip's defense of infancy?

A. Yes. An accommodation party can raise the defenses of the accommodated party.
B. Yes. The debt was void, so the liability of the guarantor is zero.
C. No. An accommodation party cannot raise the defense of infancy.
D. No. Gargery can only raise his own defenses, as if he were an infant.

ANALYSIS. An accommodation party can raise the defenses of the accommodated party, "except the defenses of discharge in insolvency proceedings, infancy, and lack of legal capacity." In effect, a guarantor takes the risk that the accommodated party is not liable because it got a bankruptcy discharge, or was too young or otherwise not legally capable. That's what a guaranty is for—to insure against the primary debtor being unable or not required to pay, which is why a party should always think twice before signing a guaranty (something lawyers need to remind their clients of). So, **C** is the best answer.

A is too broad, because not all defenses of the accommodated party can be raised. **B** likewise overstates the rights of the guarantor. Even a void debt can result in liability for the guarantor. In other words, the guarantor in effect says: "Lend to this person. If they do not pay, I will—even if they were not legally obliged to repay because of infancy or incapacity."

D errs in the other direction. A guarantor can indeed raise defenses of the accommodated party, but not all of them.

> **QUESTION 5. Defenseless.**   Shirty signs a promissory note as guarantor, to enable Obelisk to buy a shipment of inventory. The inventory delivered turns out to be faulty, giving Obelisk a defense to payment of the note. Meanwhile, the note has been negotiated to Clark, a holder in due course. If Clark sues Shirty, can Shirty raise Obelisk's defense of breach of contract?
>
> A. Yes. An accommodation party can raise the defenses of the accommodated party.
> B. No. An accommodation party can only raise its own defenses.
> C. No. Clark could not raise the defense, so Obelisk cannot raise it.
> D. Yes. Clark, as transferee, has no greater right to collect than the breaching seller had.

ANALYSIS.

Obelisk issues note → Seller → HIDC
Shirty signs as guarantor

An accommodation party may raise defenses that the principal obligor could have raised. Here, Clark could not have raised the defense of breach of contract against a holder in due course. That means Shirty cannot raise the defense. **C** is the best answer.

> **QUESTION 6. Shipwreck.**   Rastopolous lends Haddock $100,000, with Tintin indorsing the note as guarantor. When the note comes due, Haddock has no assets to pay. Rastopolous sympathetically gives Haddock another year. After the year, however, Haddock is still broke. When Rastopolous turns to Tintin, Tintin responds that by granting an extension on the debt, Rastopolous released Tintin. Is Tintin liable?
>
> A. Yes. Tintin is not released, because the extension did not cause loss to Tintin.
> B. No. Tintin guarantied to pay the debt when due. Rastopolous cannot change the terms of the guaranty.
> C. Yes. The guaranty is unconditional.
> D. No. Tintin is liable only for Tintin's debts. Rastopolous lent the money to Haddock.

ANALYSIS.

Haddock → Rasatopolous
Tintin signs as guarantor

If the creditor grants an extension of time, the guarantor is released only if that causes a loss. Haddock was broke when the debt was due and the following time. So Tintin could not have recovered from Haddock. The extension did not cause Tintin a loss, so Tintin is not released. **A** is the best answer.

E.   Waivers

Section 3-605 provides guarantors a list of protections. A guarantor may be able to say "Well, I guaranteed that debt, but my guarantee is now unenforceable because you gave them more time to pay, you settled the underlying debt therefore making me the only one who was on the hook, or you lost the collateral." Guarantors routinely sign those rights away, however. In a typical guaranty transaction, the note (or a separate guaranty contract) will provide that the guarantor waives all the protection given to guarantors. Section 3-605 makes those waivers effective:

> (f) A secondary obligor is not discharged under this section if the secondary obligor consents to the event or conduct that is the basis of the discharge, or the instrument or a separate agreement of the party provides for waiver of discharge under this section specifically or by general language indicating that parties waive defenses based on suretyship or impairment of collateral.

Likewise, guarantors may raise defenses of the accommodated party, but guarantors can waive that right as well.

Most guaranty contracts provide that guarantors waive all those defenses and discharges. In effect, the typical guarantor agrees to pay, period. So, guarantying a debt is really a serious undertaking. The guarantor is just as liable (perhaps even more liable) as the party getting the loan.

QUESTION 7. Wave that waiver. Biodiesel gets a loan from HighTech Bank. Blorafill indorses the note as "Guarantor" and signs a separate guaranty contract waiving all suretyship defenses or rights of discharge; consenting to any modifications, forgiveness, or extensions of the debt; and waiving any rights related to the collateral. Blorafill is not worried, because Biodiesel has promised there is no chance that Blorafill will have to pay on the loan. Biodiesel has plenty of money in the bank, has promised to pay on time, and has put up inventory as collateral that is worth more than the debt. Some time after Biodiesel gets the loan, lightning strikes; the silo containing the inventory burns, along with several neighboring silos, owing to Biodiesel's negligent silo maintenance. Now Biodiesel has no assets to pay. HighTech Bank sympathetically forgives the indebtedness, reserving its rights against Blorafill. Blorafill learns that HighTech Bank had agreed to purchase insurance for the inventory but negligently forgot. Blorafill argues that it can not be obliged to pay, for several reasons: unforeseen circumstances (lightning), negligence by Biodiesel, and, most of all, the lender was negligent in administering the collateral and let Biodiesel off the hook. Is Blorafill liable?

A. No. HighTech Bank forgave the debt, so there is no debt to pay.
B. No. HighTech Bank was negligent in administering the collateral and so cannot collect the debt the collateral was intended to cover.
C. Yes. Blorafill would have been off the hook but waived those rights.
D. Yes. Guarantors are always liable.

ANALYSIS. If the lender does something to increase the risk on the guaranty, that may discharge the guarantor. The guarantor may, however, waive the right to discharge—as Blorafill did. Blorafill consented to forgiveness of the debt and waived any rights with respect to the collateral, so those grounds are not available to Blorafill now. In some areas of the law, such waivers are not effective. Consumers are often unable to effectively waive such legal protections. However, for commercial parties, these waivers are effective. **C** is the best answer.

Had Blorafill not made the waivers, **B** would have been correct.

A would have been incorrect one way or the other. HighTech Bank released Biodiesel, but HighTech Bank reserved its rights against Blorafill.

D overstates things. Guarantors are only liable to the extent they take on such liability.

Why does the law enforce such harsh terms (e.g., "I agree to pay even if you lose the valuable collateral, let everybody else off the hook, and made a noncollectible loan to start with")? It does so to allow parties to structure the risks in commercial transactions as they please. Presumably, guarantors know the risks they take on and prefer them to the alternatives (e.g., not getting the loan made, borrowing the money themselves, or getting the loan on different terms). The law is certainly "guarantor beware."

F.   Scope of guaranty

A party can guaranty a debt simply by signing the promissory note. But lenders often have guarantors signs separate guaranty agreements. One reason is that the agreement will have many waivers of rights. In addition, the agreement can be much broader than the liability of the signer of an instrument. The next question is an example of this.

QUESTION 8. Scales up. Angel signs a guaranty agreement in order to help get a $100,000 loan for ArtiLife, a little biotech start-up. The guaranty reads in part: "I agree to repay all debt owed to TechBank by ArtiLife, now owed or incurred in the future." ArtiLife uses the funds to develop an iPhone-cleaning bacteria. Five years later, ArtiLife has several projects in development and has acquired some other companies—all funded by loans from TechBank. ArtiLife's debt to TechBank is now several million dollars. Is Angel on the hook for that debt?

A. Yes. Angel agreed to be liable for all ArtiLife's debt to TechBank.
B. No. Angel is only liable for the $100,000 debt incurred as consideration for the guaranty.
C. No. Angel is only liable for a reasonable amount of debt.
D. Yes, but only if Angel has a proportionate share in the company.

ANALYSIS. This problem emphasizes that a guarantor agrees to what they agree to. If the guaranty is open-ended and unlimited, so can be the liability. This can be a particular problem if the guarantor does not control the principal and so cannot limit the debt that the principal incurs. A party should always think thrice before signing a guaranty and is well advised to have maximum limits explicitly provided for in the agreement. **A** is the best answer.

G.   The closer

> **QUESTION 9. Unwavering.** Suppose that in Question 7, the waiver language read: "I, Blorafill, agree to any extensions, modifications, or forgiveness of the indebtedness." The other facts (negligence, lightning, fire) are the same. Would Blorafill be liable on the guaranty?
>
> A. No. HighTech Bank forgave the debt, so there is no debt to pay.
> B. No. HighTech Bank was negligent in administering the collateral and so cannot collect the debt the collateral was intended to cover.
> C. Yes. Blorafill would have been off the hook but waived those rights.
> D. Yes. Guarantors are always liable.

ANALYSIS. Guarantors may waive defenses and discharge. This time, Blorafill waived only some of them. Blorafill consented to any "extensions, modifications, or forgiveness of the indebtedness." So, **A** again would not be correct. Blorafill had agreed to pay even if HighTech Bank forgave the debt.

This time, Blorafill made no waivers about the collateral. So, Blorafill would have a discharge under § 3-605(d) for "failure to perform a duty to preserve the value of collateral." **B** is the best answer, meaning that **C** and **D** are both incorrect.

The lesson of this question is that where a guaranty contract is signed, it is the first place to look to determine the rights of the parties.

 McJohn's picks

1. Spot the accommodation party	C	
2. All for one, one for all	C	
3. Standby	C	
4. Parental consent	C	
5. Defenseless	C	
6. Shipwreck	A	
7. Wave that waiver	C	
8. Scales up	A	
9. Unwavering	B	

The Properly Payable Menu, Subrogation, and the Bank Statement Rule

A check should be payable properly
Not shoveling the cash out too sloppily.
If altered or stolen or forged or stopped,
The buck on the bank will surely be dropped.

CHAPTER OVERVIEW
A. Introduction
B. Customer must have authorized it
C. Bank must pay the right person (the PEEI)
D. Bank must pay the right amount (not an altered amount)
E. NSF (not sufficient funds): OK to pay, OK to dishonor
F. Stale checks: OK to pay, OK to dishonor
G. Customer may post-date but must give bank notice
H. No effective stop payment orders in effect
I. Bank may pay despite death or incompetence of customer, until notice
J. A *reasonable* clause in the deposit contract may affect bank's right to reimbursement
K. Fees—not regulated by UCC
L. Subrogation: Bank that pays by mistake may seek restitution to avoid unjust enrichment

A.   Introduction

A bank that pays a check has a right to reimbursement from its customer, provided the check was properly payable, meaning that the bank paid a check authorized by its customer, paid the right person the right amount, and there was no sufficient reason not to pay.

If the bank is not entitled to reimbursement, it may be able to recover using subrogation, if the bank's mistake is giving someone a windfall. As other chapters discuss, the bank may also have the right to recover from the presenter and prior transferors for breach of presentment warranty (for forged indorsement or alterations) or for mistake.

Customer (or forger?) → ? → Presenter → Drawee Bank pays
Drawee Bank has right to reimbursement
if check was properly payable

A typical check, properly payable:
Customer signs → Payee indorses, deposits → Depository Bank → Drawee
Bank

A check is an order, from the customer to their bank, to pay a certain amount of money to the holder of the check. From the drawee bank's point of view, checks show up, usually presented by or via depositary banks. If the bank pays a check that is properly payable, the bank has a right to reimbursement from its customer. The bank just sees a piece of paper, apparently signed by the customer, written to the payee, for a certain amount, and indorsed by the payee. The key section is Uniform Commercial Code (UCC) § 4-401.

> **§ 4-401. When Bank May Charge Customer's Account**
>
> (a) A bank may charge against the account of a customer an item that is properly payable from that account even though the charge creates an overdraft. An item is properly payable if it is authorized by the customer and is in accordance with any agreement between the customer and bank.
>
> (b) A customer is not liable for the amount of an overdraft if the customer neither signed the item nor benefited from the proceeds of the item.
>
> (c) [post-dating rule—see below]
>
> (d) A bank that in good faith makes payment to a holder may charge the indicated account of its customer according to:
>
> (1) the original terms of the altered item; or
>
> (2) the terms of the completed item, even though the bank knows the item has been completed unless the bank has notice that the completion was improper.

"Properly payable" has a lot packed into it. It requires the following:

- Customer authorized payment (e.g., signed the check)
- Bank paid the person entitled to enforce the instrument (PEEI)
- No alterations (but bank may pay original amount to holder in good faith)
- No stop payment order in effect (§ 4-403)
- No effective post-dating
- No notice of customer's death or incompetency (§ 4-405)
- Whether a clause in the deposit contract applies, and if so, whether the clause is enforceable (§ 4-103(a))
- Not sufficient funds (NSF): no wrongful dishonor if insufficient funds in account, but bank may pay
- Likewise, may pay stale check in good faith (§ 4-404)

B. Customer must have authorized it

Forger issues → Payee deposits → Depositary Bank presents → Drawee Bank pays

"An item is properly payable if it is authorized by the customer and is in accordance with any agreement between the customer and bank." UCC § 4-401. If a thief gets my checkbook and forges my name, I didn't authorize that item. So, if my bank pays that check, it is not entitled to reimbursement from me. (Note: As discussed elsewhere, if my negligence caused someone to write a check on my account, then that signature counts as my signature. Other forgeries and alterations may also be validated by those validation rules.)

> **QUESTION 1. Ghostwriter.** Cairo cleverly steals several checks from Gutman's checkbook, despite the fact that Gutman is very careful with it. When Gutman sees the checks on his next statement from Falcon Finance, he demands that the money be put back in his account. Is Falcon Finance obliged to do so?
>
> A. Yes. Falcon Finance paid checks not authorized by Gutman.
> B. No. These were authorized checks from Gutman's checkbook and so are properly payable.
> C. Yes. The person that is liable to Gutman is the bad actor, Cairo.
> D. No. The checks were written to Cairo and so are properly payable.

ANALYSIS.
A check is not properly payable if not authorized by the customer. Check forms in a checkbook are not authorizations, contrary to **B**. The authorization comes from the customer signing the check (or authorizing someone else to do so). So **A** is the best answer.

Cairo is liable. But, as in many payment systems cases, more than one person is liable. The question here is, as between the two innocent parties, who takes the loss? **C** is inaccurate.

The fact that the checks are payable to Cairo is not enough if they were not authorized by Gutman. **D** is incorrect.

The result would be different if Gutman had been negligent with the checkbook (which would validate the forged signature) or Gutman had signed the blank checks sitting in his checkbook (bad idea!).

QUESTION 2. Infirmity.   Diggs excavates a foundation for long-time client Builder, who sends a check for the fee. Diggs e-mails Builder, because Builder forgot to sign the check. Builder e-mails back, "Go ahead and sign my name to it. Thanks again." Not long after the check is paid, the hole caves in, because Diggs failed to observe basic excavation safety principles. Builder, looking to get the money back, argues that because Builder did not sign the check, it was not properly payable. Is the payor bank entitled to reimbursement?

A. No. Builder did not sign the check.
B. No. Builder was not obliged to pay, due to Diggs' breach.
C. Yes. Builder authorized payment of the check.
D. Yes. The bank cannot be expected to notice if the drawer's signature was done by someone other than the customer.
E. No. Builder has a defense to payment: breach of contract.

ANALYSIS.
Builder → Diggs signs, with Builder's authorization → Depo → Payor

To be properly payable, the check must be authorized by the customer. This does not require the customer to physically sign the check—an authorized signature is sufficient. So, **C** is the best answer, and **A** is incorrect.

Note that the check is properly payable even if the payee is not entitled to the money from the issuer. The fact that Diggs was not entitled to money from Builder does not mean the check was not properly payable. The bank need not inquire into the underlying transaction before paying the check. So, **B** is incorrect. Rather, it is up to Builder to stop payment.

D overstates things. If Builder's signature were forged, the check would not be properly payable. The drawee bank will take the loss for unauthorized signatures—even though it is true that the bank cannot determine that by looking at the signature. So, the bank must guard against this risk in other ways.

E is a red herring. Builder does have a defense that could be raised against someone enforcing the instrument; however, the bank's right to reimbursement is not enforcing the check. A bank that pays a check as authorized by its customer is entitled to reimbursement, even if the customer has a reason not to pay. The customer, as discussed below, may attempt to notify the bank and issue a stop payment order, which would make the check not properly payable.

The same rationale would hold in telemarketer situations. Acedia sells Damek a set of encyclopedias over the phone. Damek, on Acedia's request, gets a check and reads to her the numbers from the bottom of the check (which identify the bank and Damek's account). Acedia prints out a check, fills it out for the agreed amount, and gets payment from Damek's bank. Such payment would be authorized, and Damek would be obliged to reimburse his bank, even if he is now suffering from a sore back and borrower's remorse.

C.   Bank must pay the right person (the PEEI)

Customer → Payee → Thief steals, forges indorsement→ Depositary Bank → Drawee Bank

Customer writes a check payable to a car dealer. Thief steals it, forges the car dealer's indorsement, and deposits it. The check is presented and drawee pays it. If the bank pays someone other than the PEEI, the bank has paid the wrong person and is not entitled to reimbursement.

QUESTION 3. No questions asked.   Dronkers sends a $1,000 check payable to Pettito to pay for some speech-recognition software. The check is stolen by Dieb. The drawee, Labov Bank, pays Dieb and takes the money out of Dronkers' account. When Dronkers complains, Labov responds: "You wrote a $1,000 check. We paid $1,000. Checks are negotiable. Whom we pay does not affect you." May Labov keep the money?

A. No. It did not pay the PEEI.
B. Yes. It paid the amount as directed by its customer.
C. No. Payment to a thief can never be proper.
D. Yes. Labov Bank cannot be expected to know the signature of Pettito, who is not Labov Bank's customer.

ANALYSIS.

Dronkers → Pettito → Dieb steals, forges indorsement → Labov Bank pays

Labov paid the wrong person. Unless the bank pays the PEEI, the bank is not entitled to reimbursement. So, **A** is the best answer.

B overstates the bank's right to reimbursement. The bank must do more than pay the right amount. It must pay as authorized by the customer: the right amount to the right person. Although this case did not involve bearer paper, sometimes payment to a thief would be authorized — if the check were bearer paper. So **C** is incorrect. If Dronkers had written the check to Cash, or

Pettito had indorsed the check in blank, then payment to the bearer would be proper. Here, the check was payable to Pettito, so the check was not properly payable. It does not matter whether the payor bank has reason to know whether it is paying the wrong person. So **D** is incorrect.

Note that this does not give a windfall to Dronkers. Pettito is still entitled to payment from Dronkers.

QUESTION 4. Not so technical. Amy writes a check payable to Annie to pay for a shipment of macaroni and cheese. Annie gives the check to Sam Supplier, to pay off an outstanding debt. Annie does not indorse the check. Sam presents the check to Amy's Bank, Bread and Banking, who pays Sam. Not long after, Amy, unhappy with the macaroni and cheese, decides she can avoid reimbursing Bread and Banking. She wrote the check to Annie, who never indorsed it. Bread and Banking paid Sam, not Annie (the person it was payable to), so Bread and Banking is not entitled to reimbursement. Is Bread and Banking entitled to reimbursement?

A. No. Bread and Banking paid the wrong person.
B. Yes. As long as Amy signed the check, it does not matter who the bank pays (it's a negotiable instrument).
C. No. The check could be payable only to Annie.
D. Yes. Bread and Banking paid the right person.

ANALYSIS.
Amy → Annie transfers without indorsing → Sam presents → Bread and Banking pays

The bank is not entitled to reimbursement unless it pays the PEEI. One can qualify as PEEI as holder (Sam was not, because the check was not made payable to him), as ex-holder of a lost or stolen instrument (not applicable here), or transferee from a PEEI. Sam qualifies as the last type of PEEI. Annie, a holder, transferred him the check and so transferred her rights to him, indorsement or not. Sam became a PEEI, so Bread and Banking paid the right person, and **A** is incorrect. **D** is the best answer.

B is wrong, because a bank that pays a stolen check (unless the check was payable to bearer) is not entitled to reimbursement.

C is too narrow. A check may be transferred.

One frequently asked checking law question: A more common version of the above situation is where payee deposits the check in her bank without indorsing it. Remember that UCC Article 4 makes the depositary bank a holder. So, the check is properly payable to the depositary bank, even if not indorsed by its customer (much to the disappointment of many drawers of checks, who have tried to seize on the missing indorsement to argue the check was improperly paid).

D. Bank must pay the right amount (not an altered amount)

Customer → Payee alters amount of check → Depositary Bank → Drawee Bank

> **§ 4-401(d).** A bank that in good faith makes payment to a holder may charge the indicated account of its customer according to:
> (1) the original terms of the altered item; or
> (2) the terms of the completed item, even though the bank knows the item has been completed unless the bank has notice that the completion was improper.

If I write a $100 check, I authorized payment only of $100. If the check is altered to $1,000 and paid, the drawee is entitled to take only $100.

QUESTION 5. Alteration situation. Zurif gets a $300 check from Dodd. Zurif artfully adds a zero, making it a $3,000 check. Dodd's bank pays the depositary bank $3,000. Must Dodd reimburse the bank?

A. Yes, for $3,000.
B. Yes, for $300.
C. No. The check was not properly payable.
D. No. The alteration discharged Dodd.

ANALYSIS.
Dodd → Zurif alters → Depo → Payor

A bank that pays an altered check to a holder is entitled to reimbursement for the original amount of the check. So **B** is the best answer. This does not harm Dodd. Dodd wrote a $300 check to Zurif and is therefore liable to reimburse the $300 paid to Zurif's bank. So, an altered check might be called "partially properly payable."

QUESTION 6. Cognitive dissonance. Denes sends a $500 check to Pinker. Fief steals the check, alters it to $5,000, forges Pinker's indorsement, and gets payment from Denes' bank, Safire Savings. Must Denes reimburse Safire Savings?

A. Yes, for $5000.
B. Yes, for $500.
C. No. The check was not properly payable at all.
D. No. A stolen check can never be properly payable.

ANALYSIS.

Denes → Pinker → Fiet steals, alters → Safire Savings pays

Here there was an alteration—but also a forged indorsement. The check was not properly payable at all. A bank that pays an altered check *to a holder* is entitled to reimbursement for the original amount of the check. Safire Savings did not pay the holder. Unlike the preceding question, here the original payee has not transferred the check and so is entitled to payment. If Denes had to reimburse Safire Savings, and still had to write another check to Pinker, that would impose double payment on Denes, where Safire Savings is the party that paid a stolen and altered check. Safire Savings paid the wrong person and so is entitled to no reimbursement. Therefore, **A** and **B** are incorrect. **C** is the best answer.

D overstates things. A stolen check can be properly payable, if it was bearer paper.

———————

A different kind of alteration, important for anybody who deals with instruments to know about, is *completion of an incomplete instrument (such as a blank check)*: Someone signs it, making it an instrument, but they leave a material term to be completed later with words or numbers, like the name of the payee or the amount to be paid. Unauthorized completion is an alteration. If the bank pays it, however, it's properly payable *as completed.* So, if I sign a check and I leave the amount blank, no matter what amount is filled in, if my bank pays it in good faith, the bank is entitled to reimbursement from me for that full amount. Signing a blank check is not a good idea!

QUESTION 7. Exposure. Kimba owes Flammel several hundred dollars for some chemicals. She writes a check payable to Flammel, dates it, and signs it, authorizing him to fill in the correct amount when he reckons it. Flammel promises that the amount will be between $400 and $500. Flammel fills in $10,000. He deposits the check and Kimba's bank pays it. Must Kimba reimburse her bank?

A. Yes. The check was properly payable for $10,000.
B. No. The check was only properly payable up to $500.
C. No. The check was not properly payable at all.
D. No. Kimba has a defense of fraud, and the bank is not a holder in due course.

ANALYSIS. If a party signs an incomplete check, the check is properly payable *as completed.* Therefore, **A** is the best answer.

For this reason, signing a blank check is never a good idea. There are many situations where it might seem convenient, in order to get the check to a trusted party when the amount is not exactly known, or to gain credibility, or to get a closing completed. . . . But there is always a better alternative. Signing a blank check is the same as agreeing to pay whatever amount is filled in (not even limited by the amount of money in the account, because the bank can pay a check that creates an overdraft).

E. NSF (not sufficient funds): OK to pay, OK to dishonor

Customer → Payee → Depositary Bank → Drawee Bank sees not enough funds in account

> **§ 4-401(a).** A bank may charge against the account of a customer an item that is properly payable from that account even though the charge creates an overdraft.

I write a check for $10,000. There is only $1 in my account. My bank pays it. Am I obliged to reimburse the bank? Yes. A bank may pay a check that creates an overdraft, as long as the bank does so in good faith. The theory is that I am ordering my bank, with whom I have a pre-existing relationship, to pay that check when I write it. I am taking on the risk that I'll be taking on the obligation to pay an overdraft if there are not sufficient funds in my account.

The bank is entitled to reimbursement only if it pays the check in good faith. Good faith is a general requirement that we see throughout the UCC. The bank is obliged to treat items in good faith. This means it must treat items honestly and according to reasonable standards of commercial fair dealing. UCC § 3-102.

What if several checks are presented the same day and there is not enough to cover them all? Suppose seven checks written on Davis' account are presented the same day, in the amounts of $500, $200, $100, $50, $40, $30, and $10. The balance is $450. Can the bank choose to pay the $500 check first and pay the other six checks next as overdrafts, charging a hefty fee for each one (instead of paying the others first and charging one overdraft fee for the $500 check)? The UCC allows the bank to pay items "in any order." UCC § 4-303(b). So this practice, "high-low posting," is permitted.

QUESTION 8. Uncertainty. Schroedinger writes a check for $10,000 as a donation to the National Science Foundation. Schreodinger has only $50 in his checking account, but he expects a big payment to come in for a rare cat he sold. He asks the National Science Foundation to hold on to the check until he has the money. As it turns out, the cat sale does not go through. Meanwhile, the check is presented and paid, leaving Schroedinger with a $9,950 overdraft. He is shocked that his bank paid such a big check with so little in his account. Is he liable?

A. Yes. The bank is entitled to reimbursement.
B. No. The bank cannot pay money that does not exist in an account.
C. No. The bank must get prior authorization to create an overdraft.
D. No. He has a defense to payment—lack of consideration (he did not get anything for the check, which was a donation).

ANALYSIS.
Schroedinger → National Science Foundation → Drawee pays, creating overdraft

The bank that pays a check in good faith that creates an overdraft is entitled to reimbursement. Nothing here raises any questions about good faith. **A** is the best answer.

There need not be money in the account, nor need the bank get prior authorization, so **B** and **C** are inaccurate.

D's error reminds us of an important point: Whether there is a defense to payment is irrelevant to the drawee bank's right to reimbursement, which depends only on whether the check is properly payable. Schroedinger authorized the check and had not stopped payment. The check was properly payable.

A similar rule governs stale checks.

F.   Stale checks: OK to pay, OK to dishonor

§ 4-404. Bank Not Obliged to Pay Check More than Six Months Old
A bank is under no obligation to a customer having a checking account to pay a check, other than a certified check, which is presented more than six months after its date, but it may charge its customer's account for a payment made thereafter in good faith.

I write a check and it just sits there. I send it to the payee. The payee loses it. We both forget about it. The payee finds the check a year later and deposits it. If the bank pays it in good faith, it is entitled to reimbursement. If it chooses to dishonor it, it is not wrong to dishonor. There are two rationales: 1) If I did not stop payment, then no reason for my bank not to pay. And 2) the UCC does not generally expect banks to look at the date on checks. (See the section on post-dating, below).

QUESTION 9. **You snooze, you don't lose.**   Rip gets a $4,000 check from Little Red. Rip puts it in a desk drawer and forgets it. Little Red spends the money in her account on presents for Grandma. Five years later, Rip runs across the check and deposits it. Little Red's bank, Sleepy Savings, pays the check. Must Little Red pay Sleepy Savings?

> **A.** Yes. A check is an unconditional order to pay, always payable.
> **B.** Yes. Sleepy Savings simply followed Red's order.
> **C.** No. A bank could not pay a five-year-old check in good faith.
> **D.** It would depend on whether Little Red still owed the money to Rip.

ANALYSIS.

Little Red → Rip snoozes → Depo → Sleepy Savings pays

A bank may charge its customer's account if it pays an old check in good faith. Sleepy Savings has two good arguments for good faith. First, Little Red ordered payment and never counter-ordered with a stop payment, so it was following her directions, with no reason not to pay. Second, banks normally do not look at the date on a check, so it may not have even known the check was old. So, **B** is the best answer. **A** overstates things again. **C** overstates things in the opposite direction. **D** would require banks to inquire into the underlying transaction, which they need not do.

G. Customer may post-date but must give bank notice

Customer issues post-dated check → Payee → Depositary Bank → Drawee Bank pays early

I'm going to buy some artwork today but I'm a little bit leery. The painting looks authentic, but I'm not sure. I hand over the check but tell the dealer that it's not going to be good for ten days. Today is the first of the month, but the check is dated the 11th. That gives me some time to have the painting checked out. I have an expert look at the painting, who says it is a forgery. On the October 9, I check my account and see that the bank has already paid the check. I dated it for October 11. Is my bank entitled to reimbursement from me, if it prematurely pays a post-dated check? Yes — unless I had also given notice to the bank of the post-dating.

> § 4-401(c). A bank may charge against the account of a customer a check that is otherwise properly payable from the account, even though payment was made before the date of the check, unless the customer has given notice to the bank of the postdating describing the check with reasonable certainty. The notice is effective for the period stated in Section 4-403(b) for stop-payment orders, and must be received at such time and in such manner as to afford the bank a reasonable opportunity to act on it before the bank takes any action with respect to the check described in Section 4-303. If a bank charges against the account of a customer a check before the date stated in the notice of post-dating, the bank is liable for damages for the loss resulting from its act. The loss may include damages for dishonor of subsequent items under Section 4-402.

Here is the reason. These days, checks are processed largely through automated means. If I write a check to someone and they deposit it in their account, the depositary bank will encode the amount of the check. When the check is in my checkbook, it already has magnetically coded information at the bottom of the check, which gives the check number, the account number of the customer, and the routing number of the bank. A machine can read the check, the account, the drawee bank, and the check number. So, when the check is written and deposited, someone then encodes the one piece of additional information: the amount of the check. From then on, normally, no one looks at or touches that check again. Rather, it is routed around through electronic or mechanical means.

Banks are likely to have rules that say that if there are checks for large amounts, they should be looked at before payment is issued. They may also have rules that say that when a computer detects unusual activity in a checking account, those checks should also be looked at, as well as overdraft checks. In general, however, checks are handled automatically.

The law recognizes the above described automated handling in several rules, including the rule governing post-dating: A customer can post-date a check, but to make it effective the customer must tell the bank. If I post-date a check, my bank still has authority to pay it, unless I also give notice to my bank, reasonably identifying the item and giving the bank sufficient time to implement the post-dated payment (the same sort of information as with a stop payment order).

Going back to the original hypothetical, what I could have effectively done was written the check to the art dealer, post-dated it, and then immediately notified my bank with the number of the check, the amount of the check, and the fact that I post-dated it. If I don't do all of that, then post-dating is not effective. This process allows customers to post-date checks and banks can rely on automated processing of checks because they don't have to look at checks, unless they get special notice from their customer.

QUESTION 10. Premature presentation.   On May 1, McGuire agrees to buy some debentures from Looney, a securities dealer. McGuire has only a few dollars in her checking account. To get time to cover the check, and perhaps rethink her investment, she post-dates the check "May 10" and hands it to Looney, who agrees not to seek payment before May 10. Looney, who has handed McGuire worthless forged debentures, deposits the check forthwith. The drawee pays it on May 4, creating an overdraft of some $200,000. Is McGuire liable for the overdraft?

A. No. The check was not payable until May 10.
B. No. The bank lacks authority to pay money not in the account.
C. Yes. The post-dating was ineffective.
D. Yes. A check is an unconditional order to pay, so it is always properly payable.

ANALYSIS.

McGuire → Looney → Depositary Bank → Drawee Bank

This fact pattern triggers two rules. First, a customer may post-date a check, but that limits the drawee bank only if the customer gives notice to the bank. McGuire did not give notice to the drawee, so the check was payable, the postdating notwithstanding. The theory is that banks do not normally check dates before paying.

The second issue is the overdraft. "A bank may charge against the account of a customer an item that is properly payable from that account even though the charge creates an overdraft." UCC § 4-401(a). By writing the check, McGuire authorized payment and promised reimbursement, even if her account lacked the funds. So, **A** and **B** state the law inaccurately, and **C** is the best answer. **D** overstates things.

Looney did agree not to present the check before May 10, but Looney's agreement does not bind the drawee bank, which would have no knowledge of it. McGuire got the promise from the wrong person.

H   No effective stop payment order in effect

The customer may stop payment on a check by reasonably identifying the check, provided notice is given in time for the bank to avoid payment.

> **§ 4-403. Customer's Right to Stop Payment; Burden of Proof of Loss**
>
> (a) A customer or any person authorized to draw on the account if there is more than one person may stop payment of any item drawn on the customer's account or close the account by an order to the bank describing the item or account with reasonable certainty received at a time and in a manner that affords the bank a reasonable opportunity to act on it before any action by the bank with respect to the item described in Section 4-303. If the signature of more than one person is required to draw on an account, any of these persons may stop payment or close the account.
>
> (b) A stop-payment order is effective for six months, but it lapses after 14 calendar days if the original order was oral and was not confirmed in a record within that period. A stop-payment order may be renewed for additional six-month periods by a record given to the bank within a period during which the stop-payment order is effective.
>
> (c) The burden of establishing the fact and amount of loss resulting from the payment of an item contrary to a stop-payment order or order to close an account is on the customer. The loss from payment of an item contrary to a stop-payment order may include damages for dishonor of subsequent items under Section 4-402.

Customer issues, then stops payments → Payee → Depositary Bank → Drawee Bank

I write a check for an alethiometer. The next day, the alethiometer proves unreliable. I don't want the bank to pay the check. A customer can stop payment of a check by giving notice to the bank, by reasonably identifying the check, and by doing so with reasonable time for the bank to implement the stop payment order. I can stop payment, but only before the bank pays the check.

Today, that window is getting shorter and shorter. Banks are processing checks faster and faster, using electronic means and other more efficient procedures. That means customers get money faster when they deposit their own checks, but it also means they have less time to stop payment on checks they write. In the old days it might have taken a week to ten days before a check was paid—the alethiometer seller would deposit the check, perhaps in the bank's night deposit slot. Then the bank had to send it on for collection, perhaps via the Federal Reserve or a clearinghouse. Some banks actually hired "check dogs" to fly bags of checks around the country to get them processed as quickly as possible.

Now, ATMs and electronic presentment have speeded up the process considerably. If I write a check to the seller, the seller may deposit it in their account in the ATM, and their bank may take it that same night, extract the magnetically coded information, and process the check electronically—its machines can read the information off the check, add the amount of the check, put the amount in electronic form, and e-mail it to the drawee bank, whose computer may respond immediately. The check could be paid on the night it was deposited. To make things even quicker, some merchants encode the amount and send the information on electronically. The check might be paid before the customer gets out of the store, and the customer may have little time to stop payment.

QUESTION 11. With a little misdirection. Fifi burglarizes Heider's office and steals a check written to Heider from a patient. Heider, a careful sort, makes copies of all incoming checks and so is easily able to identify the drawee bank, call it, and order it not to pay the check, giving numbers of the account and the check. The drawee bank pays the check anyway, due to some miscommunication between clerks. Is the drawee entitled to reimbursement?

A. No. There was an effective stop payment order.
B. Yes. Heider lacks authority to issue a stop payment order on someone else's account.
C. No. The drawee paid the wrong person.
D. Yes. A check is an unconditional order to pay. A stop payment request cannot remove the authority to pay.

ANALYSIS.
Patient → Heider → Fifi → Depo → Payor

Heider was not Payor's customer or authorized to draw on the account, so Heider was not authorized to stop payment. But that does not matter.

The check was not properly payable to Fifi, rather, only to Heider. So, the drawee is not entitled to reimbursement, making **C** the best answer. Heider is entitled to collect, and in fact can choose to collect from Patient (on the check or the underlying transaction) or from Depo or Payor (both liable for conversion).

QUESTION 12. Bad samaritan. Deacon loses her checkbook. She contacts her bank, intending to tell it not to pay any of checks numbered 726 through 750. The bank is amenable; reminding her there is a $50 fee per check for stop payment. Deacon refuses to issue 25 stop payment fees and hangs up angrily, before identifying the numbers of the lost checks. A week later, the bank pays a $1,250 check, written by the finder of Deacon's checkbook. Is the bank entitled to reimbursement from Deacon?

A. Yes. Deacon did not issue an effective stop payment order.
B. In effect, yes. The bank is not entitled to reimbursement for the check but is entitled to the 25 stop payment fees.
C. No. The check was not properly payable.
D. Yes. Deacon should have closed her account after losing so many checks.

ANALYSIS.
Finder, signs as Deacon → Payee → Depo → Payor

This question is a variation of the preceding one. Deacon did not stop payment on the checks; however, a stop payment was not necessary. Deacon did not authorize payment, so the check was not properly payable. **C** is the best answer. Payor should have taken the tip.

QUESTION 13. Back it up. Teddy purchases a fountain for Rocky Knoll. The fountain soon springs a leak. Teddy's check has been paid. If the fountain is defective, can Teddy simply reverse the payment?

A. Yes. The customer can withdraw authorization, so that the check is no longer properly payable.
B. Yes. Teddy would have a defense to payment.
C. No. A stop payment order can only be effectively done before the check is paid.
D. No. By signing the check, Teddy promised unconditionally to pay.

ANALYSIS. A customer has the right to stop payment before the check is paid, but not to reverse payment. **C** is the best answer.

I.   Bank may pay despite death or incompetence of customer, until notice

Customer issues, promptly dies→ Payee → Depositary Bank → Drawee Bank

§ 4-405. Death or Incompetence of Customer

(a) A payor or collecting bank's authority to accept, pay, or collect an item or to account for proceeds of its collection, if otherwise effective, is not rendered ineffective by incompetence of a customer of either bank existing at the time the item is issued or its collection is undertaken if the bank does not know of an adjudication of incompetence. Neither death nor incompetence of a customer revokes the authority to accept, pay, collect, or account until the bank knows of the fact of death or of an adjudication of incompetence and has reasonable opportunity to act on it.

(b) Even with knowledge, a bank may for 10 days after the date of death pay or certify checks drawn on or before that date unless ordered to stop payment by a person claiming an interest in the account.

It would be sad indeed if someone's last words were "pay to the order of Marley Plumbing." UCC Article 4 reasons that if a check is issued and the drawer dies, the check should probably be paid anyway. It was presumably written for a debt or to make a payment the issuer intended, and the fact of death need not change that—nor does it usually discharge debts. So, rather than making payee go to probate court to collect, the checks may go through. If someone objects, then § 4-405 sends the parties to probate court to resolve things.

J.   A *reasonable* clause in the deposit contract may affect bank's right to reimbursement

§ 4-103 (a). The effect of the provisions of this Article may be varied by agreement, but the parties to the agreement cannot disclaim a bank's responsibility for its lack of good faith or failure to exercise ordinary care or limit the measure of damages for the lack or failure. However, the parties may determine by agreement the standards by which the bank's responsibility is to be measured if those standards are not manifestly unreasonable.

The bank pays a check that I didn't sign or was stolen or was post-dated. I complain about it. But our contract states that the bank may pay stolen checks and the customer will be liable. Is it enforceable?

In general, commercial law allows the parties to agree what the rules of their relationship are. However, it puts some limits on banks by saying that a bank cannot have an enforceable term in a contract that disclaims the bank's duty of ordinary care or duty of good faith. In other words, the bank's contract with its customer can't effectively allow the bank to act negligently, or in bad faith. It can allow a bank to set a reasonable standard.

> **QUESTION 14. Negligence guaranteed.**   Looking through his bank statement, Dennett finds a check paid from his account that he did not write. Dennett contacts the bank, which points out the following clause in the deposit contract: "Checks today are processed automatically. We do not examine signatures by hand, and could not feasibly check the signatures of our thousands of customers against their many checks. Customer agrees that bank is entitled to reimbursement for all checks written on the account, provided the check is not an obvious forgery. In exchange, bank offers low monthly fees. Customer is advised to guard the checkbook carefully." Is Dennett entitled to the money back?
>
> **A.** No. He assumed the risk.
> **B.** No. His bank is never liable for forgeries it could not spot.
> **C.** Yes. The clause is not enforceable.
> **D.** Yes. The deposit contract is irrelevant. Only the UCC can provide the rules that govern the parties' rights and obligations with checks.

ANALYSIS.

Not Dennet → Payee → Depo →Payor

Whenever the bank relies on a clause in the contract, we must measure it against § 4-103. The contract may set reasonable standards for the bank but may not disclaim the bank's obligations of ordinary care and good faith. This clause allows the bank to pay any checks, other than obvious forgeries. The bank may argue that this is simply setting a reasonable standard; however, it is more a disclaimer of negligence. The parties have simply shifted the risk of unauthorized checks from Payor to Dennet. Such a clause is probably not enforceable, making **C** the best answer. I say "probably," because the rule allows "reasonable" standards. This looks unreasonable to me — but whenever words like *reasonable, material, substantial,* and so forth are used, there is likely to be room for argument. **C** is not absolutely certain, but nevertheless it is the best answer.

The customer may not assume the risk of the bank's lack of ordinary care, so **A** is incorrect. Contrary to **B**, the payor normally bears the risk of forged drawer's signatures, spottable or not. **D** overstates things: The parties may agree to reasonable standards to govern the bank's obligations — just not disclaimers.

K.   Fees — not regulated by UCC

The UCC doesn't say what fees the bank can charge. In general, banks and customers are free to agree on the fees that banks charge. Courts might hold excessive fees to be invalid under unconscionability or bad faith, but either theory has a high standard of proof.

L.   Subrogation: Bank that pays by mistake may seek restitution to avoid unjust enrichment

§ 4-407. Payor Bank's Right to Subrogation on Improper Payment

If a payor bank has paid an item over the order of the drawer or maker to stop payment, or after an account has been closed, or otherwise under circumstances giving a basis for objection by the drawer or maker, to prevent unjust enrichment and only to the extent necessary to prevent loss to the bank by reason of its payment of the item, the payor bank is subrogated to the rights

(1) of any holder in due course on the item against the drawer or maker;

(2) of the payee or any other holder of the item against the drawer or maker either on the item or under the transaction out of which the item arose; and

(3) of the drawer or maker against the payee or any other holder of the item with respect to the transaction out of which the item arose.

A bank that pays by mistake may use subrogation in some cases. If it can show that it paid by mistake, that it is facing a loss, and that there is another party who is getting unjust enrichment, then the bank can use subrogation. It can step into the shoes of one of the other parties and exercise that party's right against the party that is getting unjust enrichment. We can make it a little more concrete with *McIntyre v. Harris*, 709 N.E.2d 982 (Ill. App. 1999). McIntyre owed $2,000 to Bennett as a result of a contract. McIntyre writes a check to Bennett and then immediately stops payment on it. McIntyre's bank, Twin Oaks, made a mistake and paid the check. They are not entitled to reimbursement. Subrogation, however, gives them a second bite of the apple, because they can meet all three of the requirements:

1. They paid a check by mistake.
2. They are facing a loss because they paid out $2,000, and they are not entitled to reimbursement from the customer.
3. There is a party—McIntyre—that is being unjustly enriched.

Because of Twin Oaks Bank's mistake, McIntyre is out zero dollars and will also get his $2,000 debt discharged. Twin Oaks Bank is entitled to step into the shoes of Bennett and exercise Bennett's rights against McIntyre and collect the underlying debt.

> **QUESTION 15. Subrogation situation.**   Sperber writes a check to Wilson, as the agreed payment for delivery of a library of anthropology texts. Sperber then has buyer's regret and stops payment on the check. This is a clear breach of the contract, because Wilson fulfilled all her

warranties. Sperber's bank, Forgetful Savings, inadvertently miscodes the order into its computer and pays the check when presented. Is Forgetful Savings entitled to the money from Sperber?

A. No. Payment was effectively ordered to be stopped. The contract dispute between Sperber and Wilson has no effect on the bank.
B. Yes. A check is an unconditional order to pay.
C. No. Sperber's order was ineffective, because it did not state a sufficient reason.
D. No. Sperber was liable to Wilson, so Sperber will be liable to Forgetful Savings.

ANALYSIS.

Sperber issues, and stops payment → Wilson → Depo → Forgetful Savings

Forgetful Savings should not have paid the check, because a stop payment order is in effect. This mistake could give Sperber a windfall, however. Sperber has the texts and is obliged to pay Wilson. Forgetful Savings paid Wilson's bank by mistake, so Wilson will not be seeking money from Sperber. Rather, Forgetful Savings faces a loss. This is a subrogation situation. Forgetful Savings may step into Wilson's shoes and collect for the texts. Therefore, **D** is the best answer.

A couple of variations: If Wilson had not delivered the texts, Wilson might be the one being unjustly enriched: getting the money and not delivering the books. In that case, Forgetful Savings could step into Sperber's shoes and would be entitled to the texts.

Alternatively, suppose the texts were not the ones promised, and Sperber had rejected them. Wilson breached. In that case, Sperber would not be getting unjust enrichment, nor would subrogation help. Subrogation would only give Forgetful Savings the rights Wilson had against Sperber, and Wilson did not have the right to collect.

M. Bank statement rule

A common news story: Law firm's bookkeeper has expensive tastes. Over a period of a couple years she writes checks on the firm's account without authority—to herself, or to pay her bills. Even though the checks were not authorized by the firm, it will be liable to reimburse the bank. A customer has a duty to check their account statement for unauthorized or altered checks that were paid. If the customer fails to do so, and that allows the wrongdoer to continue the course of action, the customer will be liable. As to checks improperly paid more than a year ago, the customer is not entitled to reimbursement in any case. Section 4-406 sets out the rule.

§ 4-406. Customer's Duty to Discover and Report Unauthorized Signature or Alteration

(a) A bank that sends or makes available to a customer a statement of account showing payment of items for the account shall either return or make available to the customer the items paid or provide information in the statement of account sufficient to allow the customer reasonably to identify the items paid. The statement of account provides sufficient information if the item is described by item number, amount, and date of payment.

(b) If the items are not returned to the customer, the person retaining the items shall either retain the items or, if the items are destroyed, maintain the capacity to furnish legible copies of the items until the expiration of seven years after receipt of the items. A customer may request an item from the bank that paid the item, and that bank must provide in a reasonable time either the item or, if the item has been destroyed or is not otherwise obtainable, a legible copy of the item.

(c) If a bank sends or makes available a statement of account or items pursuant to subsection (a), the customer must exercise reasonable promptness in examining the statement or the items to determine whether any payment was not authorized because of an alteration of an item or because a purported signature by or on behalf of the customer was not authorized. If, based on the statement or items provided, the customer should reasonably have discovered the unauthorized payment, the customer must promptly notify the bank of the relevant facts.

(d) If the bank proves that the customer failed, with respect to an item, to comply with the duties imposed on the customer by subsection (c), the customer is precluded from asserting against the bank:

(1) the customer's unauthorized signature or any alteration on the item, if the bank also proves that it suffered a loss by reason of the failure; and

(2) the customer's unauthorized signature or alteration by the same wrongdoer on any other item paid in good faith by the bank if the payment was made before the bank received notice from the customer of the unauthorized signature or alteration and after the customer had been afforded a reasonable period of time, not exceeding 30 days, in which to examine the item or statement of account and notify the bank.

(e) If subsection (d) applies and the customer proves that the bank failed to exercise ordinary care in paying the item and that the failure substantially contributed to loss, the loss is allocated between the customer precluded and the bank asserting the preclusion according to the extent to which the failure of the customer to comply with subsection (c) and the failure of the bank to exercise ordinary care contributed to the loss. If the customer proves that the bank did not pay the item in good faith, the preclusion under subsection (d) does not apply.

(f) Without regard to care or lack of care of either the customer or the bank, a customer who does not within one year after the statement or items are made available to the customer (subsection (a)) discover and report the customer's unauthorized signature on or any alteration on the item is precluded from asserting against the bank the unauthorized signature or

> alteration. If there is a preclusion under this subsection, the payor bank may not recover for breach of warranty under Section 4-208 with respect to the unauthorized signature or alteration to which the preclusion applies.

Normally, if a check is paid that the customer didn't sign, that's a forged drawer signature. We saw that the risk of loss for forged drawer signature usually falls on the drawer's bank. The theory is that the drawer's bank could monitor activity in that account and not pay checks that weren't authorized. If they pay checks their customer didn't sign, they are not entitled to reimbursement. Likewise, if the bank pays an altered check, the customer is liable to reimburse only for the original amount of the check.

The bank statement rule gives a different result in some situations. In the scenario described above, failure to complain about the unauthorized checks for more than a year means that the firm can't get the money back from their bank.

The bank statement rule is tricky because it has three ways for the customer to take the loss, described below. It's important for customers to know about the bank statement rule because it requires them to check their account statement regularly. Otherwise, if there's something wrong going on in the account, the customer might take the loss. The bank statement rule says that the customer has to check their account statement for two things: checks that were paid that the customer didn't sign, and checks that were paid that had been altered. It doesn't require the customer to check to see if there were checks that were paid over a forged indorsement.

What's the reason for that? The customer is in a position to detect the first two types of wrongdoing. If somebody writes a check on my account, and that check comes back in the statement, I should be able to recognize that. Likewise, if I write a check for $100 and it's changed to $100,000, I should be able to recognize that. As for a forged indorsement (e.g., I write a check to Paul and somebody forges his endorsement), I am in no better position than the bank to catch that. So, the customer has to look for forged drawer signatures and alterations.

There are three ways in which the customer can end up taking the loss. The first I call the "one-shot rule," which rarely applies. It sounds scarier than it is. Here's the rule: Suppose somebody writes a check on my account, the bank pays it and sends me my statement, and I fail to give timely notice to the bank of the disparity. If my failure caused the loss to the bank, then I take the loss. That last qualification is important, and is the reason why this rule rarely comes into effect. The sequence of events is this: somebody writes the check, my bank pays the check, then I get my statement and I fail to give my bank timely notice. Even if I fail to notify my bank within a month or two, that's usually not going to cause a loss to the bank. If I tell them within a minute after I get my account statement, it is too late. Normally, the person has the money and is gone.

The only time it is likely to cause a loss to the bank is when the following is true:

> when I get my statement;
> when the forger has an account at the bank and has money in there;

when I fail to give notice to my bank;

when the period of time goes by; and

when the forger takes the money out and leaves with it.

If I had given timely notice to my bank, they could have frozen the funds. That's not a very common situation, however. It's a lot more likely that when my bank pays the check, the person will take the funds and disappear. At any rate, my failure to give notice usually won't make a difference.

The second way a customer could take a loss is under the "multiple rule" (as I call it), which is more likely to come into effect. Say that someone writes a series of checks on my account and I don't complain about it. If I had told the bank about check number one, then the bank would have been on notice and wouldn't have paid check numbers two or three or four, or at least would have had an opportunity to not pay those checks. Here you can see it is a lot more likely that failure to give timely notice to the bank could mean that the bank loses an opportunity to prevent the loss. So, if there are multiple wrongdoings by the same person on the same account, the customer can take the loss for check number two, check number three, and check number four.

The third type of customer loss could come about under the "one-year rule," which is like a statute of limitations. If I don't give notice to my bank within a year, it's too late, and the bank doesn't even have to show that my failure to give notice caused the loss. Once the bank sends the statement, if there is an unauthorized check or an alteration, I have to give notice within a year or I lose my right to complain. Some banks by agreement shorten this period considerably—some to as little as 14 days. Courts (in the few cases touching on the issue), at least for business accounts, have tended to uphold such agreements. That is a little puzzling. Parties are allowed to set reasonable standards for rules governing the banks, but where the rule sets a specific time line of one year, one might argue that any shorter period is unreasonable. The counterargument is that businesses should be able to freely decide how they will allocate risks by agreement.

Note: The time runs from when the bank "sends or makes available" the statement. The bank is not required to show that the customer received or reviewed the statement.

QUESTION 16. Too late.   Nova has been inattentive to his checking account statements. Finally, he wonders why he seems to have several thousand less in the account than he should. Looking at a six-month-old statement, he sees a $4,000 check to "Cash," signed "Nova" by someone else. Can Nova recover the money from his bank?

A. No, due to his negligence.

B. No, due to the bank statement rule.

C. No, due to the impostor rule.

D. No, because it was bearer paper, payable to anyone in possession.

E. Yes. Nova still can complain in timely fashion.

ANALYSIS.   This question emphasizes that the bank statement rule kicks in where the customer's delay causes a loss to the bank, or where the customer delayed more than a year. Nova was slow in notifying the bank, but that did not cause the loss. By the time the statement got to Nova, the forger had the money and was long gone. The bank statement rule would kick in only if Nova's delay permitted the forger to do it again, or if Nova waited more than a year.

E is the best answer.

QUESTION 17. Too late, take 2.   Martha snags a packet of blank check forms from the mailbox of her wealthy neighbor, Brandon. Martha writes a check each month on the account to "Cash." Brandon finally notices after almost two years. Can Brandon get the money back?

A. Yes. Brandon did not sign the checks, so they were not properly payable.
B. Yes, if Brandon was not negligent.
C. Brandon can get the money back on the checks written within the last year.
D. Brandon can get none of the money back.

ANALYSIS.   This is a classic application of the bank statement rule. As to checks paid more than a year after the bank sent the first statement showing payment of one of the checks, it is too late to complain, under the one-year rule. As to checks paid within the last year, Brandon is foreclosed from complaining by the multiple-shot rule. So, Brandon gets none of the money back. Therefore, **D** is the best answer.

All the bank need show is that it sent or made the statements available. So, even if Brandon never got them (such as in cases in which the wrongdoer also steals the statement each month, to conceal the fraud), Brandon takes the loss.

N.   The closer

QUESTION 18. Reasonable I.D.?   Karel writes a check numbered "200" for $2,819.30 to Oskar to purchase some electronics equipment. On testing the equipment back in his lab, Karel determines it is extremely faulty, contrary to Oskar's express warranty. Karel quickly e-mails his bank to stop payment on "check number 200, amount $2,820." A bank employee enters the request into the system. The software, however, requires an exact match to stop a check from being paid, so the bank pays Oskar the $2,819.30 check (meanwhile watching electronically for a $2,820 check). Karel refuses to reimburse the bank. May the bank recover?

A. Yes. The bank is entitled to collect from Karel, because he authorized payment and the bank paid the correct person the right amount.
B. Yes. The bank is entitled to collect from Karel, because he did not correctly identify the check.
C. The bank is not entitled to collect from Karel, because he reasonably identified the check.
D. The bank may be entitled to collect from Oskar.
E. Both **C** and **D**.

ANALYSIS.

Karel → Oskar → Drawee Bank pays

A check is not properly payable if there is an effective stop payment order. **A** is wrong because it overlooks the ability to stop payment. The customer can stop payment of the check by giving notice to the bank, by reasonably identifying the check, and by doing so with reasonable time for the bank to implement the stop payment order. The issue here would be whether Karel reasonably identified the check. The bank would argue that he did not, because his inaccurate statement of the amount led to the computer failing to correctly flag the check. A court, however, would likely rule that Karel reasonably identified the check. He gave the correct number, and got the amount almost correct. That should be more than sufficient for the bank to avoid paying on the check. So, **B** is incorrect.

C is accurate but omits the possibility of subrogation. If Oskar is getting unjust enrichment, the drawee bank may use subrogation to exercise Karel's rights against Oskar. **D** is also true but is incomplete. **E** is the best answer.

 # McJohn's picks

1.	Ghostwriter	A
2.	Infirmity	C
3.	No questions asked	A
4.	Not so technical	D
5.	Alteration situation	B
6.	Cognitive dissonance	C
7.	Exposure	A
8.	Uncertainty	A
9.	You snooze, you don't lose	B
10.	Premature presentation	C
11.	With a little misdirection	C
12.	Bad samaritan	C

13. Back it up   **C**
14. Negligence guaranteed   **C**
15. Subrogation situation   **D**
16. Too late   **E**
17. Too late, take 2   **D**
18. Reasonable I.D.   **E**

15

Collection and Funds Availability Duties of Depositary Bank: Show Me the Money

Problem with funds availability
Is customer's checking agility.
Deposit the funny,
Depart with the money,
Leave Depo with naught but liability.

CHAPTER OVERVIEW
A. Duties of depositary bank
B. Chargeback
C. Funds availability rules
D. Depositary bank may make itself liable on a check
E. The closer
⬥ McJohn's picks

Drawer → Payee → Depositary Bank where payee has account → Drawee
                                    Bank where Payee has account

W hen a check is deposited, the depositary bank does not pay it. Rather, it acts as the customer's agent for collection. It may make the money available provisionally.

A.   Duties of depositary bank

Drawer → Payee → Depositary Bank → (may be some intermediaries) → Drawee Bank

The depositary bank (along with other banks handling the item for collection) has a duty to use ordinary care. Provided it does so, it is not liable for loss owing to other causes. As § 4-202 puts it:

§ 4-202. Responsibility for Collection or Return; When Action Timely
(a) A collecting bank must exercise ordinary care in:
(1) presenting an item or sending it for presentment;
(2) sending notice of dishonor or nonpayment or returning an item other than a documentary draft to the bank's transferor after learning that the item has not been paid or accepted, as the case may be;
(3) settling for an item when the bank receives final settlement; and
(4) notifying its transferor of any loss or delay in transit within a reasonable time after discovery thereof.
(b) A collecting bank exercises ordinary care under subsection (a) by taking proper action before its midnight deadline following receipt of an item, notice, or settlement. Taking proper action within a reasonably longer time may constitute the exercise of ordinary care, but the bank has the burden of establishing timeliness.
(c) Subject to subsection (a)(1), a bank is not liable for the insolvency, neglect, misconduct, mistake, or default of another bank or person or for loss or destruction of an item in the possession of others or in transit.

QUESTION 1. Oops.   Bagels Beyond gets a big check after catering a graduation party. Bagels Beyond deposits the check at Forgetful Bank, who lets the check sit in the vault several weeks before sending it for payment. In the intervening time, the drawer of the check has filed bankruptcy, so the check is returned, stamped "insufficient funds."
Is Forgetful Bank liable to Bagels Beyond?

A. No. Forgetful Bank did not sign the check.
B. No. Forgetful Bank did not allow the check to be damaged. It was kept safe in the vault.
C. Yes. Forgetful Bank is liable for its delay in presentment.
D. Yes. When Bagels Beyond deposited the check, it became entitled to the money.

ANALYSIS.

Drawer → Bagels Beyond → Forgetful Bank → Drawee dishonors

The depositary bank has a duty of ordinary care in handling the check for collection, including sending it for presentment. Forgetful Bank breached that duty and so is liable. **C** is the best answer.

A is irrelevant, because Forgetful Bank is not being sued as an indorser or other guarantor.

B is incorrect, because the duties go beyond simply taking care of the piece of paper. Guarding its customer's rights is Forgetful Bank's duty.

D overstates things, because depositing a check simply delivers it to the depositary bank for collection from the drawee bank.

Some common law rules also impose duties on depositary banks. If a check is written payable to the bank itself, some jurisdictions apply a common law rule requiring the bank to investigate, making sure that nothing fishy is going on. Fred from Business Corp's accounting department deposits a check, made out to Piscine Bank, in Fred's account at Piscine Bank. Piscine Bank pays the check, and Fred disappears with the money. If Fred had embezzled the funds from Business Corp., Piscine Bank could be liable for failing to investigate the case, because a check made out to a bank is a common device for diverting funds. (It would have been more suspicious at Business Corp. if the check had been made out to Fred.)

B.   Chameleon Chargeback

If a depositary bank makes funds available on a check during collection, and the check is not paid, the depositary bank has a right of chargeback (i.e., it can get the money from its customer's account, or from the customer).

Customer → Trusty → Scary Bank → Trick or Treat Bank
issues   deposits   presents   does not pay

Trusty receives a $10,000 check from Customer, drawn on Trick or Treat Bank. Trusty deposits the check in her account at Scary Bank. The next day, Scary puts $10,000 in Trusty's account. A few days later, Trick or Treat Bank dishonors the check (declines to pay it, because there are insufficient funds in Customer's account, or Customer has stopped payment, etc.). Scary can take the money back from Trusty's account. If Trusty has withdrawn the money, then Trusty is obliged to pay Scary Bank.

Receiving money when depositing a check is *not* receiving payment on the check. Rather, it is simply receiving a conditional loan of the money, and the right to keep it depends on whether the drawee bank pays the check. As § 4-214 puts it:

> **§ 4-214. Right of Charge-Back or Refund; Liability of Collecting Bank; Return of Item**
>
> (a) If a collecting bank has made provisional settlement with its customer for an item and fails by reason of dishonor, suspension of payments by a bank,

or otherwise to receive settlement for the item which is or becomes final, the bank may revoke the settlement given by it, charge back the amount of any credit given for the item to its customer's account, or obtain refund from its customer, whether or not it is able to return the item, if by its midnight deadline or within a longer reasonable time after it learns the facts it returns the item or sends notification of the facts. If the return or notice is delayed beyond the bank's midnight deadline or a longer reasonable time after it learns the facts, the bank may revoke the settlement, charge back the credit, or obtain refund from its customer, but it is liable for any loss resulting from the delay. These rights to revoke, charge back, and obtain refund terminate if and when a settlement for the item received by the bank is or becomes final.

This creates an important practical point that anyone depositing a check should know: Do not rely on the deposited funds until the check has been paid or you are confident enough that the check will be paid.

QUESTION 2. Take back. Gallery sells a Picasso drawing to Collector, for a $250,000 check drawn on Egon Bank. Gallery deposits the check in its account at Braque Bank. The next day, the funds have been credited to the account. Gallery wires the funds to buy another work. A week later, Braque Bank calls Gallery to say that the check was dishonored by Egon Bank due to a stop payment order by Collector, and Braque wants $250,000. Gallery responds that the drawing was genuine, that Collector owes the money under the contract, and that there is no reason to undo the transaction. Is Gallery liable to Braque Bank?

A. No. The stop payment is ineffective, because Collector had no reasonable basis.
B. No. Braque Bank has no defense to payment.
C. Yes. If the check is not paid, the depositary bank has a right of chargeback.
D. No. Gallery did not sign the check.

ANALYSIS.

Collector → Gallery → Braque Bank → Egon Bank
issues   deposits   presents   dishonors (Customer stopped payment)

Gallery is entitled to payment—but not from Braque Bank, who was simply handling the check on Gallery's behalf. If the check is not paid, Gallery must return funds that Gallery received provisionally from Braque Bank. **C** is the best answer.

The stop payment is a matter between Collector and Egon Bank, and does not affect Gallery's rights, so **A** is inapposite.

The right of chargeback is a different theory of liability than indorser liability. It does not matter whether Gallery signed the check or has a defense to payment, so **B** and **D** are off. This is an important practical point. When a bank takes checks deposited by its customers, it need not be concerned about whether the customer has a defense to indorser liability. Chargeback liability is much simpler and not subject to defenses arising against other people.

Note that there is probably also a clause in Gallery's deposit contract that gives Braque Bank a contractual right of chargeback.

C.   Funds availability rules

When an item is deposited (up to $5,000 in deposits per day), the bank must make the funds available in a certain amount of time. That time depends on whether the item is an ordinary check or a low-risk item (like a cashier's check), and whether it is a local or non-local check. There are exceptions, such as checks that probably will not be paid and accounts with frequent overdrafts. For such items, the bank may wait until the check is paid (if it is) before making the funds available.

Drawer → Payee → Depositary Bank → Drawee Bank

Drawer writes a check to Payee, who deposits it with Depositary Bank. How soon does Depositary Bank have to make the money available to Payee? The rule used to be, under the Uniform Commercial Code (UCC), that Depositary Bank had to give the money to Payee if and when Depositary Bank learned that the check had been paid. If it took two weeks for the check to make its way across the country, the funds to come back to Depositary Bank from Drawee, and Depositary Bank to get notice, then Depositary Bank could wait until then to make the funds available to Payee. It was not uncommon for out-of-state checks to be "on hold" for more than a month—meaning Payee could deposit the check on April 1, but not have access to the funds until sometime in May.

This caused two problems. First, the banks had use of their customers' funds as an interest-free loan ("float") for quite some time. Second, customers might write checks against the funds deposited, not realizing that the previously deposited check was on hold, resulting in bounced checks.

Congress responded with the Expedited Funds Availability Act, 12 U.S.C. §§ 4001-4010 (reinforced by the Federal Reserve's regulations in Subpart B of Regulation CC, 12 C.F.R. Part 229), which requires depositary banks to make the funds available more quickly. As amended in 2010, the timing depends on the following:

- The nature of the item (depositary banks get more time on ordinary checks than they do on low-risk items, such as cashier's checks or U.S. Treasury checks)
- The use of funds (depositary banks may get more time if a payee wants cash than if a payee is drawing with a check)

- Involvement of a third party (i.e., if the customer is depositing a check written to someone else and indorsed to the customer, then the depositary bank gets more time)
- Whether the check is deposited via ATM or over the counter (depositary banks get another day for ATM items)

One thing that is no longer a factor: where the drawee bank is located. It used to be that the depositary bank would be allowed more time for out-of-town checks. Checks, however, are increasingly processed electronically. The Federal Reserve (the biggest check clearinghouse) used to operate clearinghouses located around the country. As fewer checks are actually transported, though, the Federal Reserve has consolidated its check processing in a single location, the Federal Reserve Bank of Cleveland. It also changed the regulations, so that all checks are now treated as local checks (in effect, we all live in Cleveland now), meaning that a depositary bank has the same fund availability rules irrespective of where the drawee bank is located. It's said that all politics are local. Now all checks are local.

Borrowing from Professor Mann's concise summary of the regulations, here is the schedule for ordinary checks.

Table 1. Funds Availability Rules: Ordinary Checks

Noncash use	Day 1	$100
	Day 2	Remainder (up to $5,000)
Cash	Day 1	$100
	Day 2	$400
	Day 3	Remainder (up to $5,000)

Timing starts on the day of deposit, if it is a banking day (a day when the bank is open for business generally), or the first banking day after that. Then, the days are reckoned by business days (not weekends or holidays). Day 1 is the next business day after the clock starts ticking. Lawyers, like kids waiting for summer vacation, spend a lot of time counting off days. (When is the deadline for that motion to dismiss? Does Flag Day count as a day?) So, this is good practice.

Daffy → Custard deposits → Atlanta Depositary → Dallas Drawee

For example: Daffy writes a $1,100 check on Dallas Bank and gives it to Custard, who deposits it in the ATM at his local bank in Atlanta on Sunday, July 3. The bank is closed Sunday, and the next day for July 4. So Day 0 is Tuesday, July 5. If Custard wants cash, the Atlanta bank must make the funds available as follows: $100 on Day 1 (Wednesday), $400 on Day 2 (Thursday), and the remainder of $600 on Day 3 (Friday).

There is a tighter schedule for low-risk items. Low-risk items include electronic deposits, U.S. Treasury checks, "on-us" items (i.e., items drawn on the depositary bank itself, which can see if they are properly payable), cash, postal money orders, U.S. Federal Reserve checks, local government checks, and cashier's checks.

Table 2. Funds Availability Rules: Low-Risk Items

In-Person, Own account	
All low-risk items	Day 1
ATM Deposits, own account	
"On-us" items, U.S. Treasury Checks	Day 1
Other low-risk items	Day 2
Third-party account	
"On-us" items	Day 1
U.S. Treasury checks, postal money orders, and other low-risk items	Use check rules

For most low-risk items, the depositary bank must make the funds available (up to $5,000) on Day 1.

Note that these rules set a maximum time. If the bank knows the check has been paid sooner, it must make the provisional credit given to its customer available for withdrawal at that earlier time.

If the depositary bank does not make the funds available in time, it is liable for statutory damages to its customer. Moreover, if failure to make funds available causes it to dishonor other checks written on the account for lack of sufficient funds, then the depositary bank will be liable for wrongful dishonor.

If the depositary bank makes the funds available and the check is not paid, the depositary bank is entitled to the funds back from the payee.

Banks now get much less float on checks. Where a depositary bank makes the funds available before the drawee bank has paid the depositary bank, the customer gets a short-term, interest-free loan. If the bank has lots of customers, that cost of funds can be considerable. Moreover, a depositary bank has the risk that, if a check is not paid, the payee will not or cannot come up with the funds.

These factors gave banks a considerable incentive to speed up the check collection process: implementing clearinghouses, overnight delivery, rapid processing procedures, even using "check dogs," pilots who specialized in overnight flights carrying bags of checks. Banks have also truncated the check collection process by using electronic means. Checks formerly made their way across the country, through various mechanical means ranging from armored vans to brown paper bags to conveyor belts to pneumatic tubes. Now banks increasingly put the information into electronic form and send that, which goes quite a bit faster.

The funds availability rules require the depositary bank to advance funds for a check that may not be paid, creating a risk that the depositary bank will lose those funds if the check is not paid and the customer cannot or will not return the funds. Several rules limit the depositary bank's risk.

The rules apply only to a total of $5,000 in items per day. So, if Store sends over $500,000 of checks from shoppers, Depositary need only make $5,000 of those funds available (according to the schedules in Tables 1 and 2 above). For amounts over $5,000, Depositary must still make the funds available by the eighth business day. The funds availability regulations are more geared toward consumer protection. If Store wants faster funds availability for large deposits, it can negotiate that with its bank — and commercial parties often do seek out good services for payment systems. They want that money in their hands, too.

Depositary banks, under the regulations, need not follow the funds availability rules for all checks, however. Deposits to accounts opened within the preceding month are excluded, on the theory that new accounts are often used in check fraud schemes. Likewise, accounts with repeated overdrafts are excluded. A particular check is also excluded if it is being re-deposited after dishonor, or if the bank reasonably thinks it will not be paid (e.g., it was written by a business that just filed bankruptcy, it has apparent alterations, or it is written in crayon).

The payee also has a risk, of which the payee may be unaware. As discussed previously, the depositary bank has a right of chargeback for checks returned unpaid. When the payee receives the funds, it is likely that the check has not been paid yet. If the check is not paid, the payee will have to give the funds back. So, the payee should not rely on those funds until the check is paid. To illustrate this, we can turn to a popular fraudulent scheme, which illustrates once again that knowledge of law and practice can be an advantage.

Buyer → Seller gets $$$ from Depo, wires $ to Buyer → Depo → "Payor" dishonors

Next: After Supposed Payor dishonors, Depo is entitled to $$$ back from Seller

A typical case would work this way. Seller offers an antique table for sale via an online website. One potential buyer offers to pay $2,000, a great price. A small detail: Buyer doesn't have cash but does have a $10,000 cashier's check issued by Bank of America. Buyer says he can't cash it himself because his business is reorganizing or he is moving to a new city or does not have a bank account or. . . . So, to do this as quickly as possible, Buyer will send the Bank of America check. Seller can cash it, take his $2,000, and wire the buyer $8,000, as well as sending the table. Buyer says, "You have never heard of me before, but you don't have to trust me in the least. We'll arrange this so you need to have zero reliance on me. I'll send you the Bank of America check, and you don't have to wire me the money right away, because I trust you. Rather, you deposit the check in your account, and when it is paid, then you know you are okay. Then you can keep the $2,000 and wire me the other $8,000 and the table." The next day, Seller gets a FedEx package with the cashier's check from Bank of America, deposits it in his account, and waits. Sure enough, a day later the money is in his account.

Seller lives up to his end of the bargain. He wires the money and sends the table that afternoon. Seller is delighted to get $2,000 for that old table.

Two days later, Seller looks at his account and $10,000 has been taken out. What Seller didn't realize was that the depositary bank was making the funds available only provisionally. In the meantime, the depositary bank forwarded the cashier's check to Bank of America. Bank of America dishonored the forged cashier's check.

The distinction here is between what a bank does when it gives money as a depositary bank and what a bank does when it pays a check. All the depositary bank does is say, "Okay, you deposited a check, we'll give you the money. We're not paying that check, but we'll make that money available to you. If the other bank doesn't pay it, we'll take the money right back."

QUESTION 3. Race for the funds. El-Guerrouj gets a blue ribbon at the Local Fair, along with a check from a local dairy for $8,000, drawn on a local bank, Proximo Bank. El-Guerrouj deposits it with Nearby Savings, another local bank, the next morning, Monday. When does Nearby Savings have to make the funds available to El-Guerrouj, who needs to cover checks he has written on the account?

A. $100 on Tuesday, $4,900 on Wednesday, the remaining $3,000 when and if the check is paid.

B. When, and if, Nearby Savings receives payment on the check. Otherwise, Nearby Savings would be making a loan to El-Guerrouj.

C. Whatever the parties have agreed to in the deposit contract, which gives Nearby Savings more time than the federal regulations.

D. Cannot say — the funds availability rules apply only to small consumer transactions.

ANALYSIS.
Dairy → El-Guerrouj → Nearby Savings → Proximo Bank

B used to be the governing rule. Nearby Savings was simply forwarding the check for payment and so was not required to make money available to El-Guerrouj until and if Proximo Bank paid. However, the federal funds availability regulations now require Nearby Savings to meet a timetable, so **B** is not correct.

The parties cannot lengthen the time by agreement, so **C** is incorrect. The parties may shorten the time by agreement, and many banks do that to draw in customers.

The funds availability rules are not limited to consumer transactions, so **D** is incorrect. There is a dollar limit of $5,000 per day, so for the other $3,000, the UCC rule of "give the money when you get the money" applies.

The funds availability regulations govern the first $5,000. It is an ordinary check and a noncash use, so we look to the upper left quadrant in Table 1, shown earlier. The bank must make $100 available on Day 1 and the remainder of the $5,000 (i.e., $4,900) on Day 2. So, **A** is the best answer.

QUESTION 4. Quick service. One Monday, Ngeny deposits his $6,000 paycheck at Olympic Savings, written by his employer Rounder Records on its account at Gold Bank. Olympic Savings happens to have a messenger headed over to Gold Bank, so it sends the check right away and gets payment that same morning. When must Olympic Savings make the funds available to Ngeny?

A. $100 on Tuesday, $4,900 on Wednesday, and the remaining $1,000 when and if the check is paid.
B. That day.
C. Whatever the parties have agreed to in the deposit contract.
D. Cannot say—the funds availability rules apply only to small consumer transactions.

ANALYSIS.
Rounder Records → Ngeny → Olympic Savings → Gold Bank

This question emphasizes that the funds availability rules set a maximum time. If the depositary bank actually gets the funds sooner, then it must make them available forthwith. So, **B** is the best answer.

A would be the correct answer if the funds availability rules governed, but they only apply where the bank has not gotten the funds yet. So, **A** is incorrect.

C and **D** are not correct, for reasons already stated.

QUESTION 5. Bad rep. Lucky Morceli has had considerable problems in the last year with banking. A number of checks written to him by customers have bounced. This in turn led to Morceli himself having several of his checks dishonored for lack of sufficient funds. Just when he really needs cash, however, he receives a $20,000 dividend check from Mega Corp, drawn on a Seattle Bank. Lucky walks right over to his local Chicago bank and deposits it with a teller just before the bank closes for the weekend. When does Lucky's bank have to make the funds available against checks Lucky writes?

A. $100 on the first business day, $400 on the fifth business day, $4,500 on the sixth business day, and the rest when the check is paid.
B. $100 on the first business day, $4,900 on the fifth business day, and the rest when the check is paid.
C. When and if the check is paid.
D. Immediately.

ANALYSIS.
Mega Corp → Lucky Morceli → Chicago Depo → Seattle Drawee

The funds availability rules do not apply to all checks. The depositary bank need not follow the schedule if the customer is a new account or has had repeated overdrafts. A particular check is also excluded if it is being re-deposited after dishonor, or if the bank reasonably thinks it will not be paid. Morceli has had repeated overdrafts, so the bank is not obliged to follow the funds availability schedule with respect to his account. Chicago Depo may wait until it learns the check has been paid. So, **C** is the best answer.

If the schedule did apply, under the pre-2010 rules, it would have been treated as an ordinary check, *non-local* bank, and non-cash use, giving the result in **A**. But because all banks are now considered to be local banks, **B** would be the best answer for a local check, non-cash use, under Table 1, if the schedules applied.

D is not correct. Even if the customer really needs the money, the bank is not obliged to make funds available immediately—unless it had agreed to do so.

QUESTION 6. Low-risk item.   Ruiz sells his pickup truck to a neighbor, who pays with a $4,500 cashier's check, payable to Ruiz, from an out-of-state bank. Ruiz immediately deposits it with a teller at his bank. When must his bank make the funds available against checks Ruiz writes?

A. $100 on the first business day, $4,400 on the fifth business day.
B. When and if the check is paid. Even cashier's checks can bounce.
C. $4,500 on the first business day.
D. Immediately.

ANALYSIS.

Out-of-state → Neighbor → Ruiz → Depot → Out-of-state Bank

The time for making funds available for low-risk items is tight. This is a low-risk item (cashier's check) deposited in person. Right at the top of Table 2 we get the answer: all funds (up to $5,000) due on Day 1. **C** is the best answer. The regulations are based on the premise that low-risk items will probably be paid and that banks should readily identify ones that might not be and take steps to assess the risk (such as quickly contacting the other bank to see if the cashier's check is valid).

QUESTION 7. Variation.   Ruiz sells his pickup truck to a neighbor, who pays with a $4,500 cashier's check from an out-of-state bank. Ruiz then indorses the check to a business partner, Rono. Rono takes it down to his local bank and deposits it with a teller. When must the bank make the funds available against checks written by Rono?

A. $100 on the first business day, $4,400 on the second business day.
B. When and if the check is paid. Even cashier's checks can bounce.
C. $4,500 on the first business day.
D. Immediately.

ANALYSIS.

Out-of-state → Neighbor → Ruiz → Partner → Depositary

An item that would normally be low-risk, like a cashier's check, is riskier if it has been purportedly issued to a third party, rather than to the bank's customer. So, Table 2 sends us to the schedule for ordinary checks in Table 1. Table 1, for this check, yields the answer (non-cash use) in **A**.

D. Depositary bank may make itself liable on a check

If the depositary bank promises that a check will be paid, or is negligent in leading the customer to rely on payment, it may be liable for the amount of a check that is dishonored.

As happens every so often, common law may change the result in a case. Suppose that Custard deposits a check drawn by Magnetic Magnate on New York Bank. Custard's friendly bank officer at Local Bank promises him that the check will be paid and gives Custard the money, which Custard promptly spends. The check is returned for insufficient funds. Normally, Local Bank would have the right to charge back a check that was returned unpaid; however, Local Bank's promises could make it liable under common law. More than encouragement or vague statements about the reliability of a particular item would be required, but if Local Bank actually promised that the check would be paid, they could be bound by that promise.

E. The closer

> **QUESTION 8. Advance fee fraud.** Lyra offers her polygraph machine for sale on eBay. She accepts a bid of $10,000 from Truth or Consequences. Truth or Consequences sends her a cashier's check, apparently issued by Meta Bank to Truth or Consequences for $12,000. Truth or Consequences e-mails Lyra, asking her to deposit the cashier's check, because they have recently relocated and have not opened a bank account yet. Truth or Consequences further tells Lyra, "You don't know us, so we won't ask you to send the polygraph machine or the $2,000 difference until the check clears, of course." Lyra, uncertain, deposits the check at her bank, Solo Savings. The teller tells her, "It looks authentic, as far as I can tell."

> Two days later, Truth or Consequences e-mails again, asking if the check has been paid and, if so, could Lyra please send the machine and money as quickly as possible. Lyra checks her account, sees that $12,000 was added the day before, and sends off the polygraph with a check for $2,000. A week later, she sees that the $2,000 check has been paid—and that another $12,000 has been taken from her account, with the notation "item returned nonpaid—forgery." Can Lyra require her bank to give her the $12,000?
>
> A. No. A bank has a right to charge back items that are returned unpaid.
> B. Yes. The right of chargeback does not apply because Lyra was not the party at fault.
> C. Yes. The right of chargeback does not apply, because the teller assured Lyra the item would be paid.
> D. No. The bank breached its duty to act with ordinary care, by failing to secure payment of the cashier's check.
> E. Yes. Her bank assured her the check would be paid, so is bound to pay it.

ANALYSIS.

Truth or Consequences → Lyra deposits → Solo Savings → Meta Bank dishonors sends forged cashier's check

This fact pattern has occurred many times. A party like Truth or Consequences takes advantage of another party's lack of commercial knowledge. Lyra did not realize that when she received the money in her account, the check had not actually been paid, but rather her bank had simply advanced her the funds. If the check is not paid, the depositary bank has the right to charge back the funds advanced. Therefore, **A** is the best answer.

Chargeback applies irrespective of the customer's fault, so **B** is incorrect.

The teller simply told Lyra, "It looks authentic, as far as I can tell." That would fall short of the sort of assurances that would be binding on the bank, or representations that would be so negligent as to breach the bank's obligations of ordinary care and good faith. **C** lacks facts to support its conclusion.

D has no facts to support it. Nothing in the fact pattern suggests that the bank did not act with ordinary care. The bank does not have a duty to ensure that checks are paid. Rather, it simply has a duty to seek payment.

This reinforces the point in **C**. A bank could lose its right of chargeback by promising that Lyra could keep the funds or by promising that the check was authentic. But neither occurred here. The teller merely gave her opinion and stated it as her opinion, as opposed to an assurance by the bank. **E** is not supported by the facts.

McJohn's picks

1.	Oops	**C**
2.	Take back	**C**
3.	Race for the funds	**A**
4.	Quick service	**B**
5.	Bad rep	**C**
6.	Low-risk item	**C**
7.	Variation	**A**
8.	Advance fee fraud	**A**

16

Wrongful Dishonor

A bank that does not pay a check
Can cause a real financial wreck
Repossession, default,
Breach, discredit, tumult.
Do not dishonor less the feck.

CHAPTER OVERVIEW
A. Wrongful dishonor
B. The most common reasons banks wrongfully dishonor checks
C. Bank that wrongfully dishonors is liable to its customer (not to the unlucky presenter!) for all damages proximately caused
D. The closer
◈ McJohn's picks

Drawer/Customer → Payee/Holder → Depositary Bank → Drawee Bank
                                        presents   wrongfully refuses to pay

A drawee bank is liable for wrongful dishonor if it fails to pay a check that is properly payable. The drawee bank is not liable if it dishonors a check that was not properly payable. Wrongful dishonor liability runs to the bank's customer (who wrote the check), not to the person with the check. The liability is all damages proximately caused—which may be nothing, or may greatly exceed the amount of the check, if the wrongful dishonor causes havoc.

A. Wrongful dishonor

We have seen that a bank that pays a check by mistake may be unable to collect from its customer. A bank may also make the converse error. A bank that mistakenly does not pay a check may be liable for damages caused to its customer. Note that the bank is liable to its customer, not the unhappy holder that has the check and did not get paid. The bank did not sign the check and has no duty to the holder, but the bank has a duty to its customer to pay checks that are properly payable.

> **§ 4-402. Bank's Liability to Customer for Wrongful Dishonor; Time of Determining Insufficiency of Account**
>
> (a) Except as otherwise provided in this Article, a payor bank wrongfully dishonors an item if it dishonors an item that is properly payable, but a bank may dishonor an item that would create an overdraft unless it has agreed to pay the overdraft.

B. The most common reasons banks wrongfully dishonor checks

SF, not NSF. A bank may fail to credit its customer's account for some reason, which causes it to not pay a check, wrongly believing there are not sufficient funds ("NSF," in banking parlance). A bank may simply fail to process a wire transfer, or may deposit a check in the wrong account, or deduct payments after the mortgage is paid off, and so forth. A bank that fails to make funds available in a timely fashion when the customer deposits a check may wrongfully dishonor checks that the customer then writes on the account (i.e., failure as a depositary bank can lead to failure as a payor bank).

What if when the check is presented there is not enough money in the account to cover it, the bank decides to dishonor, but then funds come in the same day? Section 4-402(c) allows the bank to check the balance once and decide, and does not require the bank to revisit that decision.

> (c) A payor bank's determination of the customer's account balance on which a decision to dishonor for insufficiency of available funds is based may be made at any time between the time the item is received by the payor bank and the time that the payor bank returns the item or gives notice in lieu of return, and no more than one determination need be made. If, at the election of the payor bank, a subsequent balance determination is made for the purpose of reevaluating the bank's decision to dishonor the item, the account balance at that time is determinative of whether a dishonor for insufficiency of available funds is wrongful.

Failure to pay promised overdraft. Generally, a bank is not obliged to pay a check if there are not sufficient funds in the account to cover the check. But often, banks agree by contract to pay overdrafts (usually up to a certain dollar amount). If the bank unilaterally decides not to pay a check that creates an overdraft, the bank wrongfully dishonors the check (unless there is a clause in the contract allowing the bank to do so). A contract is a contract.

Freeze. A bank may wrongfully "freeze" an account, without authority. The bank may get nervous about its customer and put a "hold" on the customer's account for insufficient reasons. The checks that are then dishonored are wrongfully dishonored.

Error. Good old human (and computer) error.

Listening to the wrong person. The bank is obliged to follow its customer's instructions. Sometimes banks choose instead to follow the instructions of someone else. An officious interloper, or someone competing for funds in the account, will tell the bank not to pay a check. Only the customer has the right to stop payment. Third parties do not, and the bank obeys them at its own risk.

QUESTION 1. Mod? Over the last several years, Amiable Bank has paid overdraft checks written by its customer, Push, all in the area of $500. Push's account agreement does not provide for overdraft protection. One day, a check from Push for $20,000 is presented, while the balance is $42. Amiable Bank dishonors the check. As a result, a real estate transaction falls through for Push. Is Amiable Bank liable for wrongful dishonor?

A. No. It had no obligation to pay the check.
B. Yes. It is obliged to pay all checks authorized by its customer.
C. Yes. The parties had implicitly modified the account contract by a course of performance to include an obligation to pay overdraft checks.
D. No. A bank is never obliged to pay checks unless it signed them itself.

ANALYSIS. A bank is normally not obliged to pay a check that creates an overdraft, but the bank is obliged if it has promised in the contract to pay overdraft checks. Here, Push would argue that the parties have modified their contract by their behavior to include such an obligation. We won't go into the intricacies of contract law on modification, but here, even if there was such an implied change, it would only cover checks within the range of such behavior. Paying several $500 checks would not be taken as an implied agreement to pay a $20,000 check (and take a $20,000 risk of not getting reimbursed). The best answer is **A**.

C. Bank that wrongfully dishonors is liable to its customer (not to the unlucky presenter!) for all damages proximately caused

§ 4-402(b). A payor bank is liable to its customer for damages proximately caused by the wrongful dishonor of an item. Liability is limited to actual damages proved and may include damages for an arrest or prosecution of the customer or other consequential damages. Whether any consequential damages are proximately caused by the wrongful dishonor is a question of fact to be determined in each case.

Wrongful dishonor is different than most payment systems issues. Usually the parties are arguing about the amount of the item: whether the bank is entitled to reimbursement for a check, whether the customer is entitled to the money from a funds transfer, whether the customer can have a charge removed from a credit card bill. With wrongful dishonor, the amount of the check is not the key item. The bank left the money in the account by not paying the check. Rather, the issue is whether the bank's failure caused consequential damages. In payment systems law, banks are usually not liable for consequential damages. To encourage banks not to wrongfully fail to pay, the Uniform Commercial Code (UCC) makes them liable for consequential damages. The damages may be nothing (customer simply writes another check), but sometimes they may be big (bank's failure to pay $400 check to loan company results in repossession of vehicle, arrest of customer for "uttering" bad check, shutdown of business, pain and suffering to customer, meaning wrongful dishonor of the check leads to many thousands of dollars of liability for the bank).

QUESTION 2. Rightful dishonor.   Jackson finds a rare letter from C.S. Peirce while browsing through Swoopes Books. Jackson agrees to buy it for $1,000, a fraction of its likely price at auction. He writes a check. He knows his account has only $10 in it, but calls his bank, Nolan Bank, explains the importance of the matter, tells it to pay the check, and says that he'll deposit funds as quickly as possible. The bank responds non-committally and then dishonors the check the next day. Swoopes then refuses to let Jackson pick up the manuscript. Can Jackson recover his lost profits from Nolan Bank?

A. Yes. Nolan Bank was on notice of the possible loss and had been assured reimbursement.
B. No. Nolan Bank is not obliged to pay if there are not sufficient funds and it has not agreed to honor overdrafts.
C. Yes. Nolan Bank has a fiduciary duty toward its customer.
D. No. Nolan Bank did not sign the check. It may pay checks but is not obliged to do so.

ANALYSIS.
Jackson → Swoopes Books → Depo Bank → Nolan Bank dishonors

Not every dishonor is a wrongful dishonor, even if the customer is unhappy about it.

The drawee does not sign the check, so it has no obligation to the holder of the check. It has an obligation to its customer to pay checks that are properly payable. So, **D** misstates the drawee's obligation.

This check was not properly payable. As **B** states, a drawee is not obliged to pay if there are not sufficient funds and it has not agreed to honor overdrafts. **B** is the best answer.

Contrary to **C**, the bank does not have an additional duty to generally look out for its customer.

Contrary to **A**, the bank may refuse to pay even though its customer wants it to pay. Rather, the customer must get the bank to agree to honor an overdraft (either a general agreement in the deposit contract or a specific agreement as to that check, which the bank in this question did not make).

QUESTION 3. Do not pass go. Hat writes out a check for $50,000, to pay off the mortgage on his hotel. Hat's Bank, Community Chest Savings, does not pay the check. A clerk at Community Chest Savings had mistakenly coded the check as $500,000, and Hat's account had $80,000 in it. The mortgage holder informs Hat, who writes another check, which is duly paid. This costs Hat $20 for a reprocessing fee and $40 extra interest. Is Community Chest Savings liable for wrongful dishonor?

A. Yes, for the amount of the item, $50,000.
B. Yes, for the damages of $60.
C. No. It did not sign the check.
D. No. It did not intentionally make a wrongful dishonor.

ANALYSIS.

Hat → Lender → Depositary → Community Chest Savings dishonors

Wrongful dishonor means the bank is liable for damages proximately caused, which may be large, but which usually will be small or nonexistent.

In many cases, a wrongful dishonor will result in little or no damages. Here, Community Chest Savings wrongfully failed to pay or sign the check but caused only $60 in damages to Hat (unless Hat could show that it increased his costs of credit, or otherwise could prove damages caused by the wrongful dishonor). This is different from where the bank makes the opposite mistake, paying a check by accident. There, the bank has paid out the money and may lose that amount (unless it can get it back). With wrongful dishonor, the bank refuses to pay, and the money is still sitting in the account. So, unless there are consequential damages, the bank will have no liability. Of course, it may have other ill effects: Hat may close the account, or the bank may get a bad reputation. **B** is the best answer.

A is incorrect, because the amount of the item is not the amount of liability (unlike many cases in payment systems).

C points to an irrelevant fact. Community did not pay the check, so it has no liability *as a signer, to the person entitled to enforce the check.* Unlike someone who signs (the drawer or an indorser), the drawee bank is not liable to the holder of the check. The drawee does have a different type of obligation, however, to a different person. The bank has promised its customer to pay checks written by the customer on the account. So the bank's failure to do so makes it liable to its customer for wrongful dishonor, and **C** is incorrect.

D states the wrong standard. Section 4-402 does not require that the bank *intentionally* wrongfully dishonored. Rather, it imposes a form of strict liability. A bank that wrongfully dishonors a check is liable. No mental state is required.

QUESTION 4. Diversion—or disholder. Reading Railroad, in dire financial straits, sends a check for $350,000 to Holdsclaw Finance, to pay off a mortgage. There are sufficient funds in the account to cover the check when presented. The drawee, Timorous Bank, dishonors the check, because it hates to see money leave the account when so many other creditors have been calling to ask about Reading Railroad's financial status. Not long after, Reading Railroad's treasurer has all the funds in the account wired overseas—and disappears along with the money. Holdsclaw is left holding the check. Can Holdsclaw collect its lost $350,000 from Timorous Bank?

A. No. The check was not properly payable, because there were serious questions about Reading's financial condition.
B. No. Holdsclaw has no damages to show, because it still had the claim against Reading Railroad.
C. No. Timorous did not wrongfully dishonor the check.
D. No. Timorous has no duty to Holdsclaw.
E. It depends on whether the wrongful dishonor proximately caused the loss.

ANALYSIS.

Reading → Holdsclaw → Depositary → Timorous

This question reminds us where wrongful dishonor fits in (and does not fit in). This was a wrongful dishonor. But that was not the question posed. The question is, "Can Holdsclaw collect its lost $350,000 from Timorous Bank?" Holdsclaw was the holder of the check, entitled to collect from anyone that signed the check. Timorous did not sign the check and so has no liability to Holdsclaw. Whether Timorous's dishonor was wrongful or not does not affect Holdclaw's rights against Timorous. So, **D** is the best answer. This raises the question: What about Reading's rights against Holdsclaw?

QUESTION 5. What about Reading's rights against Holdsclaw?
Can Reading collect its lost $350,000 from Timorous Bank?

A. No. The check was not properly payable, because there were serious questions about Reading's financial condition.

B. No. Reading has no damages to show, because it still had the claim against the treasurer.

C. No. Timorous did not wrongfully dishonor the check, because a bank always may refuse to pay in its discretion.

D. No. Timorous has no duty to Holdsclaw.

E. It depends on whether the wrongful dishonor proximately caused the loss.

ANALYSIS.

Reading → Holdsclaw → Depositary → Timorous

Timorous wrongfully dishonored the check. The check was duly authorized and there was money in the account to cover it. Timorous' concern about the other creditors does not give Timorous authority to breach its obligation, so **A** is incorrect.

The bank has a valid claim against the missing treasurer, but that is worth nothing. **B** is likewise incorrect.

Timorous is liable for consequential damages proximately caused by the wrongful dishonor. The question would be whether the loss of the $350,000 was proximately caused by Timorous. The UCC does not define proximate cause, rather, leaving it to each state to apply its own law. Some courts would likely hold that there was not proximate cause here, because another party's evil act caused the act more directly (i.e., was an intervening cause). Another court might hold that Timorous' failure left the money available to tempt the treasurer and therefore proximately caused the loss. At any rate, **E** states the issue well and is the best answer.

D talks about irrelevant factors. Timorous is liable for wrongful dishonor only to its customer, not to Holdsclaw, the payee.

QUESTION 6. Chain Reaction. Augusta sends her monthly check of $2,000 to Earth Friendly Excavators, who sold her a specialized backhoe on credit. Her bank, Twin Savings, does not pay the check, owing to a careless mistake about the customer's identity. Earth Friendly immediately repossesses the backhoe, as its contract entitles it to do. That causes Augusta to miss out on her biggest job of the year, the annual repairs at Nobby Stiles Gardens. Stiles then cancels Augusta's contracts for other jobs. The dishonored check leads to $50,000 in economic losses to Augusta. Twin Savings apologizes but argues that it cannot be held accountable for the others. Can Augusta recover from Twin Savings?

A. Yes, Twin Savings is liable for all damages proximately caused by the wrongful dishonor.

B. Yes, Twin Savings is liable for the amount of the item, $2,000.

C. No. Twin Savings did not sign the check.

D. No, the chain of events was not within the control of Twin Savings.

ANALYSIS.

Augusta → Earth Friendly → Depositary → Twin Savings dishonors

Twin Savings is liable for damages caused by its wrongful dishonor. When Twin Savings dishonored the check, it set into motion a chain of events naturally flowing from nonpayment of the check: Earth Friendly repossessed the backhoe, causing Augusta to breach her contract, causing Stiles to cancel the contract. That is exactly the sort of consequential damages that customers may recover. **A** is the best answer.

B is incorrect, because wrongful dishonor liability is not measured by the amount of the item.

C is incorrect, for reasons already given.

D is incorrect. Twin Savings need not control the events; it need merely proximately cause them.

QUESTION 7. Wrongful?   Stonewall strives to keep his little restaurant afloat. He writes a check for $500 for vegetables, then goes to the bank the next day to put enough in the account to cover it. The bank had already checked the balance, however, and decided to dishonor the check. The next day, the bank dishonors the check, even though there is plenty in the account to cover the check. This causes a breach with the vegetable vendor, whose complaints lead other suppliers to change their terms of business with Stonewall. Between raised fees, called loans, and cash-on-delivery demands, the dishonor results in $5,000 in costs to Stonewall. Can Stonewall recover from the bank?

A. No. There was no wrongful dishonor.
B. Yes, but only to the extent of $500, the amount of the item.
C. No. The dishonor was wrongful but innocent.
D. Yes, for all damages proximately caused.

ANALYSIS.

Stonewall → Veggie vendor → Depo → Drawee dishonors

The bank is not obliged to pay if there are not sufficient funds in the account. The UCC permits the bank to check the account once and go by the balance:

> A payor bank's determination of the customer's account balance on which a decision to dishonor for insufficiency of available funds is based may be made at any time between the time the item is received by the payor bank and the time that the payor bank returns the item or gives notice in lieu of return, and no more than one determination need be made.

UCC § 4-402(c). So, the fact that funds subsequently came into the account does not make for wrongful dishonor. **A** is the best answer.

This may seem a little unfair to the customer. The bank could have paid the check at the same time as it checked the balance, so the customer has no basis to rely on the bank waiting the maximum time for funds to be in the account before dishonoring. More practically, a customer may agree with the bank to have overdrafts covered. Otherwise, the customer bears the risk if the customer does not get funds into the account on time.

QUESTION 8. Death before dishonor. Amis' last action in life, before a pig fatally falls on him on the way back from the mailbox, is to send a check to pay off a bar bill. The bank dishonors the check despite ample funds in the account, angering Amis' estate. His executor sues for wrongful dishonor, arguing that the untimely blow to Amis' credit reputation has cost the estate considerable funds, by making it difficult to get credit and to hire suppliers. Is the bank liable?

A. Yes. The bank is liable for wrongful dishonor.
B. No. The bank did not wrongfully dishonor the check.
C. No. A bank may always reasonably decline to pay a check.
D. Yes. A bank must always pay a check that is properly presented.

ANALYSIS. This question reminds us that there is no liability for rightful dishonor. As discussed in an earlier chapter, a bank may decline to pay checks after the customer dies (although it may also choose to pay them). So, a bank that does not pay such a check is not liable for wrongful dishonor. Nor would it be if the check was stale, or there were insufficient funds, or the check was presented by a thief, or altered, and so on. So, **A** is incorrect and **B** is the best answer.

C overstates things — the bank does not get to decide if the check is properly payable. **D** overstates things the other way. The question is not whether it was properly presented, rather whether it was properly payable.

D.   The closer

QUESTION 9. Reasonable clause? Lee, producing a film, writes a check to the caterer that feeds the cast and crew. There is plenty of money in Lee's account to cover the check. Meanwhile, a disgruntled former business partner of Lee contacts Lee's bank and tells it not to pay any more checks on the account, on the grounds that the money in the account belongs to the partner. The bank, concerned about paying money out that it will not get back, stops paying checks on the account. The angry caterer stops delivering food, as do other suppliers. Soon, production is at a halt. The movie founders, because it had to be shot during the first weeks of November. Lee has huge losses: cash, debts to investors, and loss of business reputation. The bank justifies its actions by pointing to a clause in the deposit contract: "Bank may at any time in its discretion decline to pay checks drawn on the account." Is the bank liable?

A. No. The parties have agreed that the bank may decline to pay checks.
B. No. The bank did not sign the checks, so it has no obligation to pay.
C. Yes. The clause is not effective.
D. Yes. The bank must pay all checks written on the account.

ANALYSIS. This question reminds us of § 4-103. That rule permits the parties to set a reasonable standard for the bank's duties but does not allow enforcement of a disclaimer of the duties of ordinary care or good faith. The clause in this question is an ineffective disclaimer, not an effective reasonable standard-setter. It purports to completely relieve the bank of its duty to pay checks that are properly payable. It would be closer if the clause were limited, such as allowing the bank to dishonor, where the specific check was questionable, or the bank faced unusual risks, or there were valid questions about whether the customer had authority over the funds. This one is far too broad.

C is the best answer.

 ## McJohn's picks

1.	Mod	A
2.	Rightful dishonor	B
3.	Do not pass go	B
4.	Diversion — or disholder	D
5.	What about Reading's rights against Holdsclaw?	E
6.	Chain reaction	A
7.	Wrongful?	A
8.	Death before dishonor	B
9.	Reasonable clause?	C

17

Check Payment (The Tale of the Midnight Deadline)

~

Listen my children and you shall hear
The midnight deadline, a time to revere
To avoid a loss baronial
Don't you dither like Colonial.

~

CHAPTER OVERVIEW
A. Final payment and the midnight deadline
B. How final payment occurs
C. The effects of final payment
D. When does the midnight deadline pass?
E. Today becomes tomorrow at teatime
F. The midnight deadline is extended by federal regulations
G. Branch banks
H. Return and notice of nonpayment
I. The closer
✦ McJohn's picks

With wrongful dishonor, we saw that a bank does not want to mistakenly refuse to pay a check. The bank also does not want to make the opposite mistake, to mistakenly pay a check. If the bank pays a check, it may be out the funds if the customer is not good for the funds, or the customer's signature is forged, or a stop payment is in effect, or the customer has expired, or the check is properly post-dated. This chapter deals with the following question: When a check is presented for payment, how quickly does a bank have to act if it decides not to pay the check? As we will see, the bank generally has to send the check back by midnight of the day following presentment.

Drawer → Payee → Depositary Bank presents → Drawee Bank becomes
obliged to pay
if final payment occurs

When a check is presented, the drawee bank becomes obliged to pay if "final payment" occurs. Final payment normally occurs when the drawee bank makes the funds available, then does not dishonor effectively before its midnight deadline (as extended by some federal regulations). So if the drawee bank does not wish to pay a check (NSF, forged drawer's signature, stop payment, etc.), the bank must act in time or is stuck with the obligation to pay. Unless it can get reimbursement from the customer or can recover the funds from the presenting bank (for breach of presentment warranty if there is an alteration or forged indorsement) or from someone else (through subrogation, or for mistake), the drawee bank will be out of luck.

The midnight deadline passes at midnight the day after presentment. The bank may have a policy stating that items presented after 2 p.m. are treated as presented the following day, giving it more time to act. In addition, branch banks are treated as separate banks, so delivery to one branch does not set the clock ticking for payment by another branch.

Final payment also occurs if the drawee bank pays the check in cash or irrevocably makes the funds available. So a bank that pays the check over the counter in cash has no time to revoke that payment.

A.   Final payment and the midnight deadline

World Commodities → Shelly International → First National Bank → Colonial Bank
Drawer, kiter   Payee, confederate   Innocent depository   Too-slow drawee

The *Colonial Bank* case gives a nice example of what's at stake with the midnight deadline. See First Nat'l Bank in Harvey v. Colonial Bank, 898 F. Supp. 1220 (N.D. Ill. 1995). Colonial Bank was presented with some $1.5 million in checks written by its customer, World Commodities. The next day, before Colonial Bank had decided whether to pay the checks, a number of checks that World Commodities had deposited were returned unpaid. There was then not enough money in the account to cover the checks written by World Commodities. If Colonial Bank paid the $1.5 million in checks, World Commodities was obliged to reimburse it—but might not have the money. If Colonial Bank dishonored the checks, World Commodities (who seemed to be a customer with lots of business for Colonial Bank) would be disappointed, and might even sue if it could come up with a theory for wrongful dishonor. World Commodities' comptroller and attorney both assured Colonial Bank that funds would soon be on the way. Colonial Bank decided to sleep on it.

The next day, Colonial Bank decided not to pay the checks and mailed them back, but it was too late. The midnight deadline had passed. As discussed below, if a check is presented and the drawee bank does not dishonor before the midnight deadline, the bank becomes obliged to pay the check. So, banks must affirmatively act to avoid getting stuck with checks they do not want to pay. If the checks were presented on a Tuesday, Colonial Bank could avoid liability by sending them back before midnight Wednesday (or even by sending them by courier on Thursday, as discussed below with the federal regulations that extend the midnight deadline). Here, Colonial Bank sat on its hands too long. It was obliged to pay the checks, even knowing there were not funds on deposit to cover the checks. Colonial Bank had a right to reimbursement from its customer, World Commodities. As it turned out, though, World Commodities was running a check-kiting scheme and had no funds to get.

Wobbly → Payee → Depositary Bank → Hamlet Bank

Wobbly writes a check to Payee, who deposits it with Depositary Bank, who presents it to Hamlet Bank, the drawee.

"Final payment" refers to the fact that the drawee bank has to make up its mind. When a check is presented, under the *pay or return rule*, on the first day the bank must pay, make a provisional settlement, or return the item. (Banks routinely make a provisional settlement, so we will not discuss pay or return in detail.) The drawee bank then has until the midnight deadline (as extended by some federal regulations) to make up its mind. It must send back the check and dishonor it, or it becomes obliged to pay it. This is another example of the fact that commercial law is an activity that really favors those who know the rules of the game.

Note that final payment occurs irrespective of whether the check is properly payable. A bank that waits too long must pay, even if there are not sufficient funds to cover it; if the check is forged or stolen, or there is a stop payment or post-dating in effect; or if there is any other valid reason not to pay. If the problem breaches the presentment warranty (i.e., it is a stolen or altered check), then the bank may be able to put the loss back on the presenter. The presentment warranty does not, however, cover other reasons for nonpayment. The presenter (and earlier transferors, who make the presentment warranty as well) does not warrant such matters as to whether there are funds to cover the check or whether a stop payment order is in effect.

B.   How final payment occurs

Section 4-215 sets out the several ways that final payment can occur.

§ 4-215. Final Payment of Item by Payor Bank; When Provisional Debits and Credits Become Final; When Certain Credits Become Available for Withdrawal.
(a) An item is finally paid by a payor bank when the bank has first done any of the following:
(1) paid the item in cash;

(2) settled for the item without having a right to revoke the settlement under statute, clearing-house rule, or agreement; or

(3) made a provisional settlement for the item and failed to revoke
the settlement in the time and manner permitted by statute, clearing-
house rule, or agreement.

(b) If provisional settlement for an item does not become final, the item
is not finally paid.

In other words, final payment can occur as follows:

1. If the check is presented and the drawee bank pays it in cash, then final
   payment has occurred.
2. If the check is presented and the drawee bank settles unprovision-
   ally (that is, puts the money in an account without a right to revoke),
   then final payment has occurred. In practice, this one rarely (if ever)
   occurs. Banks almost always say, "I'll put the money in the account
   provisionally."
3. If the check is presented and the drawee bank does not dishonor the
   check by the midnight deadline, then final payment has occurred.
   Usually this means that the bank has made a provisional settlement
   and does not revoke it by the midnight deadline.

Note that "final payment" is a misleading term. Final payment occurs not necessarily when the bank actually pays cash or otherwise pays the check, but
rather when the bank loses its ability to dishonor the check. If final payment
occurs, the bank becomes obliged to pay the check.

C.   The effects of final payment

When final payment occurs, several results are triggered:

1. The drawee bank can no longer dishonor the check. It's accountable for
   the check, meaning it has to pay the check.
2. If the check is properly payable, the bank has a right to reimbursement
   from its customer. With most checks, final payment occurs and the bank
   is reimbursed by its customer. Only if there is a problem (e.g., no funds
   in the account) will final payment become an issue, because then the
   bank must avoid final payment to avoid being stuck with a loss. There
   may be a problem as to whether the check is properly payable or not. If
   the check is properly payable, but there are no funds in the customer's
   account and none forthcoming from the customer, then the bank may
   be unable to get reimbursed. If the check is not properly payable, then
   the bank is not entitled to reimbursement from the customer.
3. Because the drawee bank is obliged to pay the check, it gets a presentment warranty from the person who presented it and from previous

people who transferred the check. If the check is stolen or altered, the bank is entitled to recover for breach of presentment warranty from the presenting bank. If, rather than paying another bank, the bank paid over the counter, then it may be difficult to find the presenter. The presentment warranty only covers forged indorsements and alterations. For other problems (NSF, stopped payment, effective post-dating, etc.), the drawee bank may be stuck.

4. The third result is a little more subtle. If the drawee bank becomes obliged to pay the check, then the depositary bank is entitled to get the money from drawee bank. Remember, the check was deposited at the depositary bank. The depositary bank in effect said to its customer, "Okay, here's the money, but if this isn't paid I'm going to take the money right back out of your account." The depositary bank now loses that right of chargeback. Because the drawee bank is obliged to pay the check and give the money to the depositary bank, the depositary bank then in turn is obliged to give the money to its customer. If the depositary bank has made the money provisionally available to its customer, then that money now becomes unconditional—the customer gets to keep the money.

D.   When does the midnight deadline pass?

The midnight deadline is defined as "midnight on its next banking day following the banking day on which it receives the relevant item." UCC § 4-104(10). If the bank gets the check on a Tuesday, the midnight deadline occurs at midnight on Wednesday. Only banking days count. If the bank does not get the check on a banking day (i.e., not "the part of a day on which a bank is open to the public for carrying on substantially all of its banking functions," from § 4-104(3)), the clock will not start running until the next banking day. So, if the bank gets the check on a Saturday (or after the close of business Friday) and is closed on Saturday and Sunday, the clock will start running on Monday and the midnight deadline will occur Tuesday at midnight.

Under the UCC, which is state law, if the check is presented today, payor bank has until its midnight deadline to send it back.

> **§ 4-301. Deferred Posting; Recovery of Payment by Return of Items;**
> **Time of Dishonor; Return of Items by Payor Bank**
>
> (a) If a payor bank settles for a demand item other than a documentary draft presented otherwise than for immediate payment over the counter before midnight of the banking day of receipt, the payor bank may revoke the settlement and recover the settlement if, before it has made final payment and before its midnight deadline, it

(1) returns the item;

(2) returns an image of the item, if the party to which the return is made has entered into an agreement to accept an image as a return of the item; and the image is returned in accordance with that agreement; and

(3) sends a record providing notice of dishonor or nonpayment if the item is unavailable for return.

To meet the midnight deadline, the bank need only send it by that time. UCC § 4-301(d). The item need not arrive back before the midnight deadline.

E.   Tomorrow becomes today at teatime

§ 4-108. Time of Receipt of Items

(a) For the purpose of allowing time to process items, prove balances, and make the necessary entries on its books to determine its position for the day, a bank may fix an afternoon hour of 2 P.M. or later as a cutoff hour for the handling of money and items and the making of entries on its books.

(b) An item or deposit of money received on any day after a cutoff hour so fixed or after the close of the banking day may be treated as being received at the opening of the next banking day.

If an item is presented today after 2 p.m., a bank may treat it as being presented tomorrow. The midnight deadline is relatively tight, so the UCC says that a bank may make a policy that items presented after 2 p.m. or later are treated as presented the next day. That gives the bank one more day to meet its midnight deadline. Therefore, today may not be until tomorrow. Banks may apply this rule to other deadlines for dealing with checks.

F.   The midnight deadline is extended by federal regulations

The UCC rule requires the payor bank to decide relatively quickly whether it's going to pay the check. It must send the check back before midnight the following banking day. It doesn't, however, require the bank to communicate that decision very quickly. The bank must *send* the check back by midnight tomorrow. They can (and banks often did, less so now for reasons we will see) send it via U.S. mail. They may on, say, Thursday decide not to pay a check and drop it in the mail. Then a week later, it arrives back at the other bank. Now the other bank says, "Oh, okay, that check that we sent out a week ago, it's not going to be paid." They communicate that to their customer. So, the rule put a tough deadline on the drawee bank but did not give much benefit to the depositary bank, because the news could take a long time in coming.

The Federal Reserve then decided that it could help both banks (sometimes a bank acts as a depositary bank and sometimes it acts as a drawee bank). The Federal Reserve issued regulations that give a little bit more time to the payor bank, provided it uses a means of communication that get the news through a little quicker.

Here's how it works: Suppose the check is presented on a Wednesday. The next day the check is still in the hands of the payor bank. To meet the midnight deadline under the UCC, it has to send it back by midnight on Thursday. However, under the federal regulations the bank has two more options, added to encourage the bank not just to send the check, but to see that the check is delivered quickly: The bank can get up on Friday and actually deliver the check to the other bank — which makes sense, because why say you'll only meet the deadline by dropping it in the mail, even though it may not show up for another week, if you can get up the next day and messenger it over? — Alternatively, the bank can send back the check via "highly expeditious means." In other words, on Friday, send the check via overnight delivery for arrival Saturday morning.

G.   Branch banks

§ 4-107. **Separate Office of Bank**
    A branch or separate office of a bank is a separate bank for the purpose of computing the time within which and determining the place at or to which action may be taken or notice or orders must be given under this Article and under Article 3.

A check, drawn on Bank of America's branch in Woburn, is deposited in a branch in Saugus. Those are two separate banks for the purposes of the midnight deadline. It takes time to get pieces of paper from one branch to another. So, the clock does not start running until the relevant branch receives that piece of paper.

H.   Return and notice of nonpayment

If a bank decides to dishonor a check, to do so effectively it has to meet the midnight deadline. If it does not meet that deadline, it has to pay the check. In addition to that, under federal banking regulations, it has to send the check back. That is called a "return requirement." It basically has to get the check back to the other bank within two days for a local bank, or four days for a non-local bank. In addition to that, if the check is for more than $2,500, it has to get an actual notice of dishonor to the other bank by the second business day after receipt. In practice, banks use electronic messaging systems to get those messages around.

There's a key difference between the midnight deadline and the return and notice of nonpayment rules. If the bank misses the midnight deadline, the bank must pay the check. If the bank instead does not comply with the return and notice of nonpayment rules, it is liable for actual damages. Those damages are very likely to be zero, though, because the odds are that the other bank doesn't have any damages. The presenting bank has the right of chargeback and can get the money from its customer. Only if the depositary bank could show that the failure to give timely notice resulted in a loss of funds would there be damages.

QUESTION 1. After midnight. Layla gets her royalty check from Peerless Music. She deposits it with Blues Bank, who presents it to the drawee bank, Sylvan Savings, on Monday morning. Peerless does not have enough in the account to cover the check, but Sylvan Savings decides to see if funds come in to cover the check. On Wednesday, the account is still bare, so Sylvan Savings mails the check back. Layla demands the money. Is she entitled?

A. No. Sylvan Savings is not obliged to pay a check if there are not sufficient funds.
B. No. Layla did not present the check to Sylvan Savings, so she has no rights against it.
C. No. Sylvan Savings did not sign the check, so it is not liable on the check.
D. Yes. Sylvan Savings must pay due to its delay. Blues Bank is obliged to give the money to Layla.

ANALYSIS.
Peerless → Layla → Blues Bank → Sylvan Savings

If final payment occurs, the presenter is entitled to the money—and the person that deposited the check is likewise entitled to the money. This is true whether there are funds in the account or not. When the check is presented, Sylvan Savings is not obliged to pay it. To avoid becoming obliged, however, Sylvan Savings must dishonor the check in timely fashion. Because Sylvan Savings failed to do so, final payment occurred, meaning Sylvan became obliged to pay Blues Bank and Blues Bank became obliged to give the money to Layla. So, **D** is the best answer. Layla's rights are against Blues Bank, the bank she deposited the check with, so **B** is incorrect.

C emphasizes the effect of the midnight deadline. Sylvan Savings did not sign the check, so it was not obliged to pay the presenter. But if Sylvan Savings fails to send the check back by the midnight deadline, it becomes obliged to pay.

This is true even if there are not funds to cover the check, **A** not withstanding.

QUESTION 2. **Midnight at the oasis.**   In the previous question, Sylvan Savings had to pay because it waited too long to mail the check back. What result if, instead of mailing the check on Wednesday, Sylvan had sent it back via courier?

A. No change. Wednesday is still too late, because it would be after the midnight deadline.
B. No change. The check must always be returned via U.S. mail.
C. Sylvan Savings would not be liable.
D. Sylvan Savings would not be liable, provided it can show that there was not money in the account to cover the check on Wednesday.

ANALYSIS.   This question illustrates the extra time the federal regulations give to drawee banks. The UCC midnight deadline says that to dishonor, the drawee bank must send the check back no later than midnight the day after presentment. The federal regulations extend this by saying that the drawee bank may send it back up to two days after presentment, provided it uses the most expeditious means. So, a courier on Wednesday would be timely. Therefore, **C** is the best answer.

QUESTION 3. **Midnight rambler.**   Angie gives Mick a big fat check for his birthday. Mick deposits it with Rolling Bank on Monday morning. Rolling Bank presents it to Tumbling Bank on Tuesday. Tumbling Bank decides not to pay the check (because Angie has zero in her account), and drops it in the mail Wednesday evening. The check arrives in Rolling Bank's mailbox Monday afternoon. Rolling Bank mails it back to Mick, who receives it on Thursday. Mick complains that ten days is much too long and that he is entitled to the money. Is he?

A. Yes. Rolling Bank must pay him, because it did not meet the midnight deadine.
B. Yes. Tumbling Bank failed to meet the midnight deadline, so it must pay the check, and Rolling Bank then must give the money to Mick.
C. No. Tumbling Bank met the midnight deadline.
D. No. Even if Tumbling Bank was obliged to pay, there was a breach of presentment warranty, because no money was in the account.

ANALYSIS.
Angie → Mick → Rolling Bank presents Tuesday → Tumbling Bank mails
Wednesday

The midnight deadline governs only the interaction between the presenter and the drawee bank. Tumbling Bank dishonored the check in a timely fashion, by dropping it in the mail before midnight of the day after presentment.

So, even if it took ten days for Mick to get the news, that does not matter. **C** is the best answer.

Rolling Bank is not subject to the final payment rule. Rolling Bank does have the obligation to act with ordinary care, but it met that here by forwarding the check in a timely fashion.

Note that this does involve possible breach of the return and notice rules, but likely damages could not be sufficiently shown.

QUESTION 4. Midnight robbery. Peerless mails a check to Barack for $2,008. Cousin Dick steals the check from the mailbox, forges Barack's indorsement, and deposits it with Hampshire Bank. Hampshire Bank gives the money to Cousin Dick and presents the check one chilly Tuesday morning to the drawee bank, Change Bank. Distracted employees ignore the check for a week. Change Bank then contacts Hampshire Bank, stating that it will not pay the check. Hampshire Bank, realizing that Cousin Dick has skipped town, demands the money. Is Change Bank obliged to pay?

A. No. Final payment occurs only for valid checks.
B. No. Final payment occurred, but Change Bank has a counterclaim for breach of presentment warranty.
C. Yes. If Change Bank wishes to avoid liability, it must dishonor in timely fashion.
D. Yes. The drawee bank is obliged to pay whomever has the check.

ANALYSIS.

Peerless → Barack → Cousin Dick steals → Hampshire Bank → Change Bank

Final payment occurred when Change Bank failed to dishonor before the midnight deadline, so they were obliged to pay. Final payment does not, however, affect presentment warranty liability. Hampshire Bank presented a stolen check, so it breached the presentment warranty. That would negate the obligation of Change Bank to pay. Technically, Change Bank would be liable for the amount of the check, but Hampshire Bank would be liable in return for the same amount for breach of presentment warranty. So, final payment is not always the last word, and **B** is the best answer.

A bank that is obliged to pay a check because final payment has occurred can seek to recover

- from its customer, if the check is properly payable (indeed, this is normally what occurs);
- for breach of presentment warranty if the check is stolen or altered;
- under subrogation, if someone is getting unjust enrichment; and
- under mistake (§ 3-418; but that does not apply very often, because it cannot be used against one that, in good faith, took the instrument for value or changed position in reliance on the payment).

> **QUESTION 5. Midnight rider.**   Revere, a silversmith, gets a check in the mail for a set of mugs. Revere deposits the check with Minuteman Bank, who presents it on Tuesday just before midnight to the drawee bank, Redcoat Bank. Wednesday morning, the fickle customer contacts Redcoat Bank and stops payment. Redcoat Bank ponders whether to pay the check. And ponders . . . and ponders. . . . Finally, on Thursday of the following week, Redcoat Bank sends the check back via courier. Minuteman Bank responds that it does not want the check; it wants the money. Must Redcoat Bank pay the check?
>
> A. No. Payment was effectively stopped.
> B. No. Minutemen Bank breached the presentment warranty.
> C. Yes. Redcoat Bank waited too long to dishonor the check.
> D. Yes. Redcoat Bank must pay the check if the proper person presents it.

ANALYSIS.

Customer → Revere → Minuteman Bank presents Tuesday p.m. → Redcoat
Bank dithers

Redcoat Bank waited too long before dishonoring the check. A stop payment order had been issued, but that affects only the relationship between Redcoat Bank and Customer. It does not affect the rights of Minuteman Bank to payment on the check. Redcoat Bank could have dishonored, but it failed to do so in timely fashion. So, Redcoat Bank is obliged to pay.

Like the preceding question, the check was not properly payable. But unlike the preceding question (where a stolen check was presented), there is no breach of the presentment warranty. Minuteman Bank was the party entitled to enforce the instrument and the check had not been altered, so the presentment warranty was not breached. Minuteman Bank does not warrant that no stop payment is in effect. So, Redcoat Bank must pay, even though it is not entitled to reimbursement from Customer. (Although, it's possible that Redcoat Bank could use subrogation against Customer, or Revere—see the Properly Payable chapter.) **C** is the best answer.

> **QUESTION 6. Midnight in the garden of good and evil.**
> Franklin is running a check-kiting scheme. He opens up accounts at Harmonium Bank and at Almanac Bank. Franklin writes checks on the Harmonium Bank account and deposits them with Almanac Bank, and vice versa, creating balances out of thin air. He deposits a $1 million check with Harmonium Bank drawn on Almanac Bank. Harmonium Bank presents the check on Monday evening to Almanac Bank. Almanac Bank sees that there is not enough in the account to pay the check. Almanac Bank calls Franklin on Tuesday, who assures them the

funds will arrive via wire transfer on Wednesday. Thursday comes and the funds are still not there, so Almanac Bank mails the check back. In the meantime, Harmonium Bank has made the funds available to Franklin, who quickly withdrew them and disappeared. Harmonium Bank demands the money from Almanac Bank. Must Almanac Bank pay?

A. No. The check was not properly payable, for lack of funds.

B. No. The check was fraudulent, so Harmonium Bank need not pay.

C. No. The midnight deadline rule is a consumer protection rule. So at most, Almanac Bank need only pay $5,000.

D. No. Franklin was not entitled to the money, so his bank, Harmonium Bank, cannot be entitled to the money.

E. Yes. Harmonium Bank missed the midnight deadline.

ANALYSIS.

Franklin → Franklin as payee → Harmonium Bank → Almanac Bank mails
                                          presents Mon. p.m.   Thurs.

The check was not properly payable for lack of funds. The check was part of a fraudulent scheme. The funds availability rules apply only up to $5,000 in deposits per day; however, all that is irrelevant to the issue of whether Almanac Bank is obliged to pay the check to Harmonium Bank.

Harmonium Bank presented it on Monday evening. That would be deemed presentment on Tuesday. Almanac Bank could dishonor by mailing it back Wednesday or sending it via courier as late as Friday. Almanac Bank mailed it Thursday, however, meeting neither form of the midnight deadline (too late via mail, and not sent via highly expeditious means). So, Almanac Bank is stuck with it.

Even though final payment occurred, that would not prevent presentment warranty liability. Harmonium Bank did not breach the presentment warranty; Harmonium bank was the party entitled to enforce the instrument, and the check had not been altered. **E** is the best answer.

I.   The closer

QUESTION 7. Once upon a midnight dreary, while I pondered, weak and weary. Alex ambles into Tinky Bank with her paycheck, drawn on Tinky Bank by Phonic Sounds. Tinky Bank pays the check over the counter. That afternoon, Tinky Bank finds that Phonic Sounds has no funds to cover the check, and likely never will. Can Tinky Bank prevent final payment by sending the check back to Alex?

A. Yes. The drawee bank has until midnight the day after presentment to send the check back (or can even courier it back the next day).

B. Yes. Final payment did not occur because it was a wrongful honor of a check that was not properly payable.

C. No, but Alex breached the presentment warranty by presenting a worthless check.

D. No. Final payment occurred when the check was paid in cash over the counter.

ANALYSIS.

Phonic Sounds → Alex → Tinky Bank
issues   presents   pays over counter

Final Payment (making bank obliged to pay) can occur three ways, under UCC § 4-215:

(a) An item is finally paid by a payor bank when the bank has first done any of the following:

(1) paid the item in cash;

(2) settled for the item without having a right to revoke the settlement under statute, clearing-house rule, or agreement; or

(3) made a provisional settlement for the item and failed to revoke the settlement in the time and manner permitted by statute, clearing-house rule, or agreement.

Final payment normally occurs under the third provision, when the drawee bank, having given provisional credit for a check, fails to revoke by its midnight deadline (as extended by federal regulations). Final payment, however, can also occur if the drawee bank pays the item in cash, per subsection (a)(1). Tinky Bank paid the item in cash, so final payment occurred.

A bank that becomes obliged to pay can enforce any breach of the presentment warranty. Recall, however, that the presentment warranty will generally cover only stolen checks or altered checks. Alex presented a check with neither problem. Tinky Bank was not obliged to pay it, but it did. Alex did not breach the presentment warranty, so Tinky Bank is not entitled to its money back, contrary to **C**. The correct answer is **D**.

There is no such thing as "wrongful honor," contrary to **B**. Rather, if a bank mistakenly pays a check, the check is still paid. The bank then must try to find a theory, such as breach of presentment warranty or subrogation, that will enable it to recover the funds. Neither is applicable here.

 McJohn's picks

1. After midnight   **D**
2. Midnight at the oasis   **C**

3. Midnight rambler   **C**
4. Midnight robbery   **B**
5. Midnight rider   **C**
6. Midnight in the garden of good and evil   **E**
7. Once upon a midnight dreary, while I pondered weak and weary   **D**

18

Truncation and Electronic Processing of Checks

~

I wandered lonely like a check
With float for banks through tubes pneumatic.
Now I go in form electric—
Faster, if not acrobatic.

~

Drawer → Payee → Depository Bank → presents directly or through others, like clearinghouses or Federal Reserve → Drawee

T his chapter discusses several ways that law and practice have speeded up the check collection process.

A.   Odyssey of a check

In days of yore, all checks physically traveled around the country, from drawer to payee to depositary bank, through various intermediaries to drawee bank for payment, and then back to drawer with the checking statement. Some still follow this path.

Drawer → Payee → Depositary Bank → perhaps via Federal Reserve → Drawee Bank,
returns to Drawer
or other clearinghouse

Once upon a time, checks were processed by sending them around the country. I wrote a check on my Seattle bank and mailed it across the country to my supplier in Boston. She might deposit it in her account in Boston, who would likely send it over to the Boston Federal Reserve. In that big building, they zoomed checks around in little containers through pneumatic tubes, to be sorted and allocated. The sorted checks might get packed up and sent off to another clearinghouse or to other Federal Reserve branches across the country, and then from there processed until they wind up at the Seattle bank, which would then look at the check and decide whether to pay it or not.

If the Seattle bank decided to pay the check, it would give the funds to the Boston bank through the Federal Reserve. (More accurately, the Seattle bank would simply not revoke the provisional credit that had already been made.) The check itself would be sorted and saved and mailed out with the customer's monthly statement.

The checking system relied on pieces of paper being handled and mailed several times during their lifetime. But that is no longer necessary. Not that a national network of pneumatic tubes is in place; rather, banks and their customers can do all of the same actions electronically, faster and cheaper.

This chapter discusses several ways law and practice have changed to speed things up.[1] There are benefits for all parties to speed up the check collection process. Customers making deposits get their money faster; depositary banks, who are subject to the funds availability rules, can find out more quickly if a check has been paid (and have less exposure from advancing funds on checks deposited, while waiting to see if the check is paid); drawee banks can get presentment in electronic form, with lower cost in handling.

There are costs to parties as well, however. Customers can no longer write checks against empty accounts, with the assumption that they have several

---

1. I follow the thoughtful organization of the issues in James Brooks, *Examples and Explanations: Payment Systems* (Third Edition, Aspen Publishers, 2007).

days to deposit funds to cover the check. (Although they can get overdraft protection, where the bank agrees for a fee to pay checks despite insufficient funds on deposit.) A check may be presented for payment electronically on the same day it is received by the payee. Banks may have less "float," or interest-free use, of their customers' funds because checks no longer lumber slowly around the country. Loss of the paper check may be difficult for some consumers to adjust to. In cases of forgery, it may make investigating and proving the case more difficult.

B.   Drawee → drawer: truncation

The drawee bank may retain the checks paid and send back information (e.g., images of the front and back of the check, or just the check number, amount, and date paid) to the drawer.

Drawee banks, if they send a monthly statement or make the information otherwise available, now need not send back the paid check itself, but rather may simply send information about checks paid, such as images of the checks. Under Uniform Commercial Code (UCC) § 4-406:

> (a) A bank that sends or makes available to a customer a statement of account showing payment of items for the account shall either return or make available to the customer the items paid or provide information in the statement of account sufficient to allow the customer reasonably to identify the items paid. The statement of account provides sufficient information if the item is described by item number, amount, and date of payment.
>
> (b) If the items are not returned to the customer, the person retaining the items shall either retain the items or, if the items are destroyed, maintain the capacity to furnish legible copies of the items until the expiration of seven years after receipt of the items. A customer may request an item from the bank that paid the item, and that bank must provide in a reasonable time either the item or, if the item has been destroyed or is not otherwise obtainable, a legible copy of the item.

Under the present version of UCC § 4-406, payor banks are now allowed to truncate the process. The Seattle bank now no longer has to mail that check back to their customer — so that saves them some processing. They don't have to keep track of that piece of paper, get it in an envelope, and send it to their customer. The bank has to either return the check to the customer, or else send a statement to the customer that reasonably identifies the item paid: the number of the check, the amount of the check, and the date of payment.

During the process of revising UCC Articles 3 and 4, consumer advocates said that people are used to getting their checks back with their statements and that shifting to simply getting information about the check posed risks for consumers. In particular, the information that the bank is required to give the consumer is pretty bare bones: the number of the check, the amount, and the date of payment. A consumer, if they get the checks back, can flip through the checks and see if any of them look suspicious or if there's one they didn't sign. Numbers alone, some said, are insufficient. You can't look through the statement and see who was paid on the checks (as you can with a credit card statement); all you have is a list of the amounts. Unless a consumer has a perfect memory, they are not going to remember all of the exact dollar amounts of the checks that they wrote.

In theory, if the consumer notes their checks in their checkbook's register, they can then compare the numbers and amounts listed there to the checks listed on their bank statement and catch any discrepancy—that is, if the consumer is perfect in keeping their check register. So, because many consumers don't keep perfect check registers, or perhaps any check register at all, consumer advocates on one side said that truncation would be dangerous for consumers. Banks of course argued, "Because we don't have to send checks back to customers, it will save us money. That, in turn, will save consumers money because the lower our costs are, the lower our costs can be for providing checking accounts."

The number one priority for a state legislature from year to year isn't revising the UCC. Legislators may understand that the UCC helps commerce, but it's not a pressing political issue. In many states, the entire revision of UCC Articles 3 and 4 was stymied because of debate about the truncation provision. In some states, it eventually got through only after a non-uniform provision was added. In Massachusetts, for example, the bank must return checks on request without a fee.

QUESTION 1. Just the facts.   When Rembrandt Bank sends its customer a monthly checking account statement, it sends this info about each check paid: the number of the check, the amount paid, and the date paid. Rembrandt Bank does not send the checks back or identify the payee or the presenting bank. Is that sufficient to meet its obligations under the UCC?

A. Yes. That is all the UCC requires.
B. No. The bank must send the checks back, so the customer can see if they were paid to the right person, and use them as proof of payment (for the IRS, suppliers, etc.).
C. No. The bank must send back either the checks or images of the checks.
D. The bank need send nothing at all. The customer has a record of checks written in the customer's checkbook.

ANALYSIS.   As **A** correctly puts it, that is all the UCC requires: "The statement of account provides sufficient information if the item is described by item number, amount, and date of payment."

So why do banks normally send more information? Banks now usually send back the checks themselves or images of the checks. Some banks send back the checks themselves because the customers prefer that—and providing checking services is a competitive industry. As discussed later, sometimes the bank does not get the check itself but receives only an image of the check (or even just the identifying information about the check, for some electronic presentments). In that case, the bank will usually send along the information that it has.

B is incorrect because the UCC does not require the bank to send the checks, even though banks often do. **B** does list some reasons why customers might like to have the checks. Section 4-406 deals with this by requiring banks to retain the checks, or copies, for seven years, and, on a customer's request, provide the check or a legible copy.

C likewise overstates the UCC's rule. Name, rank, and serial number are sufficient—actually, date of payment, amount, and item number.

D errs in the opposite direction. That would be a poor rule. The issue is not telling the customer what checks the customer wrote; the issue is what checks were paid. The bank is in the better position to provide information that would indicate whether it paid checks the customer did not write, or has not paid checks the customer did write, or paid the wrong amount on checks the customer wrote that were altered, or paid the same check twice (you can think up more possibilities—they all happen).

QUESTION 2. Copy me on that. One of Rembrandt Bank's customers has a dispute with his landlord, who claims not to have received the rent for March or April. The customer provides the checking statement showing that checks for the amount of the rent were paid near the beginning of each month. The landlord counters that the checks could have been cashed by anybody. Customer requests the check from Rembrandt Bank, who points to § 4-406(a), which requires the statement to show only date of payment, amount, and check number. Is Rembrandt Bank required to do more?

A. No. Rembrandt Bank has met its obligations to provide information.
B. Yes. On request, Rembrandt Bank must provide the check.
C. Yes. On request, Rembrandt Bank must provide the check or a legible copy.
D. No. Rembrandt Bank is not a party to the dispute between Customer and Landlord.
E. Yes. Rembrandt Bank must return all paid checks to customer.

ANALYSIS. The question emphasizes the balance struck when allowing truncation. Banks may use truncation but must practice retention:

> § 4-406(b). If the items are not returned to the customer, the person retaining the items shall either retain the items or, if the items are destroyed, maintain

the capacity to furnish legible copies of the items until the expiration of seven years after receipt of the items. A customer may request an item from the bank that paid the item, and that bank must provide in a reasonable time either the item or, if the item has been destroyed or is not otherwise obtainable, a legible copy of the item.

So Rembrandt Bank must provide the check or a legible copy of the check. So **C** is the best answer.

Rembrandt Bank's duties do not end with providing the information in the statement. Rather, Rembrandt Bank also has duties to retain checks (or copies) and to provide them on request. So **A** is incorrect.

Rembrandt Bank need not return the checks with the statement, so **E** is not correct. Rembrandt Bank also need not retain the checks themselves, so **B** is not correct. Customer is entitled only to a copy of the check—whether or not that will be sufficient to convince Landlord (or a court, if there is litigation) may depend on making them aware of the state of the law with respect to checks.

D is also incorrect, because Rembrandt Bank has a duty to Customer, whether Rembrandt Bank is a party to the dispute or not.

C.   Collecting bank→drawee bank

1. *Electronic presentment*

Banks may agree to do presentment electronically.

Suppose that every day Banco Chicago presents hundreds of checks drawn on Banc New York. These are all checks deposited by Banco Chicago's customers, written by customers of Banc New York. Similarly, Banc New York presents hundreds of checks to Banco Chicago. The two banks could send a lot of checks back and forth every day. They could save time by agreeing to put all the information in electronic form: "That's easy, we can scan the account number and bank routing number from the check, and have someone encode the amount. On many commercial checks, the drawer encodes the amount. Then we'll just send that electronic info and you can decide whether to pay or not. Actually, your computers can do that for you, by checking the account balance, and making sure no stop payment or other irregularity is in effect. We'll send the checks themselves along later (or perhaps just pictures of them, front and back, as we agree)." This is an agreement to do electronic presentment. Such agreements are very common, because they considerably reduce costs for both banks. Of course, the banks should be careful to specify in the contract their respective rights and responsibilities.

2. *Check 21*

A federal statute now authorizes the depository bank (or other parties), to make an image of both sides of the check, transmit it electronically, print it out, and present a "substitute check," which is treated as the legal equivalent of the original check.

Banco Chicago might like to do electronic presentment with all the checks it handles, but it would be tricky to get a contract in place with every bank in the country. The United States has lots of banks, whereas in many countries there may be just a few banks, with branches in every town. The plethora of banks in the United States is a legacy of banking regulation laws, which once practically required every town to have its own bank. Those regulations are gone and banks have consolidated, but they are still numerous. So, it would be hard for Banco Chicago to get an agreement with every bank in the country to do electronic presentment.

Congress stepped in to facilitate things with Check 21, a federal statute. If you revise the UCC, you have to go through the whole UCC revision process, and then you have to get it through 50 state legislatures. A more efficient way to change payment law is to go through one legislature, the federal legislature.

Check 21 does not require banks to accept electronic presentment. There are still lots of little banks that do not have very sophisticated technology and that might not like to accept electronic presentment. Congress did not choose to impose a requirement on them. In addition, mandating that banks accept electronic presentment would require someone to come up with technical standards. What if Bank Silicon Valley sent its presented checks in a format that Banco Chicago could not read? Check 21 allows electronic transmission but retains a low-tech standard for presentation: a piece of paper that looks like a check.

3. *Substitute checks*

Check 21 allows the use of substitute checks. The substitute check must look and function like the original:

> Substitute check. The term "substitute check" means a paper reproduction of the original check that—
> (A) contains an image of the front and back of the original check;
> (B) bears a MICR line containing all the information appearing on the MICR line of the original check, except as provided under generally applicable industry standards for substitute checks to facilitate the processing of substitute checks;
> (C) conforms, in paper stock, dimension, and otherwise, with generally applicable industry standards for substitute checks; and
> (D) is suitable for automated processing in the same manner as the original check.

12 U.S.C. § 5002(16).

Check 21 allows the bank in Boston, instead of mailing the check across the country, to take a picture of the check in Boston, transmit a file containing that image across the country, print out a picture of the check at the other end—including the MICR (Magnetic Ink Character Recognition) info—and present that substitute check for payment. So it speeds things up (by allowing electronic files rather than pieces of paper to be transported) but keeps presentment simple (by allowing presentment of a piece of paper, but not an electronic file). Banks can choose to do electronic presentment, and many do so choose. They don't have to, however.

A substitute check is the legal equivalent of the original check.

> (b) Legal equivalence. A substitute check shall be the legal equivalent of the original check for all purposes, including any provision of any Federal or State law, and for all persons if the substitute check—
>> (1) accurately represents all of the information on the front and back of the original check as of the time the original check was truncated; and
>> (2) bears the legend: "This is a legal copy of your check. You can use it the same way you would use the original check."

12 U.S.C. § 5003(b).

The collecting person or entity may present the substitute check, and the drawee bank is not entitled to require the original:

> (a) No agreement required. A person may deposit, present, or send for collection or return a substitute check without an agreement with the recipient, so long as a bank has made the warranties in section 5 with respect to such substitute check.

12 U.S.C. § 5003(a).

QUESTION 3. Stand-in. Dara writes a check to pay off a loan. She has no money in the account to cover the check. Not long after, a collection agency seeks to recover on the check, which has been dishonored. Dara represents herself in small claims court. As evidence, the plaintiff submits a Check 21 substitute check, rather than the original check. Dara argues to the judge that the substitute check should be rejected as evidence, because the real check may be out there. The court, Dara contends, should not make her pay this plaintiff, when another plaintiff may show up in time with the original check. Should the court rule for Dara?

A. Yes. To collect on an instrument, a party must have the instrument (or prove that it has been lost, stolen, or destroyed).
B. Yes. The check embodies the right to payment.
C. No. The substitute check is the legal equivalent of the original check.
D. No. Dara has not paid her loan and so is still liable.

ANALYSIS. A substitute check is indeed the legal equivalent of a real check, under the federal statute known as Check 21. So, the plaintiff is entitled to collect using the substitute check. Therefore, **C** is the best answer. **A** and **B** have been displaced by federal law in this regard.

Having said that, it may take some time for this rule to be reflected in practice. Parties may not treat substitute checks as the legal equivalent. Even in court, it may take some time for judges to learn about Check 21 and apply it. If Dara's opponent is not prepared to educate the judge in short order, Dara's spurious argument could take the day.

D is a red herring. Dara may indeed be liable on the original debt, but that liability would run to the holder of that debt (presumably, the same person who was the payee on the check). The holder of a check does not have the right to enforce the underlying obligation.

4. *Substitute check warranties*

What about the original check? What if the bank makes a mistake?

> A bank that transfers, presents, or returns a substitute check and receives consideration for the check warrants, as a matter of law, to the transferee, any subsequent collecting or returning bank, the depositary bank, the drawee, the drawer, the payee, the depositor, and any endorser (regardless of whether the warrantee receives the substitute check or another paper or electronic form of the substitute check or original check) that—
>> (1) the substitute check meets all the requirements for legal equivalence under section 4(b) and
>> (2) no depositary bank, drawee, drawer, or endorser will receive presentment or return of the substitute check, the original check, or a copy or other paper or electronic version of the substitute check or original check such that the bank, drawee, drawer, or endorser will be asked to make a payment based on a check that the bank, drawee, drawer, or endorser has already paid."

12 U.S.C. § 5004.

Banks warrant that 1) that the substitute check is accurate and 2) that there are "no duplicates." The bank in Boston takes the original check, makes an image, and sends that out to Seattle and prints out a substitute check. You now have a substitute check out there. The Boston bank has to warrant, "I'll hold on to the original. Nobody's going to show up and present this one and try to get paid twice. And I also promise that I won't print out a second version or a third version or a fourth version at the other end, so there are no duplicate substitute checks." Check 21 essentially says, "Bank, you can take this check, print out exactly one copy at the other end, and then you have to lock this one up, and make sure there is only one check at any given time floating around out there."

5. *Re-credit provision*

If a consumer customer claims an irregularity, the bank within ten days is obliged to re-credit the customer's account, if it is a check of up to $2,500. The bank gets 45 days if it is more than $2,500. Later on, the bank can take the money back out again if it disproves the irregularity to its own satisfaction, or if it proves that the customer's check was correctly processed. It is only a provisional re-credit requirement. Unless the bank can show that the check was valid, while it investigates, it has to put the money back in the customer's account.

The last protection is an *indemnity*.

6. *Indemnity*

(a) Indemnity. A reconverting bank and each bank that subsequently transfers, presents, or returns a substitute check in any electronic or paper form, and receives consideration for such transfer, presentment, or return shall indemnify the transferee, any subsequent collecting or returning bank, the depositary bank, the drawee, the drawer, the payee, the depositor, and any endorser, up to the amount described in subsections (b) and (c), as applicable, to the extent of any loss incurred by any recipient of a substitute check if that loss occurred due to the receipt of a substitute check instead of the original check.

12 U.S.C. § 5005(a).

The bank is allowed to take the nice, original check that its customer wrote and essentially transform that into a picture of a check at the other end. If somehow that causes customer a loss, that's a risk that the bank takes, even if the check was a legitimate check. In other words, the statute just says, "We won't try to think of all the weird things that could happen or the unlikely scenarios that will happen to a few people out there. There's probably some risk that something could go wrong. If that causes a loss to the customer, the bank will indemnify them for that loss, at least up to the amount of the check, even if the check was properly payable." In effect, it is as though the customer has the right to have the check in its original form and processed in its original form. If the bank chooses to process it differently, and that causes a loss to the customer, the bank takes that loss.

QUESTION 4. Nothing like the original.   Ansel sends a check to Yosemite to pay for a shipment of silver nitrate. Yosemite deposits the check in Degas Bank. Degas Bank converts it to a Check 21 substitute check and presents the substitute to the drawee bank, Durer Bank, which pays it. A couple of months later, Yosemite sues Ansel for payment, denying receipt of the check. Ansel produces the substitute check as evidence. The presiding judge grants judgment to Yosemite, ruling that the substitute check is insufficient evidence of payment, because anyone could forge one on a home computer. Yosemite takes the money and runs. Does Ansel have any recourse against the banks?

A. Yes, against Durer Bank, which paid a copy of a check, as opposed to the check.
B. Yes, against Degas Bank, who is liable for any loss caused by converting the check.
C. No. A substitute check is the legal equivalent of an original check.
D. No, only Yosemite is liable.
E. Both **A** and **B**.

ANALYSIS.

Ansel → Yosemite → Degas Bank converts to substitute check → Durer Bank pays

This question plays out the indemnity provision. The substitute check is the legal equivalent of an original check; however, Check 21 recognizes that in practice, the use of the substitute check could cause problems. Check 21, in effect, says that banks may choose to convert checks but will bear any loss that flows from that. So, Degas Bank is liable to Ansel for the loss caused by the substitute check. **B** is a correct answer.

A is also correct. Durer Bank is entitled (indeed, required) to pay the substitute check, the legal equivalent of the original check; Durer Bank also indemnifies its customer against loss. Durer Bank can then turn around and recover from Degas Bank on its indemnity. So, **E** is the best answer.

C is incorrect. It states a legal rule correctly, but another legal rule (the indemnity provision) governs.

D is incorrect, because the indemnity provision makes Durer Bank liable.

7. *Truncation by payee*

There are several ways that the payee can speed up the check collection process.

 a. Payee could make a Check 21 image.
 b. Payee could digitize the information from the check (such as by swiping the check in a scanner; if the amount is only handwritten, the payee could type that into a scanner or other computer) and send it electronically to Payee's bank. The information may be used either for electronic presentment or to initiate an automated clearinghouse request (a wire transfer of funds from Drawer's account). In other words, if Drawer pays with a check, Payee may in effect use the account number and bank identifying information from the check to initiate a debit from Drawer's account, almost as if Drawer had used a debit card to pay.
 c. An individual who is payee on a check might be able to make a deposit over the phone, by reading the information to a bank employee or voice recognition program.

D. Note: patents on payment system methods

After banks started using check imaging more widely, as encouraged by Check 21, a company named Data Treasury claimed that patents that it held covered the process permitted by Check 21. In other words, it claimed that any bank using the new process permitted by the statute would infringe its patents—meaning that such banks would have to pay licensing fees to Data

Treasury or not use substitute checks. The question of whether the patents are valid and therefore infringed is working its way through the courts.

E.   The closer

QUESTION 5. **Whither draft?**   Fiona in Philadelphia deposits her paycheck, drawn on a Los Angeles Bank, in the local ATM. The machine shows her an image of the check, along with the amount. She realizes that the machine has read the info (amount, bank, drawer's account number) from the check. What, she wonders, will happen from here?

A. Fiona's bank will send the information electronically to the Los Angeles bank, to present the check for payment.
B. Fiona's bank will transmit the image to Los Angeles, print it out there, and present the printout as a substitute check, for payment.
C. Fiona's bank will send on the check itself (probably via a clearing-house) and present it for payment.
D. Any of the above.

ANALYSIS.   This question simply highlights the various ways in which banks speed up the check collection process. **D** is the best answer.

 McJohn's picks

1.	Just the facts	A
2.	Copy me on that	C
3.	Stand-in	C
4.	Nothing like the original	E
5.	Whither draft?	D

19

Credit Cards: Policy Issues

A. Introduction

Here we turn to credit cards, a payment system quite different from checks. A check is an order to the customer's bank to pay funds out of the customer's checking account. A credit card is a device used to order a bank (or other card issuer) to make a loan to the customer—to pay the amount of funds to the merchant and then add that amount to the balance owed on the customer's revolving line of credit with the bank.

Customer → Merchant → Merchant's Bank → Card issuer (via network)

Credit cards are used to borrow money. Customer uses a credit card to buy lecterns or artwork or software (or whatever else) from Merchant, and gets a quick loan. Merchant processes the transaction by sending a credit slip (which may be electronic) to Merchant's bank (or other credit card acquirer), whoever has access to the credit card network. Merchant's bank sends the transaction through the network to the card issuer, who sends the funds back through the network. Merchant's bank then transmits the funds to Merchant (just when and on what terms depends on their contract). Customer may pay that loan in full when the statement comes, pay a minimum payment and leave that as an outstanding balance accruing interest, or pay nothing at all (although that will trigger fees, and if repeated, collection efforts).

Why do all the parties to the transaction do it? Each party incurs costs and obtains benefits. Customer promises to pay the card issuer, which is a big cost. But Customer gets whatever they are purchasing in the transaction, they don't have to pay cash, and they can pay the charge over time.

The card issuer gives funds to Merchant, which is a big cost. But the card issuer gets a slice of each transaction; it also accrues debt from Customer. Customer promises to pay the purchase price, plus interest, plus fees. Merchant's bank charges Merchant a percentage for each transaction and may have a relationship with Merchant that involves selling other banking services.

Merchant will likely end up with around $96 per $100 in sales paid via credit card, after the banks take their percentage. So, Merchant gets less than if it took $100 cash for the same item. Many merchants honor credit cards, however, and there must be a reason for that. In some ways, credit cards are safer than cash. As a merchant, you don't have to monitor your employees as much. You don't have to take any money down to the bank. You also don't have to count it. It makes a merchant more attractive to potential customers if they can say, "You don't have to carry around big wads of cash all the time; rather, you can come and buy from me and just pay with that little piece of plastic that you already have in your pocket." Most of all, buyers now expect most merchants to honor credit cards. A merchant that does not take credit cards may be at a distinct disadvantage.

B.   Most of credit card law is contract law

Federal law does not regulate most aspects of credit cards: fees, interest rates, conditions under which fees can be charged, and other contractual provisions are generally left to the card issuer and the customer. The Credit Card Accountability, Responsibility, and Disclosure Act of 2009 (discussed below) sets some specific limitations on credit card practices. The Truth in Lending Act, discussed in later chapters, further provides that cardholders can be liable for only $50 of unauthorized use (such as stolen credit cards), that consumer cardholders need not pay the bill for transactions where the merchant did not perform as promised, and provides rules governing errors and requiring disclosures.

But contract law governs most of credit card practice. There is a contract between the card issuer and the cardholder—the credit card contract. There is also a contract between the cardholder and the merchant (it could be a sales contract, or a sale of services, like a semester of education). The merchant, to get their credit card slips processed at the merchant bank, signs a contract with merchant bank. The card issuer and merchant bank, to be part of the credit card network, in effect, sign a *very big* contract. All the banks and other card issuers that are part of that network all agree to a set of network rules that govern the credit card network. The merchant bank agrees to be bound by those rules, as does the card issuer and the merchant, indirectly, in their contract with the merchant bank. So, the network rules are likened to a privately created commercial code for credit cards.

C.   Policy issues

1.   *Credit cards: good or bad?*

A credit card enthusiast might say that credit cards have been a great benefit to consumers and to businesses large and small. They provide a cheap and efficient form of payment, which means that more mutually beneficial transactions can occur; they also allow customers to borrow funds when needed, and to decide when to repay it. Credit cards are much better for consumers than the systems they have replaced (or are replacing), such as payday loans and even checks. Finally, for small business borrowers, credit cards have provided a form of financing that is vastly better than bank loans in terms of convenience, cost, and availability.

A credit card skeptic might say that credit cards have fueled a harmful level of borrowing and permitted manipulative practices by issuers. Because credit cards are so easy to obtain and use, consumers often incur much more debt than is advisable. Consumers often cannot understand the implications of credit card use, due to confusing arrays of fees, rules, and changing interest rates. Credit cards also facilitate impulsive or misinformed purchases, through such devices as affinity programs, in which a customer earns "points" by accruing debt, at a hefty interest rate. The network power of credit card companies allows them to control the terms on which merchants honor cards, even where merchants would prefer cash.

Some have argued that there should be more regulation of the items discussed in the following sections.

2.   *Fees and interest*

There is some question as to whether the fees and interest card issuers charge should be regulated more. Some contend that card issuers are so sophisticated about figuring out how to extract fees from customers that regulation is required.

In 2009, Congress enacted a number of regulations affecting consumer credit cards. The Credit Card Accountability, Responsibility, and Disclosure Act of 2009, along with Federal Reserve regulations, limits card issuers in a number of ways. Issuers must give clearer disclosure to consumers in various ways, such as stating how long it would take to pay off the balance if only minimum monthly payments are made. Issuers must give 45 days notice of changes in interest rates, fees, or other key provisions of the credit card agreement. There are limits on when over-the-limit fees may be charged, on the size of late fees, and on interest rate increases. There are limits on marketing of credit cards to persons under age 21, such as requiring proof of ability to pay. Certain affinity cards may not be issued to students. Nor may card issuers give "freebies" like T-shirts or gift cards to students at campus promotions. "Universal default clauses" are prohibited. Under such a clause, if the customer was in default with any of the customer's creditors, then the card issuer could raise the customer's interest rate to the default rate. If a customer missed a payment on their electric bill, for example, that could raise the rate on their credit card.

3. Disclosure

A credit card issuer has to make lots of disclosures, but they are all made when the credit card is issued. Issuers send a packet to the customer with approximately 30 pages of rules, regulations, and terms. It is the rare cardholder who reads it all. Some say it would be much better to give a shorter, clearer set of disclosures to consumers about the factors that really affect them the most, and to give disclosures when consumers are making the relevant decisions, such as at a point of sale or in the monthly statement.

4. Minimum payments

Some common credit card provisions have been criticized, as described in this and the following sections.

A cardholder has to make a minimum payment every month. A consumer might think of that as being the amount that they should prudently pay if they are going to pay off that credit card debt. With some credit cards, however, the minimum is set so low that if the consumer pays their minimum amount every month, it will take them decades to pay off that outstanding debt. Rather, the function of a minimum is more likely to ensure that the issuer hears from that person every month, that the person is accustomed to paying off the debt to a certain extent, and that they don't disappear off of the radar screen. Consumer advocates say there should be some disclosure to consumers about the role of a minimum payment and the effect the minimum payment has on the amount of debt the consumer is accruing.

5. Freedom to change terms

Credit card contracts often provide that the card issuer, with notice to the customer, may change terms of the contract unilaterally.

6. Affinity programs

One policy debate about credit cards now is whether they facilitate too much use of consumer credit—namely, whether consumers borrow too much because credit cards make it so easy and attractive to do so without understanding the real ramifications of their actions. Some also argue that affinity programs (reward miles, etc.) lead to excessive use of credit.

7. Arbitration clauses

Agreements routinely provide that disputes will be sent to arbitration, not to court. Card issuers appear to win an overwhelming majority of arbitration cases. Some argue this shows that arbitrators favor card issuers, because that makes it more likely the arbitrators will get work. Others respond that the cases are being decided on the merits, and that issuers have just as high a success rate in court, just at greater expense to all.

In 2008, federal regulators issued proposed regulations governing various matters, such as how fees are assessed for late payment, and how interest and finance charges can be calculated. The professors at www.creditslips.org provide lively commentary and analysis on developments in this and credit issues generally.

8. Product liability

Some people have even argued that credit cards should be subject to product liability lawsuits. If you sell something that can be dangerous, or that can cause harm to somebody who uses it under the wrong circumstances, then the seller should be liable for the harm caused. By analogy, some argue that if someone who gets a credit card is not sophisticated enough to use it and they run up large bills, then maybe the issuer should be liable under product liability law.

D. The closer

> **QUESTION 1. The best and the brightest.** What sort of expert would be helpful in deciding whether and how to regulate credit cards?
>
> **A.** An economist.
> **B.** A psychologist.
> **C.** A marketing analyst.
> **D.** A lawyer.
> **E.** All of the above and more.

ANALYSIS. Credit cards raise issues all across the spectrum:

> *Economic:* How does credit card use affect the level of saving and debt in the economy? Con—consumers rack up excessive debt; pro—many

small businesses thrive using the flexibility of credit cards as a source of capital.

Psychology: How does the use of a credit card affect the decision-making process (long-term versus short-term, level of information and understanding, cognitive biases)?

Marketing: Credit cards are the subject of millions of dollars in marketing. Some have questioned campaigns to sign up such customers as first-year college students or people who have recently emerged from bankruptcy. Others would say that consumers benefit from having options, and from becoming more sophisticated about their own finances.

Lawyers: Regulation is a tricky process—to achieve its goals, and to avoid making the problem actually worse.

E is the best answer—and there are many other sides to the credit card story.

 ## McJohn's picks

1. The best and the brightest   **E**

Credit Cards: Unauthorized Use and Errors

Swifty with fingers quite nifty
Gave Abigail's Amex a lifty.
Must she pay his charges?
The little and larges?
Not Priceless. Just up to fifty.

CHAPTER OVERVIEW
A. Liability for unauthorized use: capped at $50
B. Business cardholder may take risk of unauthorized use
C. Use is "unauthorized" when there is no actual, applied, or apparent authority
D. Negligent monitoring of account may be deemed granting apparent authority
E. Issuer may charge back to merchant in card-not-present transactions, not in face-to-face transactions (provided merchant follows network rules)
F. Billing errors
G. The closer
✦ McJohn's picks

For credit cards, the federal Truth in Lending Act (TILA) sets a $50 maximum liability for unauthorized use. A business that sets up cards for employee use can waive this limit by agreement (a risky thing to do). "Unauthorized use" means use without actual, apparent, or implied authority, so a cardholder can be liable for use by others. Some courts have held that negligence (failing to properly monitor the use of an account) can give apparent authority.

The card issuer will generally take the loss for unauthorized use in face-to-face transactions, provided the merchant followed the network rules, but card issuers have developed numerous security measures to reduce credit card fraud. The card issuer may charge back the loss to the merchant in card-not-present transactions (e.g., in telephone, online, or mail-order transactions), which means that such merchants often are a little more careful.

The Truth in Lending Act also sets out a procedure for dealing with billing errors. The cardholder must give notice of irregularity within 60 days of when the statement is transmitted. The card issuer then must investigate and respond, within certain time limits.

A.   Liability for unauthorized use: capped at $50

This chapter looks at a risk in every payment system: *unauthorized use*. This could refer to forging a check, using a stolen credit or debit card, or even hacking into a system and sending wire transfers.

With checks, the overall policy toward fraud is to put the loss on the party—asking, with respect to a particular check, who was in the best position to avoid the loss? If someone was negligent, and that caused a forged signature or alteration of the check, then they should take the loss. If someone accepts a check from a forger or thief, then they are likely to take the loss. Those rules are fine-tuned by the validation rules. If you write a check to an impostor, or you employ someone and give them responsibility with respect to instruments, then you take the loss. Likewise, if a customer fails to monitor his account, and that causes a loss with respect to a particular check or a series of checks, then the customer takes the loss. For checks, there is a whole set of relatively fine-tuned rules that zero in on the problem with a particular check and try to say, "The wrongdoer is gone. On which one of the innocent parties should we put the loss?"

Credit card law uses a much simpler approach. The card issuer takes the loss, beyond the first $50.00. The following states the liability that the customer has under credit card law:

> Liability of holder of credit card
>   (a) Limits on liability.
>   (1) A cardholder shall be liable for the unauthorized use of a credit card only if—
>   (A) the card is an accepted credit card;
>   (B) the liability is not in excess of $50;

(C) the card issuer gives adequate notice to the cardholder of the potential liability;

(D) the card issuer has provided the cardholder with a description of a means by which the card issuer may be notified of loss or theft of the card, which description may be provided on the face or reverse side of the statement required by section 127(b) or on a separate notice accompanying such statement;

(E) the unauthorized use occurs before the card issuer has been notified that an unauthorized use of the credit card has occurred or may occur as the result of loss, theft, or otherwise; and

(F) the card issuer has provided a method whereby the user of such card can be identified as the person authorized to use it.

(2) For purposes of this section, a card issuer has been notified when such steps as may be reasonably required in the ordinary course of business to provide the card issuer with the pertinent information have been taken, whether or not any particular officer, employee, or agent of the card issuer does in fact receive such information.

TILA § 133 (15 U.S.C. § 1643).

The customer is liable for *unauthorized use* of the card up to $50. If my card is stolen and somebody charges $5,000 on my card, I'm only liable for $50. The parties cannot contract around this limitation.

The checking law regime says to be careful with checks. If you're not, and somebody steals, forges, or alters one, you can take the loss. The credit card regime doesn't do that. It might look like it skews the incentives to cardholders because it does not give much incentive to be careful with the card, but there are other reasons for people to be careful with their credit cards. If they lose their credit card, they can't use it. They've got to have it replaced, which gives them an incentive to contact the issuer anyway. If a card is lost and someone other than the cardholder runs up a number of charges, the cardholder is not liable for those charges, provided they convince the card issuer that the card was lost and that those are unauthorized charges. If the bank and the court (or more likely, an arbitrator) don't believe the cardholder, then the cardholder will take those losses. These things can cause a lot of practical problems. So, from a cardholder's point of view, if they lose their card, they have a good incentive to notify the issuer. Also, when they have their card, they have a certain incentive to take reasonable care with it, because it is relatively simple to keep track of where the credit card is and not let it fall into somebody else's hands.

Having said all that, in general, this is a rule that puts the onus on card issuers. It says to card issuers: You're going to take the loss from credit card fraud. Your customers aren't going to take the loss — only up to $50.

Card issuers have reacted to that by instituting all kinds of security measures. On the card itself there are several security measures: the number, the expiration date, and the cardholder's signature. There is also another security number on the signature strip. The signature strip itself is often made out of some kind of special material. Increasingly, credit cards have the cardholder's picture on them, or a hologram to help identify counterfeit cards.

Beyond the cards themselves, card issuers use many methods to detect unauthorized use. Card issuers run pattern-detection software that monitors the activity on accounts. If an account normally has a pattern of activity within a certain geographic area, with certain types of merchants, and for certain dollar amounts, but all of a sudden pops up in a different location with different types of charges for much different amounts, the software may issue an alert. The issuer won't necessarily cut off the card, but it may follow up and investigate.

Who pays for credit card losses is a complex question. As a first-order risk allocation, the card issuer takes the loss. That doesn't mean that the card issuer ultimately takes the loss, though. The card issuer may be able to pass on the loss in the form of higher charges to cardholders or merchants, in lower returns to its investors, or by other means. The approach is more analogous to having card issuers insure against losses.

The legal rule is $50 of unauthorized use liability applies only if the card has been accepted. If someone sends me a card but I don't accept that card and then someone uses it anyway, my liability is zero. The $50 liability limit applies only to those charges made before notice to the issuer. So, if I lose my card and give notice to the issuer before the thief uses it, even the $50 liability does not apply.

QUESTION 1. Choose one. Ada mislaid a credit card. She waited a few weeks before notifying the issuer. In the meantime, Fiona found it and ran up $5,400 in charges. For how much is Ada liable?

A. $50

ANALYSIS. **A** is it. This question is simply to emphasize the simple risk allocation for credit cards: The customer is liable for a maximum of $50.

B. Business cardholder may take risk of unauthorized use

The $50 limit applies not just to consumers, but to business credit cards as well—unless the business agrees to bear the risk of unauthorized use (and not pass the risk on to the employees):

> Business credit cards; limits on liability of employees
> [A] card issuer and a business or other organization which provides credit cards issued by the same card issuer to ten or more of its employees may

by contract agree as to liability of the business or other organization with respect to unauthorized use of such credit cards without regard to the provisions of section 133 but in no case may such business or other organization or card issuer impose liability upon any employee with respect to unauthorized use of such a credit card except in accordance with and subject to the limitations of section 133.

TILA § 135 (15 U.S.C. § 1645).

C.   Use is "unauthorized" when there is no actual, applied, or apparent authority

A cardholder is liable for $50 of *unauthorized use*. Unauthorized use means "a use of a credit card by a person other than the cardholder who does not have actual, implied, or apparent authority for such use and from which the cardholder receives no benefit." TILA § 103(o).

So the cardholder is liable for use that was made with actual, implied, or apparent authority, or use where the cardholder received a benefit. If I authorize someone to use my card, I'm liable. If I ask someone to do something that naturally requires use of the card, I have given them *implied authority*. If I give someone *apparent authority* to use my card, I'm also liable. Say that I hand my card to an employee or a family member or a friend and tell them, "You can use this, but I'm going to limit my permission. You can use this just to go out to lunch and spend $20, then you have to give it back to me." I've only given them actual authority to charge $20 for lunch, but by giving them the card and saying, "Go ahead and use it," I've given them *apparent authority*. I don't have to sign anything or say any special words to give them authority.

To use a classic payment systems situation, let's look at the embezzling employee: I have a small business or a big business, and I have a credit card issued to an employee in the employee's name. That employee has authority to make charges to the account. I may limit the actual authority (e.g., "You can use this only for job-related expenses"), but by giving them the card with their name on it, and allowing them to go out in the world and use it, I have given them *apparent authority* to do so. If the employee uses that card to run up $5,000 in unauthorized home decorating and entertainment and travel expenses, I'm liable for it.

D.   Negligent monitoring of account may be deemed granting apparent authority

Minskoff v. American Express, 98 F.3d 703 (2d Cir. 1996), opens up a hole in the $50 liability limit, using reasoning similar to what we saw with respect to checks. In *Minskoff*, the newly hired assistant to the president of a real estate firm handled the credit card bills and the checking account statements when they came in — including solicitations for getting more cards on the account. A solicitation came in saying, "Why don't you upgrade your American Express card to a platinum one?" The assistant sent back an application for a couple of platinum cards: one with the firm president's name on it, and another one with the assistant's name on it. The assistant used the second card for approximately $300,000 in personal credit card transactions. The real estate firm took the position that it was an unauthorized use of the credit card account, and the assistant had no authority to make any actual charges on the account. Therefore, of the $300,000, they would be liable to the extent of $50. That would seem to be the result under the literal terms of the statute; there's nothing in the statute that makes the firm liable for its negligence in failing to notice months of account statements with the employee's lavish personal charges.

The court, however, reasoned that by allowing the employee to do whatever she wanted with the checking and credit card accounts, by not monitoring what was going on, by allowing her to walk around with that credit card for months on end while using it repeatedly, and by having those charges go through repeatedly without objection while getting paid off by the bookkeeping department, the firm gave her *apparent authority* to use the card.

The court even borrowed a little bit from the bank statement rule. The court reasoned that just as a customer has a duty with respect to a checking account to be monitoring that account, they should do the same thing with respect to a credit card account. So *Minskoff* says that even though there isn't a negligence rule, an employee forger rule, or an impostor rule in the credit card statute, you can find one in the concept of *apparent authority.* Negligence can create apparent authority. *Minskoff* has, in turn, been followed by other courts.

The big question is how broadly other courts would take that holding. *Minskoff* has been followed on similar facts. See *DBI Architects, P.C. v. American Express Travel-Related Services. Co., Inc.,* 388 F.3d 886 (D.C. Cir. 2004), and *Azur v. Chase Bank, USA, National Association,* 601 F.3d 2012 (3d Cir. 2010) (both decisions emphasizing that repeatedly paying credit card debt incurred by employee gave apparent authority to employee). But that would not extend to most types of negligence with respect to a credit card. For example, if I just leave my credit card where someone can steal it, or if I'm somehow otherwise negligent with my credit card and someone uses it, one might argue that I gave them *apparent authority* to use it and therefore am liable for all of the use that was made of it. That approach hasn't been taken in any other case, however.

Minskoff is likely to be applied in a limited situation in which someone permits continuing use of a credit card account, despite repeated sending of information to the account holder, the ignoring of which is negligent.

E.   Issuer may charge back to merchant in card-not-present transactions, not in face-to-face transactions (provided merchant follows network rules)

Suppose a thief steals a credit card and buys $2,000 worth of merchandise. The merchant does what they are supposed to do under the credit card rules. The rules tell the merchant what to do (such as getting a signature or checking identification) for various categories of transactions. That $2,000 charge goes through. The cardholder isn't liable for that charge, as we have seen, because the charge is unauthorized use. The merchant doesn't take the loss, either. The card issuer doesn't have the right to charge that back through the network: It takes the loss in face-to-face transactions. This is not something in the federal statute or the federal regulations. This is in the network rules that the various credit card networks have adopted.

The reason the networks have adopted this rule is to get merchants to honor credit cards. If the rule was that the merchants are liable for unauthorized charges, then merchants might be a little bit more reluctant to do so. Presumably, banks with pattern-detection software are the ones who are in the business of identifying the risks associated with credit card losses. This is risk they can manage better than merchants.

That is only the risk allocation rule for face-to-face transactions. For online, mail-order, and phone transactions, the merchant can be subject to chargeback. Such merchants often have more security in place than face-to-face merchants.

QUESTION 2. Dis-carded.   Sneaky picks Sleepy's pocket, getting a credit card and some postcards. Sneaky runs up $5,000 in charges over the next few weeks. Sleepy finally notices the missing card some time after that, after paying all the charges that Sleepy has made. What liability does Sleepy have for the $5,000 in charges by Sneaky?

A. $50.
B. $5,000, because Sleepy has paid the charges.
C. $5,000, because Sleepy was slow in noticing that the card was stolen.
D. $0. Sleepy did not authorize any of the charges.

ANALYSIS.   Sleepy is liable for unauthorized charges only up to $50. **A** is the best answer.

Note that with a checkbook, the answer might be different. The bank statement rule and the negligence rule would potentially put the loss on Sleepy. The court would have to assess the respective fault of Sleepy, as well as the various merchants and card issuer. Credit card law gives a much simpler, customer-friendly rule: $50.

QUESTION 3. **Brother's keeper.**   Happy, excited about his parents'
golden wedding anniversary, hands his credit card to his brother, Chipper,
and tells him to get something nice. Chipper signs Happy's name to
a credit card slip for a $10,000 golden garden gnome. When the bill
comes, Happy has second thoughts. He refuses to pay, on the grounds
that someone else signed his name. Is Happy liable?

A. Yes, for $50.
B. Yes, for the entire $10,000.
C. No. Happy is not liable, because he did not make the charge.
D. No. Happy was not even present at the transaction.

ANALYSIS.   Happy is liable only for $50 of unauthorized use. Unhappily for
him, though, "unauthorized use" is use without actual, apparent, or implied
authority. In this case, Chipper had implied, or at least apparent, authority. So
Chipper made an authorized charge for $10,000. Happy is liable for the full
amount, and **B** is the best answer.

QUESTION 4. **Long leash.**   Happy forgets to get his card back from
Chipper. Chipper resisted temptation for a couple of weeks, then went on
a $6,600 shopping spree. Is Happy liable for Chipper's charges?

A. Yes, for $50.
B. Yes, for the entire $6,600.
C. No. Happy is not liable, because he did not make the charge.
D. No. Chipper authorized only the charge for their parents' present.

ANALYSIS.   This one is less certain. Happy is liable if Chipper had implied
or apparent authority. Chipper did not have implied authority, but he probably had apparent authority. By giving Chipper the card with authority (albeit
limited) to use it, and by failing to limit his use (by not getting the card back),
Happy likely gave apparent authority to Chipper to use the card. Therefore, **B**
is the best answer.

QUESTION 5. **Discard card.**   Prodigious Credit mails credit cards to
prospective customers. The typical prospect, however, tosses the card into
the trash. If someone retrieves the card and uses it, is the discarder liable?

A. Yes, for $50.
B. Yes, for the entire amount.
C. It would depend on whether the court decided that by tossing the
   card, the person gave apparent authority to the finder.
D. Yes. Finders keepers.
E. No.

ANALYSIS. The rules on unauthorized use apply only to accepted cards. The prospective customer never accepted the card and so would be liable for zero dollars. **E** is the best answer.

QUESTION 6. Discard. Dopey is careless with his credit card. At a bar one night, he tosses it with a flick, trying to get a friend's attention. He watches the card glide down the stairwell but cannot be bothered to retrieve it. Subsequently, $4,000 of charges for bar bills and purchases at electronic stores show up on Dopey's next bill. He pays the minimum payment and forgets to contact the credit card issuer. After $4,500 more charges appear on the next bill, Dopey finally notifies the card issuer. What is his liability, with respect to the $8,500 in charges by the lucky finder of the card?

A. $8,500, because his negligence substantially contributed to the making of the charges.
B. $4,000, for the charges he has paid and cannot now rescind.
C. $0. He did not make the charges.
D. $50.

ANALYSIS. Dopey is liable for only $50 of unauthorized use. The TILA (unlike the Uniform Commercial Code rules on checks) does not apply liability according to fault for unauthorized use.

There is an argument that the use was authorized. One could argue that by negligently flicking and failing to retrieve his card, and by ignoring the unauthorized charges on his first bill, Dopey gave apparent authority to whoever picked up the card. Some courts have applied the "negligence creates apparent authority" theory, but only in the context of an employer that negligently fails to monitor credit card use by employees. Extending it to this sort of case would effectively change the bright-line, $50 rule into a fact-specific negligence standard — quite contrary to the statute, which puts the onus on card issuers to minimize unauthorized use. **D** is the best answer.

QUESTION 7. Carded. Dopey has to bear only $50 of the $8,500 in charges. Who takes the loss for the other $8,450?

A. The various merchants who took the card from the wrong person, even if they took the minimum security measures required.
B. The card issuer, who authorized payment on the various charges.
C. The banks of the various merchants, who processed payment for ill-chosen customers.
D. It would depend on who was deemed to be more at fault.

ANALYSIS. Under the credit card network rules, card issuers bear the risk of unauthorized use in face-to-face transactions (as long as the merchant follows the rules in processing the transactions such as requiring signatures for certain transactions). So, **B** is the best answer. Note that the rule is different for card-not-present transactions (e.g., online, mail-order, or phone transactions), so those sorts of merchants need to be more careful.

QUESTION 8. Without commercial break. Doc hires Grumpy as a receptionist for Doc's medical office. Within a week, Grumpy steals a credit card that Doc uses for business purposes, such as purchasing supplies. Grumpy runs up $9,000 in charges for furniture. Must Doc pay the bill?

A. No. Doc is liable for only $50.
B. Yes. The $50 limit protects only consumers, not commercial card users.
C. Yes, if Doc was negligent in hiring or supervising Grumpy.
D. No. Grumpy is liable, not Doc.
E. Yes. The employee forger rule places the loss on Grumpy's employer, Doc.

ANALYSIS.   Some courts have held that an employer's negligence can give the evil employee apparent authority. Business employs Bookkeeper and then negligently permits her to get and use a credit card on Business's account. Business then fails to take note of numerous bank statements over the next year or so setting forth Bookkeeper's many transactions (ranging from vacations to vacuum cleaners). Some courts would hold that Business's inaction gave Bookkeeper apparent authority.

But would those courts extend that rationale to Doc's failure to keep track of a card and a single transaction? Doc did not ignore numerous statements. Holding Doc liable would seem to create a general negligence exception to the $50 limit, which would seem a job for Congress, not the courts. So **A** is the best answer.

The $50 limit applies to business cards, not just consumer transactions, so **B** is incorrect.

Courts have only interpreted negligence to give apparent authority where there is repeated failure to monitor the activity on an account, so **C** takes the case law too far.

Grumpy is liable, but that does not reduce Doc's liability to the card issuer, contrary to **D**.

The employee forger rule is part of negotiable instrument law, not credit card law, so **E** is incorrect.

QUESTION 9. Disregard.   Sneezy Auto sells luxury cars. Lopes has the job of opening the mail and delivering items to the proper person or department (e.g., Sales, Service, or Accounting). Lopes takes the credit card bills to Accounting; she uses this opportunity to apply for a new company credit card. When the card comes, Lopes pockets it. She uses it frequently over the next two years, at couturiers and casinos. The bills come each month, reflecting these unusual charges on Sneezy Auto's account. Sneezy is very lax in keeping track of expenditures, however, and no one takes action. Finally, a new accountant finds that over $200,000 has been charged by Lopes. Sneezy demands reimbursement from the card issuer. What is the credit card issuer's strongest argument that it has no liability to Sneezy?

A. Sneezy authorized Lopes to use the card by giving her access to the envelopes containing credit card bills.
B. Sneezy is liable for negligence.
C. Sneezy gave Lopes apparent authority to use the card by doing nothing despite receiving monthly statements reflecting her charges.
D. Sneezy cannot get the money back once paid.

ANALYSIS. Some courts, as discussed above, have imposed liability on an apparent authority theory, in just this fact setting. The cases are few but (so far) have not been rejected by other courts. So, following the trend of authority, **C** is the best answer.

QUESTION 10. Disclaim. Golden Apple Mining signs a credit card contract with Queenly Bank. Golden Apple will get 40 credit cards issued to various employees. The rates charged will be low. Golden Apple agrees to bear the risk of unauthorized use. One of the cards is stolen, and $6,000 in charges is run up. Golden Apple rethinks the deal and refuses to pay. Is it liable (beyond $50)?

A. Yes. The $50 limit applies only to consumer credit cards.
B. Yes. Golden Apple waived the $50 limit.
C. No. The parties' contract cannot override federal law.
D. It would depend on whether Golden Apple's employee was negligent with the card.

ANALYSIS. The $50 limit applies to all cards (business or consumer), except a business may agree to waive the limitation. A business with at least ten employee cards may agree to take liability for unauthorized use (presumably in exchange for favorable terms from the issuer). It's a pretty risky way to get a good deal on credit cards but is a risk that federal law allows businesses to take. Golden Apple agreed to such a deal and so is liable for the unauthorized use. **B** is the best answer.

F.   Billing errors

The TILA also sets out a procedure for dealing with billing errors. The card-holder must give notice within 60 days of when the statement is transmitted. The issuer then must investigate and respond, within certain time limits.

Here's the detailed rule, which defines billing errors and sets out the procedure to address them.

§ 1666. Correction of Billing Errors

(a) Written notice by obligor to creditor; time for and contents of notice; procedure upon receipt of notice by creditor. If a creditor, within sixty days after having transmitted to an obligor a statement of the obligor's account in connection with an extension of consumer credit, receives at the address disclosed under section 127(b)(10) a written notice (other than notice on a payment stub or other payment medium supplied by the creditor if the creditor so stipulates with the disclosure required under section 127(a)(7) from the obligor in which the obligor—

(1) sets forth or otherwise enables the creditor to identify the name and account number (if any) of the obligor,

(2) indicates the obligor's belief that the statement contains a billing error and the amount of such billing error, and

(3) sets forth the reasons for the obligor's belief (to the extent applicable) that the statement contains a billing error, the creditor shall, unless the obligor has, after giving such written notice and before the expiration of the time limits herein specified, agreed that the statement was correct—

(A) not later than thirty days after the receipt of the notice, send a written acknowledgment thereof to the obligor, unless the action required in subparagraph (B) is taken within such thirty-day period, and

(B) not later than two complete billing cycles of the creditor (in no event later than ninety days) after the receipt of the notice and prior to taking any action to collect the amount, or any part thereof, indicated by the obligor under paragraph (2) either—

(i) make appropriate corrections in the account of the obligor, including the crediting of any finance charges on amounts erroneously billed, and transmit to the obligor a notification of such corrections and the creditor's explanation of any change in the amount indicated by the obligor under paragraph (2) and, if any such change is made and the obligor so requests, copies of documentary evidence of the obligor's indebtedness; or

(ii) send a written explanation or clarification to the obligor, after having conducted an investigation, setting forth to the extent applicable the reasons why the creditor believes the account of the obligor was correctly shown in the statement and, upon request of the obligor, provide copies of documentary evidence of the obligor's indebtedness. In the case of a billing error where the obligor alleges that the creditor's billing statement reflects goods not delivered to the obligor or his designee in accordance with the agreement made at the time of the transaction, a creditor may not construe such amount to be correctly shown unless he determines that such goods were actually delivered, mailed, or otherwise sent to the obligor and provides the obligor with a statement of such determination.

After complying with the provisions of this subsection with respect to an alleged billing error, a creditor has no further responsibility under this section if the obligor continues to make substantially the same allegation with respect to such error.

(b) Billing error. For the purpose of this section, a "billing error" consists of any of the following:

(1) A reflection on a statement of an extension of credit which was not made to the obligor or, if made, was not in the amount reflected on such statement.

(2) A reflection on a statement of an extension of credit for which the obligor requests additional clarification including documentary evidence thereof.

(3) A reflection on a statement of goods or services not accepted by the obligor or his designee or not delivered to the obligor or his designee in accordance with the agreement made at the time of a transaction.

(4) The creditor's failure to reflect properly on a statement a payment made by the obligor or a credit issued to the obligor.

(5) A computation error or similar error of an accounting nature of the creditor on a statement.

(6) Failure to transmit the statement required under section 127(b) of this act to the last address of the obligor which has been disclosed to the creditor, unless that address was furnished less than twenty days before the end of the billing cycle for which the statement is required.

(7) Any other error described in regulations of the Board.

One could read this 60-day limit as applying to unauthorized charges. The definition of "billing error" includes unauthorized charges. So, a customer who waits too long to complain (i.e., more than 60 days from when the statement is transmitted) may lose the right to contest the charge. Under this reading, a customer is liable for only $50 of unauthorized charges *provided she does not wait too long to give notice of the unauthorized charge*. With that in mind, the $50 cap may easily be lost. The better reading of the statute as a whole, however, could be that the billing error procedure is just one way to raise an unauthorized charge and does not limit the broad language in § 133, which limits liability to $50.

QUESTION 11. Not my job?   Rowena gets her credit card statement, including a charge for $4,500 to Fred and Circus Foods. Rowena suspects a mistake. Her typical purchase there is $45 and never more than $100. She contacts the card issuer immediately. The card issuer responds that it never gets involved in the underlying transaction and suggests that Rowena contact Fred and Circus Food to get her money back. May the card issuer punt like that?

A. Yes. The card issuer is merely a conduit, not a party to the sales contract.
B. Yes. It would impose considerable costs if card issuers had to investigate every question that cardholders have about their statement.
C. Yes. Before raising defenses against the card issuer, Rowena must make a reasonable effort to resolve the dispute with Fred and Circus.
D. No. The card issuer is required to investigate the matter and report results to Rowena.

ANALYSIS. The card issuer is obliged to investigate and report. **D** is the best answer.

QUESTION 12. Bar date. Jakub lets his credit card statements pile up on his desk. He goes through them in December and sees a six-month-old charge of $5,000 for the annual credit card fee. Jakub knows his annual fee is $50, so he contacts the card issuer to have the $4,500 reimbursed. The card issuer refuses, on the grounds that Jakub has waited too long. Does federal law require the card issuer to reimburse Jakub?

A. Yes. A $5,000 fee is unconscionable.
B. Yes. Jakub did not agree to the charge, so he is not liable.
C. No. Jakub must report a billing error within 60 days of transmission of the statement.
D. It depends on whether Jakub has paid the charge yet.

ANALYSIS. The statute requires the creditor to respond if the creditor receives written notice of a billing error from the consumer obligor "within sixty days after having transmitted to an obligor a statement of the obligor's account in connection with an extension of consumer credit." The federal statute, on its face, requires the card issuer only to correct errors if it receives notice from the consumer within 60 days. So, **C** is the best answer.

A might be correct under state law, but the question is specifically limited to federal law. This emphasizes that federal law provides limited regulation of credit cards.

Having said that, there might be remedies available at state law, under such theories as unjust enrichment or breach of contract. So, Jakub might not be out of luck. The trickier situation would be where the original billing error was by the merchant, who received the money from the card issuer, via the credit card network. In that case, the card issuer would not be getting unjust enrichment (as opposed to previous question, in which it accidentally gave itself $5,000 at the customer's expense).

G.   The closer

> **QUESTION 13. 60 days and $50?** Liev purloins one of Filip's credit cards, using it to purchase some $10,000 of antique lecterns. Filip does not notice the card's absence for several months. He finally notifies the credit card issuer some four months after the statement showing the charges. The credit card issuer declines to reverse the charges, on the grounds that Filip acted too late. Did Filip lose his rights under federal law?
>
> **A.** Yes. He must notify the card issuer before paying the relevant charges.
> **B.** Yes. He must notify the card issuer no later than 60 days after the statement is sent.
> **C.** Yes. He must notify his card issuer within a reasonable time of losing his card.
> **D.** No. Filip cannot be liable for more than $50 of unauthorized charges on a credit card.

ANALYSIS.   The definition of billing error includes, in subsection (b)(1): "A reflection on a statement of an extension of credit which was not made to the obligor or, if made, was not in the amount reflected on such statement." One could make the argument that the 60-day limit would apply here. But such a reading of the statute would ignore the clear rule that a consumer may be liable only for up to $50 of unauthorized use. **D** is the best answer.

 # McJohn's picks

1.	Choose one	A
2.	Dis-carded	A
3.	Brother's keeper	B
4.	Long leash	B
5.	Discard card	E
6.	Discard	D
7.	Carded	B
8.	Without commercial break	A
9.	Disregard	C
10.	Disclaim	B
11.	Not my job?	D
12.	Bar date	C
13.	60 days and $50?	D

Credit Cards: Consumer Buyer Protections

An unschooled lad with a Visa,
Bought a bogus but belle Mona Lisa.
No problem for laddie.
They'll charge it back gladly
And lean on the merchant like Pisa.

CHAPTER OVERVIEW
A. Buyer protection for consumer credit card transactions
B. Applies only for consumer transactions
C. Must make good faith effort to resolve the dispute with the merchant
D. Applies only to transactions over $50
E. Geographical limitation: transactions in state or within 100 miles of residence
F. Time limit: must give notice before paying the credit card bill
G. Card issuer can charge back to merchant
H. Contract law again: card issuer may provide greater protections or waive limits
I. Comparison to other payment systems
J. The closer
⟐ McJohn's picks

If a consumer buys something with a credit card, the Truth in Lending Act (TILA) mandates some buyer protection. If the consumer has a valid reason not to pay the merchant (e.g., the goods paid for were defective or were not delivered), the consumer may raise that defense against the credit card issuer—meaning the consumer is not required to pay that charge on the bill. Not all transactions get this protection, and the consumer loses the right if she pays the charge.

A.   Buyer protection for consumer credit card transactions

The federal TILA gives more protection to credit card holders than any other payment system, with respect to the ability to raise defenses.

Consumer → Merchant → Merchant's Bank → Card Issuer (via network)

If Consumer does not get what Merchant promised, Consumer is not required to pay the bill from Card Issuer. Credit cards thus provide a form of buyer protection that is not provided by payment systems that take payment from a consumer's checking account (i.e., checks, debit cards and other electronic fund transfers). Here's the rule in gory detail.

> § 1666i. Assertion by cardholder against card issuer of claims and defenses arising out of credit card transaction; prerequisites; limitation on amount of claims or defenses
>
> (a) Claims and defenses assertable. Subject to the limitation contained in subsection (b), a card issuer who has issued a credit card to a cardholder pursuant to an open end consumer credit plan shall be subject to all claims (other than tort claims) and defenses arising out of any transaction in which the credit card is used as a method of payment or extension of credit if (1) the obligor has made a good faith attempt to obtain satisfactory resolution of a disagreement or problem relative to the transaction from the person honoring the credit card; (2) the amount of the initial transaction exceeds $50; and (3) the place where the initial transaction occurred was in the same State as the mailing address previously provided by the cardholder or was within 100 miles from such address, except that the limitations set forth in clauses (2) and (3) with respect to an obligor's right to assert claims and defenses against a card issuer shall not be applicable to any transaction in which the person honoring the credit card (A) is the same person as the card issuer, (B) is controlled by the card issuer, (C) is under direct or indirect common control with the card issuer, (D) is a franchised dealer in the card issuer's products or services, or (E) has obtained the order for such transaction through a mail solicitation made by or participated in by the card issuer in which the cardholder is solicited to enter into such transaction by using the credit card issued by the card issuer.
>
> (b) Amount of claims and defenses assertable. The amount of claims for defenses asserted by the cardholder may not exceed the amount of credit outstanding with respect to such transaction at the time the cardholder first notifies the card issuer or the person honoring the credit card of such claim

or defense. For the purpose of determining the amount of credit outstanding in the preceding sentence, payments and credits to the cardholder's account are deemed to have been applied, in the order indicated, to the payment of: (1) late charges in the order of their entry to the account; (2) finance charges in order of their entry to the account; and (3) debits to the account other than those set forth above, in the order in which each debit entry to the account was made.

We can contrast this with checks. If I write a check to buy a defective whirlpool, I can stop payment on the check, but I have just a couple of days to do that. Once the check is paid, it's too late. I can't call up my bank a week later and tell the bank to un-pay the check. That's how it is with most payment systems.

With credit cards, it's different — at least for consumer transactions. If I buy that whirlpool, I retain my defenses to payment against the seller and against the card issuer. In terms of paying the credit card bill, the card issuer stands in the shoes of the seller. When it comes to paying the bill, if I don't have to pay the seller, I don't have to pay the card issuer. In legal terms, any defense or claim I can raise against the seller, I can likewise raise against the card issuer: "Seller didn't deliver the lectern; the lectern was defective; it was an unconscionable contract; there was a mistake, so the contract is unenforceable; or, I was able to avoid the contract under consumer protection laws."

The following sections describe the conditions for buyer protection rights.

B.   Applies only for consumer transactions

This buyer protection applies only for consumer accounts, not to "credit transactions involving extensions of credit primarily for business, commercial, or agricultural purposes."

C.   Must make good faith effort to resolve the dispute with the merchant

The customer must make a good faith effort to resolve the dispute with the merchant.

D.   Applies only to transactions over $50

The transaction must exceed $50 — a de minimus rule.

E.   Geographical limitation: transactions in state or within 100 miles of residence

To meet the geographical limitation requirement, the transaction has to be in my state of residence, or within 100 miles. If I live in Chicago, I have that protection anywhere in Illinois, or anywhere within 100 miles of Chicago (e.g., Milwaukee, Wisconsin).

What if I order something from somebody in Oregon over the phone, online, or by sending them an order through the mail? Where do these transactions occur? This hasn't been resolved—pretty surprising, because there are so many mail-order, internet, and phone transactions—but there just hasn't been that much litigation about it.

Note: The geographical limit and the $50 limit do not apply where the merchant is affiliated with the card issuer.

F.   Time limit: must give notice before paying the credit card bill

This is the limitation that has the most bite. It's a right to retain defenses against enforcement of the debt, or payment of the debt. If I charge a $10,000 whirlpool on my credit card bill and it turns out to be defective, I retain the right to raise that against the seller and against the card issuer. I have that defense when I get the bill. I have that defense until I pay that particular charge. If the bill comes and *I pay the whole thing, then I lose my right to retain defenses.*

Say that I charge a $10,000 lectern, and when I get the credit card bill there's $15,000 in charges, of which I pay $7,000. How much of that $7,000 goes toward the charge for the lectern, and how much goes toward the other charges? The payment first goes to interest and fees and then to the individual charges—first in, first out.

G.   Card issuer can charge back to merchant

What does the card issuer do? The card issuer has a right of chargeback. Under the network rules, if the customer calls up the card issuer and says, "Take that off of my credit card bill, please," the card issuer in general has the right to turn around and get its money back from the merchant bank, who then in turn has the right to get its money back from the merchant.

H. Contract law again: card issuer may provide greater protections or waive limits

Card issuers can waive the various limits. Some card issuers actually do that as a matter of routine in the contract. They say, "We will give you buyer protection, even if you buy the stuff out of state more than 100 miles away, and even if there is nothing wrong with it, and you just take it home and drop it and break it." Presumably, that makes the credit card more attractive to customers.

I. Comparison to other payment systems

Consumer→Merchant→Merchant's Bank→Card Issuer (via network)

If Consumer does not get what Merchant promised, Consumer is not required to pay the bill from Card Issuer. Credit cards thus provide a form of buyer protection not provided by payment systems that take payment from the consumer's checking account (e.g., checks, debit cards and other electronic fund transfers). Note that there are analogous protections for promissory notes given in consumer credit transactions (due to rules like the Federal Trade Commission regulations barring application of the holder in due course doctrine), non-negotiable promissory notes (which are not subject to the holder in due course doctrine, whether issued by consumers or anyone else), and letters of credit (where the buyer, who is likely to be a business rather than a consumer, can build protections into the conditions of the letter of credit).

> **QUESTION 1. Status quo.**   Carl lives in Chicago, Illinois. He drives approximately 400 miles south to visit Cairo, in southern Illinois. There, his car's muffler makes some funny noises. Using his credit card, Carl pays a local service station for a new muffler and tailpipe, some $500. Back in Chicago, Carl looks under his car and sees his old muffler and tailpipe still there. His regular mechanic explains that the southern station just changed a $5 part and listed some fictitious charges. Carl's call to the mechanic in Cairo is fruitless. Carl would not be obliged to pay the fraudulent service station. Is Carl obliged to pay the credit card bill?
>
> A. Yes. The credit card issuer is like the holder in due course of a negotiable instrument. It is not subject to defenses arising out of the underlying transaction.
> B. No. The customer can always raise a defense to payment.

> **C.** Yes. Federal law does not protect him here, because he was more than 100 miles from home (unless his card issuer gives greater rights to customers than required by law).
>
> **D.** No. He can raise his defenses to payment, because the transaction was in state.

ANALYSIS.   Carl may raise defenses against the card issuer that he could raise against the merchant. If the fraudulent mechanic sued Carl for the repair bill, Carl could raise the defenses of fraud, breach of contract, lack of consideration, consumer protection (etc., etc.). In short, if the consumer was not obliged to pay the merchant, the consumer need not pay the credit card charge.

None of the limitations would apply here. Carl can raise defenses as long as the transaction was in state *or* within 100 miles (not *and*, contrary to **C**). Cairo is 374 miles from Chicago, but both are in Illinois. The charge is for more than $50. Carl raised his objection in timely fashion. He must object before paying the charge, and he did. So **D** is the best answer.

QUESTION 2. Gold-bricker shale game. On vacation in California, Clementine uses her credit card to buy some "gold ore" for $500. Back in Miami the next week, a geologist friend tells her it is actually worthless shale. Clementine wonders if she can somehow stop payment. What rights does she have?

A. Under federal law, she has the right not to pay the charge.

B. Federal law does not help her, but her credit card contract might give her the right to avoid paying the charge.

C. She can have no right to avoid payment to the credit card company, who did not sell her the shale.

D. She can always refuse to pay, where the merchant defrauded her.

ANALYSIS.   Clementine does not have to pay the merchant, but she may have to pay the credit card bill. The statutory right to raise defenses only applies to transactions in state or within 100 miles. Clementine was out of state, thousands of miles from home. Many card issuers waive that limitation, however, giving protection to cardholders irrespective of the location of the transaction. So, **B** gets it right.

QUESTION 3. Rubbish delivery.   Sam visits a local merchant and puts $5,000 on her credit card to order some custom-made exercise equipment for her home. She pays the charge the next month as usual, to avoid high interest rates. A few months later, several heavy boxes arrive from the seller. Inside are some defective, second-hand treadmills. Sam immediately contacts her credit card company to have the charges reversed. Does federal law give her that right?

A. No. The TILA is consumer protection law. Its protections do not apply to luxury purchases.

B. Yes. A cardholder need never pay if she does not get the promised goods or services.

C. No. Sam has waited too long.

D. Yes. Sam still has the right to raise defense to payment, as long as she acts within a reasonable time after learning of the breach by the seller.

ANALYSIS. This was a consumer transaction, because it was for personal, family, or household use. Rich people are consumers, in the eyes of the TILA. The transaction occurred in state, so the geographic limitations do not bar Sam. She has, however, paid the charge, so she no longer has the right to raise defenses. Therefore, **C** is the best answer.

Nor could Sam use the 60-day limit for billing errors. One type of billing error is where the goods are rejected or not delivered, but the 60 days run from transmission of the statement reflecting the charge. That time has passed, and so **C** still is best. Note a little irony: If someone never pays a credit card bill, they do not lose the right to raise defenses. Of course, they may have other problems.

A couple of practical notes: The protection disappears when the charge is paid. So, the buyer protection is less useful for goods and services that will not be delivered for some time, or on which the buyer will not know about defects until long after the bill is paid. In addition, as with other limitations in the federal scheme, the card issuer could waive the time limit. Issuers routinely waive the geographic restrictions, but not the time limit. The credit card network rules make it much more difficult to unwind a payment.

QUESTION 4. Nantucket. Stinks Plumbing uses its credit cards to buy a shipment of buckets for inventory from a local seller, Dubious Supplies. When Stinks Plumbing realizes that it has purchased rusty buckets, does federal law give it the right to avoid paying the credit card charge?

A. No. The TILA is a consumer protection law. Its protections do not apply to business accounts.

B. Yes. The TILA applies to consumers and small businesses.

C. It depends on whether Stinks Plumbing has paid the charge yet.

D. Yes. A cardholder never has to pay if the promised goods or services are not delivered.

ANALYSIS. The protections of TILA § 170 (and the billing error procedure) apply to consumer credit card accounts, not business accounts. Federal law does not give Stinks Plumbing the right to raise defenses in this business transaction. The card issuer might, allow Stinks Plumbing to raise defenses to payment (such as by providing warranties or other money-back guaranties on purchases made with the card), either in the contract or with respect to the particular transaction, but the question asks about federal law. So, **A** is the best answer.

Note that the card issuer may not always know which transactions are covered. If a lawyer buys some curtains for the office, that charge looks just like a purchase for the home. So, if the card holder requests a chargeback, she may get it, even though she is not entitled to it.

QUESTION 5. Dabbling. Gates usually uses her credit card for family purposes. One day, she uses the credit card to purchase a 3D printer for her fledgling home business, making falcon figurines. The printer, however, is unable to render more than 2.718 D. When Gates gives notice to the credit card issuer, it responds that buyer protections do not apply to business purchases. Is Gates obliged to pay the card issuer?

A. Yes. The TILA is a consumer protection law. Its protections do not apply to business transactions.
B. No. The TILA applies here, because it is a consumer account.
C. No. The cardholder never has to pay if the promised goods or services are not delivered.
D. No. The transaction was unauthorized, because the goods were defective.

ANALYSIS. The TILA buyer protections apply if the account is a consumer account. This was a consumer account, so Gates has buyer protections, even if the particular transaction was for business purposes. Otherwise, consumers who make the occasional business charge (such as a work-related purchase) would not get appropriate protection. The best answer is **B**.

QUESTION 6. Where in the world? Waldo, of Washington State, purchases a nifty helmet online, for $100, from the website of Hatterdasher of Hatteras, North Carolina. Hatterdasher sends an entirely worthless helmet, not at all what was promised. Does federal law give Waldo the right to avoid payment of the credit card charge?

A. No. The TILA protections apply only to parties residing in the same state.
B. Yes. The TILA protects consumers in all transactions.
C. It would depend on where the transaction is deemed to have occurred.
D. No. The consumer protections of the TILA apply only to transactions of $50 or less.

ANALYSIS. The TILA protections apply only to transactions in state or within 100 miles of the consumer's residence. Where did this transaction occur? One could argue for several locations: Washington State, where Waldo ordered; Hatteras, North Carolina, where the order was received and accepted; halfway between; or cyberspace, a notional location. The TILA does not say, and courts have not definitely addressed the issue. So, **C** is the best answer—for now.

J.   The closer

> **QUESTION 7. Too late?**   Marlon, trying to remember the name of a restaurant, flips through his recent credit card bills. He notices a charge to Eastern Mountain Snorts, a snuff company. The bill was mailed to Marlon 47 days ago. Marlon got the bill two days after that and paid it in full right away. Marlon has never bought anything from Eastern Mountain Snorts. Is it too late to complain about the charge?
>
> A. Yes. The customer has the right to raise defenses to payment, but not to revoke payment.
> B. Yes. To raise a defense, Marlon must notify the card issuer within a reasonable time of receiving the statement.
> C. Yes, but Marlon will be liable for the first $50 of unauthorized charges.
> D. No. Marlon may contest this charge, even though he already paid it.

ANALYSIS. It's not too late. Marlon is not simply raising defenses to a charge—he is contesting an unauthorized charge. The limitations in TILA § 170 are not applicable. Marlon is not obliged to pay unauthorized charges, even if he unwittingly paid them or if the charges were made out of state, more than 100 miles away. Therefore, **D** is the best answer. As the previous chapter discussed, Marlon has at least until 60 days after the bill was sent (and probably more).

 # McJohn's picks

1. Status quo	D
2. Gold-bricker shale game	B
3. Rubbish delivery	C
4. Nantucket	A
5. Dabbling	B
6. Where in the world?	C
7. Too late?	D

22

Debit Cards and Other Consumer Wire Transfers: The Electronic Funds Transfer Act

~

How do I debit thee?
Let me count the ways.
A card,
Point of purchase (POP),
Direct deposit,
Online banking,
Automatic bill pay,
It's EFTA what's lefta
My ACHy breaky heart.

~

CHAPTER OVERVIEW
A. Electronic Funds Transfer Act (the EFTA)
B. When does the EFTA apply?
C. Liability for unauthorized use
   1. Federal law has step-up to theoretically unlimited liability for unauthorized use
   2. Most debit card issuers, by contract, agree not to impose liability
   3. Other EFTs (electronic fund transfers) remain subject to unlimited liability

D. Authorized use includes use by others furnished card by consumer
E. Network rules on allocating risk
F. Preauthorized transfers
G. No right to raise defense from underlying transaction against card issuer bank
H. Error resolution process: 60 days, from transmission of statement, to give notice to bank
I. Limits on fees charged to merchants by debit card network
J. The closer
✥ McJohn's picks

A.   Electronic Funds Transfer Act (the EFTA)

This chapter is about the law governing electronic fund transfers to and from a consumer's checking account, such as debit card transactions; automated clearinghouse (ACH) transfers; point-of-purchase (POP) check conversion, where the merchant uses the check to initiate a wire transfer (called "ACH POP"); online transactions using a checking account; direct deposit; telephone checks and telephone bill payment; and preauthorized bill payment. The federal Electronic Funds Transfer Act (EFTA) provides a number of rules governing the area.

Using a debit card is like writing a check. A check is an order to the bank to pay the holder of the check. Using a debit card or making any other funds transfer is an order to the bank to pay whoever has authorized and sent the transaction through. In fact, a lot of check collection is done electronically. It's not unlikely today that handing a check to a merchant means that the merchant takes it, and in essence just swipes the check and sends it right through for payment electronically—maybe even across the same network that they use for some of their debit card transactions.

B.   When does the EFTA apply?

The EFTA applies to an "electronic funds transfer" defined as follows:

> any transfer of funds, other than a transaction originated by check, draft, or similar paper instrument, which is initiated through an electronic terminal, telephonic instrument, or computer or magnetic tape so as to order, instruct, or authorize a financial institution to debit or credit an account. Such term includes, but is not limited to, point-of-sale transfers, automated teller machine transactions, direct deposits or withdrawals of funds, and transfers initiated by telephone.

EFTA § 903(6).

"Account" is a defined term:

the term "account" means a demand deposit, savings deposit, or other asset account (other than an occasional or incidental credit balance in an open end credit plan as defined in section 103(i) of this Act as described in regulations of the Board, established primarily for personal, family, or household purposes.

EFTA § 903.

The EFTA governs any transfer of funds to or from a consumer's account that originates from an electronic terminal. This means that checks aren't covered by the EFTA, even though you might have a lot of electronic messages going around. A check transaction is initiated by writing a check. The EFTA applies only when the transfer is initiated from an electronic terminal to take funds out of or put funds into a consumer's account.

C.   Liability for unauthorized use

The EFTA has a tricky-to-read provision providing the limits on liability for unauthorized use. Here's the rule in detail—it is summarized below.

Consumer Liability

(a) Unauthorized electronic fund transfers; limit. A consumer shall be liable for any unauthorized electronic fund transfer involving the account of such consumer only if the card or other means of access utilized for such transfer was an accepted card or other means of access and if the issuer of such card, code, or other means of access has provided a means whereby the user of such card, code, or other means of access can be identified as the person authorized to use it, such as by signature, photograph, or fingerprint or by electronic or mechanical confirmation. In no event, however, shall a consumer's liability for an unauthorized transfer exceed the lesser of—

(1) $50; or

(2) the amount of money or value of property or services obtained in such unauthorized electronic fund transfer prior to the time the financial institution is notified of, or otherwise becomes aware of, circumstances which lead to the reasonable belief that an unauthorized electronic fund transfer involving the consumer's account has been or may be affected. Notice under this paragraph is sufficient when such steps have been taken as may be reasonably required in the ordinary course of business to provide the financial institution with the pertinent information, whether or not any particular officer, employee, or agent of the financial institution does in fact receive such information.

Notwithstanding the foregoing, reimbursement need not be made to the consumer for losses the financial institution establishes would not have occurred but for the failure of the consumer to report within sixty days of transmittal of the statement (or in extenuating circumstances such as extended travel or hospitalization, within a reasonable time under the circumstances) any unauthorized electronic fund transfer or account error which appears on the periodic statement provided to the consumer under section 906. In addition, reimbursement need not be made to the consumer for losses which the financial institution establishes would not have occurred but for the failure of the consumer to report any loss or theft of a card or other means of access within two business days after the consumer learns of the loss or theft (or in extenuating circumstances such as extended travel or hospitalization, within a longer period which is reasonable under the circumstances), but the consumer's liability under this subsection in any such case may not exceed a total of $ 500, or the amount of unauthorized electronic fund transfers which occur following the close of two business days (or such longer period) after the consumer learns of the loss or theft but prior to notice to the financial institution under this subsection, whichever is less.

EFTA § 909.

To put the foregoing in a nutshell:

1. *Federal law has step-up to theoretically unlimited liability for unauthorized use*
2. *Most debit card issuers, by contract, agree not to impose liability*
3. *Other EFTs (electronic fund transfers) remain subject to unlimited liability*

These are explained in more detail below.

1. *Federal law has step-up to theoretically unlimited liability for unauthorized use*

The possible limits are more risky to consumers than credit cards. For credit cards, we saw that a cardholder is liable for $50, period, of unauthorized use. For debit cards and other consumer wire transfers, if the consumer delays long enough, she can (in theory, if not often in practice) face unlimited liability.

If timely notice is given, within two business days of learning of the loss of the card, the cap is $50. The two days run from when the customer knows or should have known that they lost their card. If timely notice isn't given, then the limit goes up from $50 to $500. Then, if they continue to fail to give notice for a long time—say, the statement is sent to them, 60 days goes by from transmittal of the statement, and they still haven't given notice—then the cap comes off. The consumer can be liable without limit.

This looks like pretty scary, potentially unlimited liability for losing your debit card. In practice, it really doesn't often take effect when use of a debit card requires a PIN (personal identification number). If a person just loses their card and someone else picks it up, unless they manage to guess the PIN, it won't help them. There is also a natural limit. The person having lost the card is likely to recognize that and give notice to their bank, because they want to stop outflows and get a new card. Even if they don't give notice, the outflow would likely be capped by the amount of money in their checking account (unless the bank funds overdrafts, which banks often do by agreement, sometimes with a considerable fee). There is also protection in the statute against mishaps, forgiving delayed notice "in extenuating circumstances such as extended travel or hospitalization, within a reasonable time under the circumstances." Having said that, the issue does concern consumers and there have been some cases in which people had considerable losses.

2. Most debit card issuers, by contract, agree not to impose liability

Things changed when the credit card networks began to issue PIN-less cards, which do not require a PIN for many uses. At first, consumers were worried about debit cards because money comes right out of their checking account and, in theory, they faced unlimited liability. Some consumers were therefore reluctant to have PIN-less debit cards. In addition to that, there was a possibility that Congress would step in and regulate things.

MasterCard and Visa responded. They gradually provided by contract that consumers would have no liability for unauthorized use. That allows the card issuers to make debit cards more attractive to consumers and rely on their own ability to reduce fraud, rather than relying on the ability to go after consumers for unauthorized charges. The networks ran many advertisements to get this across to consumers.

3. Other EFTs (electronic fund transfers) remain subject to unlimited liability

The greater liability still potentially applies to other consumer funds transfers using other means of access: debit cards issued by entities that have not agreed to take the loss for unauthorized use, online banking, online purchases, POP check conversion, and so on.

Unlimited liability risk goes beyond cards, however. It can apply to any consumer EFT, such as transfers from a bank account. A wealthy Wall Street investor lost approximately $300,000 because he did not give timely notice as an unknown malefactor made a series of transfers from his account over some 15 months. "The Bank Account that Sprang a Leak," *New York Times* (Aug. 30, 2008).

D. Authorized use includes use by others furnished card by consumer

What is unauthorized use? The statute, as with credit cards, defines unauthorized use:

> the term "unauthorized electronic fund transfer" means an electronic fund transfer from a consumer's account initiated by a person other than the

consumer without actual authority to initiate such transfer and from which the consumer receives no benefit, but the term does not include any electronic fund transfer (A) initiated by a person other than the consumer who was furnished with the card, code, or other means of access to such consumer's account by such consumer, unless the consumer has notified the financial institution involved the transfers by such other person are no longer authorized, (B) initiated with fraudulent intent by the consumer or any person acting in concert with the consumer, or (C) which constitutes an error committed by a financial institution.

EFTA § 903(11).

In plain terms, it is authorized use if 1) the cardholder gives actual authority, 2) the cardholder receives a benefit, or 3) the cardholder furnishes the card (or other means of access) to the person making the use. Although phrased differently, in practical terms this is similar to credit card law, where use is authorized if there is actual, apparent, or implied authority. Likewise, with debit cards (and other consumer electronic fund transfers), the consumer will not be shielded by the limits for unauthorized use, where the consumer knowingly provides someone the means to make the funds transfer.

QUESTION 1. Astray.   Collector learns that a rare Bowie baseball card is for sale at a local store. Collector's brother-in-law offers to go get it. Collector hands over her debit card and PIN number, strictly telling him to withdraw no more than $100. Over the next few days, the brother-in-law drains $10,000 from the account an fritters it away. Is Collector entitled to have the money put back?

A. No. Collector has no rights against the bank.
B. Yes, beyond $50.
C. Yes, beyond $500.
D. Yes, if the card was a Visa or MasterCard.

ANALYSIS.   Collector is liable for all authorized use, and this was all authorized use. Collector only gave express authority to withdraw $100, but authorized use also includes any use by someone furnished the card and the means to use it. So **A** is the best answer.

The $50 (for use within three days) and $500 (for use after three days, but before 60 days from when the statement is sent showing unauthorized use) are limits on liability for unauthorized use. This is authorized use, so the limits do not apply. Therefore, **B** and **C** are out.

Visa and MasterCard do not apply any liability for unauthorized use. But, again, this is authorized use, so **D** is out.

QUESTION 2. Benefits. Sundance buys a new bicycle for his friend, Butch, as a birthday present. After crashing the bicycle, Butch is further dismayed to learn that Sundance paid for the skis by surreptitiously making an online payment from Butch's checking account. Butch demands that the bank put the money back in the account, on the grounds that he did not authorize the transfer. Must the bank comply?

A. No. The transfer was authorized.
B. No. Butch was negligent with his account.
C. Yes. Butch did not authorize the transfer, because he did not furnish the means of access to Sundance.
D. Yes. Butch is not obliged to pay, because the bicycle has been destroyed.

ANALYSIS. The use is deemed to be authorized. Butch did not furnish the means of access to Sundance. But use is unauthorized if the cardholder gives actual authority (not applicable here), the cardholder receives a benefit (applicable here), OR the cardholder furnished the means of access (not applicable here). **A** is the best answer.

QUESTION 3. Ribbit. After using her debit card to buy some groceries, Debbie notices that the card must have fallen from her wallet. Due to a crazy work schedule, Debbie does not get around to notifying her bank for almost a month, when a statement arrives showing $10,000 in purchases and ATM withdrawals, evenly spread over the month. For how much is Debbie potentially responsible under federal law?

A. $50.
B. $500.
C. $10,000, because she waited too long to give notice.
D. $10,000, if she is held to have been negligent.
E. $10,000. The use is authorized, because she furnished the card to the bad actor.

ANALYSIS. Debbie, under federal law, is potentially liable for $500. The scale is $0 for notice before unauthorized use, $50 for timely notice (within two days of learning of loss of card), and $500 for untimely notice; then the cap comes off 60 days after the bank sends the statement giving notice of unauthorized use (but Debbie hasn't reached that date yet). **B** is the best answer.

That is the liability federal law allows banks to impose on customers. If Debbie's card is a Visa or MasterCard, however, her exposure is $0. By contract, Visa and MasterCard (and many other issuers) do not impose any liability for unauthorized use.

Debbie would be liable for all use of the card if she furnished the card to the user, because that would make it authorized use. But "furnishing" the card means more than losing it, contrary to **E**.

QUESTION 4. Wayward wallet. Wally's wallet is stolen at the ballpark. Wally had written his PIN on a sheet of special numbers kept in the wallet, along with various passwords and phone numbers. Within hours, the thief withdraws $6,000 from an ATM, emptying Wally's account. Moping, Wally waits over three months before finally notifying his bank. For how much of the loss is Wally liable?

A. $50.
B. $500, due to his delay in giving notice.
C. $6,000, due to his delay in giving notice.
D. $6,000, due to his negligence in leaving the PIN written on a paper kept with the card.

ANALYSIS. The key here is timing. Wally has waited so long that he is past the 60-day mark, giving him potentially unlimited liability. But he would be liable for such use only if it occurs after the 60-day mark. The only unauthorized use occurred right after his loss, within the 2-day window. So, lucky Wally is liable for only $50 (under federal law; again, Visa and MasterCard do not impose any liability, by contract). **A** is correct.

QUESTION 5. Stealthy. Debon keeps his rarely used debit card in a locked desk drawer. Voleuse burglarizes Debon's home and steals the card, but leaves little trace. Debon does not notice anything amiss until the next bank statement arrives, showing $5,000 gone from his account in various transactions over that time. He calls his bank forthwith. For how much is Debon responsible?

A. $50.
B. $500.
C. $10,000.
D. $10,000, if he is held to have been negligent.

ANALYSIS. The limit is $50 for timely notice. Here, the card was stolen a month ago. But the clock starts ticking only when the consumer learns of the theft. Debon gave timely notice. **A** is the best answer, and it is unlikely the bank would seek the $50.

> **QUESTION 6. Electronic fun transfer.**   Irena owes $100 to her room-
> mate, Aoi. Irena hands him her debit card, tells him the PIN, and says he
> can get the money from an ATM. Irena does not see him around for a few
> days, by which time Aoi has withdrawn some $2,500. For how much is
> Irena liable?
>
> A. $50
> B. $100
> C. $150
> D. $500
> E. $2,500

ANALYSIS.   The limits apply to unauthorized use. This is authorized use, which includes any transfer "initiated by a person other than the consumer who was furnished with the card, code, or other means of access to such consumer's account by such consumer." Irena is liable for the whole amount, making **E** the best answer.

> **QUESTION 7. Give me liberty or give me debit.**   Prithvi is just
> about to put his debit card into an ATM, when a stranger flashes a gun
> and demands the card and the PIN. The stranger withdraws $800 and
> disappears. Prithvi notifies his bank the next day. The bank takes the hard
> line that Prithvi is liable for the entire $800. For how much is Prithvi liable
> under federal law?
>
> A. $50
> B. $500
> C. $800
> D. $0

ANALYSIS.   Where Prithvi gave the card and PIN at gunpoint, it would be unauthorized use—even if Prithvi gave the stranger the card and number. Coercion does not give authorization. The same would be true if Prithvi operated the ATM himself, at gunpoint. As long as Prithvi gave timely notice, the applicable limit would be $50 (assuming it was neither a Visa nor a MasterCard, nor another debit card where the issuer has agreed to zero liability for unauthorized use—which is a likely scenario). **A** is the correct answer—but it would be a foolish bank that enforced the $50 in a case like this.

E.   Network rules on allocating risk

We have seen the consumer is generally not liable for unauthorized use. Who is—the merchant that honored the card or the bank that issued that card?

Risk of loss is not governed by the federal statute or state common law. Rather, the risk of loss is governed by the rules of the relevant debit card network: If somebody steals a debit card and uses it to buy something from a merchant the network rules generally put that loss not on the merchant, but on the issuer, in face-to-face transactions. For online, telephone, and other "card-not-present," transactions, the merchant may take the risk.

As with credit cards, to encourage merchants to honor debit cards, the bank networks say, "If you honor a stolen card or somebody makes unauthorized use of a card with you, or our network is malfunctioning and authorizes transactions by mistake, the banks take the loss. As long as you (merchant) process the card correctly, we take the loss for stolen cards, for unauthorized use, and for network malfunctions."

QUESTION 8. Loss falls on whom? MOV sells an ATV for $5,000 to a new customer, who pays with a debit card. MOV checks the customer's identification and processes the transaction by the book. It turns out that the debit card belonged to Bilski, who had lost it hours ago and reported the loss just minutes after the sale went through. Who takes the loss?

A. MOV, which dealt with the fraudulent actor.
B. Bilski, who lost her debit card, making the fraud possible.
C. The issuing bank, which authorized the transaction.
D. Whichever party is held to be most at fault.

ANALYSIS. Bilski would be liable for $50 at most, and zero if the issuer has agreed to zero liability, like Visa and MasterCard. The network rules would then allocate the loss, as between MOV and the issuing bank. The network rules generally place the loss on the issuer (not the merchant) in face-to-face transactions. So, the best answer is **C**.

F.   Preauthorized transfers

The EFTA also provides some limits on preauthorized transfers. The consumer must authorize in writing and be able to stop payment, by notice, up to three days before the transfer. The payee or bank must give prior notice to the consumer for repeating transfers, such as where the credit card bill states the payment will be made automatically from a designated account.

§ 1693E. Preauthorized Transfers

(a) A preauthorized electronic fund transfer from a consumer's account may be authorized by the consumer only in writing, and a copy of such authorization shall be provided to the consumer when made. A consumer may stop payment of a preauthorized electronic fund transfer by notifying the financial institution orally or in writing at any time up to three business days preceding the scheduled date of such transfer. The financial institution may require written confirmation to be provided to it within fourteen days of an oral notification if, when the oral notification is made, the consumer is advised of such requirement and the address to which such confirmation should be sent.

(b) In the case of preauthorized transfers from a consumer's account to the same person which may vary in amount, the financial institution or designated payee shall, prior to each transfer, provide reasonable advance notice to the consumer, in accordance with regulations of the Board, of the amount to be transferred and the scheduled date of the transfer.

G.   No right to raise defense from underlying transaction against card issuer bank

If a consumer buys a kayak with a credit card and it is defective, she doesn't have to pay. Any defense the consumer had arising out of that transaction she could raise against the bank. There is no counterpart to that with respect to funds transfers, such as debit cards or online funds transfers. If a consumer uses a funds transfer to buy the kayak, that tells her bank to give her money to the merchant, period. If she finds out the kayak is deficient, she can't take it up with the bank. Rather, she must take it up with the merchant.

Perhaps that's one reason Craigslist (www.craigslist.org) advises users as follows: "**Avoid scams and fraud by dealing locally!** Beware of any deal involving Western Union, Moneygram, wire transfer, cashier check, money order, shipping, escrow, or any promise of transaction protection/certification/guarantee." If the consumer uses any of those forms of payment, she will not be able to raise her defenses against the bank, if the goods are defective or are not delivered. There are other reasons, as well, not to use such irreversible forms of payment, or to agree to receive payment by such means, when proffered by persons unknown.

QUESTION 9. **Buyer protection?** Buyer purchased a car for her family from Seller. Seller promised Buyer that the car is in perfect working order. If the car turns out to be completely defective, which of the following is true?

A. If Buyer paid with a check that has been paid, Buyer may rescind payment.

B. If Buyer paid with a debit card, then Buyer can require that the money be refunded by the bank.

C. If Buyer paid with a credit card and Seller refuses to compensate Buyer, then Buyer can refuse to pay the credit card issuer because the car is defective.

D. If Buyer paid with a business wire transfer, then Buyer can require the money be refunded by the bank.

ANALYSIS.   This question emphasizes that a credit card transaction is the only one of the payment systems discussed with a right to raise defenses against the paying bank. If Buyer wrote a check, Buyer has a limited right to stop payment. As long as the bank has not paid the check yet, Buyer can stop payment. That ability is likely to last only a matter of a few days, and that window is shrinking as merchants and banks increasingly process checks electronically. With wire transfers, payment becomes final very quickly. Debit cards, unlike credit cards, have no right to raise defenses. We will see in later chapters (sorry, makes this question sort of unfair to ask here) that the same is true for wire transfers by businesses. So, the best answer is **C**.

QUESTION 10. Credit card.   Janus purchases a video game system for his home. At the checkout counter, he hands over his MaestroCard (a dual credit–debit card). Asked "Debit or credit?", Janus responds, "Credit." Within two weeks, the game system crashes and burns. The merchant refuses to give Janus his money back. Janus waits for the credit card bill, intending to tell the issuer to remove the charge. The charge does not, however, appear on the bill. At first, Janus thinks that he got the system for free—exactly what it was worth. Then he checks his checking account, and realizes that the clerk processed the sale as a debit card transaction. Can Janus raise his defense against payment of the credit card charge?

A. No. It was processed as a debit card transaction.
B. Yes. He agreed with the merchant to treat it as a credit card transaction.
C. No. The consumer protection rules apply only to purchases of necessities, not frivolities like video game systems.
D. The law is unclear on this point.

ANALYSIS.   The protections in TILA § 170 apply to a "transaction in which the credit card is used as a method of payment or extension of credit." Was that the case here? Janus would argue that he handed over a credit card and so identified it. The bank, if it resisted, would argue that Janus handed over a debit card and that the method of payment was a debit card, because that is how the network processed it. Both arguments are plausible, and this has not been resolved. Under the present state of the law, **D** is the best answer.

H. Error resolution process: 60 days, from transmission of statement, to give notice to bank

Error Resolution

(a) Notification to financial institution of error. If a financial institution, within sixty days after having transmitted to a consumer documentation pursuant to section 906(a), (c), or (d) or notification pursuant to section 906(b), receives oral or written notice in which the consumer—

(1) sets forth or otherwise enables the financial institution to identify the name and account number of the consumer;

(2) indicates the consumer's belief that the documentation, or, in the case of notification pursuant to section 906(b), the consumer's account, contains an error and the amount of such error; and

(3) sets forth the reasons for the consumer's belief (where applicable) that an error has occurred,

the financial institution shall investigate the alleged error, determine whether an error has occurred, and report or mail the results of such investigation and determination to the consumer within ten business days. The financial institution may require written confirmation to be provided to it within ten business days of an oral notification of error if, when the oral notification is made, the consumer is advised of such requirement and the address to which such confirmation should be sent. A financial institution which requires written confirmation in accordance with the previous sentence need not provisionally recredit a consumer's account in accordance with subsection (c), nor shall the financial institution be liable under subsection (e) if the written confirmation is not received within the ten-day period referred to in the previous sentence.

(b) Correction of error; interest. If the financial institution determines that an error did occur, it shall promptly, but in no event more than one business day after such determination, correct the error, subject to section 909, including the crediting of interest where applicable.

(c) Provisional recredit of consumer's account. If a financial institution receives notice of an error in the manner and within the time period specified in subsection (a), it may, in lieu of the requirements of subsections (a) and (b), within ten business days after receiving such notice provisionally recredit the consumer's account for the amount alleged to be in error, subject to section 909, including interest where applicable, pending the conclusion of its investigation and its determination of whether an error has occurred. Such investigation shall be concluded not later than forty-five days after receipt of notice of the error. During the pendency of the investigation, the consumer shall have full use of the funds provisionally recredited.

(d) Absence of error; finding; explanation. If the financial institution determines after its investigation pursuant to subsection (a) or (c) that an error did not occur, it shall deliver or mail to the consumer an explanation of its findings within 3 business days after the conclusion of its investigation, and upon request of the consumer promptly deliver or mail to the consumer reproductions of all documents which the financial institution relied on to conclude that such error did not occur. The financial institution shall include notice of the right to request reproductions with the explanation of its findings. . . .

(f) Acts constituting error. For the purpose of this section, an error consists of —

(1) an unauthorized electronic fund transfer;

(2) an incorrect electronic fund transfer from or to the consumer's account;

(3) the omission from a periodic statement of an electronic fund transfer affecting the consumer's account which should have been included;

(4) a computational error by the financial institution;

(5) the consumer's receipt of an incorrect amount of money from an electronic terminal;

(6) a consumer's request for additional information or clarification concerning an electronic fund transfer or any documentation required by this title; or

(7) any other error described in regulations of the Board.

As with unauthorized transfers, there is a 60-day time period to resolve errors. Here, however, the time period means something somewhat different. If there's a billing error—say that my bank puts an erroneous $500 charge on my account—I'm liable for zero of that. Of course, it's an error. I have to give notice within 60 days of when the statement is transmitted, however. When the bank gets notice from the customer, the bank has to act quickly—within ten business days.

The bank has to re-credit the customer's account or else respond and explain why it isn't an error. This is a relatively tight time frame—the theory being that this is money taken out of the consumer's account. This isn't just an extra charge that's been put on the credit card bill. So, unless the bank can show that there isn't an error, the bank has to re-credit the account while it is doing the investigation. It has just ten days to do that.

QUESTION 11. Time to reflect. Divine checks her account balance online, and sees that the bank has made a mysterious charge of $5,000 for "Mortgage Payment." Divine has no mortgage to pay. She immediately contacts the bank, demanding the money be put back right away. The end of the month is nigh, and Divine needs the money to cover her rent check and other bills. How quickly must the bank replace the erroneously charged account?

A. As soon as reasonably possible.
B. After a reasonable investigation, up to ten days.
C. Within ten days.
D. When the bank is reasonably certain there has been a mistake.

ANALYSIS. The bank must make a provision re-credit "within ten business days" while it investigates. Therefore, **C** is the best answer. This gives banks a little protection against frivolous claims used to get cash but can be harsh on consumers who need access to the money.

I.   Limits on fees charged to merchants by debit card network

In 2011, the Federal Reserve issued regulations limiting the portion of a debit card transaction fee that is paid to the card issuer (the debit card interchange fee). Generally, the debit card issuer may charge no more than 24 cents per transaction, a limit that was set after considerable debate before the Federal Reserve between merchants and banks.

J.   The closer

QUESTION 12. Out of town. Major Tom goes on a two-year mission to Mars, spending much of the time in suspended animation to save oxygen, food, and water. On returning, Major Tom learns that Yuri has used Major Tom's debit card without authority and emptied the $60,000 balance. Major Tom's debit card was issued by Little Local Bank, which does not limit liability to zero dollars (unlike Visa and MasterCard). Is Tom entitled to get the money back from his bank?

A. Not for any funds transfer that occurred more than 60 days after the bank sent a statement showing unauthorized transfers.
B. Yes, because Tom is excused by an extenuating circumstance: extended travel.
C. Not unless the bank transmitted the statement to him in space.
D. Umm . . .

ANALYSIS. The statute extends the deadline for delay, requiring notice for "extenuating circumstances such as extended travel or hospitalization, within a longer period which is reasonable under the circumstances." Major Tom would not be liable beyond $50, as long as he gave timely notice on his return. **B** is the correct answer.

 # McJohn's picks

1.	Astray	**A**
2.	Benefits	**A**
3.	Ribbit	**B**
4.	Wayward wallet	**A**
5.	Stealthy	**A**
6.	Electronic fun transfer	**E**
7.	Give me liberty or give me debit	**A**
8.	Loss falls on whom?	**C**
9.	Buyer protection?	**C**
10.	Credit card	**D**
11.	Time to reflect	**C**
12.	Out of town	**B**

23

Commercial Wire Transfers

Sending money down a wire
Makes a funny thing transpire.
Money gone in one account
Appears elsewhere, the same amount.
Spooky action at a distance?
Just a fund transfer acceptance.

A.   When Article 4A applies, along with some key terms

A funds transfer (commonly called a "wire transfer") is a transfer of funds from one party's account to another. It's the payment system of choice for larger transfers of money. If one company buys another company, or a company gets a loan, or a bank is moving funds around, or a company is moving funds from one account to another, or a debtor is

paying off a billion dollars in bonds that it owes to a consortium of investors . . . et cetera, et cetera, et cetera. The larger the amount of money that
is involved in a transaction, the more likely it is that the parties arrange for
a wire transfer. For consumer wire transfers, the Electronic Funds Transfer
Act (EFTA) governs, as discussed earlier in the book. For other wire transfers, the governing law is Uniform Commercial Code (UCC) Article 4A.

Wire transfers are quick (can be done in a matter of seconds, and almost
always are done on the same day) and relatively cheap. Efficiency and low cost
make wire transfers an attractive payment system. However, the technologi-
cal systems that implement them can be very sophisticated, because there's so
much money at stake. It's worth putting a lot of money into encryption and
other security measures to prevent a person from just logging on and sending
$100 million to a bank account on a sunny island with no extradition treaty.

From a legal point of view, Article 4A provides a nice clear framework. A
couple of decades ago, someone thought, "There's trillions of dollars a day in
wire transfers, and nobody knows what law governs them, because the states
haven't developed a comprehensive set of rules governing them. So, if something goes wrong with a wire transfer, it's not at all clear who takes the loss."
Interested parties therefore drafted a brand-new Article 4A of the UCC and
squeezed it in between Article 4 (banking) and Article 5 (letters of credit).

As § 4A-102 states, Article 4A applies to any "funds transfer," defined in
§ 4A-104 to mean

> the series of transactions, beginning with the originator's payment order,
> made for the purpose of making payment to the beneficiary of the order. The
> term includes any payment order issued by the originator's bank or an inter-
> mediary bank intended to carry out the originator's payment order. A funds
> transfer is completed by acceptance by the beneficiary's bank of a payment
> order for the benefit of the beneficiary of the originator's payment order.

In short, a funds transfer is accomplished by a series of "payment orders." A
payment order is defined as

> an instruction of a sender to a receiving bank, transmitted orally, electroni-
> cally, or in writing, to pay, or to cause another bank to pay, a fixed or deter-
> minable amount of money to a beneficiary if:
>   (i) the instruction does not state a condition to payment to the benefi-
> ciary other than time of payment,
>   (ii) the receiving bank is to be reimbursed by debiting an account of, or
> otherwise receiving payment from, the sender, and
>   (iii) the instruction is transmitted by the sender directly to the receiving
> bank or to an agent, funds-transfer system, or communication system for
> transmittal to the receiving bank.

§ 4A-103(a)(1).

So, a payment order is an unconditional instruction transmitted to
a bank to put money into somebody's account, where the bank will have

a right of reimbursement for sending that money. Note that it must be unconditional: Article 4A will not apply if the order is conditional, such as, "Wire $500,000 to Seller if the agreed-upon goods are shipped." Also, it need not be electronic. Article 4A generally applies to wire transfers but could also apply to a funds transfer initiated by a handwritten note or by spoken word.

Section 4A-108 then ensures that consumer funds transfers are not governed by Article 4A: "This Article does not apply to a funds transfer any part of which is governed by the Electronic Fund Transfer Act of 1978." Article 4A gives a set of rules intended to govern transactions by commercial parties. The rules here are governed by the policy that commercial parties are sophisticated and know the risks that they take on. They aren't a set of consumer protection rules; these are rules that give sophisticated commercial parties a framework with which to deal with each other.

Let's make these terms more concrete. A simple wire transfer can be illustrated as follows:

Boston Bank	→	Seattle Bank
↑	P.O.2	↓
P.O.1		funds to
Buyer		Seller, Account #2001

To use a simple, two-bank example: Buyer is in Boston, and Seller is in Seattle. The only information that Buyer needs from Seller to wire the money is: who you are, what bank you use, your bank account number, and how much I owe you. Buyer sends a payment order to Buyer's bank: "Wire $100,000 to Seller, Account #2001 at Seattle Bank." (Of course, actual payment orders use more formal terms.)

Boston Bank happens to have a direct relationship with Seattle Bank. Boston Bank sends a payment order to Seattle Bank: "Put $100,000 into Seller's account at your bank, Account #2001." Seller's bank, also known as the beneficiary's bank, can implement that by crediting Seller's account.

As with other payment systems, there's a need for reimbursement. Seattle Bank is entitled to reimbursement from Boston Bank, who is in turn entitled to reimbursement from its customer, Buyer.

I say "has a right of reimbursement" because in most transactions, originator's bank won't actually send out the fund transfer until it has the money. If the customer says, "Send $100,000 to Seller in Seattle," the originator's bank will say (more diplomatically than this), "First, you give me $100,000; then I'll send out that payment order. Otherwise, I could send the payment order, it gets put in effect, I'm obliged to reimburse the other bank, and I have to rely on your promise to reimburse me."

Here are the same parties, with their Article 4A terms added in italics:

Boston Bank   →   Seattle Bank
Originator's bank   *Beneficiary's bank*

↑   P.O.2   ↓
P.O.1   funds to
Buyer   Seller
Originator   *Beneficiary*

Each bank receiving a payment order is a *receiving bank*, so here that would be Boston Bank and Seattle Bank.

Often, a funds transfer requires more than the two parties' banks.

Boston   →   Federal   →   Seattle
Bank   Reserve   Bank
↑   P.O. 2   P.O. 3   ↓
P.O. 1   funds to
Buyer   Seller
Originator   *Beneficiary*

Buyer in Boston will contact its bank and say "Send $100,000 to Seller, Account #2001 at Seattle Bank." Boston Bank does not have any regular dealings with Seattle Bank but can implement that through an intermediary, likely to be the Federal Reserve. Boston Bank sends a payment order: "Federal Reserve, put $100,000 in Seller's account, Account #2001 at Seattle Bank." The Federal Reserve contacts Seattle Bank directly, or might contact a big bank in Seattle that then contacts a smaller bank in Seattle. It's an elegant, nested framework. The originator just sends out a payment order and the first bank sends it to a bank that is a little bit closer to the target bank. That party in turn sends it to another bank that is a little bit closer to the target bank until the money actually hits the bank at which you're aiming, and the money goes into the person's account.

The most common intermediary is the Fedwire Funds Service, a service provided by the Federal Reserve System (America's central banking system, with 12 branches in major cities). Many banks have accounts at the Federal Reserve, and those that don't, generally have relationships with banks that do. Fedwire handles around $3 trillion a day in wire transfers.

Two other common intermediaries are CHIPS (a private clearinghouse in New York for large-value wire transactions, whose members are large banks) and Swift (an international financial messaging system often used to set up bilateral international wire transfers).

QUESTION 1. 4A or not 4A, that is the question. Tonxtu Education Inc. sends a letter to Ana Bank, instructing the bank that whenever the balance in Tonxtu's low-interest checking account exceeds

$50,000 to wire the excess to Tonxtu's higher-yield investment account at another bank. Ana Bank loses the letter and fails to follow the instructions. Meanwhile, Ana Bank sends a letter to its customers, including Tonxtu, saying, "We are changing our wire transfer setup. If you want to keep your wire transfers going, you have to send in a new agreement." Tonxtu didn't do that. Because Ana Bank was not transferring funds from the low-interest account, the balance went from $10,000, to $110,000, to around $20 million, just sitting in the account getting zero interest—in effect, a $20 million interest-free loan to the bank. Tonxtu sues for lost interest.

Tonxtu's lawyers decide that a breach of contract action against Ana Bank will not succeed (because the contract between the parties, drafted by Ana Bank, protects Ana Bank against such claims). But if Article 4A applies, Tonxtu might win (owing to some provisions in Article 4A that we have not looked at in this chapter). When Tontxu sues Ana Bank, does Article 4A apply to the case?

A. Yes, because the case involves wire transfers, or lack thereof.
B. Yes, because the letter is a payment order.
C. No, because the letter is not a payment order.
D. No, because the letter is a check, governed by Article 4.

ANALYSIS. This question is based on *Trustmark Ins. Co. v. Bank One*, 48 P.3d 485 (Ariz. App. 2002). It gives a nice example of a case in which the determinative legal issue is an issue of scope: "What body of law governs this case?"

Article 4A applies to "funds transfers." A funds transfer is "the series of transactions, beginning with the originator's payment order, made for the purpose of making payment to the beneficiary of the order." So, Article 4A will apply only if the letter qualified as a payment order. In order to be a payment order, Article 4A requires, among other things, that "the instruction does not state a condition to payment to the beneficiary other than time of payment." Tonxtu's letter stated a condition: wire funds out whenever the balance exceeds $50,000. The letter was not a payment order, so Article 4A does not apply.

This result is not a sheer technicality. Article 4A does not have provisions to deal with conditions. Rather, it is drafted to deal with unconditional orders. When there are conditions, contract law is better adapted.

The best answer is **C**.

QUESTION 2. Which? Of the following transactions, which would be subject to Article 4A?

A. Customer, a business, sends an e-mail, instructing Bank to pay $10,000 into Supplier's account from Customer's account.
B. Customer, a business, sends an encrypted wire transfer order to Bank, to pay $10,000 into Supplier's account from Customer's account.

> **C.** Customer, a business, shouts across the street to Bank, to pay $10,000 into Supplier's account from Customer's account.
> **D.** Customer, a business, sends an e-mail, instructing Bank to pay $10,000 into Supplier's account from Customer's account, provided that Supplier's credit rating is at least A minus.
> **E.** Client sends an encrypted wire transfer order to Bank, to pay $10,000 in Microcenter's account, to pay for a new home computing network.
> **F.** All of the above.
> **G.** A–C only.

ANALYSIS. Article 4A applies broadly to commercial funds transfers, whether initiated electronically or otherwise. Answers **A** through **C** are all commercial funds transfers, making **G** the best answer.

Article 4A does not apply to conditional orders to pay, ruling out **D**.

Nor does it apply to consumer funds transfers, ruling out **E**.

QUESTION 3. Terminology. Ollie Hardware directs Roach Bank to wire $50,000 to Boffo Gardening's account #0002627 at Vaudeville Bank, a little bank in San Francisco. Roach Bank does not have a direct relationship with Vaudeville Bank, but Roach Bank does often deal with Trolley Bank, a big San Francisco bank, on such matters. Roach Bank implements the payment order by sending an electronic message to Trolley Bank, saying, "Put $50,000 in Boffo Gardening's account #0002627 at Vaudeville Bank." Roach Bank then sends a payment order to Vaudeville Bank, saying, "Put $50,000 in Boffo Gardening's account #0002627 with you." Which banks are receiving banks?

A. None. Nobody has received any money yet.
B. Roach Bank, which received the initial payment order.
C. Roach Bank, Trolley Bank, and Vaudeville Bank, which all received payment orders.
D. Vaudeville Bank, which is going to receive the money.

ANALYSIS.

Roach Bank	→	Trolley Bank	→	Vaudeville Bank
↑	P.O. 2		P.O. 3	↓
P.O. 1				funds to
Ollie Hardware				Boffo Gardening
Originator				*Beneficiary*

A bank that receives a payment order is a receiving bank. Roach Bank, Trolley Bank, and Vaudeville Bank each received payment orders, so each is a receiving bank. **C** is the best answer.

The other answers give plausible readings of the term "receiving bank," but the term is not open to such interpretation. It is a defined term in Article 4A. So, this question emphasizes an important skill in applying a statute. If a term is defined, that is the meaning that governs.

B. Acceptance by the beneficiary's bank: the key moment

The central concept in Article 4A is acceptance by the beneficiary's bank.

Boston Bank	→	Seattle Bank
Originator's bank		*Beneficiary's bank*
↑	P.O.2	↓
P.O.1		funds to
Buyer		Seller
Originator		*Beneficiary*

A receiving bank, other than the beneficiary's bank, accepts a payment order simply by executing it, meaning it issues a payment order intended to carry out the order it received. UCC §§ 4A-209(a), 4A-301(a). Acceptance by the beneficiary's bank is more momentous. There are two key questions: When does acceptance occur, and what are the effects of acceptance?

C. What constitutes acceptance by beneficiary's bank?

Section 4A-209(b) defines what triggers acceptance by the beneficiary's bank:

a beneficiary's bank accepts a payment order at the earliest of the following times:

(1) when the bank (i) pays the beneficiary as stated in Section 4A-405(a) or 4A-405(b), or (ii) notifies the beneficiary of receipt of the order or that the account of the beneficiary has been credited with respect to the order unless the notice indicates that the bank is rejecting the order or that funds with respect to the order may not be withdrawn or used until receipt of payment from the sender of the order;

(2) when the bank receives payment of the entire amount of the sender's order pursuant to Section 4A-403(a)(1) or 4A-403(a)(2); or

(3) the opening of the next funds-transfer business day of the bank following the payment date of the order if, at that time, the amount of the sender's order is fully covered by a withdrawable credit balance in an authorized account of the sender or the bank has otherwise received full payment from

the sender, unless the order was rejected before that time or is rejected within (i) one hour after that time, or (ii) one hour after the opening of the next business day of the sender following the payment date if that time is later. If notice of rejection is received by the sender after the payment date and the authorized account of the sender does not bear interest, the bank is obliged to pay interest to the sender on the amount of the order for the number of days elapsing after the payment date to the day the sender receives notice or learns that the order was not accepted, counting that day as an elapsed day. If the withdrawable credit balance during that period falls below the amount of the order, the amount of interest payable is reduced accordingly.

UCC § 4A-209(b).

If it pays the beneficiary, then it has accepted the payment order. If it notifies the beneficiary that the money is available, then it has accepted the payment order. If it receives the money (in other words, originator's bank sends it a payment order saying, "Give money to customer," and also sends it the money, or puts the money in its account), then it has accepted the payment order. Or, and this is analogous to final payment with checks, if the beneficiary's bank receives the payment order, and the funds are available to it, and it doesn't reject the payment order within two business days, then it accepts the payment order through inaction, the same way that a drawee bank can become obliged to pay a check by inaction.

D.   Effects of acceptance by beneficiary's bank

If beneficiary's bank accepts the payment order, that has these effects:

- It has to give the money to its customer, the beneficiary. UCC § 4A-204(a).
- It has to notify its customer, the beneficiary, that it has the money or that the customer is entitled to the money. UCC § 4A-204(a).
- Because it has to pay the beneficiary, the beneficiary's bank is entitled to reimbursement from the sending bank. The sending bank, in turn, is entitled to reimbursement from the originator, which makes sense. Each of them sends payment orders. Those payment orders have been given effect, so now they have to pay them. UCC § 4A-202.
- The underlying obligation is discharged, unless use of a payment order was inconsistent with an underlying contract. For example, if I had a contract to buy a lectern and the Seller and I agreed I can't pay by wire transfer and I go ahead wire the funds anyway, acceptance by the Seller's bank doesn't discharge me. UCC § 4A-206.
- There is a right to stop payment, but only until the payment order is accepted. UCC § 4A-211(b). It could get paid quickly. So, again, acceptance is the key moment for the overall funds transfer. Once a payment order is accepted, the Seller no longer has a right to stop payment. It's a very limited right to stop payment.

The beneficiary bank (as with any of the receiving banks) can reject a payment order by transmitting a notice orally, electronically, or in writing. UCC § 4A-210(a). If the beneficiary bank effectively rejects the payment order, it doesn't become subject to any of those consequences.

QUESTION 4. Didactic. Continuing from the previous question, how could Vaudeville Bank (the beneficiary's bank) accept the payment order?

A. Pay Boffo Gardening.
B. Notify Boffo Gardening that Vaudeville Bank has received a payment order for Boffo Gardening.
C. Receive the payment order, along with the funds from Trolley Bank.
D. Receive the payment order, have the funds available, and fail to make a timely rejection.
E. All of the above.

ANALYSIS.

Roach Bank	→	Trolley	→	Vaudeville Bank
↑	P.O. 2	Bank	P.O. 3	↓
P.O. 1				funds to
Ollie				Boffo Gardening
Hardware				
Originator				*Beneficiary*

This question emphasizes the several ways there are to accept a payment order. Any of the listed events would trigger acceptance, so **E** is the best answer. If Vaudeville Bank wishes to reject (and avoid the consequences of acceptance), it must avoid all the modes of acceptance.

QUESTION 5. Instructive. Continuing on again from the preceding questions, what would be the effects of acceptance by Vaudeville Bank (the beneficiary's bank)?

A. Vaudeville Bank would be obliged to pay Boffo Gardening.
B. Vaudeville Bank would be obliged to notify Boffo Gardening that Boffo Gardening was entitled to the funds.
C. Vaudeville Bank would be entitled to reimbursement from Trolley Bank, who would be entitled to reimbursement from Roach Bank, who would be entitled to reimbursement from Ollie Hardware.
D. Ollie Hardware's obligation to pay Boffo Gardening would be discharged.
E. Trolley Bank has no right to cancel the funds transfer.
F. All of the above.

ANALYSIS.   This question emphasizes why acceptance by the beneficiary's bank is the key moment. It gives effect to the overall funds transfer and triggers rights and obligations for all the parties. Therefore, **F** is the best answer.

QUESTION 6. **Reluctant.** Vaudeville Bank notifies Boffo Gardening that it has received a payment order of $50,000 for it. Within the hour, Vaudeville Bank learns that Trolley Bank has become insolvent. Vaudeville Bank realizes that Trolley Bank very likely will not reimburse Vaudeville Bank if Vaudeville Bank pays Boffo Gardening. Vaudeville Bank regretfully informs Boffo Gardening that it will not receive any money after all. Boffo Gardening claims that Vaudeville Bank must stick by its word. Must it?

A. No. Vaudeville Bank received no consideration.
B. No. Vaudeville Bank made no promise to pay. It merely informed Boffo Gardening that a payment order had arrived.
C. No. Vaudeville Bank need not pay, where it has little chance of being reimbursed.
D. Yes. Vaudeville Bank accepted the payment order, so it must pay Boffo Gardening.

ANALYSIS.   This question puts the two previous questions together and illustrates the risk to beneficiary's bank of acceptance. By notifying Boffo Gardening that it had received a payment order, Vaudeville Bank accepted the payment order. To accept, Vaudeville Bank need not say, "I accept" or "OK." It need only do only one of the listed things that constitute acceptance: pay Boffo Gardening, notify Boffo Gardening, get the money, or fail to reject in timely fashion.

Once acceptance occurs, that triggers the listed effects: Vaudeville Bank must pay Boffo Gardening, Vaudeville Bank must notify Boffo Gardening, Vaudeville Bank is entitled to reimbursement from Trolley Bank, and the underlying obligation is discharged. So, Vaudeville Bank must pay Boffo Gardening, and so **D** is the best answer. Vaudeville Bank is entitled to reimbursement, but that may not be worth much.

QUESTION 7. **Always accepted.** Powder Game Inc. sends a payment order to its bank, Iron Bank, to put $100,000 into the account of Conductor Corp. at Lava Bank. Iron Bank sends a matching payment order to Fedwire, which sends a matching payment order to Lava Bank. At the end of the day, Fedwire puts the money into Lava Bank's account at Fedwire. Fedwire always pays its wire transfers the same day and is reimbursed from the sending bank by taking the money out of that bank's

account at the end of the day. Lava Bank has done nothing and is not
sure if it should accept the wire transfer. What must occur for Lava Bank
to accept the wire transfer?

A. Lava Bank must pay Conductor Corp.
B. Lava Bank must notify Conductor Corp. that Lava Bank has received a
   payment order for it.
C. Nothing else, because Lava Bank has received the funds from Fedwire.
D. Lava Bank must receive the payment order, have the funds available,
   and fail to make a timely rejection.
E. All of the above.

ANALYSIS. This problem emphasizes an important practical aspect of
Fedwire. When Fedwire sends a payment order to a bank, Fedwire always
gives the bank the money at the end of that day. So here, Lava Bank accepted
the payment order (even though it did nothing), because the money was put
into Lava Bank's account at the Federal Reserve. Therefore, the best answer
is **C**. So Lava Bank cannot reject the payment order. It is obliged to pay the
money to Conductor Corp.—but it has no risk, because Lava Bank has already
received the money. What if Iron Bank is unable to pay the payment order?
Then Fedwire would take the loss. In short, Fedwire accepts the credit risk of
participating banks. This makes Fedwire a very attractive system for banks to
use, because they can always count on being paid. Fedwire manages this risk
carefully by limiting the net amount of funds transfers it will make for a bank
during any day and charging banks a fee for certain overdrafts.

QUESTION 8. **Discharged?** Dedham Industries owes $1 million to
Needham Finance. Dedham wires $1 million to Needham's account
at Swan Bank. As luck would have it, Swan Bank goes into insolvency
proceedings the next day, before Needham can get the money out. Is
Dedham's debt discharged?

A. No. The debt has not been paid.
B. No. Dedham was negligent in sending money to a shaky bank.
C. Yes (unless the contract prohibited payment by wire transfer).
D. Yes. Needham was negligent in banking at a shaky bank.

ANALYSIS.
Dedham → Dedham's Bank → Swan Bank puts the money → Needham
in Needham's account

Acceptance of a payment order discharges the underlying obligation,
unless the underlying contract prohibits payment by wire transfer. **C** is the
best answer. **A** is incorrect.

The rule turns on the parties' contract, not on their respective level of care, so **B** and **D** are incorrect.

QUESTION 9. Seizure. Bonzi sends a payment order to his bank, Alewife Savings, to put $100,000 into Jack's account in Central Bank. Alewife implements it by sending a payment order to Porter Bank, who sends a payment order to Harvard Bank, who sends a payment order to Central Bank. Jack's creditors get wind of this windfall and attempt to seize the money in the hands of Harvard Bank. Can they do that?

A. No. Harvard has no property of Jack's to seize.
B. Yes. Harvard has the right to reimbursement, a valuable property right.
C. No. Intangible rights are not property.
D. Yes. Banks have an unlimited amount of money.

ANALYSIS.   This problem emphasizes the legal nature of funds transfers. A funds transfer is implemented by a series of discrete transactions. Harvard Bank acts as an intermediary in the funds transfer, but does not deal with Jack or ever has property of Jack's. Rather, Harvard Bank gets a payment order from Porter Bank and sends a payment order to Central Bank, and has rights and liability with respect to those parties. Intangible property is property, but Harvard Bank at no point controls any intangible property of Jack's. Jack's creditors have to look elsewhere for property of Jack's to seize. Jack's account at Central Bank would be a likely target (provided Central Bank is not located on some distant, judgment-proof island). The best answer is **A**.

E.   The closer

QUESTION 10. Avoiding commitment.   Vaudeville Bank, stung by a loss from accepting a payment order that was not reimbursed by the sending bank, decides to reform its wire transfer practices. Which course of action will protect it from being obliged to pay a wire transfer without being reimbursed?

A. Upon receiving a payment order, wait until it receives the money before notifying the customer or making funds available.
B. Upon receiving a payment order, wait until it receives the money before notifying the customer or making funds available. Reject the payment order if it does not get the funds in time.
C. Do not accept a payment order until the sending bank promises to reimburse Vaudeville.
D. Accept all payment orders.

ANALYSIS.   To avoid acceptance, Vaudeville Bank must avoid all the modes of acceptance: paying its customer, notifying its customer, getting the money, or waiting too long to reject a payment order. The third mode (getting the money) is hard to avoid, because it can be accomplished without Vaudeville Bank doing anything, by a bank putting money in Vaudeville Bank's account. There's no problem, however—if Vaudeville Bank gets the money, it has no risk of not being reimbursed (it has already been reimbursed). So, Vaudeville Bank, until it is assured of getting the money on a payment order, needs to avoid the other three modes of acceptance. For banks that Vaudeville trusts, it might be willing to accept before it actually has the money, its bad experiences notwithstanding.

A is insufficient. Avoiding payment and notification is not enough, if Vaudeville Bank waits so long that it accepts by inaction.

B is the best answer.

C is insufficient. A promise to reimburse adds nothing. A promise may not be enforceable, if the bank does not have the money.

D is exactly the opposite of what Vaudeville seeks. It wants to accept only those payment orders where it is assured of payment.

 # McJohn's picks

1.	4A or not 4A, that is the question	C
2.	Which?	G
3.	Terminology	C
4.	Didactic	E
5.	Instructive	F
6.	Reluctant	D
7.	Always accepted	C
8.	Discharged?	C
9.	Seizure	A
10.	Avoiding commitment	B

24

Commercial Wire Transfers: Errors and Fraud

~

I. Wrong name, no blame.
Number wrong; sad song.
II. Money hackered?
Customer knackered.

~

CHAPTER OVERVIEW
A. Introduction
B. Fraud (a.k.a. unauthorized use)
C. Customer normally agrees to risk of security breach (!)
D. Errors: party that gets account number wrong may take loss (even if name was correct)
E. Subrogation and restitution
F. Limited right to request cancellation of accepted payment order due to error
   1. Bank's liability
   2. Notice of error
G. The closer
❖ McJohn's picks

A.   Introduction

A funds transfer is just a way to change the balances in two bank accounts. The originator sends a payment order to their bank saying, "Put $100,000 in Seller's account, Account #2001 at Seattle Bank." Then the originator's bank sends the order to someone and says, "Put $100,000 in Seller's account, Account #2001 at Seattle Bank." It keeps going until it arrives at Seller's bank, which is the critical moment. If Seller's bank rejects the order, then the funds transfer simply doesn't occur; no one owes anything. If Seller's bank accepts the order, then that effectuates the overall funds transfer and gives everyone the respective rights and responsibilities. Seller's bank has to give Seller the money; Seller's bank also has a right to reimbursement from the bank that sent it the payment order. There's a right to reimbursement all the way along the line, back to the originator of the payment order. The underlying obligation to pay is discharged. Buyer owed money to Seller. If Seller's bank is obliged to pay Seller, that discharges the obligation to pay.

But what if something goes wrong? Someone puts down the wrong name or the wrong account number, someone realizes that they were sent two payment orders instead of one, or perhaps even an impostor sent a fraudulent payment order. We will look at risks that we have seen with other payment systems (errors and unauthorized use), and we will see how those risks are allocated for business-to-business wire transfers.

B.   Fraud (a.k.a. unauthorized use)

Boston Bank	→	Seattle Bank
Originator's bank		*Beneficiary's bank*
↑	P.O.2	↓
P.O.1		funds to
Someone with authority		Seller, Acct. #2001
to act for Buyer?		*Beneficiary*
Originator (a.k.a.		
Customer)		

As with other payment systems, Customer must reimburse Customer's bank for payment orders authorized by Customer. That includes payment orders that Customer actually authorized, and ones that Customer is bound by under the law of agency. So Buyer/Customer could be liable if an employee acting with apparent or implied authority sent a payment order. That much is pretty similar to other payment systems.

QUESTION 1. Strange loop. Jeremy Corp. wires $12,000 to Hector Engineering. Jeremy's bank, Repeater Savings, accidentally enters the payment order as a recurring payment, so Repeater Savings sends $12,000 to Hector Engineering from Jeremy Corp.'s account on the fifth of every month for several months. Is Jeremy Corp. entitled to get the money back?

A. Yes. Jeremy Corp. did not authorize the payments (other than the first one).

B. No. Jeremy Corp. gave authority to wire funds to Hector Engineering.

C. No. Repeater Savings acted in good faith.

D. Yes, provided that Repeater Savings can first recover the money from Hector Engineering.

ANALYSIS. As **A** correctly and succinctly puts it, Jeremy Corp. is obliged to reimburse Repeater Savings only for the funds transfer it authorized—the first one. Repeater Savings is entitled to use restitution to get the funds from Hector Engineering.

QUESTION 2. Reckoning. Impatient Bank informs Repeater Bank that Jeremy Corp. has failed to pay the mortgage on a local investment property. Impatient Bank instructs Repeater Bank to wire the overdue funds directly from Jeremy Corp.'s account. Repeater Bank, seeing justice in this, complies. When Jeremy Corp. objects, is Repeater Bank obliged to reimburse Jeremy Corp.?

A. Yes. Jeremy Corp. did not authorize the transfer.

B. No. Jeremy Corp. owed the money.

C. Yes. Repeater Bank ultimately controls accounts at its bank.

D. No. Jeremy Corp. is not obliged to pay a debt.

ANALYSIS. Jeremy Corp. did not authorize the transfer, and so is not obliged to reimburse the bank (and is entitled to have the money put back in its account). So **A** is the best answer.

However, all is not lost for Repeater Bank. Because it paid the debt owed to Impatient Bank, it would be subrogated to Impatient Bank's rights against Jeremy Corp. But if Jeremy Corp. had a defense to payment of that debt, or if the debt was not due yet, then Repeater Bank would be subject to those defenses. (Subrogation is discussed later in this chapter.)

C.   Customer normally agrees to risk of security breach (!)

There is a rule specially tailored to wire tranfers. A payment order will be deemed authorized by Customer if the payment order is processed by the bank in accordance with a security procedure agreed to by Customer (unless Customer can somehow prove that the evil sender did not get the information, directly or indirectly, from Customer). So, if Customer agrees to a security procedure, Customer will be bound by payment orders complying with that procedure, even if sent by some clever Norwegian teenager. Scary, right?

§ 4A-202. Authorized and Verified Payment Orders

(a) A payment order received by the receiving bank is the authorized order of the person identified as sender if that person authorized the order or is otherwise bound by it under the law of agency.

(b) If a bank and its customer have agreed that the authenticity of payment orders issued to the bank in the name of the customer as sender will be verified pursuant to a security procedure, a payment order received by the receiving bank is effective as the order of the customer, whether or not authorized, if (i) the security procedure is a commercially reasonable method of providing security against unauthorized payment orders, and (ii) the bank proves that it accepted the payment order in good faith and in compliance with the security procedure and any written agreement or instruction of the customer restricting acceptance of payment orders issued in the name of the customer. The bank is not required to follow an instruction that violates a written agreement with the customer or notice of which is not received at a time and in a manner affording the bank a reasonable opportunity to act on it before the payment order is accepted.

(c) Commercial reasonableness of a security procedure is a question of law to be determined by considering the wishes of the customer expressed to the bank, the circumstances of the customer known to the bank, including the size, type, and frequency of payment orders normally issued by the customer to the bank, alternative security procedures offered to the customer, and security procedures in general use by customers and receiving banks similarly situated. A security procedure is deemed to be commercially reasonable if (i) the security procedure was chosen by the customer after the bank offered, and the customer refused, a security procedure that was commercially reasonable for that customer, and (ii) the customer expressly agreed in writing to be bound by any payment order, whether or not authorized, issued in its name and accepted by the bank in compliance with the security procedure chosen by the customer.

§ 4A-203(2). The receiving bank is not entitled to enforce or retain payment of the payment order if the customer proves that the order was not caused, directly or indirectly, by a person (i) entrusted at any time with duties to act for the customer with respect to payment orders or the security procedure, or (ii) who obtained access to transmitting facilities of the customer or who obtained, from a source controlled by the customer and without authority of the receiving bank, information facilitating breach of the security procedure, regardless of how the information was obtained or whether the customer was at fault. Information includes any access device, computer software, or the like.

§ 4A-201. Security Procedure

"Security procedure" means a procedure established by agreement of a customer and a receiving bank for the purpose of (i) verifying that a payment order or communication amending or cancelling a payment order is that of the customer, or (ii) detecting error in the transmission or the content of the payment order or communication. A security procedure may require the use of algorithms or other codes, identifying words or numbers, encryption, call-back procedures, or similar security devices. Comparison of a signature on a payment order or communication with an authorized specimen signature of the customer is not by itself a security procedure.

Because there's so much money involved with wire transfers, there are often a number of different security procedures used. One nice, simple, and old-fashioned one is a four-way calling system. For a business to send a wire transfer, Person A at the business has to call Person B at the bank. Person B has to give the payment order to Person C at the bank, who then calls back to Person D at the business to verify it. That way, you can't have any unauthorized wire transfers where just one bad actor at the business and the bank are involved—you need four together. This discourages fraud, or at least encourages teamwork.

By agreeing to use a commercially reasonable security procedure, the customer agrees to take the loss of unauthorized wire transfers, unless the customer can show that the information didn't come from the customer.

The rule applies only to a commercially reasonable security procedure. A security procedure has to be a system to verify orders or to detect errors, and it has to be something more than just comparing signatures. A commercially reasonable system is one that the court finds to be reasonable, or, if a customer is offered a commercially reasonable system and chooses a different one, the customer's choice is then deemed to be commercially reasonable. As with the other rules, Uniform Commercial Code (UCC) Article 4A allows customers to take on risks if they so choose.

QUESTION 3. Risky business. Self Storage's comptroller notices with horror one Friday morning that the operations account at Northerly Bank is missing hundreds of thousands of dollars. Self Storage calls the bank, which freezes the account and investigates. It turns out that an unknown cracker managed to get past the various security measures and ordered the bank to wire the funds to an account in Seattle, from whence the funds rapidly went overseas. Everyone is shocked, because the bank used a set of highly sophisticated security procedures that exceed industry standards. In its contract with Northerly Bank, Self Storage had agreed to use of this procedure to authenticate payment orders. Despite many hours of analysis, technical experts are unable to figure out how the intruder got access to necessary codes and passwords. Self Storage is even more surprised when the bank refuses to re-credit the account. Who takes the loss?

A. Northerly Bank, because the transfers were not authorized by Self Storage.
B. Northerly Bank, because banks assume the risk of security breaches.
C. Self Storage, because it agreed to use the security procedure.
D. Northerly Bank, because the security procedure was not commercially reasonable.

ANALYSIS. This question illustrates the risk to customers of agreeing to a security procedure. Where the parties agree to use a commercially reasonable security procedure to verify the authenticity of payment orders, a payment order will be effective, provided the bank acts in compliance with the security procedure. So, the payment order is binding on Self Storage, who must reimburse Northerly Bank. **C** is the best answer.

This rule applies even if the payment order was not actually authorized, so **A** is incorrect.

Banks do not assume the risk; rather, customers bear the risk (even though many customers may not realize this). **B** is incorrect.

The rule applies only if the security procedure is commercially reasonable. Here, the security procedure would be deemed commercially reasonable, even if not perfect. So, **D** is incorrect.

QUESTION 4. **Substandard.** Westerly Bank convinces its new customer, General Storage, to use Westerly's wire transfer service, including new security software. The software was developed by Bugs, Westerly's chief of information services. Bugs has made great claims for the software, talking about encryption, neural networks, and counterintuitive passwords. But the software is a mash, well below commercial standards and full of holes. Before long, persons unknown direct wire transfers from General Storage's account to places unknown. Who takes the loss?

A. Westerly Bank, because the transfers were not authorized by General Storage and the security procedure was not commercially reasonable.
B. Westerly Bank, because banks assume the risk of security breaches.
C. General Storage, because it agreed to use the security procedure.
D. General Storage, which was negligent in banking with Westerly.

ANALYSIS. The customer bears the risk only if the security procedure is commercially reasonable. This one was not. So, even though Westerly followed the security procedure, the payment order would not be effective. General Storage therefore would not be required to reimburse Westerly. **A** is the best answer.

QUESTION 5. Take your chance. Easterly Bank offers wire transfer services to a new customer, Particular Storage. Easterly advises the use of Standard Security, a widely used security package. Particular Storage, however, prefers to use a buggy security procedure recently developed by its newly hired chief of technology, Bugs. Particular Storage agrees in writing to be bound by orders processed in conformity with the system. Soon, an anonymous user has circumvented the security procedure, logged on as Particular Storage, and sent wire transfers from Particular Storage's account to Spa Island. Who takes the loss?

A. Easterly Bank, because the transfers were not authorized by Particular Storage.
B. Easterly Bank, because banks assume the risk of security breaches.
C. Particular Storage, because it refused Standard Security and proposed use of Bugs' work.
D. Easterly Bank, because the security procedure was not commercially reasonable.

ANALYSIS. As this question illustrates, the UCC allows the customer's choice to deem a security procedure commercially reasonable. If the bank offers a commercially reasonable security procedure, and the customer chooses a different security procedure, then the chosen procedure is deemed commercially reasonable. As with other rules in Article 4A, parties are allowed to choose their risks. Therefore, **C** is the best answer.

D. Errors: party that gets account number wrong may take loss (even if name was correct)

When it comes to wire transfers, MAKE SURE THE ACCOUNT NUMBER IS CORRECT. If someone sends a payment order with the correct name but the wrong account number, they take the loss if the money goes into the wrong account and the recipient disappears with it. The loss falls not on the beneficiary bank (even though the account name and number did not match), but on the party that supplied the incorrect account number. One false digit can lead to a big loss.

Section 4A-207 sets out the rule governing mistakes in identifying the beneficiary.

§ 4A-207. Misdescription of Beneficiary.

(a) Subject to subsection (b), if, in a payment order received by the beneficiary's bank, the name, bank account number, or other identification of the beneficiary refers to a nonexistent or unidentifiable person or account, no person has rights as a beneficiary of the order and acceptance of the order cannot occur.

(b) If a payment order received by the beneficiary's bank identifies the beneficiary both by name and by an identifying or bank account number and the name and number identify different persons, the following rules apply:

(1) Except as otherwise provided in subsection (c), if the beneficiary's bank does not know that the name and number refer to different persons, it may rely on the number as the proper identification of the beneficiary of the order. The beneficiary's bank need not determine whether the name and number refer to the same person.

(2) If the beneficiary's bank pays the person identified by name or knows that the name and number identify different persons, no person has rights as beneficiary except the person paid by the beneficiary's bank if that person was entitled to receive payment from the originator of the funds transfer. If no person has rights as beneficiary, acceptance of the order cannot occur.

(c) If (i) a payment order described in subsection (b) is accepted, (ii) the originator's payment order described the beneficiary inconsistently by name and number, and (iii) the beneficiary's bank pays the person identified by number as permitted by subsection (b)(1), the following rules apply:

(1) If the originator is a bank, the originator is obliged to pay its order.

(2) If the originator is not a bank and proves that the person identified by number was not entitled to receive payment from the originator, the originator is not obliged to pay its order unless the originator's bank proves that the originator, before acceptance of the originator's order, had notice that payment of a payment order issued by the originator might be made by the beneficiary's bank on the basis of an identifying or bank account number even if it identifies a person different from the named beneficiary. Proof of notice may be made by any admissible evidence. The originator's bank satisfies the burden of proof if it proves that the originator, before the payment order was accepted, signed a writing stating the information to which the notice relates.

This is a rule that is unique to the business wire transfer system. If I write a check and the bank pays the wrong person, I would not have to reimburse my bank. If I write a check to Harold Holt, it is payable only to him (or a transferee from him, direct or indirect), even if I misspell the name, or use a trade name. However, wire transfers are a little bit different. Instead of just writing the name of the payee, the originator gives two pieces of identification: the name of the payee and the payee's account number at a particular bank.

O's Bank   →   B's Bank
Originator   Beneficiary

Suppose the originator, or one of the banks along the way, makes a mistake. They correctly name the beneficiary and the beneficiary's bank, but get the account number slightly wrong. Originator's bank okays the payment order as is and sends out the payment order that matches it to beneficiary's bank, which accepts it. Beneficiary's bank then puts the money into the account with that account number, which is the account of a completely different person. That person takes the money and disappears with it.

The rule could be that the beneficiary's bank takes the loss. It had a payment order that said, "John Logon Smith Inc.," with an account number that didn't match. All it had to do was check and see if it was the right account.

One could argue that failure to take this basic precaution caused the loss. A risk allocation system might say that the entity that was in the best position to avoid this loss was the bank—it didn't recognize that its customer's name didn't match the account number on the slip and could have easily avoided the loss. That's not the risk allocation rule for wire transfers, however.

The risk allocation rule for wire transfers says that banks can rely on the account number and ignore the name on the account. If the customer (the originator) was the one who got it wrong in the first place, then the customer takes the loss. This assumes that the customer was given prior notice by their bank, which would have been done in a customary wire transfer agreement. The agreement would say, "If the account number is wrong, you (customer) take the loss." The drafters of Article 4A chose the rule because it matched banking practices.

An alternative rule would be that the beneficiary bank would take the loss if the name and the account do not match. In that case, beneficiary banks would be a lot more careful. If the name and the account number didn't exactly match, they would reject the payment order. The problem is that the name and the account number often do not match. If I'm dealing with a seller who is going to ship me some hardwood trees or provide pony ride services, I may have their name on the contract. I wire them the funds, but the name on the account may not exactly match the name on the contract. They may be doing business under another name, or they may have a slightly different name listed on the account—for example, instead of "Incorporated," it might say "Inc." If there are several related entities that all do business together, it's possible that one name is on the account, and that name may not be the one that dealt with me.

There are a lot of transactions in which the name that a party is using is not their exact legal name, or is not the exact name that appears on their bank account. So, to avoid a lot of rejections by beneficiary banks, the theory is that this rule is a nice bright line rule: Go by the account number. We don't have to argue about who made the mistake or whether the names match. It gives all the parties a strong incentive to double- and triple-check the account number, which is unambiguous. If you get the number right, the money will go into the right account. The theory here is to have a rule that clearly allocates risks. As long as everybody knows about that, then they will be careful not to make any mistakes with the account numbers and risk having the money put in the wrong account.

The big question is the customer, because the customer isn't a bank. The customer therefore may not know this rule. They signed a contract agreeing to this rule, probably with their bank, but they still may not know about it. Yet, it is a risk that they take on. Article 4A governs business-to-business wire transfers. So, an entity that uses wire transfers has to be sophisticated enough to know about the risks of using wire transfers and to guard against possible losses from those risks.

The bank isn't entitled to reimbursement if it is aware of the error.

E.   Subrogation and restitution

If there's a mistake in payment, the party facing the loss may use subrogation or restitution. Suppose Customer purchases a painting from Gallery and sends a payment order with an execution date of next week; the bank mistakenly sends the money today. Gallery gets the money, keeps it, and doesn't send the painting. Customer cancels the payment order before the payment date and therefore isn't obliged to pay it. The bank can then use subrogation. The bank can step into the shoes of Customer and use its rights to collect from Gallery.

Restitution may also be available. Someone who gets unjust enrichment or a gift as a result of a mistake may be obliged to hand it back under principles of restitution. In a typical case in which a bank mistakenly sends the money to the wrong person, the bank can get the money back. If somebody accidentally drops $1 million in my bank account because they put the wrong number in a wire transfer, under principles of restitution, I wouldn't be entitled to keep it. I would have to give it back to the person who was facing the loss.

There is one exception to restitution that courts have recognized, in which the party that gets the money by mistake was owed the money. Say Business owes $1 million to Lender. Business's bank mistakenly wires $1 million to Lender. Business owed the money, but they hadn't sent a payment order to the bank. Business is not liable to reimburse the bank.

The bank would go after the recipient of the mistaken wire transfer on the principle of restitution, saying, "We put $1 million in your account by mistake. Give it back." In this situation, courts have held that restitution does not apply, because the lender was actually owed the money (even though paid by mistake). There is no unjust enrichment. Mistaken payment of a debt is not unjust enrichment. The bank would then have subrogation rights. It would now be owed the $1 million debt—but subject to the terms and conditions on that debt.

F.   Limited right to request cancellation of accepted payment order due to error

In the preceding chapter we saw that there is a very limited right to stop payment of a wire transfer. If the beneficiary's bank hasn't yet accepted the wire transfer, the sender has a right to cancel it.

After acceptance, there's a second type of stop payment available. It's not an order to stop payment; it is a *request to stop payment.*

> § **4A-211(c).** After a payment order has been accepted, cancellation or amendment of the order is not effective unless the receiving bank agrees or a funds-transfer system rule allows cancellation or amendment without agreement of the bank.
>
> (1) With respect to a payment order accepted by a receiving bank other than the beneficiary's bank, cancellation or amendment is not effective unless a conforming cancellation or amendment of the payment order issued by the receiving bank is also made.
>
> (2) With respect to a payment order accepted by the beneficiary's bank, cancellation or amendment is not effective unless the order was issued in execution of an unauthorized payment order, or because of a mistake by a sender in the funds transfer which resulted in the issuance of a payment order (i) that is a duplicate of a payment order previously issued by the sender, (ii) that orders payment to a beneficiary not entitled to receive payment from the originator, or (iii) that orders payment in an amount greater than the amount the beneficiary was entitled to receive from the originator. If the payment order is canceled or amended, the beneficiary's bank is entitled to recover from the beneficiary any amount paid to the beneficiary to the extent allowed by the law governing mistake and restitution.

If beneficiary's bank has accepted the wire transfer, it can go ahead and pay the beneficiary. If it has paid them already, it can let them keep the money. If it wants to, however, it can choose to cancel the wire transfer, but only for these specified reasons: if it was an unauthorized payment order, if there's a duplicate, or if there's an error in the amount or in the name of the beneficiary. So, if originator's bank realizes that it sent the same wire transfer twice, and the beneficiary's bank has accepted it already, the beneficiary's bank can choose to cancel it. If it does, it can then get the money back from the beneficiary, subject to restitution law.

If Business owes $1 million to Lender and wires it that amount, and then mistakenly wires another $1 million, it can request the beneficiary's bank to cancel the second transfer. Beneficiary's bank doesn't have to, but it can choose to cancel it, and then may be entitled to get the money back from the beneficiary under the law of restitution.

QUESTION 6. Slight error.   To pay a debt, Lanes & Games instructs Westford Bank to wire $100,000 to Johann Gombolputty von Hautkopf of Ulm, account number 1212200110 at Charisma Bank. Westford Bank sends a payment order to Charisma Bank, instructing it to credit its customer Johann Gombolputty von Hautkopf of Ulm, account number 12122201010. Westford gets the beneficiary's name exactly correct, but makes a slight error in the account number. Charisma Bank plops $100,000 in account number 12122201010 (the incorrect account), which happens to be Lucky Jim's account. He withdraws the money with a poker face and absconds with a big smile. Who will take the loss?

A. Lanes & Games, who started the chain of events.
B. Westford, who got the account number slightly wrong.
C. Charisma, who didn't notice the slight difference between "Johann Gombolputty von Hautkopf of Ulm" and "Lucky Jim."
D. Johann Gombolputty von Hautkopf of Ulm. Lanes & Games' debt is discharged, because Charisma accepted the payment order.

ANALYSIS.

Lanes & Games → Westford Bank gets bank account # wrong → Charisma Bank

This question illustrates that with wire transfers, banks are entitled to go by the account number and ignore the name of the beneficiary. Charisma relied on the account number sent by Westford and put the money in that account. Charisma is entitled to reimbursement from Westford. Westford is not entitled to reimbursement from Lanes & Games, because it sent the correct account number. So, Westford takes the loss and **B** is the correct answer.

A is incorrect, because Lanes & Games may have sent the initial payment order, but did not include an incorrect account number.

C is incorrect, because Charisma Bank may rely on the account number and need not compare it to the named beneficiary.

D is incorrect. The debt to Johann Gombolputty von Hautkopf of Ulm is not discharged, because Charisma did not accept a payment order payable to Johann Gombolputty von Hautkopf of Ulm's account.

QUESTION 7. Standard waiver.   Continuing from the previous question, suppose that Lanes & Games had gotten the account number wrong to start with, and that Westford used that account number in its payment order to Charisma Bank. Lanes & Games has signed a standard funds transfer agreement with Westford Bank. Under those facts, who would take the loss?

A. Lanes & Games, because it supplied the incorrect account number.
B. Westford Bank, because it used the incorrect account number without making an effort to verify it. Customers are not bound by the same rule as banks.
C. The entity that should have required some other form of payment in the contract.
D. Johann Gombolputty von Hautkopf of Ulm.

ANALYSIS. Lanes & Games is liable. The rule that banks may rely on the account number applies even against non-banks (like customer Lanes & Games), provided the non-customer has agreed to that risk—and banks routinely include a clause to that effect in wire transfer contracts. So, **A** is the best answer.

QUESTION 8. Don't tell, ask. In addition to changing the facts in the earlier question, let's go back in time. Lanes & Games has just sent the payment order with the incorrect account number, and Westford Bank immediately executed it by sending a payment order with the same error to Charisma Bank. Westford Bank sent the money along with the payment order. Lanes & Games realizes its error. What are its legal options?

A. It can stop payment.
B. It can ask Westford Bank to ask Charisma Bank to cancel the order.
C. It has no option other than to pay up.
D. It has a reasonable period of time to cancel the order.

ANALYSIS.
Lanes & Games → Westford Bank → Charisma Bank

The right to stop payment is very limited indeed with wire transfers. Before acceptance, a bank can cancel. In this case, however, acceptance has occurred (Westford Bank sent the money with the order, triggering one type of acceptance), so it is too late for that. After acceptance, there is no right to cancel, only the right to *ask*, for specified grounds. So, **B** is the best answer. **C** is just a little too pessimistic. **D** is decidedly too optimistic.

QUESTION 9. Restitution resistant. Krane Cranes owes $2,000,000 on a construction loan to Good Harbor Finance, who has been pushing for full payment. Krane instructs Singing Bank to transfer $200,000 to Good Harbor's account at Plum Bank. Singing Bank mistakenly sends a payment order for $2,000,000, thinking its customer intended to pay off the full amount. Good Harbor is delighted to get payment in full. When Singing Bank demands return of the mistakenly paid $1,800,000, Good Harbor refuses. Is Good Harbor required to return the money mistakenly transferred to it?

A. Yes. The payment order may be cancelled, due to mistake.
B. No. Good Harbor received payment on a bona fide debt and so is not subject to restitution.
C. Yes. Anyone that receives payment by mistake must return it.
D. No. Wire transfers are unconditional.

ANALYSIS. If payment is made by mistake, the recipient is subject to the law of restitution. So, **D** is too broad.

Not all recipients of mistaken payment are required to return it, however. So **C** is too broad at the other extreme.

Courts have held that where a party is paid on a bona fide debt by mistake, the party is not subject to restitution. So **B** is the best answer.

The payment order may be cancelled due to mistake, if Singing Bank agrees. Singing Bank would then have the right to recover the money from Good Harbor subject to the law of restitution, so the result would not change. **A** does not get us a better result.

1. Bank's liability

What if the bank does something wrong? In general, if the bank violates the rules or makes a mistake, it is not liable for consequential damages. If the underlying transaction falls through because of a wire transfer mistake by the bank, such as a failure to execute, the bank isn't liable for those consequential damages. Rather, it has to hold on to its customer's money for a period of time, and it has to hand over interest on that money. If it is a situation in which the beneficiary's bank refuses to pay, then it is liable for attorney's fees.

2. Notice of error

If there is an error, the customer has 90 days, from the date their statement was received, to give notice to the bank in order to retain the right to get interest. In addition to that, it has one year to give notice, to retain the right to get the money from the transfer. The big difference here from other payment systems that we've seen is that the time period starts running when the statement is received by the customer.

For checks, debit cards, and credit cards, the time period starts running when the statement is sent, not when it is received. So, if a statement was sent but never received, the time period still started ticking. The best rationale I've heard for this difference is that with a bank statement, you send it every month, so the customer should expect it every month. With wire transfers, however, statements are sent when there is a wire transfer, so they only come periodically. The customer therefore may not have the expectation to receive their statement at the same time every month.

G.   The closer

QUESTION 10. **Sneaky review question.**   Martha Millionaire uses her bank account to fund her lavish lifestyle. Someone intercepts messages between Martha and her bank, despite a state-of-the-art security procedure agreed to by the parties. Using that information, the person directs the bank to wire $5 million to an overseas bank, whence it soon disappears. The bank contends that Martha takes the loss, because she agreed to the security procedure. Does she?

A. Yes. Article 4A places the risk on her.
B. No. The procedure was not commercially recoverable if some could circumvent it.
C. No, because Martha uses the account for personal purposes.
D. It would depend on who was negligent.

ANALYSIS. When we talk about big-money wire transfers, we expect Article 4A to provide the rules. Under Article 4A, as discussed previously, the customer normally must bear the risk for an erroneous wire transfer if the bank complied with the security procedure and the customer cannot prove that the information did not come from the customer. Article 4A does not apply here, however. The account is used for "personal, family, or household purposes," so this is a *consumer* wire transfer, governed by the Electronic Funds Transfer Act (the same rules that govern debit cards). Under this act, Martha's liability here would be $50. The best answer is **C**.

This question reminds us that the threshold question is, "What body of law governs?"

 McJohn's picks

1.	Strange loop	A
2.	Reckoning	A
3.	Risky business	C
4.	Substandard	A
5.	Take your chance	C

6.	Slight error	**B**
7.	Standard waiver	**A**
8.	Don't tell, ask	**B**
9.	Restitution resistant	**B**
10.	Sneaky review question	**C**

25

Letters of Credit

To draw on a letter of credit,
Have documents needless of edit.
Unless their compliance is strict,
Its payment is nitpicked and nixed.

CHAPTER OVERVIEW

A. Letters of credit
B. A payment letter of credit transaction
C. A standby letter of credit transaction
D. Bank's right to reimbursement after payment (where documents strictly comply or customer agreed)
E. Bank's obligation to pay, where documents strictly comply or bank waits more than seven days to give notice of defects
F. Bank that wrongfully dishonors may be liable for attorney's fees
G. Fraud
H. What amounts to fraud?
I. Subrogation
J. The closer
❖ McJohn's picks

A.   Letters of credit

A letter of credit represents a definite undertaking by a bank, issued for the account of an applicant, to honor a documentary presentation by payment. In short, a letter from the bank, promising to pay upon presentation of specified documents. With other payment systems, the customer simply orders the bank to pay. With letters of credit, the customer has the bank issue a letter of credit, payable only when documents are presented that comply with terms in the letter of credit. So, it is a device for payment upon occurrence of certain conditions.

The two most common uses of letters of credit are *payment letters of credit* and *standby letters of credit*. Letters of credit are often used as payment devices in sales transactions, especially international business transactions. "Trade letter of credit" is the standard term, but I'll use "payment letter of credit" to distinguish them from standby letters of credit, which are used as financial guaranties in a variety of transactions.

Legally, a letter of credit is a letter of credit. They can be used in many different ways, but the same rules apply.

B.   A payment letter of credit transaction

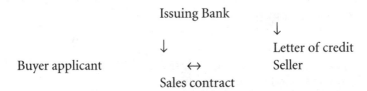

Suppose Buyer in Budapest wants to buy lecterns from Seller in San Diego. Buyer is willing to pay for the lecterns, but does not want to pay in advance. If Seller does not ship (or ships late, or ships the wrong lecterns, or ships faulty ones, or ships podiums), Buyer could face the prospect of trying to sue Seller in San Diego. It is a costly nuisance, however, to find a lawyer, win a lawsuit, and enforce a judgment in another jurisdiction. Seller wants to sell the lecterns but does not want to ship without assurance of payment, for the same reason. A payment letter of credit allows banks to act as intermediaries, providing a payment mechanism and reducing the risk to both parties at the same time.

A letter of credit is one way to accomplish payment in the transaction and also to allow the parties to tailor the allocation of risk so neither party bears the entire credit risk. Buyer's bank issues a letter of credit to Seller. The letter of credit says, "I, Bank will pay you, Seller, $10,000, when you present the following specified documents." Seller doesn't get paid in advance but gets a letter of credit, which is a definite undertaking by Bank to pay, as opposed to just a promise enforceable against Buyer in some other jurisdiction. It is payable when Seller can produce the documents specified in the letter of credit. That will make Seller much more comfortable in shipping the goods, because Seller knows they will get paid as long as they can produce those documents. Buyer doesn't get the goods before Buyer pays; rather, before getting the goods, Buyer promises the bank to pay. (Very likely, the bank will take the money in advance or get other collateral from Buyer.) Buyer does get some assurance that Buyer will not pay unless Buyer receives the goods. Buyer can draft the letter of credit with terms Buyer is comfortable with. A typical letter of credit might require a certificate of inspection, the bill of lading, and specified customs documents. That way, Buyer knows that the goods were shipped and they have been inspected by an inspection service Buyer trusts. Buyer has the documents needed to get them out of customs; that's much better than Buyer just wiring off the money and hoping that Seller performs.

C.   A standby letter of credit transaction

Issuing Bank

↓

Letter of Credit

Construction Co.   ↔   School Board

Construction

Contract

There are many situations in which someone says, "I'd love to do business with you, if you can increase your credibility a bit. I'd like to make you a loan (or give you a big contract, or . . .), but I'll charge you a very high interest rate or you'll have to put up some collateral or do something else that will increase my chances of getting paid." One answer is a guarantee from a third party. To get a loan from a finance company or a construction contract with a local school board, one might need a reliable guaranty (or surety). It could be with an affiliated entity or a surety company. A bank that does business with a debtor and has security interests in some of debtor's property would be willing to act as a guarantor, but it can't. Regulatory law in the United States bars banks from signing guarantees.

Someone at some point figured out that a letter of credit could function as a guarantee. Suppose that Construction Company wants to get a contract with School Board. School Board requires a surety bond of a $100,000. A letter of credit can do the same thing. Construction Company has its bank issue a $100,000 letter of credit that says (except in more formal terms), "I, Bank, will pay you, School Board, $100,000 if you present a certificate signed by the architect that Construction Company has failed to meet the deadlines in the construction contract." Likewise, for Obligor to put up collateral for a loan from Stranger Bank, they could have their bank issue a letter of credit to Stranger

Bank that says, "We will pay you $100,000 if you present a certificate saying that Obligor has failed to make one of the payments as scheduled in the loan."

A standby letter of credit is different in several functional ways from a payment letter of credit. A payment letter of credit is the payment means for the transaction. If everything goes right, the seller ships the goods, draws on the letter of credit, and gets the money. A standby letter of credit is the opposite. If everything goes right, then Construction Company builds the new school and School Board rips up the letter of credit, or the borrower pays its loan according to the schedule of payment in the promissory note and the lender bank rips up the letter of credit. A standby letter of credit stands by in the background to be drawn on if things go wrong, as opposed to providing the payment mechanism if things go right.

A standby letter of credit is likely to differ in several ways from a payment letter of credit. The term of a payment letter of credit is usually just a matter of weeks or months, because it is often used in an international transaction for a sale of goods. The buyer orders the goods, gets the letter of credit issued, and then the seller ships the goods, so the letter of credit might be outstanding for just a few weeks. A standby letter of credit often acts as a guarantee in a long-term transaction, such as the construction of a school or an extended financing agreement. It can therefore be outstanding for years. This means that when the bank issues the letter of credit, it is less likely to require reimbursement in advance, because this would mean the bank would have the money for years. It is more common that a standby letter of credit will be issued without the bank actually getting reimbursement in advance. It is likely to do something to protect itself and protect its right to get reimbursement. So, instead of actually getting payment in advance it might get collateral, or only issue standby letters of credit for very, very solid customers.

A standby letter of credit may also be simpler, calling for one certain document, as opposed to several documents. A payment letter of credit may well require a bill of lading, customs documents, the invoice, and the certificate of inspection; a standby letter of credit is likely just to call for one certificate. It could be a certificate signed by the architect that the Construction Company has failed to meet the deadlines set forth in the construction contract. It makes a big difference what certificate is required and who has to sign it. For example, Construction Company might not want School Board to be able to draw on a letter of credit if Construction Company is a couple of weeks late meeting a deadline. The party that signs the certificate matters, too. Construction Company might reason that the architect works for School Board, so the parties should nominate a neutral third party.

Lastly, a standby letter of credit is designed to be drawn on when there is a big problem in the underlying transaction (e.g., school built backward, loan not paid). That's what it's there for. The chances are higher that by the time the letter of credit is drawn on the parties will be at odds with each other and the applicant will be trying to prevent payment to the beneficiary. In drafting and in dealing with a standby letter of credit, the parties should bear this in mind,

> **QUESTION 1. Role reversal.** Would it ever make sense for a buyer in a sales transaction to be the beneficiary of a letter of credit?
>
> A. Yes. The buyer could provide a standby letter of credit, to enhance buyer's credibility.
> B. No. Buyer pays in a sales transaction. A letter of credit is a payment device.
> C. No. The letter of credit would have to be payable for a negative amount.
> D. Yes. The letter could be a letter of reference from other satisfied sellers.

ANALYSIS. Letters of credit are often used as payment devices in international sales transactions. But they can serve many other purposes.

Suppose Buyer in Buffalo really needs to purchase one hundred smart boards for its new building. This is not an international transaction, so Buyer may be content to pay with a cashier's check. Buyer is willing to enter into a contract with Seller from Syracuse but wants assurance that the boards will be delivered on time for the opening of the building. The parties can agree that Seller will provide a standby letter of credit for, say, $10,000, to cover Buyer's damages if the delivery is late. **A** is the best answer.

D. Bank's right to reimbursement after payment (where documents strictly comply or customer agreed)

Uniform Commercial Code (UCC) Article 5 provides rules that govern letters of credit, whether standby or payment.[1] The key rule in Article 5 is that a bank may and must pay a presentation if and only if the documents presented strictly comply with the terms of the letter of credit. UCC § 5-108, Issuer's Rights and Obligations. As § 5-108 puts: "An issuer shall honor a presentation that, as determined by the standard practice [of financial institutions that regularly issue letters of credit], appears on its face strictly to comply with the terms and conditions of the letter of credit. . . . [A]n issuer shall dishonor a presentation that does not appear so to comply."

This is known as the rule of *strict compliance*. The bank may and must pay if the documents presented match the documents specified in the letter

---

1. There is also the Uniform Customs and Practices for Documentary Credits (UCPDC). Many letters of credit in the United States and abroad provide that they are governed by the UCPDC, and courts will honor this choice of governing rules. The UCPDC rules are similar to the present version of UCC Article 5 (although they are termed quite differently and are more detailed in some respects, especially with respect to the meaning of specific commercial terms). So, the text will stick to UCC Article 5, for simplicity's sake.

of credit. The underlying policy is the *independence principle*, which states that the letter of credit is legally independent of the underlying obligation. That means the job of the bank is to deal with documents, not to determine the merits of the underlying sales contract. The bank is not the right party to determine whether the seller has complied with the contract; its tellers are not trained to test lecterns, to judge whether they are made of the promised Arthurian Oak, and to measure whether they fit the contract specifications. Likewise, the bank would not be an appropriate party to judge whether there has been performance of a contract to sell wine, computers, MP3 players, or other goods. Banks deal with documents. As § 5-108(f) puts it:

> An issuer is not responsible for:
> (1) the performance or nonperformance of the underlying contract, arrangement, or transaction,
> (2) an act or omission of others, or
> (3) observance or knowledge of the usage of a particular trade.

QUESTION 2. Nice bank.   Bene makes a presentment under a letter of credit issued by Cordial Savings. Bene's documents do not match exactly: the inspection certificate is from the wrong service and the bill of lading shows too few boxes of goods shipped. But Cordial Savings pays anyway, knowing that Bene is a reputable seller and probably had good reason for the changes. Is Cordial Savings entitled to reimbursement from its customer, the applicant on the letter of credit?

A. No. The bank paid over nonconforming documents and therefore is not entitled to reimbursement from the customer.

B. Yes. Just like a check, a letter of credit is an order to pay, along with an obligation to reimburse.

C. Yes. The bank paid as its customer's agent.

D. No. The customer always can choose whether to reimburse the bank.

ANALYSIS.   The bank paid over a nonconforming presentation and so is not entitled to reimbursement. So **A** is the best answer. The rule of strict compliance protects the applicant, by ensuring that the bank is entitled to reimbursement only if it pays over documents as specified by the customer. In this case, for example, it may matter greatly to the customer that a different inspection service was used, or that the number of boxes of goods shipped differed from the number specified. If the bank is inclined to pay (such as where it thinks a discrepancy is not material), it should ask its customer. If the customer instructs the bank to pay despite the discrepancy (maybe the inspection service used is okay with the customer, or the customer had notified the seller to change the number of boxes shipped), then the customer will be obliged to reimburse the bank.

E. Bank's obligation to pay, where documents strictly comply or bank waits more than seven days to give notice of defects

The rule of strict compliance and the independence principle insulate the bank from the underlying transaction—and likewise increase the credibility of the bank's promise to pay, because Seller is assured of payment if Seller can provide the promised documents.

Strict compliance does not mean perfect compliance, though. A bank must observe "the standard practice of financial institutions," meaning that if banks normally overlook certain discrepancies, the bank may not reject for such a discrepancy.

After payment, the bank is entitled to reimbursement from its customer, provided the presentation complied with the terms of the letter of credit. How quickly must the bank decide? Not as quickly as with checks, where the midnight deadline requires the bank by about midnight the day after presentation.

> (b) An issuer has a reasonable time after presentation, but not beyond the end of the seventh business day of the issuer after the day of its receipt of documents:
> (1) to honor,
> (2) if the letter of credit provides for honor to be completed more than seven business days after presentation, to accept a draft or incur a deferred obligation, or
> (3) to give notice to the presenter of discrepancies in the presentation.

UCC § 5-108.

The bank has seven business days to decide. In practice, presentations often do not strictly comply. The seller often has a document that does not quite match the specification in the letter of credit (e.g., goods were shipped a day early, or a different inspection service was used, or there were some typographical errors). Banks often try to avoid *wrongful payment* by using the seven days to decide by consulting with the applicant. If the documents are presented and the bank isn't sure whether the beneficiary is entitled to payment, it can simply contact the applicant and say, "You know, these documents don't look right. Shall I pay? Do you waive any defects in the documents?" If the applicant says "go ahead and pay," then the bank can pay and it is entitled to reimbursement.

If the bank does not pay, it must give the reason during the seven-day period. This prevents banks from scrutinizing the documents later on to justify dishonor after the fact.

> (c) Except as otherwise provided in subsection (d), an issuer is precluded from asserting as a basis for dishonor any discrepancy if timely notice is not given, or any discrepancy not stated in the notice if timely notice is given.

(d) Failure to give the notice specified in subsection (b) or to mention fraud, forgery, or expiration in the notice does not preclude the issuer from asserting as a basis for dishonor fraud or forgery as described in Section 5-109(a) or expiration of the letter of credit before presentation.

UCC § 5-108.

F. Bank that wrongfully dishonors may be liable for attorney's fees

Section 511 of Article 5 provides that a bank that wrongfully dishonors a letter of credit may be liable for attorney's fees, to the beneficiary or to the bank's customer. This rule imposes a risk on banks, but it also increases the value of letters of credit by making the bank's promise to pay more credible: "I promise to pay, and if I do not, I'll pay your lawyer's fee when you sue me."

> **QUESTION 3. Must what?** Impish Imports signs a sales contract to buy 20 riding lawnmowers from Extrovert Exports. As agreed, Impish Imports has Bashful Bank issue a letter of credit to Extrovert Exports. The letter provides for a payment of $10,000 upon presentation of a bill of lading, an invoice, customs documents, and an inspection certificate, all specifically described. What must Extrovert Exports do to be entitled to payment under the letter?
>
> **A.** Meet all of its obligations under the sales contract.
> **B.** Meet substantially all of its obligations under the sales contract.
> **C.** Present documents that strictly comply with the terms of the letter of credit.
> **D.** All of the above.

ANALYSIS. The bank's right and obligation to pay is determined by the terms of the letter of credit, which call for specified documents. Whether Extrovert Exports has met all or substantially all of its obligations under the sales contract with Impish Imports is legally irrelevant to Extrovert Exports' right to collect from Bashful Bank. The question is whether Extrovert Exports has presented to Bashful Bank documents that comply with the terms of the letter of credit. So, **C** is the best answer, and **A**, **B**, and **D** are incorrect.

> **QUESTION 4. Same as the old boss?** Deconstruction gets a big contract to demolish Town Hall in Psalm Springs, to make way for a new municipal complex. Deconstruction's contract with the town requires it to indemnify the town against any damages from faulty operations. The

contract also calls for Deconstruction to put up a letter of credit to cover such damages. The letter of credit provides that Psalm Springs may draw up to $100,000, provided it presents "a certificate signed by the town comptroller, Keith Moon, that the town is entitled to damages under the contract." Deconstruction has dealt with Moon for many years, and trusts him not to make a draw without justification. Deconstruction puts a little too much oomph into the demolition charges and breaks half the windows in the business district. The town makes a draw on the letter of credit, presenting a certificate signed by the new town comptroller, Bonham. There is evidence that banks normally require such certificates to be signed by the party named in the letter of credit. Is the bank obliged to pay?

A. Yes, because Deconstruction is obliged to pay.
B. Yes, because the substitution signatory was reasonable.
C. No, because the certificate was not signed by Moon.
D. The bank should perform an independent assessment of whether the town is entitled to damages.

ANALYSIS.   The governing rule is the rule of strict compliance:

> An issuer shall honor a presentation that, as determined by the standard practice of financial institutions that regularly issue letters of credit standard practice, appears on its face strictly to comply with the terms and conditions of the letter of credit.

UCC § 5-108.

The letter of credit requires presentation of "a certificate signed by the town comptroller, Keith Moon, that the town is entitled to damages under the contract." The beneficiary presented a certificate signed by the new comptroller, Bonham. So, the issue is whether that strictly complies with the terms of the letter of credit, as determined by the standard practice of financial institutions that regularly issue letters of credit. One might argue that this is a minor discrepancy that banks should disregard, but we are told that banks normally do not disregard such discrepancies. Moreover, in this case, the parties specifically named Moon, rather than simply referring to the town comptroller, where Deconstruction had experience with him and trusted him. The purpose of the rule of strict compliance is to give effect to the independence principle, and not make it necessary for the bank to consider whether Bonham is as qualified to sign as Moon. Therefore, the best answer is **C**.

A is definitely incorrect. Whether Deconstruction is obliged to pay is legally irrelevant to whether the bank is obliged to pay on the letter of credit. For that reason, **D** is also incorrect.

B is closer, but names the wrong standard. There is no rule providing for a reasonable substitute for the required documents. Rather, the documents must strictly comply, subject to standard banking practices. So, it would be necessary to show that banks normally pay in the face of such a discrepancy.

QUESTION 5. Close doesn't count.   Rivera agreed to sell Trotsky an order of special acrylic paint. As required by the contract, Trotsky provided a $20,000 letter of credit issued by Villa Bank. The letter of credit required presentation of several documents, including a bill of lading showing shipment of 100 cases of paint. Because of a factory fire, Rivera was able to ship only 86 cases of paint. Rivera presented documents complying with the letter of credit, except that the bill of lading showed shipment of only 86, rather than 100, cases of paint. Rivera stated that he would accept $17,200 to reflect the reduction in quantity. Is Villa Bank required to pay Rivera?

A. Yes. Villa Bank must pay for the paint delivered at the agreed-on price.
B. It depends on sales contract law—in particular, whether the change in circumstances partially excused Rivera's obligation to deliver 100 cases.
C. No. Rivera did not strictly comply with the terms of the letter of credit.
D. No. The presentation is fraudulent.

ANALYSIS.   It may well be that under contract law, Rivera is entitled to $17,200. However, contract law governs the rights of Rivera against the buyer, Trotsky. Under letter of credit law, Rivera is entitled to payment, from the bank on the letter, if and only if the presentation strictly complies with the terms of the letter. The presentation clearly did not, so Rivera is not entitled to payment from Villa Bank.

This result may seem unfair but is a risk that Rivera should have taken into account when agreeing to the sales contract. The purpose of the independence principle is to avoid requiring the bank to determine whether there has been compliance with the underlying contract. To determine that, the bank would have to know the relevant law, the relevant practice in the trade, and the relationship between buyer and seller. If banks had to play such a role, letters of credit would be more expensive to obtain, because the fee would include arbitration and mediation services.

Having said that, Rivera may still be able to obtain payment. If Trotsky agrees, then Villa Bank can pay the letter of credit, in full or in part. If Trotsky accepts 86 cases, Trotsky is obliged to pay for them, and the easiest way to do that is likely to tell Villa Bank to go ahead and pay. If Trotsky does not agree that it is obliged to pay, then there is a contract dispute between Trotsky and Rivera, and letter of credit law keeps the bank out of it. The correct answer is **B**.

> **QUESTION 6. Close enough.**   Renege Bank issues a letter of credit to
> Trump Cards, at the direction of Overbid Stores, who has put in a big
> order for playing cards. Trump Cards ships the cards and makes a pre-
> sentation on the letter of credit. Overbid Stores, meanwhile, has fallen
> into a financial abyss. Renege Bank does not want to pay the letter of
> credit, knowing that Overbid Stores has no means to reimburse Renege
> Bank. Renege Bank scrutinizes the documents presented, hoping to find a
> nonconformity to eliminate its obligation to pay. It notices a typographi-
> cal error in the bill of lading, which means it does not exactly match the
> requirements of the letter of credit. This sort of discrepancy is common,
> and banks uniformly ignore it and pay the letter of credit anyway. Not this
> time, however. Is Renege Bank obliged to pay Trump Cards?
>
> A. No, because Renege Bank will not be reimbursed.
> B. No, because there was a discrepancy in the presentation.
> C. No, because that would be fraud.
> D. Yes, because Trump Cards has complied with the terms and condi-
>   tions of the letter of credit.

ANALYSIS.   Here is the flip side of the independence principle, which can
also aid the beneficiary. Renege Bank's obligation to pay is independent of the
underlying contract, and independent of its ability to get reimbursed. Renege
Bank does not want to pay, but it must. **A** is incorrect. The documents presented
comply with the terms of the letter of credit, according to standard banking
practices. Because banks routinely ignore such trivial typos, the documents
conform. **B** is incorrect and **C** is not even close. So, **D** is the best answer.

> **QUESTION 7. Frozen?**   Henry sends a large shipment of nails to an
> overseas buyer, then presents the letter of credit to the issuing bank,
> Lionheart Trust, for payment. Henry provides exactly the documents
> required, but Lionheart Trust refuses to pay. The buyer has gone into
> bankruptcy, and Lionheart Trust knows it will not be repaid if it pays the
> letter of credit. Is Lionheart Trust liable to Henry?
>
> A. No. Lionheart Trust is only an intermediary and need not pay if it will
>   not be reimbursed.
> B. No. Henry has no damages, because under sales law, Henry owns the
>   nails that have not been paid for.
> C. Yes. Lionheart Trust is liable for the amount of the letter of credit,
>   plus Henry's attorney's fees in enforcing it, plus Henry's consequential
>   damages.
> D. Yes. Lionheart Trust is liable for the amount of the letter of credit, plus
>   Henry's attorney's fees in enforcing it.

ANALYSIS. Lionheart Trust's right to reimbursement is independent of its obligation to pay the letter of credit. Article 5 backs this up by making a bank that wrongfully dishonors liable for attorney's fees, so **D** is the best answer.

G.   Fraud

Fraud is where it gets very difficult to apply the *independence principle*. Suppose that a seller presents documents that comply with the terms of the letter of credit: invoice and bill of lading for 100 cases of wine, at $140 per case; shipped on October 16; and with the necessary customs certificates. By the time the seller makes the presentation, however, the shipment has already reached the buyer. The buyer has opened it up and looked inside. The cases are empty, or the bottles have been filled with water. The buyer calls up the bank and says, "Don't pay that letter of credit. Seller has defrauded me."

If we took the independence principle to its logical extreme, the bank couldn't refuse payment. If the underlying transaction was absolutely independent of the letter of credit, the bank would be stuck with the terms of the letter of credit. The beneficiary would be able to say, "Listen, here are the required documents. I presented those documents, so you have to pay me." That's an unjust result if the seller is truly being fraudulent.

The fraud rules address this procedurally. In the case of fraud, even if the customer tells the bank, "Don't pay seller. Seller is defrauding me," the bank may still choose to pay. If it is a fraudulent presentation, the bank is not obliged to pay, but the bank might not be able to decide whether it is fraudulent or not. So, the bank, if it pays in good faith, is entitled to reimbursement, even if its customer has claimed that there is fraud. The bank may dishonor if the presentation is fraudulent. This means the bank need not get involved in the underlying transaction but may choose to do so.

The customer, however, can get an injunction. If there's a court order telling the bank not to pay, then the bank can't pay and isn't obliged to pay. This scheme serves the policy behind the independence principle. The independence principle insulates the bank from the underlying transaction. The fraud rule—on its face an exception to the independence principle—still serves the policy of insulating the bank from the underlying transaction. It says to banks, "You don't have to figure out if there's fraud or not. If your customer says there's fraud and you believe him, then don't pay, because the fraudulent presentation doesn't entitle the seller to payment. You can pay if you want; you don't have to figure out if there's been fraud or not. But the customer has the option of going to court, and then if the court orders you not to pay, then you're off the hook. You just do whatever the court tells you to do, and then you don't have to worry about the underlying transaction." The onus is on the customer, not the bank, to seek injunctive relief.

H.   What amounts to fraud?

Fraud means fraud. Not every unhappy buyer can go to court and get an injunction on the basis of fraud. Mere breach of the contract is not fraud. It is not fraud if the wine is not quite good enough, or if it is a few bottles short, or if the buyer bought one type of wine and the seller thinks the contract calls for another type of wine. Fraud is where a seller ships bottles of water instead of wine, or instead of shipping brooms, a seller ships trash. If there is a good faith attempt to comply with the contract, it is likely that the court will not hold that there is fraud.

QUESTION 8. Strictly speaking.   Macaw Industries, wiring a new factory, orders five industrial reels of Grade AAA copper wire from Quetzal Copper. Due to a surge in demand, Quetzal Copper is unable to fill the order in time, and instead ships Grade AA copper wire. Quetzal Copper's engineers believe that the Grade AA wire will meet Macaw Industries' needs, although it will require some changes in the planned wiring system. Quetzal Copper makes a demand on the letter of credit issued by Jaguar Bank on behalf of its customer Macaw Industries. Jaguar Bank contacts Macaw Industries, informing it that a presentation has been made and that the documents comply with the letter of credit. Macaw Industries tells Jaguar Bank not to pay, because it does not want the Grade AA wire. Is Jaguar Bank obliged to pay?

A.   It depends on whether, under sales contract law, Macaw Industries would be obliged to pay.

B.   No. Quetzal Copper has made a fraudulent presentation.

C.   No. Jaguar Bank is not obliged to pay if its customer makes a stop payment order.

D.   Yes. Quetzal Copper has complied with the terms of the letter of credit. It does not matter if Quetzal Copper is breaching the underlying contract.

ANALYSIS.   Jaguar Bank is obliged to pay a conforming presentation. One exception is fraud. A bank may choose to dishonor in the case of fraud, and Macaw Industries might argue that there is fraud here. The contract calls for Grade AAA wire and Quetzal Copper shipped Grade AA wire. Fraud is more than breach of contract, however. Fraud would be seeking payment for shipping trash instead of wire. Here, Quetzal Copper reasonably believes that Grade AA wire is a reasonable substitute under the circumstances. Therefore, **D** is the best answer. Contrary to **C**, there is no such thing as a stop payment order for letters of credit. Otherwise, they would be far less reliable. There is such a thing as a revocable letter of credit, but few commercial parties would take such a thing—which is not really a commitment to pay.

> **QUESTION 9. Out of time.** Cortes Enterprises signs a contract with La Malinche Hardware to purchase 450 handheld, special purpose computers. Cortes Enterprises provides a letter of credit issued by Tardy Bank. A draw under the letter of credit requires an inspection certificate from Aguilar Inspection Services (along with a bill of lading, invoice, and customs documents). La Malinche Hardware makes a presentation to Tardy Bank for payment. All of the documents are in order, except that the inspection certificate is from Jeronimo Inspection Services. Tardy Bank, from past experience, knows that Jeronimo Inspection Services is just as well regarded in the industry as Aguilar Inspection Services. Tardy Bank decides to ask Cortes Enterprises whether to pay the letter of credit. Cortes Enterprises, after a long delay, tells Tardy Bank not to pay. Two weeks after the presentation, Tardy Bank informs La Malinche Hardware that it will not pay. La Malinche Hardware insists on payment. Is Tardy Bank obliged?
>
> A. Yes. The presentation complies, despite the non-substantial difference.
> B. Yes. Tardy Bank has waited too long to refuse payment.
> C. No. La Malinche Hardware did not present conforming documents.
> D. No. La Malinche Hardware did not comply with the letter of credit.

ANALYSIS. This question emphasizes that the bank must act in time to effectively dishonor. The bank is not obliged to pay if the documents presented do not comply with the terms of the letter of credit, but it must give notice of any discrepancy within seven days of presentation. Here, Tardy Bank waited too long to give notice and may not rely on that reason to justify nonpayment. **B** is the best answer.

I.   Subrogation

As with other payment systems, a bank that pays for the benefit of someone else may be able to use their rights. Subrogation may be used to avoid someone getting a windfall.

§ 5-117. Subrogation of Issuer, Applicant, and Nominated Person

(a) An issuer that honors a beneficiary's presentation is subrogated to the rights of the beneficiary to the same extent as if the issuer were a secondary obligor of the underlying obligation owed to the beneficiary and of the applicant to the same extent as if the issuer were the secondary obligor of the underlying obligation owed to the applicant.

(b) An applicant that reimburses an issuer is subrogated to the rights of the issuer against any beneficiary, presenter, or nominated person to the same extent as if the applicant were the secondary obligor of the obligations owed to the issuer and has the rights of subrogation of the issuer to the rights of the beneficiary stated in subsection (a).

(d) Notwithstanding any agreement or term to the contrary, the rights of subrogation stated in subsections (a) and (b) do not arise until the issuer honors the letter of credit or otherwise pays and the rights in subsection (c) do not arise until the nominated person pays or otherwise gives value. Until then, the issuer, nominated person, and the applicant do not derive under this section present or prospective rights forming the basis of a claim, defense, or excuse.

If Bank pays a letter of credit to the beneficiary, it gets the beneficiary's rights. If Bank pays Seller by mistake (i.e., the documents did not match the specifications in the letter of credit), Bank is not entitled to reimbursement from Buyer, but Bank receives Seller's rights against Buyer. So, if Seller shipped goods for which Buyer is obliged to pay, Buyer is now obliged to pay Bank.

Note that a bank gets subrogation rights only if it pays the letter of credit. A bank may not use the rights of another party to avoid payment. This means that Bank may not argue something like, "Although Seller presented complying documents, Seller did not comply with the sales contract with Buyer. I will use Buyer's rights on the breach to refuse to pay Seller." This rule preserves the independence principle and raises the credibility of banks issuing letters of credit by assuring sellers (and other beneficiaries, such as lenders or other contract parties on standby letters of credit) that the bank will be bound by its commitment.

QUESTION 10. Give it back?   Bonds borrowed $755,000 from Aaron. As security, Bonds provided a letter of credit issued by Ruth Bank, with Aaron as beneficiary. A draw on the letter of credit required a certificate, signed by Aaron's general counsel, that "Bonds has failed to pay the debentures when due." Bonds did not pay the loan when due, and Aaron drew the full amount of the letter of credit. Ruth Bank paid and then belatedly realized that Aaron had not provided the required certificate. Is Bonds required to reimburse Ruth Bank?

A. Bonds is not required to reimburse Ruth Bank, because the necessary certificate was not presented.
B. Bonds is required to reimburse Ruth Bank, because Ruth Bank issued the letter of credit on Bonds' behalf.
C. If Aaron was entitled to collect from Bonds, then Ruth Bank is now entitled to collect from Bonds.
D. A and C are correct.

ANALYSIS.   Ruth Bank paid by mistake. The required certificate was not provided. Ruth Bank is not entitled to reimbursement from Bonds, but Ruth Bank may use subrogation to exercise Aaron's rights against Bonds. So, **A** and **C** are correct, meaning that **D** is the best answer.

J.   The closer

> **QUESTION 11. A little review.**   Is a typical letter of credit a negotiable instrument?
>
> **A.** Yes, because the right to proceeds can be freely assigned.
> **B.** No, because a letter of credit is conditional.
> **C.** Yes, because it is a definite promise to pay money.
> **D.** No, because it is a writing.

ANALYSIS.   This question compares negotiable instruments and letters of credit. The twain do not meet. A negotiable instrument must be unconditional. Otherwise, it is simply a conditional promise to pay. A letter of credit is conditional. The right to payment depends on presenting the required documents (in most cases, a letter of credit could be drafted to be effectively payable on demand). So, a typical letter of credit would not be a negotiable instrument because it is conditional. So **B** is the best answer.

 # McJohn's picks

1.	Role reversal	**A**
2.	Nice bank	**A**
3.	Must what?	**C**
4.	Same as the old boss?	**C**
5.	Close doesn't count	**B**
6.	Close enough	**D**
7.	Frozen?	**D**
8.	Strictly speaking	**D**
9.	Out of time	**B**
10.	Give it back?	**D**
11.	A little review	**B**

26

Closing Closers

The questions in this concluding chapter fall in two categories. Most call on material from more than one chapter, to help the reader pull together the material in the book. Some simply emphasize key points in payment law.

QUESTION 1. Personal. As part of an investment offered by Phoney Bone, Mackerel signs a promise note that reads, "I hereby unconditionally promise to pay Phoney Bone or assignee the amount of $10,000 on demand. Dated October 8, 2009." Phoney Bone indorses the note to Frigate Finance, who gives $8,500 in good faith. Phoney Bone absconds with the proceeds. Mackerel soon learns that the representations made by Phoney Bone were completely false, and the investment is worthless. When Frigate Finance sues on the note, must Mackerel pay?

A. Yes. The fraud is not a defense that can be raised against a holder in due course.
B. Yes. A defense can only be raised against the party who caused the problem, so fraud by Phoney Bone could not be raised as a defense against anyone else.
C. No. Fraud is a defense that can be raised against a holder in due course.
D. No. No one could be a holder in due course of this promissory note.

QUESTION 2. Personable. Same facts as in Question 1, except the note reads, "I hereby unconditionally promise to pay to *the order of* Phoney Bone or assignee the amount of $10,000 on demand. Dated October 8, 2009." Must Mackerel pay?

A. Yes. The fraud is not a defense that can be raised against a holder in due course.

B. Yes. A defense can only be raised against the party who caused the problem, so fraud by Phoney Bone could not be raised as a defense against anyone else.

C. No. This fraud is a defense that can be raised against a holder in due course.

D. No. No one could be a holder in due course of this promissory note.

QUESTION 3. Personal, family, or household. Suppose the facts are the same as in Question 2, with one new tweak: The transaction was the sale on credit of a mystery cow, which Mackerel purchased to provide milk for the family and to frolic with the kids. Now, must Mackerel pay?

A. Yes. The fraud is not a defense that can be raised against a holder in due course.

B. Yes. A defense can only be raised against the party who caused the problem, so fraud by Phoney Bone could not be raised as a defense against anyone else.

C. No. This fraud is a defense that can be raised against a holder in due course.

D. No. No one could be a holder in due course of this promissory note.

QUESTION 4. Hot potato. One last variation. Suppose that, before Frigate Finance learned of Mackerel's defense, Frigate Finance sold the note to Prime Factor. Frigate Finance received cash, and indorsed the note "Pay Prime Factor, Frigate Finance, Without Recourse." Prime Factor next learns that it cannot recover from Mackerel (who can raise the defense of fraud) or Phoney Bone (who is not to be found). Frigate Finance denies liability, pointing at the indorsement made "Without Recourse." Is Frigate Finance liable to Prime Factor?

A. No. Frigate Finance has no liability because it indorsed "Without Recourse."

B. Yes. The "Without Recourse" language is without effect. An indorser always guaranties payment. (That's the meaning of "indorse.")

C. No. Frigate Finance did not know of the Mackerel's defense to payment.

D. Yes. Frigate Finance transferred, for consideration, an instrument subject to a defense.

QUESTION 5. Failure to stop.   Phoney Bone (back from a pleasant interlude) writes a check to purchase a Red Dragon from Barrelhaven Exports. Phoney Bone likes the Dragon, but would rather not pay for it. Phoney Bone sends a stop payment order to his bank, Valley Savings. A few days later, Barrelhaven Exports' bank presents the check, and Valley Savings pays it. Can Valley Savings recover from Phoney Bone?

A. No. A bank that pays over a stop payment order is not entitled to reimbursement.

B. Yes. The stop payment order is not effective, because Phoney Bone lacked reasonable grounds to stop payment.

C. Yes. Valley Savings paid by mistake but may recoup its loss from Phoney Bone, who is getting unjust enrichment (getting his dragon without paying for it).

D. No. Phoney Bone may be liable to Barrelhaven Exports but is not liable to his bank, which failed to give effect to the stop payment order. Valley Savings caused its own loss here.

QUESTION 6. Theft.   Crowbar Construction gets a big check from Lucky Lode Resort as payment for completing a loggia project. That evening, Big Al burglarizes Crowbar Construction's office, expertly opens the safe, and makes off with the check. Big Al goes directly to an ATM and deposits the check with Hardly Savings, who is paid by the drawee, Dawson Bank. A couple of days later, Crowbar Construction realizes the check is gone. Who is liable to Crowbar Construction?

A. Lucky Lode Resort, who wrote the check on which Crowbar Construction has not been paid.

B. Hardly Savings, who took the check from the thief, Big Al.

C. Dawson Bank, who paid the bank collecting on Big Al's behalf.

D. Big Al, who stole the check.

E. All of the above.

QUESTION 7. Embezzlement. In an alternate universe, which also has adopted UCC Articles 3 and 4, Crowbar Construction gets a big check from Lucky Lode Resort as payment for completing a loggia project. Little Lulu, Crowbar Construction's comptroller, has the job of keeping track of the checks that come in. She steals the Lucky Lode check, signs Crowbar Construction's name, and deposits it in her account at Hardly Savings, who gets payment from the drawee, Dawson Bank. A couple of days later, Crowbar Construction realizes the check is gone. Who is liable to Crowbar Construction?

A. Lucky Lode, who wrote the check on which Crowbar Construction has not been paid.
B. Hardly Savings, who took the check from the thief, Little Lulu.
C. Dawson Bank, who paid the bank collecting on Little Lulu's behalf.
D. Little Lulu, who stole the check.
E. All of the above.

QUESTION 8. Limited warranty. Slipgun steals Nancy's checkbook, writes a check to Bearer, and uses it to purchase some camping gear at Hilton Tent City. Ben Tinker, shopping at Hilton Tent City, slips the check out of the cashier's drawer. Ben cashes the check at Check Republic. Check Republic presents the check and the drawee, River Bank, pays it. Nancy refuses to reimburse River Bank. Slipgun and Ben Tinker are not to be found. Can River Bank collect from anyone else?

Slipgun → *Hilton Tent City* → *Ben Tinker* → *Check Republic* → *River Bank*
forges   steals and   presents   pays
Nancy's   forges
signature   indorsement

A. Nancy is liable to River Bank, because one of her checks was actually used.
B. Check Republic is liable for breach of presentment warranty, because the check was stolen.
C. Check Republic is liable for breach of presentment warranty, because the check had a forged drawer's signature.
D. Check Republic is liable for breach of presentment warranty, because it presented a check that was subject to a claim (by Hilton Tent City, the owner of the check).
E. None if the above.

QUESTION 9. **"Closing time, every new beginning comes from some other beginning's end."**   Carla carelessly fails to pick up her credit card, after paying for several rounds of drinks. Walt, the bartender, pockets the card. Over the next two months, Walt uses the card liberally. Carla carelessly pays only the minimum payment the first month, not noticing the balance has grown large. Carla finally gives notice to the card issuer after getting a huge bill the next month. Is Carla obliged to pay Walt's charges, beyond $50?

A. Yes. By handing the card over to Walt to pay for dinner, Carla gave Walt apparent authority to use the card.

B. Yes. By failing to retrieve the card that night, Carla gave Walt apparent authority.

C. Yes, for the charges made after the first bill was sent. By failing to retrieve the card and failing to object to Walt's charges, Carla gave apparent authority to Walt.

D. Yes, but only for any charges on the bill that Carla paid. The customer loses the right to object to charges after paying the bill for those charges.

E. No. Carla is liable only for $50 of Walt's charges.

QUESTION 10. **Slow leak.**   Terra, a wealthy businesswoman, uses her account at Liberty Bank to fund a busy life. Liberty Bank sends Terra her monthly statement on March 1. Terra does not notice, among her many checks and electronic transfers, an entry for a $1,000 transfer to Svalbard Bank. That entry reflects the fact that Harriet Hacker has managed to figure out Terra's username and password. Over the next year, despite the bank's use of a commercially reasonable security procedure, Harriet makes monthly withdrawals of increasing size. After a year, an entry for a transfer of $300,000 finally gets Terra's attention. A total of $1.5 million has been transferred out over the year. No one is ever able to figure out how Harriet Hacker got the necessary info. Is Liberty Bank liable to reimburse Terra?

A. No. The customer takes the loss, where the bank followed a commercially reasonable security procedure.

B. Yes. A customer can only be liable for authorized transfers.

C. No. Terra is liable, because her inattention gave Harriet Hacker apparent authority to use the account.

D. Partially. Terra takes the loss for any unauthorized transfers that occurred more than 60 days after March 1, plus $550.

QUESTION 11. Jump the gun. Wobbly Bank sends a payment order instructing Helpful Bank to put $280,000 into the account of Helpful Bank's customer, Joe the Plumber. Helpful Bank quickly calls Joe at the office to share the good news. Then, Helpful Bank realizes that Wobbly Bank is not the most reliable counterparty. Later that afternoon, Helpful Bank hears that Wobbly Bank has gotten a visit from bank regulators with grim expressions. Helpful Bank decides not to handle the payment order until and unless it receives the funds from Wobbly Bank. When Joe asks for the money, Helpful Bank tells him that he will not get it unless Wobbly Bank comes through. May Helpful Bank do that?

A. Yes. A bank is not required to accept a payment order.
B. Yes. A bank is not entitled to pay its customer unless it has adequate assurance of reimbursement.
C. Yes. Joe has not shown any reliance on the bank's representations.
D. No. Helpful Bank accepted the payment order by notifiying Joe. Once the payment order is accepted, the beneficiary's bank is obliged to pay the beneficiary.

QUESTION 12. Scrutinize. Old Faithful Bank issues a letter of credit for its long-standing customer, Canyon Goods, which is buying some goods from a seller in Budapest. The letter of credit is pretty typical and specifies the documents required for payment: a bill of lading, an inspection certificate, customs documents, and an invoice, all described in detail. Because Canyon Goods has a sterling record, Old Faithful Bank does not require collateral or payment up front. Pretty soon, however, Canyon Goods goes broke and clearly will not be able to reimburse Old Faithful Bank if the letter of credit is paid. Old Faithful Bank realizes that it might at least get the goods but does not want to be in the goods business, and also might have to fight for them with Canyon Goods' bankruptcy trustee. The U.S. bank that handles the Budapest seller's affairs calls to say the documents are on their way over, two days before the letter of credit expires. Old Faithful Bank does not want to pay the letter of credit. What may it do?

A. Revoke the letter of credit.
B. Refuse to pay, because its right to reimbursement no longer provides adequate assurance of payment.
C. Check the documents presented very carefully, to see if there is a discrepancy that justifies nonpayment.
D. Rely on its right of subrogation to refuse payment.

QUESTION 13. Antepenultimate closing closer. Tuesday, visiting her local travel agent, gets a great deal for the family on a holiday package on a sunny island. She pays with her credit card and then, when the statement comes, pays the bill in full. A few months later, the great deal turns out to be a rip-off. The "four-star hotel" is really the Ratty Tatty Hotel, with inedible food, broken glass for a beach, and a pool that's a scary shade of purple. Tuesday immediately calls the travel agent, who is now out of business. Tuesday next calls her credit card company to reverse the charges. The card issuer declines. Does Tuesday have the right to have the charge rescinded?

A. No. Tuesday's objection comes too late.
B. No. Credit card buyer protection does not apply, because the vacation is out of state and more than 100 miles from her home.
C. No. She authorized the charges.
D. No. The card issuer is not required to cancel the charge, because it cannot get the money back from the defunct travel agent.
E. Yes. If a consumer is not obliged to pay the merchant, then the consumer is not obliged to pay the card issuer.

QUESTION 14. An old chestnut. Daphne writes Piet a $500 check as a gift—one she soon regrets. She checks her account online the next month and sees the check was paid. She notices the check was not indorsed by Piet, but rather only by Check Casher, where Piet often takes his business. Because Piet never indorsed it, Daphne thinks her bank paid the wrong person and is not entitled to reimbursement. Was the check properly paid?

A. No. It was payable to Piet, who never indorsed to anyone else, so the bank paid the wrong person.
B. Yes. Checks are negotiable, so a bank may pay anyone who presents a check.
C. Yes. Checks are bearer paper, so a bank may pay anyone who presents a check.
D. Yes. Piet transferred it to Check Casher, so Check Casher was the PEEI. Daphne's bank paid the right person.

QUESTION 15. **Closing closing closer.** Thorn Tech gets a big order from a new overseas customer, Overadvance, followed up with a $500,000 cashier's check. The day the check arrives, Overadvance calls to reduce the size of the order by 20 percent, and to ask Thorn Tech to wire back $100,000. Overadvance reassures Thorn Tech: "Of course you need not send the money back until the check is paid to you. But please send it as quickly as you can, once you have the money." Thorn Tech deposits the check that day in its account at Rainy Day Bank. The next day, $500,000 has been credited to Thorn Tech's account. The following day, prompted by some friendly but urgent calls from Overadvance, Thorn Tech wires Overadvance $100,000.

Three days later, Thorn Tech sees that its account is overdrawn by $100,000. Rainy Day Bank has charged $500,000 to the account. Thorn calls Rainy Day Bank, and learns that the cashier's check was dishonored by the purported issuer as a forgery.

May Rainy Day Bank do that?

A. No. Rainy Day Bank paid the check.

B. No. Rainy Day Bank waited too long to dishonor the check, because its midnight deadline passed.

C. No. Rainy Day Bank was negligent in allowing Overadvance access to the funds before its was assured that the money was forthcoming.

D. Yes. If a check is not paid, the depositary bank may charge back the item.

E. It does not matter. Thorn Tech can simply cancel its wire transfer to Overadvance and gets its funds back from Overadvance's bank.

 McJohn's picks

1. Personal.
Mackerel → Phoney Bone → Frigate Finance

This question reminds us that the rules of Article 3, especially the holder in due course rule, apply only to negotiable instruments. This note is not negotiable. To be a negotiable instrument, a writing must meet several requirements:

- A promise (e.g., promissory note) or order (e.g., check) to pay, in a signed writing
- A fixed amount of money, with or without interest or other charges
- Unconditionally (the "unconditional" condition)

- Consumer credit sale notes: may be negotiable, but must preserve defenses
- Payable to bearer or to "order" (checks don't need the word "order")
- Payable on demand or at a definite time
- No extra promises (does not state any other undertaking or instruction by the issuer)

A negotiable note must be payable to bearer or "order," and this one is neither. The note is payable to "Phoney Bone or assignee," which makes it assignable, but to be negotiable it must be payable to bearer (i.e., use words indicating it is payable to whoever is in possession) or use that magic word "order." So, **D** is the best answer.

2. Personable.
Mackerel → Phoney Bone → Frigate Finance

This note is negotiable, subject to the holder in due course doctrine, along with the rest of Article 3. So, **D** is incorrect.

A party that signs an instrument promises to pay it but can raise their defenses against whoever enforces the note (other than a holder in due course), so **C** is incorrect.

The holder in due course doctrine applies. The question is whether that helps Frigate Finance. Frigate Finance qualifies as a holder in due course, because it is a holder that took for value, in good faith, with no notice of the defense. One of the few defenses that can be raised against a holder in due course is "real fraud": "fraud that induced the obligor to sign the instrument with neither knowledge nor reasonable opportunity to learn of its character or its essential terms." UCC § 3-305(a)(2)(iii). The fraud in this case does not qualify. Mackerel had ample opportunity to learn what he was signing. The fraud induced him to sign, as opposed to making him think he was signing something other than a promise to pay money. **A** is the best answer.

3. Personal, family, or household.
Mackerel → Phoney Bone → Frigate Finance

A promissory note given in a consumer credit sale may be negotiable—meaning it is subject to the rules of Article 3—but the holder in due course doctrine may not be applied to such notes. FTC regulations provide that such notes bear language to that effect, saying that any holder of the note is subject to the consumer's claims or defenses. Even if the required language is omitted, however, no one may be a holder in due course. So **D** is the best answer.

4. Hot potato.
Mackerel → Phoney Bone → Frigate Finance → Prime Factor

This one reminds us that there are other theories of liability beyond that for signing an instrument. When Frigate Finance indorsed "Without

Recourse," that did indeed mean that Frigate Finance would not be liable as an indorser. An indorsement can be made to negotiate an instrument, to guaranty payment, or to restrict payment. Article 3 allows the parties to structure their transaction and choose which of those functions the indorsement fulfills. Here, Frigate Finance indorsed without recourse, which served to negotiate the instrument but not to guaranty payment. The signature made the note payable to Prime Factor but did not also serve to guaranty payment. **B** is incorrect.

Frigate Finance has no indorser liability, but it is liable for breach of the transfer warranty. A transferor for consideration warrants that there is no legal reason why the instrument would not be paid (i.e., transferor is PEEI, instrument is not stolen, no forgeries, not altered, no defenses to payment, no claims to instrument). Here, there was a defense to payment. So, **D** is the best answer. Transfer warranty liability is a form of strict liability. Frigate Finance is liable, even if it did not know of the problem with the instrument. **C** is incorrect.

Frigate Finance has no indorser liability but is liable for breach of transfer warranty. **A** is also incorrect.

The result would be the same if there had been some other legal problem with the note, such as alteration, forgery, or theft. The result would be different if there had been no legal problem (i.e., Mackerel was not defrauded) but rather a financial problem (both Mackerel and Phoney Bone lacked money to pay). The transfer warranty does not guarantee that the previous signers can pay, rather that they are obliged to pay and have no legal reason not to pay.

5. Failure to stop.
Phoney Bone → Barrelhaven → Barrelhaven's Bank → Valley Savings

Phoney Bone made an effective stop payment order. He gave notice to Valley Savings, reasonably identified the check, and did so in time for Valley Savings to avoid payment. The check was not properly payable, so Valley Savings is not entitled to reimbursement. A party need give no reason for stop payment, so **B** is incorrect (even though it purports to rely on a legal rule, by invoking the word "reasonable").

Phoney is not off the hook, however. A bank that pays by mistake may use subrogation if it is facing a loss and another party is getting unjust enrichment. Had Valley Savings dishonored the check, the check would have gone back to Barrelhaven, who would have been entitled to collect from Phoney Bone. But that will not happen. Valley Savings mistakenly paid the check, so Barrelhaven got its money and has no complaints. Phoney Bone is getting his dragon bill paid by Valley Savings' mistake. So Valley Savings may use subrogation, step into the legal shoes of Barrelhaven, and collect the price of the dragon from Phoney Bone. **C** is the best answer. Subrogation allows Valley Savings to use Barrelhaven's rights, so **D** is incorrect. **A** states a correct proposition, but does not address the key issue of subrogation and so is not as good an answer as **C**.

6. Theft.

Lucky Lode Resort → Crowbar Construction → Big Al steals, forges → Hardly
        Savings→ Dawson Bank Crowbar Construction's indorsement

This question reminds us that there are several ways to use the various theories of liability to unravel the multiple party fact patterns in payment systems. Crowbar Construction can recover from any of the other parties. Crowbar Construction can enforce the instrument under § 3-309, as the owner of a lost, stolen, or destroyed instrument, so **A** is true. Crowbar Construction would have to provide protection against Lucky Lode Resort against any risk of paying twice. There is no risk here, however, where the parties have the check and Dawson Bank would be required to give the money back to Lucky Lode (because Dawson Bank paid the wrong person).

Crowbar Construction could recover from Big Al for conversion. Theft is conversion and Big stole Crowbar Construction's check. **D** is true.

Section 3-320 also provides broader theories of conversion. A party that takes a check from someone who is not entitled to enforce it is liable to the person who is entitled to enforce it. Hardly Savings is liable to Crowbar Construction, so **B** is true. A party that pays a check to someone not entitled to enforce the check is also liable for conversion. Dawson Bank is liable to Crowbar Construction, and so **C** is true.

As **A**, **B**, **C**, and **D** are all true, **E** (all of the above) is the best answer.

That answers the question posed but does not tell the whole story. Crowbar Construction could recover from Big Al, which would be the just resolution. If Big Al is gone or lacks funds, Crowbar Construction could recover from Hardly Savings, who took the check from Big Al. Alternatively, Crowbar Construction could collect from Dawson Bank, who would then collect from Hardly Savings for breach of presentment warranty. Or, Crowbar Construction could collect from Lucky Lode Resort, which would then seek its money back from Dawson Bank (which paid a check that was not properly payable), which would then collect from Hardly Savings. In short, Hardly Savings will take the loss, unless, miraculously, Big Al can be found and has funds.

7. Embezzlement.

Lucky Lode Resort → Crowbar Construction → Little Lulu steals, forges → Hardly
        Savings→Dawson Bank Crowbar Construction's indorsement

This question shows how the validation rules can shift the allocation of loss. Crowbar Construction employed Little Lulu and gave her responsibility with respect to instruments. So when she steals a check and forges Crowbar Construction's indorsement, the employee forger rule validates the forged indorsement. That means the forged signature is effective to make the check payable to Hardy Savings. When Dawson Bank pays Hardy Savings, Dawson Bank is paying the entity entitled to enforce the instrument, so the check is properly payable.

Hardly Savings is not liable for conversion, because the forged signature nevertheless counts as Crowbar Construction's signature. Dawson Bank is not liable for conversion, because it paid a party entitled to enforce the instrument (because the forged signature was validated). Lucky Lode Resort is not liable on the check, because it has been properly paid. The only party liable to Crowbar Construction is Little Lulu. **D** is the best answer.

In the previous version of the question, the loss fell on the party that took the check from the thief. The theory is that, as between all the innocent parties, the one that took the check from the thief over a forged indorsement was in the best position to avoid the loss. This time, the loss falls on the party that employed the thief and put her in position to steal the check and make the forgery.

8. Limited warranty.   This convoluted fact pattern serves to emphasize how limited the presentment warranty is. Anyone who transfers a check or presents it for payment makes a presentment warranty to the bank that pays it. The presentment warranty covers only two things: (1) I am the PEEI (i.e., no necessary indorsement is forged) and (2) the check has not been altered. Here, there were lots of problems with the check. The drawer's signature was forged, the check was stolen (so subject to a claim from Hilton Tent City), and Hilton Tent City's indorsement was forged. Check Republic was the PEEI, however, because the check was bearer paper, making any person in possession of it the PEEI. The check was not altered. There was a forged indorsement, but that indorsement was not necessary to negotiate a bearer instrument. There was also a forged drawer's signature, but the presentment warranty does not include drawer's signatures, on the theory that River Bank is in a better position to deal with the risk of its customer's signature being forged. So the best answer is **E**.

9. "Closing time, every new beginning comes from some other beginning's end."   The credit card customer is liable for only $50 in unauthorized charges. Unauthorized charges are charges made without actual, apparent, or implied authority. Carla did not give Walt actual or implied authority to make the charges, so the issuer would need a theory to show that Carla gave Walt apparent authority.

The one fact setting where courts have done that is where an employer permits an employee to have access to a card, then obliviously ignores months of statements reflecting the employee's use of the card without permission. That view (which other courts may reject, because it stretches the idea of "apparent authority" pretty far) would not apply here. Carla handed the card to the bartender to pay the tab. No carelessness there—or granting of any authority to use the card. Carla did neglect to get the card back, did not do anything about her missing card, and failed to note the unauthorized charges on her next bill. But that falls short of the failure to monitor an employee or the credit card bills for a period of months. Even the broadest reading of "apparent authority" would not apply here. So **E** is the best answer.

D refers to the wrong rule. If a consumer buys something and then claims it is defective, she must object before paying the relevant charge. That is a limitation that applies only to the buyer protection rules. This is a different issue: unauthorized use.

10. Slow leak. The first issue here is "what body of law governs?" Funds transfers may be governed by Article 4A, for commercial parties, or by the EFTA, for consumers. Although Terra is a wealthy businesswoman, this account is used for personal, family, or household uses. It is a consumer account, so the EFTA governs, not Article 4A.

A would be correct if Article 4A governs. Article 4A places the loss on the commercial customer, where the parties have agreed to use a commercially reasonable security procedure. That rule does not apply here, however, because Article 4A does not apply, so **A** is incorrect.

B overstates things. Customers are generally liable only for authorized transfers but can end up taking the loss.

C provides a plausible-sounding theory, but it is without any legal basis. There is no rule or case law that creates apparent authority for a complete stranger from a failure to monitor an account. Such a rule would swallow up the specific step-up liability scheme in the EFTA ($50 for timely notice, $500 if late, no cap if no notice 60 days after statement sent).

D applies the correct rule. A consumer's liability is limited to $50 for unauthorized funds transfers—but only if the consumer gives timely notice. It goes up to $500 dollars for late notice, and then the cap comes off 60 days after the initial statement is transmitted. So, Terra is liable for $50 plus $500 plus all transfers made more than 60 days after March 1. Compared to credit cards ($50 cap), the risks for electronic funds transfers are potentially great, if there is enough money in the account and the customer sufficiently inattentive.

11. Jump the gun. The key moment for a commercial funds transfer is acceptance of a payment order by the beneficiary's bank.

The beneficiary's bank accepts a payment order

- if it pays the beneficiary;
- if it notifies the beneficiary that the money is available;
- if it receives the money for the beneficiary; or
- if it receives the payment order, the funds are available for reimbursement, and the bank waits too long to reject (not unlike final payment for checks).

Acceptance by the beneficiary's bank has several effects:

- The beneficiary's bank has to give the money to its customer, the beneficiary.
- It has to notify its customer of the order.
- The beneficiary's bank is entitled to reimbursement from the sending bank, as are the parties all the way back to the originator.

- Acceptance by the beneficiary's bank discharges the underlying obligation, unless use of a payment order was inconsistent with an underlying contract.
- The sending bank no longer has the right to cancel the payment order.

Helpful Bank accepted the payment order from Wobbly Bank, so Helpful Bank is obliged to pay Joe. As **D** correctly puts it, Helpful Bank accepted the payment order by notifying Joe. Once the payment order is accepted, the beneficiary's bank is obliged to pay the beneficiary. Helpful Bank is entitled to reimbursement from Wobbly Bank and so had better hope things were not as grim as the bank examiners seemed to think. **D** is therefore the best answer.

A bank is not required to accept a payment order, so **A** states a correct legal rule. If the bank does accept the payment order, however, it is bound. So, **A** is inapposite.

Once a bank accepts, it must pay. Its right to reimbursement is distinct and is not a condition to its obligation. **B** is incorrect.

The beneficiary is entitled to the money. The beneficiary need not show reliance or an underlying right to payment. **C** is incorrect.

12. Scrutinize.   As in the previous question, we have a bank that wants to avoid payment—not an uncommon case in payment system law. When Old Faithful Bank issued the letter of credit, it made a definite commitment to pay, when the required documents were presented. If the letter of credit states that it is revocable, then Old Faithful Bank can revoke it. Such letters of credit are very rare, however. Few sellers would accept a letter of credit that said, in effect, "I promise to pay, unless I decide not to." This, we are told, is a typical letter of credit, which would not be revocable. **A** raises false hopes.

As with a bank that accepts a wire transfer, the bank that issues a letter of credit cannot renege even if its source of reimbursement dries up. That is a risk that it must address before issuing the letter of credit, and here Old Faithful Bank put too much trust in Canyon Goods' creditworthiness. **B** is not correct.

C, however, is an option. Unlike some other payment systems, a letter of credit is a conditional obligation. Old Faithful Bank has to pay only if the documents presented strictly conform to the terms of the letter of credit, under standard banking practices. Old Faithful Bank is entitled to refuse payment if the documents do not comply. In practice, the documents presented often do not comply. In a typical case, the bank would check with its customer, who would approve payment over noncomplying documents, if the customer was nevertheless satisfied with the seller's performance. The bank may also simply refuse to pay if the documents do not comply. If the documents do comply, Old Faithful Bank is obliged to pay (and see if it has a right to the goods, and can find a buyer). It could also simply ask the seller to take the goods back (Old Faithful Bank paying for shipping). It never hurts to ask.

C is the best answer.

D is not an option. First, a bank that does not pay cannot use subrogation. Second, If Old Faithful Bank pays, then it could use subrogation to have the rights to the goods, or to sue Seller if there has been a breach. Subrogation may not be used to deny payment, however, because that would open a huge hole in the independence principle.

13. Antepenultimate closing closer.   Generally speaking, if a consumer is not obliged to pay the merchant, then the consumer is not obliged to pay the card issuer. So, **E** is incorrect. Credit cards give a form of buyer protection that checks and debit cards do not.

Those protections are subject to certain limits. The transaction must occur in state or less than 100 miles from home. Here the transaction was local, even if the vacation was not. The geographic limitation would not be triggered, so **B** is incorrect.

The consumer gets buyer protection precisely for charges she authorizes (but does not get the promised goods or services), so **C** is incorrect (and misleading, by trying to get us thinking about the rules for unauthorized use). Bad **C**.

D invents a rule. The right to raise defenses does not depend on an ability to pass on the charge to the merchant. To the contrary, it is a protection against shaky merchants, putting the risk on banks that deal with them.

One key limitation is triggered here, however. The right applies only until the charge on the bill is paid. It is a right to raise defense against payment, not a right to get a refund of payment from the issuer. **A** is the best answer.

14. An old chestnut.
Daphne → Piet → Check Casher → Daphne's bank pays

To be entitled to reimbursement, the bank must (among other things) pay the right person, the PEEI. The PEEI can be

(i)   the holder of the instrument;
(ii)   a non-holder in possession of the instrument who has the rights of a holder; or
(iii) a person not in possession of the instrument who is entitled to enforce the instrument pursuant to § 3-309 or § 3-418(d).

Piet transferred the check to Check Casher, so Piet transferred his rights as a holder to Check Casher. Check Casher is a PEEI, under category (ii). The check was properly paid. **D** is the best answer.

Note that if Piet had deposited the check in a bank, we would have the same result. Section 4-205 automatically makes the depositary bank the holder of an unindorsed item (only if the customer was a holder—if the customer stole a check payable to someone else, then the customer does not have rights to pass on).

15. Closing closing closer.

Forger/Overadvance → Thorn Tech → Rainy Day Bank → Purported issuer
dishonors and returns

This question illustrates a key risk in payments law and practice. A party that has received money may be obliged to return it. A merchant that honors a credit card may be subject to charge back, if the buyer has a defense. A bank that receives payment on a check may have breached a presentment warranty; a bank that has improperly paid a check may have to put the money back in its customer's account.

More specifically, this question emphasizes an important distinction in check collection (one with parallels in other payment systems). When a party delivers a check to the depositary bank (Rainy Day Bank, in this case) and gets money, the check has not been paid. The depositary bank does not pay the check and is not subject to the rule of final payment (a.k.a., the midnight deadline). Rather, the depositary bank (Rainy Day Bank) simply handles the check on behalf of the customer. If the check is not paid, the customer is not entitled to the money from the depositary bank. If the depositary bank has advanced funds to the customer, it is entitled to charge those funds back. **D** is the best answer.

E illustrates another important principle. Sometimes you cannot get your money back. There is no right to cancel a payment order that has been completed.

In short, payments law is about such risks as not getting paid and paying without recourse. A lawyer that understands those risks can do a lot for a client, whether in advising, in negotiating, in litigation—and in changing public policy.

Index